Industrial Innovation Excellence in the 21st Century

SCIENCE, INNOVATION, TECHNOLOGY AND ENTREPRENEURSHIP

Series Editors: Elias G. Carayannis, *Professor of Science, Technology, Innovation and Entrepreneurship, School of Business, George Washington University, USA* and Aris Kaloudis, *NIFU STEP Studies in Innovation, Research and Education, Oslo, Norway*

There is ample and growing evidence that intangible resources such as knowledge, know-how and social capital will prove to be the coal, oil, and diamonds of the twenty-first century for developed, developing, and emerging economies alike. Moreover, there are strong indications and emerging trends that there are qualitative and quantitative differences between the drivers of economic growth in the twentieth and twenty-first centuries.

This new era is punctuated by:

- Development of a service-based economy, with activities demanding intellectual content becoming more pervasive and decisive.
- Increased emphasis on higher education and life-long learning to make effective use of the rapidly expanding knowledge base.
- Massive investments in research and development, training, education, software, branding, marketing, logistics, and similar services.
- Intensification of competition between enterprises and nations based on new product design, marketing methods and organizational forms.
- Continual restructuring of economies to cope with constant change.

This valuable new series concentrates on these important areas by focusing on the key pillars of science, technology, innovation, and entrepreneurship.

For a full list of Edward Elgar published titles, including the titles in this series, visit our website at www.e-elgar.com.

Industrial Innovation Excellence in the 21st Century

Theory, Policy, Practice and Politics

Edited by

Elias G. Carayannis

Professor of Science, Technology, Innovation and Entrepreneurship, School of Business, George Washington University, USA

Nikos R. Zotas

PhD Candidate and Researcher, Business Strategy and the New Digital Era, University of the Aegean, Greece

Pantelis C. Kostis

Department of Economics, National and Kapodistrian University of Athens (NKUA), Greece

Aris Kaloudis

Department of Industrial Economics and Technology Management, Norwegian University of Science and Technology, Norway

Halvor Holtskog

Department of Industrial Economics and Technology Management, Norwegian University of Science and Technology, Norway

SCIENCE, INNOVATION, TECHNOLOGY AND ENTREPRENEURSHIP

EE Edward Elgar PUBLISHING

Cheltenham, UK • Northampton, MA, USA

Published by

Edward Elgar Publishing Limited
The Lypiatts
15 Lansdown Road
Cheltenham
Glos GL50 2JA
UK

Edward Elgar Publishing, Inc.
William Pratt House
9 Dewey Court
Northampton
Massachusetts 01060
USA

Authorised representative in the EU for GPSR queries only: Easy Access System Europe – Mustamäe tee 50, 10621 Tallinn, Estonia, gpsr.requests@easproject.com

A catalogue record for this book is available from the British Library

Library of Congress Control Number: 2025951143

This book is available electronically in the **Elgar**online
Business subject collection
https://doi.org/10.4337/9781839109188

MIX
Paper | Supporting responsible forestry
FSC® C014540
FSC www.fsc.org

ISBN 978 1 83910 917 1 (cased)
ISBN 978 1 83910 918 8 (eBook)
ISBN 978 1 0353 9243 8 (ePub)

Printed and bound in the UK by Short Run Press Ltd, Exeter EX2 7LW

Contents

List of contributors

Elias G. Carayannis, Professor, Department of Information Systems and Technology Management, School of Business, George Washington University, and Director, European Union Research Center, Washington, D.C., USA

Halvor Holtskog, Professor, Department of Industrial Economics and Technology Management in the Faculty of Economics and Management, Norwegian University of Science and Technology (NTNU), Gjøvic, Norway

Aris Kaloudis, Professor, Department of Information Security and Communication Technology, Norwegian University of Science and Technology (NTNU), Gjøvic, Norway

Sokratis Katsikas, Professor, Department of Information Security and Communication Technology, Norwegian University of Science and Technology (NTNU), and Director, Norwegian Centre for Cybersecurity in Critical Sectors, Gjøvik, Norway

Pantelis C. Kostis, Assistant Professor of Economic Development, Department of Economics of the National and Kapodistrian University of Athens (NKUA), Athens, Greece

Nikos R. Zotas, PhD Candidate and Researcher, Business Strategy in the New Digital Era, University of the Aegean, and Strategy and Innovation Consultant, Ioannina, Greece

1. Introduction: Mapping the landscape of industrial innovation in the digital age

Elias G. Carayannis and Nikos R. Zotas

The 21st century has seen industrial innovation rise not merely as a technical or economic function but as a structural driver of global change. Innovation now operates at the intersection of digital transformation, geopolitical turbulence, societal demands, ecological imperatives, and ethical complexities. It is not only an engine of competitiveness, but a contested arena—one that shapes futures, allocates power, and reflects values. This book embarks on a comprehensive journey across this landscape, mapping the critical theories, emerging paradigms, systemic disruptions, and governance challenges that define the new contours of industrial innovation.

The chapters that follow build a multi-perspective, cross-disciplinary analysis of how industrial innovation evolves, how it is measured, how it is governed, and how it must adapt to meet the demands of an increasingly complex world. Collectively, they advance the understanding that innovation is no longer an isolated input or output—it is a systemic, ecosystemic, and socio-technological process.

Chapter 2 provides the foundational entry point, offering a contemporary perspective on the concept of industrial innovation. It traces its evolution from narrow techno-product paradigms to expansive, multi-layered processes that encompass digitalization, user co-creation, sustainability, and ecosystem collaboration. Central to this chapter is the notion that innovation today operates within—and transforms—broader technological and societal systems. It introduces the core motifs that will reappear throughout the book: the rise of Industry 4.0 and 5.0, the shift toward inclusive and distributed innovation, and the systemic thinking embedded in frameworks like the Quintuple Innovation Helix and Society 5.0. In doing so, it sets the intellectual scaffolding for the book, positioning innovation as a driver not only of growth but of systemic change.

While theoretical models are important, innovation cannot be meaningfully understood without effective measurement. Chapter 3 confronts the challenge of quantifying innovation in ways that reflect both its traditional dimensions and its emerging dynamics. It critiques outdated indicators such as patent counts and research and development (R&D) spending, which often fail to capture collaborative, cross-sectoral, or intangible value creation. The chapter then proposes more holistic and dynamic tools—including the M4 Framework, big data analytics, and network analysis—as pathways toward more actionable, real-time, and system-aware metrics. These new methods offer the possibility of aligning innovation assessment with strategic foresight, economic impact, and ecosystem health.

Measurement leads directly into governance, and Chapter 4 addresses how innovation policy is deeply entangled with global political and economic shifts. It frames industrial innovation as a site of geopolitical competition, strategic autonomy, and policy convergence. No longer are industrial and innovation policies separable; rather, they have merged into hybrid strategies that seek to secure technological leadership while embedding sustainable development goals. The chapter argues that nations increasingly recognize innovation as a tool for not only industrial renewal but also economic sovereignty and global influence. Environmental sustainability is presented as not merely a constraint but as a generative principle that can reshape innovation agendas toward long-term societal resilience.

Governance, however, is not just a state function—it is a distributed activity shaped by multi-actor networks. Chapter 5 shifts focus toward the emergent models of innovation ecosystems and the transition toward human-centric transformation. Drawing on the conceptual frameworks of Industry 6.0 and Society 6.0, it asks how innovation can move beyond smartness and efficiency toward equity, inclusion, and planetary well-being. By introducing the Insight–Innovation–Execution (I2E) framework and themes such as digital humanism and ethical foresight, the chapter lays the groundwork for a normative reframing of innovation. It explores how interdisciplinary collaboration, collective intelligence, and value-based design can shift the innovation paradigm toward a more just and regenerative future.

Chapters 6 and 7 delve into the fundamental enablers of trust and security in innovation systems: cybersecurity, privacy, and safety. Chapter 6 positions cybersecurity not as a reactive necessity but as a proactive driver of industrial competitiveness and research excellence. It presents the Norwegian SFI model and Norwegian Centre for Cybersecurity in Critical Sectors (NORCICS) as exemplars of how national strategies can align academia, industry, and public institutions around shared cybersecurity goals. By safeguarding intellectual property, ensuring system integrity, and enabling open innovation, cybersecurity is shown to be the backbone of digital and industrial resilience.

Chapter 7 expands this focus by weaving together cybersecurity, privacy, and safety into a unified lens. As Industry 4.0 technologies introduce new efficiencies, they also expose new vulnerabilities. The chapter explores how the integration of artificial intelligence (AI), the Internet of Things (IoT), and automation has increased the attack surface of industrial systems, making cyber-physical security and ethical data practices indispensable. It argues for integrated security architectures that balance operational agility with responsible governance, and highlights how these concerns are central not only to technical implementation but to the social license to innovate.

The architecture of innovation also extends to industrial networks and supply chains, the subject of Chapter 8. This chapter explores the evolution from linear supply models to interconnected, globally distributed, and digitally mediated industrial networks. Through case studies and theoretical frameworks, it illustrates how technologies like AI, blockchain, digital twins, and cloud platforms are reshaping value creation, collaboration, and resilience. Special emphasis is placed on circular economy principles and sustainable manufacturing practices. These are not only environmental imperatives but also strategic opportunities for differentiation and systemic efficiency in volatile global contexts.

As innovation systems grow in complexity, decision-making becomes more fraught. Chapter 9 addresses the core problem of making decisions under conditions of uncertainty and multiple, often conflicting criteria. It outlines both classical and contemporary approaches to decision-making—including bounded rationality, multi-criteria decision analysis (MCDA), scenario planning, and AI-driven analytics. The chapter shows that industrial innovation is increasingly a behavioral, organizational, and ecological challenge. Decisions must account for technical, financial, regulatory, and sustainability constraints while remaining agile, inclusive, and responsive to unforeseen events. It is in this messy middle—between rational planning and adaptive improvisation—that real innovation governance occurs.

The complexity of this landscape culminates in Chapter 10, which introduces an integrative model for navigating disruption through strategic foresight and the I2E framework. Disruption is reconceived not as a singular crisis, but as a systemic, converging force that reshapes innovation ecosystems. Drawing on contemporary cases—such as generative AI, pandemic-induced supply chain shocks, and geopolitical realignments—the chapter illustrates how strategic foresight can transform disruption into a driver of innovation readiness. The I2E model connects anticipation with scalable execution, offering a practical, dynamic tool for governing innovation in turbulent times.

Chapter 11 closes the arc by addressing the long-term trajectories of technological evolution in the age of Industry 6.0 and Society 6.0. It interrogates the dual imperative of enabling innovation while ensuring ethical integrity, ecological balance, and public accountability. Anticipatory and adaptive governance models are proposed as essential tools for steering emerging technologies toward inclusive and sustainable outcomes. The chapter reaffirms the I2E framework as a governance architecture that aligns exponential technologies with democratic values and planetary boundaries. In doing so, it offers a vision of responsible innovation grounded in reflexivity, collaboration, and systemic foresight.

Together, these chapters form a comprehensive narrative of industrial innovation in the digital age—a narrative that is at once empirical, conceptual, and strategic. The book does not propose a single model or solution but instead offers a cartography of frameworks, case studies, and critical questions. It argues that innovation is no longer a matter of discrete breakthroughs or isolated ventures; it is a continuous process of system design, governance, and sense-making. It is embedded in networks, values, and futures.

Innovation, as this book insists, must be accountable—not only to the market, but to society, to the environment, and to the generations yet to come. It must be governed—not through rigid control, but through adaptive, participatory, and foresight-driven architectures. And it must be inclusive—mobilizing the knowledge, creativity, and legitimacy of diverse actors across the helix of innovation.

In an era marked by simultaneous transformation and fragility, this book serves as both a reflection and a roadmap. It invites readers to reimagine industrial innovation not as a race to disruption, but as a shared commitment to human flourishing, ecological stewardship, and institutional resilience. The chapters that follow offer the conceptual tools and strategic insights to navigate this commitment—with clarity, with urgency, and with care.

PART I

Foundations and frameworks of industrial innovation

2. What is industrial innovation? A current perspective

Elias G. Carayannis and Pantelis C. Kostis

2.1 INTRODUCTION

Innovation is a buzzword that is thrown around in several contexts. It generally refers to the process of introducing something new or significantly improved. It could be a product, a service, a method, or even how one thinks. Innovation is a critical driver of economic and social development, pushing the boundaries of progress and competition in a rapidly changing economy. Innovation has developed into a distinct field. Throughout history, innovation was primarily concerned with the commercialization of an invention, or in other words, new, engineered, commercialized things. Belief in innovation, on the other hand, expanded over time. Innovation presently encompasses a variety of phenomena, from incremental enhancements to the use of current technologies in fresh contexts and the conversion of ideas into feasible applications. Since 1994, the conception of innovation has altered.

In the mid-1990s, the first adjustments occurred in the field of innovation. It was the dawn of the digital era, and it had a transformative influence on how we innovate. The utilization of the internet and digital technology has spawned new goods, new kinds of activities, and new techniques of innovation. There has been a transition from closed to open innovation, in which companies look outside their boundaries for fresh ideas and resources. Another important adjustment in people's attitude to innovation was made in 1994 (Francis & Woodcock, 2024). This adjustment emphasized speed and flexibility. In the fast-paced digital economy, rapid innovation is required. For this reason, companies have adopted efficient start-up management methods and agile development processes, including quick prototyping, iterative development, and constant improvement.

Another important change is the democratization of innovation, which is emphasized by Euchner (2023): due to the invention of the internet, cloud computing, and open-source technologies, large companies and research institutions are not the only ones that get to innovate. Start-ups, individual entrepreneurs, and consumers are significant contributors to innovation. In addition, the author defines the globalization of innovation as an important change. Innovation has increasingly become global; ideas, talent, and resources flow across borders. Through global innovation networks, companies tap into insights and expertise worldwide. User-driven innovation is considered critical (Fursov & Linton, 2022). Users, rather than just producers, are a valuable source of innovative ideas and solutions. Companies increasingly work with customers and users as partners to generate new ideas and improve products.

Sustainability is highlighted as driving many innovations (Nidumolu et al., 2013). The history of innovation reveals increasing environmental concerns and the pressing need for sustainable development, which emphasizes eco-innovation: developing marketable solutions that address environmental challenges.

The role of data in innovation has also changed markedly. The era of big data and advanced analytics has demanded data-driven innovation, and the confluence of the two has resulted in a critical aspect. By gathering records and statistics, companies can now obtain new and deep insights and make more accurate short-term forecasts of innovative areas than ever before. Big data (Shahid & Sheikh, 2021) impacts innovation, competitive advantage, productivity improvement, and assisting decision-makers. Finally, innovation has attracted many more industries due to the emergence of artificial intelligence and machine learning. These organizations produce new products or services, alter innovation, conduct more sophisticated analyses and predictions, or automate moderately sophisticated operations.

At the same time, collaboration and networking have increasingly emerged as crucial ingredients for the success of innovation. Many present-day technological and societal problems are so hard and multifaceted that they call for integrated solutions integrating diverse capabilities and viewpoints. It has subsequently triggered the inception of innovation ecosystems, which refer to networks of industry players, academia, and government organizations geared toward fostering innovation. In a similar vein, the emergence of social innovation has grown prominently, emphasizing the creation of solutions to social concerns, and enhancing the quality of life of the people. Social innovations predominantly occur in informal relationships between public, private, and non-profit players.

Since 1994, innovation has evolved tremendously, transcending traditional areas such as product and technological innovation to encompass processes, business models, and social and environmental issues. Therefore, innovation has changed as the global economy influences it, and in the face of competition, the world seeks to be more innovative. The first section of this chapter provides a comprehensive examination of how industrial innovation interacts with technological change and how that interaction is changing the world. The section touches on various topics, including the rise of the fourth industrial revolution, the transition from analog to digital production processes and mechanisms, the development of industrial innovation paradigms, and the creation and development of mature industrial innovation ecosystems. The section goes further and examines how these key players are altering business models and operational paradigms and subsequently analyzes how these changes affect the social and economic landscape. Finally, the section covers the future of industrial innovation, exploring critical topics such as the pentalogy of innovation: the Quintuple Innovation Helix, Industry 5.0, and Society 5.0, and how they are anticipated to enhance industrial innovation to create sustainable and inclusive industrial futures.

Due to the abovementioned, the chapter is designed in such a way as to ensure a sequential and detailed examination of the discussed themes. Thus, the first module examines Industry 4.0 and digital transformation, noting the integration of digital technologies into manufacturing and the rise of the smart factory. On the other hand, the second section delineates the concept of industrial innovation ecosystems, comparing traditional, schematic interpretations with dynamic and non-linear models while accentuating the significance of collaboration and cohort adaptiveness. Next, the chapter addresses the progression of industrial innovation outlooks from linear, one-dimensional models to complex and interconnected frameworks. Finally, the last section studies the advanced concepts considering future development and refinement concerning industrial innovation, namely the innovation helix and the relationship between Industry 5.0 and Society 5.0. This design allows a reader to navigate multiple layers and interdependent elements of industrial innovation and technological transformation, facilitating the development of current comprehension and future conceptualization.

2.2 INDUSTRIAL INNOVATION AND TECHNOLOGICAL DYNAMICS

All in all, it is hard to overestimate technology's contribution to the rapidly changing environment of industrial innovation. Technological progress has profoundly influenced this key element of economic growth and competitiveness. The interaction between technology and industrial innovation is multilateral and dynamic, molding the industrial background. For this reason, it is essential to be more flexible and responsive regarding benefits, which may be typical for each industry exposed to innovation pressure. This involves investing in research and development, fostering a culture of innovation (Petrakis et al., 2015, Kostis et al., 2018, Kostis, 2021), and continuously adapting to the evolving technological landscape.

2.2.1 Understanding Disruptive Technologies

Disruptive technologies refer to a type of innovation that disrupts businesses, industries, or markets by displacing established norms and practices (Christensen, 1997). Innovations, which take place incrementally, only make minor improvements to systems or operations. They mostly create new industries and reframe competition by challenging mature technologies, allowing new leadership to establish new business models (Bower & Christensen, 1995).

Major disruptive technologies' characteristics include the creation of new products, a shift in customer expectations on quality, and the replacement of existing technology. These technologies often start small, gradually improve, and fall in cost and quality, eclipsing more mature technologies (Downes & Nunes, 2013).

The internet, for instance, has transformed how information is disseminated and received, resulting in improved communications, and thus breaking geographical barriers and enabling real-time interaction (Katz, 2015). It has also revolutionized commerce, including e-commerce, by changing consumers' procurement and spending patterns. The internet-based supply chain has replaced all old models. This new market trend compelled traditional industries to adapt or face extinction (Rifkin, 2014).

Moreover, they also establish new business models that prioritize the customer's well-being and participation, as in custom design (Westerman et al., 2014). Additionally, the energy sector is currently affected due to recently introduced renewable energies (Green & Newman, 2017). For example, renewable energy technologies have proven to be a vital innovation, given the current energy models that rely heavily on fossil fuels. This is because the traditional energy models have adverse effects on the environment. For instance, solar and wind energy innovations are threatening the traditional energy model. Renewable energy promotes democratization due to decentralized production. When renewable energies produce energy on a small scale, consumers can produce their own energy. This means there is no need to connect consumers to the central utilities, as energy is consumed locally (Perez, 2002).

Therefore, the industry needs to ensure there are regulatory frameworks in place for sustaining innovations and disruptive innovations. Regulatory policies, which are based on current infrastructure, should be dismantled to retain pure disruptive or sustaining innovations (Gobble, 2014). Between them, there exists a wasteland that invites a labyrinthine legal system to protect established industries against irrelevance. Since many businesses were established long before these laws were enacted, few have the provision and processes in place to avoid competitive slaughter (Christensen, 1997).

2.2.2 The Nature of Discontinuous Innovations

The defining characteristic of discontinuous innovations is that they are not incremental. Rather than refining existing technologies, they are "game changers" that do not merely improve current markets or technologies but frequently create completely new ones or change the landscape of existing ones radically (Tushman & Anderson, 1986). They are, in other words, expansive and penetrating, surpassing small increments of existing goods or techniques. They have more in common with the disruptive type in that they topple established practices, but it is important to recognize that not all disruptives are discontinuous (Christensen & Bower, 1996). While disruptives may insinuate their way into markets incrementally, discontinuous is akin to a sudden, radical realignment of the playing landscape (Anderson & Tushman, 1990).

Because of their character, discontinuous innovations frequently necessitate modifications in the technologies and customer behaviors and operations. In some cases, they compel the total replacement of present practices, demanding consumers to adopt new habits or requiring the complete rethinking of operations by businesses (Utterback, 1994). For example, the smartphone was a discontinuous innovation. It was not simply an improvement of the earlier cellphone; it fundamentally redefined the device and what it could do, opening the door to a new type of human–machine communication (Perez, 2002). This necessitated that consumers learn behaviors like tapping a screen and that businesses establish strategies for an ecosystem driven by internet-connected technology.

The trajectory of discontinuous innovation is frequently fraught with difficulties since it necessitates a significant amount of change. It may encounter opposition from policymakers and stakeholders in the current system while also necessitating a significant investment of resources to develop infrastructural needs. The potential, on the other hand, is transformative (Arthur, 2009). Discontinuous innovations open new markets and avenues for advancement that previously did not exist. They are how transformational progression is brought about. Therefore, grasping and mastering discontinuous innovations is not just a valuable strategy for businesses and industries seeking to stay ahead—it is critical.

2.2.3 The Impact of Digitalization

Digitalization has become an all-encompassing force and a key factor that defines industrial innovations, reorganizing how modern business is done (Schwab, 2017). The integration of digital technology into various spheres facilitated not only the acceleration of processes but also the emergence of completely new business models and opportunities for creating value

(Brynjolfsson & McAfee, 2014). Digitalization is a concept that goes beyond what was traditionally called the sphere of application. It refers to small-scale processes and overarching corporate strategies (Westerman et al., 2014).

Most importantly, the digitalization process significantly impacted the efficiency of business operations. Digital technologies promote the automation of multiple processes and enable unhindered communication, leading to optimized performance and resource-saving (Porter & Heppelmann, 2014). This efficiency measure is not limited solely to the pace at which things are done; it also includes doing them smarter. Digital tools allow more precise control over every aspect of the process, producing better quality output and enhancing overall productivity.

Another aspect influenced by the emergence of digital technologies is business models. In the digital sphere, there is a rise in the number of platforms and ecosystems that create new value streams (Iansiti & Lakhani, 2020). Previously, businesses were limited to linear models; today, they can leverage network effects and achieve economies of scale that were previously unattainable. This means a novel approach to capitalizing and monetizing the efforts and many new ways to engage with customers.

Another transformation factor is digitalization's role in enabling the collection and analysis of staggering amounts of data. In the digital economy, data today stand as powerful assets. Businesses have used the opportunity to gather and store tremendous data, defining customer behavior, market trends, and performance (McAfee & Brynjolfsson, 2012). The data-driven approach to decision-making allowed for eliminating guesswork and increased the accuracy of strategies. It informs every business sphere, from production, where assets facilitate manufacturing processes, to services that capitalize on platforms to connect with customers. Digitalization remains a constant development process as technology evolves and industries find novel applications.

2.2.4 The Role of Artificial Intelligence

Artificial Intelligence (AI) has become a transformative power in modern industries. It redefines what machines can do merely by simulating human intelligence. Machines are now capable of conducting the complex tasks that only humans could (Russell & Norvig, 2016). Such abilities include informed judgment, visual pattern recognition, and understanding and interpretation of languages (Jordan & Mitchell, 2015). AI has expanded beyond the simple act of automating to one of augmentation and enhancement. More so, it makes the building of new capabilities and more business models a reality (LeCun et al., 2015).

One of the most complicated applications of AI in the modern world is in the decision-making process (Goodfellow et al., 2016). Machines using machine learning algorithms and overwhelming information make decisions based on patterns and trends that may go unnoticed by human beings. In the field of finance, algorithms of AI study trends and predict market course (Bughin et al., 2017). In healthcare, AI helps in diagnosing diseases and developing personalized treatment plans (Davenport & Ronanki, 2018).

Considering the visual abilities, AI has made advancements. Machines can look at and explain the visual world using computer vision (Marr, 2016). Machine learning provides the vehicle for machine vision technology to see in multiple dimensions while retail utilizes AI more with visual image recognition.

Another aspect that AI has helped with is the ability to speak and make the machine talk. The technologies called downstream processing allow machines to interpret human languages to their means of understanding (Hirschberg & Manning, 2015). Chatbots utilize AI in customer service, while the translation system that breaks the language barrier is also an AI invention.

Moreover, IT also creates new business models besides automating current ones. For instance, analytics and predictive modeling design new ways upon which one can offer services and products that are unique to an individual (Agrawal et al., 2018).

For the manufacturing company, AI enhances the growth of smart factories through the proven factory where predictions and optimization of the production process minimize downtime (Manyika et al., 2013).

AI always exists independently. Nonetheless, as times move, it integrates with other technologies like the Internet of Things (IoT) and blockchain, which makes the system efficient and smart with high levels of automation (Schwab, 2017). The entire system has synchronization and high coordination with super autonomy. The vital impact of the above-discussed views is definite. AI transforms what workers do and changes possibilities, opening new windows for innovation. Its development will enhance the influence of nature in industries but is not limited. So, one should consider it when conducting research in the overlooked complex environment.

2.2.5 The Emergence of the Internet of Things

The Internet of Things (IoT) is one of the most transformative trends in the field of industrial innovation, and it represents an exciting end of the spectrum of how technology interacts with the physical world. The IoT is a network of physical objects that contains embedded technology to sense and communicate or interact with their internal states or the external environment (Ashton, 2009), usually connected via the Internet with various sources, systems, and devices. The concept of an IoT was first implemented with a working system in 1999 due to Kevin Ashton, the cofounder of the Auto-ID Center at MIT.

Since then, the IoT and the number of IoT devices have grown significantly. Such interconnectivity holds great potential for creating more efficient, flexible systems.

The emergence of the IoT is closely associated with breakthroughs made in sensor technology, wireless connections, and the development of cloud services. Essentially, it has become possible to gather and unpack useful data from an immense quantity of devices, which has the effect of generating conditions for automation and efficiency. In industrial manufacturing, IoT is reshaping the process by enabling real-time control of manufacturing processes (Al-Fuqaha et al., 2015). Furthermore, it increases the majority of supply chain processes: from monitoring goods in inventory to monitoring the state of food products in transportation (Borgia, 2014).

The implementation of IoT solutions in various processes, however, brings some challenges, including security issues, software to store, and work with vast amounts of data (Gubbi et al. 2013).

Similarly, as is already happening now, the IoT's integration with AI and machine learning is expected to create more intelligent and independent systems in the future. This intersection indicates a trend toward automation and smart automation: systems are learning, adapting, and making decisions (Alpaydin, 2016). The social impact also promises to be huge: the IoT will improve healthcare and make smart cities possible (Atzori et al., 2010).

2.2.6 The Advancements in Robotics

Robotics technology has evolved significantly. While in the past robots were only used to carry out repetitive tasks, nowadays they perform more complex tasks. The evolution of robotics has several implications in different sectors, including manufacturing, healthcare, and many more. These sciences and beyond are influenced by the ability to ensure the safety of robots and to utilize their potential.

The development is focused on improving the safety of robots, ensuring their efficiency, and revealing new possibilities. Moreover, the ability of simple programmable machines to develop into complex systems with the help of AI and machine learning represents a significant change within the field. The robots are able to easily adapt to the environment, rely on sensory data to make decisions, and learn from their experiences (Siciliano & Khatib, 2016). The transformation has enabled the implementation of robots in every aspect of manufacturing work. Robots started being used separately in production and needed to be distinguished between basic tasks and complex operations that require more hard work (Zhang et al., 2016). From that perspective, robotics utilization extended the utilization of the process, which is essential for increasing success and reducing human input.

Robotic technology contributes to transforming the face of patient care in the healthcare system (Taylor et al., 2016). It includes, for example, surgical robots to operate with a higher percentile of accuracy and lower invasiveness. Rehabilitation robots help patients with movement, sickness, or disorders by suggesting more treatable options (Krebs & Volpe, 2015).

Robotic technology developments started to be recognized in the social field. Robots started performing an important role in our daily lives (Ford, 2015). From home robots in the home workplace to social robots that keep us company or relieve and aid patients, they decided to help (Lin et al., 2012).

2.2.7 The Evolution of 3D Printing

Three-dimensional (3D) printing, or additive manufacturing, has undergone a significant transformation since it was first developed. Developed as a method of rapid prototyping, it is now one of the most innovative and powerful production methods in different industries. This technology has changed manufacturing, providing for the development of more complicated designs, minimizing waste, and increasing the capacity for produce-to-order manufacturing.

Surmen et al. (2023) consider 3D printing to be like other conventional manufacturing processes but is distinguished by the repeated addition of material layers based on the 3D geometric data of the workpiece, interchangeably moving from design to production. The authors point to the different characteristics of 3D printing compared with traditional manufacturing—for example, 3D printing does not produce debris through material cutting, and it is unnecessary to use molds, unlike manufacturing plastic injection or molding, or creating molds. This technology is widely used in the manufacturing of prototypes and produce-to-order design, with 3D printer technology using an increasing number of materials, such as plastic, metal, composite, and organic materials.

Nandakumar and Raja (2019) describe the use of Fused Deposition Modeling to build scaffolding constructs out of polylactic acid filament for orthopedic devices. They demonstrate the structural integrity, porosity, and mechanical properties which are compatible with biomedical applications.

Adam et al. (2017) discuss the maturation of polymer-based additive manufacturing from rapid prototyping to a full-fledged industrial production method. They describe how this technology transforms and challenges the automotive industry, stressing the easier access to parts supply chains and the possibility of multi-material, multi-use design.

2.2.8 The Significance of Blockchain Technology

Originally, blockchain was developed as the underlying technology of cryptocurrencies, such as Bitcoin. However, its application goes beyond cryptocurrencies and has implications in many areas, including industrial innovation. Blockchain technology presents numerous possibilities for changing traditional business processes due to its features of decentralization, transparency, and security.

One of the crucial uses of this technology in industry is the concept of supply chain management. Blockchain technology provides a secure, decentralized, and immutable method of recording information, which allows real-time tracking of products throughout their entire production and shipment (Tian, 2017). Given that this option is not purely theoretical, and several companies have already employed blockchain to streamline product traceability, the time it takes from farm to table has significantly decreased.

Blockchain can present a new approach to intellectual property rights. This is largely achieved through the establishment of copyright on the network and as a result, the eradication of the need to prove ownership. The music industry is currently employing blockchain to reduce instances where musicians do not receive full compensation for their work (De Filippi & Wright, 2018).

Furthermore, blockchain is notably useful in the field of smart contracts. They are self-actualizing contract clauses that can expedite various processes (Christidis & Devetsikiotis, 2016). In the real estate industry, for instance, smart contracts can make the real estate acquisition process much more straightforward by automatically executing contracts when specific conditions are met.

Blockchain is revolutionizing the finance industry. Apart from its application in cryptocurrencies, it is used to increase speed and efficiency, and reduce costs of traditional banking operations. For example, Ripple is a project that aims to transform the way global payments are made by developing a faster, cheaper, and more secure system (Schwartz et al., 2014). Other industries that can benefit from this technology include the energy sector, healthcare, and education (Grech & Camilleri, 2017).

2.2.9 The Convergence of Technologies

The broad trend shaping the technology landscape is the convergence of several of the most innovative technologies, including AI, the IoT, and big data analytics. This progress redefines the basis of industrial innovation and opens the potential for the development and implementation of more developed intelligent systems operating in numerous fields and areas of people's lives. For instance, the emergence of the Artificial Intelligence of Things (AIoT), or a combination of AI with the IoT, significantly increases the intelligence potential of IoT systems by allowing AI algorithms to streamline and interpret extensive amounts of data collected by IoT devices to make systems more self-efficient. This progress is particularly relevant for smart cities characterized by the prevalence of AIoT-driven systems used to manage traffic and energy use more effectively (Al-Fuqaha et al., 2015).

Similarly, the integration of big data analytics, AI, and other technologies results in a radical transformation of decision-making evident in the success experienced by certain industries, such as finance and healthcare, to date. For example, AI analytics and big data integration underpin the innovative patient diagnosis and risk assessment applications noted by Wang et al. (2018). Equally impressive is the integration of blockchains with the IoT, optimizing security and transparency of networks. A more recent work by Reyna et al. (2018) suggests that such applications render connections more reliable and shield them from tampering, with supply chain operations and cryptocurrencies supported by smart contracts reaping great benefits.

Cloud computing is another convergence involving IT and the IoT, where the former uses the latter to develop data analysis algorithms that analyze data from IoT devices. In this case, cloud platforms provide the necessary infrastructure to support the dynamic management of the enormous amounts of data generated by IoT devices and analyzed by IT algorithms (Marjani et al., 2017). Robotics and AI also converge to create a new revolution in automation where the latter enables robots to learn and adapt. The hemisphere of AI is integrated with robotics to enable the robots to learn and adapt to the environment, which is critical to the manufacturing and health sectors.

Nanotechnology and biotechnology also converge, leading to significant breakthroughs in medicine, proper materials engineering, and production (Serrano et al., 2009). Virtual and augmented reality combine with AI, revolutionizing the user experience, gaming, training, and education, providing rare realism elements.

Crucially, 5G technology is involved in all these convergences, offering the high-speed, low-latency connections needed for the Artificial Intelligence of Things (AIoT) connectivity and autonomous vehicles (Shafi et al., 2017). AI is also integrated with the renewable energy sectors, offering the transformational convergence in energy and sustainable energy management through renewable technologies (Zhang et al., 2016).

AI and high data analytics also converge in monitoring the environment, an efficient way to control climate change and reduce biodiversity loss. Such broad integration of technologies touching on all technology sectors signifies a different era powered by efficiency and safety.

2.2.10 The Challenge of Technological Adoption

The fast pace at which technology advances presents significant impediments to its implementation across various sectors. The potential of these innovations to accelerate efficiency and promote ingenuity cannot fully be realized due to the numerous challenges faced by previously established systems, prompting the need for technology integration. The skill gap is a major barrier to technology. With many industries evolving, firms need more personnel who have knowledge of emerging technologies such as artificial intelligence, big data analytics, and IoT. This forces companies to incur more costs in training and onboarding, as well articulated by Bughin et al. (2018), who compared the skill gap in the digital era and stressed the urgency of reskilling.

Moreover, the culture of an organization has a significant impact on the acceptance of new technology. New business models and methodologies have been shown to resist new technological integrations. Data concerns, especially with systems that manage large amounts of data, are particularly relevant with the rise of cybercrimes. Therefore, security frameworks and regulations must be all-encompassing, as strongly advocated by Roman et al. (2013).

Additionally, financial challenges in developing new technologies hinder their acceptance. According to Mazzucato (2013), institutions may be unwilling to invest in new technologies due to the fear of unknown factors involved. Interoperability can also pose a challenge. Moreover, the pace of technological change is a barrier.

The hyperinflation of technological evolution has the potential to outpace a business's ability to adjust to the new norms, thus stalling the acceptance process (Perez, 2010). The regulatory framework of adopting a new technology is another impediment. The compliance and cost of new regulatory standards complete technology adoption. This is in accordance with Yeung (2017), who also discussed AI systems.

Additionally, emerging environmental issues, caused by the non-utilization of environmentally friendly technology, contribute to stalling acceptance of new technology. User resistance to new technology, caused by uncertainty and fear, contributes to the difficult acceptance of technology, as previously highlighted by Venkatesh et al. (2012).

Finally, data integrity remains an issue in technological development as a major factor. Complete applications require the availability of quality data, as highlighted by Wang and Strong (1996) in their early research on the quality of data. These combine to form the various constraints entities face when trying to implement new technological approaches.

2.3 THE EMERGENCE OF INDUSTRY 4.0 AND DIGITAL TRANSFORMATION

Industry 4.0 refers to a major shift in industrial production and operations that has spurred the fourth industrial revolution. Industry 4.0 is when digital technology is integrated into the production and operations of enterprises. As Kagermann et al. (2013) explain, the concept originated from Germany and describes a vision where factories are connected while production processes are monitored via intelligent systems and installed sensors. It has set up a revolution in the manufacturing sector.

At the heart of Industry 4.0 is the digitalization of manufacturing through the advanced technology of the IoT, AI, robotics, and cloud computing. The resulting "smart factories" have machines and systems that can optimize, configure themselves, and make decisions (Lasi et al., 2014). Because of this, the manufacturing industry has made technology work for it (Rüßmann et al., 2015). This includes more and more automation that comes with increased efficiency and the possibility of getting highly customized products in vast amounts.

Industry 4.0 has made the manufacturing sector centered on data. Big data and analytics make it possible to make more strategic decisions in the field. This has increased productivity and innovation, as access to data helps manufacturers gain a better and more profound understanding of their production processes and customers (Brettel et al., 2014). Industry 4.0 has also made operations easier by enhancing the connectivity and communication between different players in the sector.

Among the crucial trends in modern industries is the re-creation of traditional manufacturing companies to service-oriented ones. The rationale behind this transformation is that combining services with products increases the customer's perceived value and competitive advantage (Vandermerwe & Rada, 1988). Under Industry 4.0, the nature of such service is broadened, and manufacturers can now develop new commercial offerings, like real-time monitoring, predictive maintenance, or customized solutions that were previously unavailable (Baines et al., 2009).

The incorporation of services into manufacturing does not require the mere addition of new services to traditional product lines. The trend is an opportunity for companies to change the business model to a single holistic approach to providing a finished solution. Thus, top-rated companies such as aerospace and automotive do not just produce products; they already solve the problem: selling products and services that bring complete ideas from maintenance and data analytics to fully integrated project management (Neely, 2008).

Simplicity, a term popularized in the lectures of Elias Carayannis at George Washington University, has the meaning of the effortlessness of looking ambitious. One of the requirements in Industry 4.0 is simplicity, which covers coping with integrated sophisticated technological systems' inherent complexity. Kristina Hoffman's article attempts to decipher this notion in technological systems and simplifies such complexity at the user level. This is especially true when designing the user interface or creating the system's functionality that animates when interaction is done without human intervention. In one smart factory, the fourth industrial revolution, factory operators were battling with highly automated machines, which were complex, to pull down the interface for easy interaction and workarounds.

Insight–Innovation–Execution (I2E) also has the opposite—Excellence in Industrial Innovation—dimension—which delves into the concept of simplification. In the context of Industry 4.0, simplification means high innovation performance and sensitivity to a high level of firepower, as well as complexity of new technologies. These systems and processes must be at a state-of-the art level yet be simplified and possible to manage. This is achieved through a philosophy that innovation is determined by minimizing complexity and maximizing simplicity. However, to attain I2E, not only is a profound understanding of what is truly possible using technology needed, but also experience in overcoming the practical challenges and organizational impediments that implementation imposes. It is as summarized above about the mindset that appreciates simplicity in a complex world. And it is essential for this challenging era.

2.4 THE INDUSTRIAL INNOVATION ECOSYSTEM VS. THE INDUSTRIAL INNOVATION SYSTEM

In most introductory definitions, the concept of an industrial innovation ecosystem remains a multidimensional system outside industry's conventional boundaries. It refers to a broad spectrum of participants—companies, research organizations, governments, and others. Through their complex interaction, these participants generate a complex system that promotes innovation. The system-wide definition of an industrial innovation ecosystem relies on the idea of mutual dependence and coevolution of system participants (Jackson, 2011).

Local innovation ecosystems are highly regarded as a critical source of innovation, as evidenced by the increased concentration of technology businesses, venture capital (VC), and academic institutions. Such systems are founded on the principle of "propinquity," which emphasizes proximity and promotes collaboration and knowledge exchange (Saxenian, 1994).

Regional innovation ecosystems operate at a higher organizational level and spread beyond the local level. Although such ecosystems may still be limited to a few cities, they are more likely to cross state boundaries. These systems are built on regional strengths and designed to maximize the potential where certain industries or technologies are more developed. For example, the biotech center is integrated into a network of higher education, and research is called an economic cluster (Porter, 1998).

Industry-specific clusters and ecosystems are sectoral innovation ecosystems which focus on specific industries. Industry clusters include organizations, suppliers, service companies, and clients collaborating within one industry sector (Malerba, 2002).

A nation's innovation ecosystem is based on policy decisions and cultural, economic, and scientific determinants (Nelson, 1993).

Global innovation systems encompass networks from everywhere in the world. Global ecosystems are driven by globalization and the increasing economic connection. They are characterized by transnational cooperation, transnational supply chains, and huge multinational corporations (Gereffi et al., 2005).

The shift from sectorial systems to dynamic, non-linear ecosystems is a significant paradigm change in the comprehension of industrial innovation. In the traditional perception, industries were seen as isolated systems with a linear form of value chains. However, global complex challenges and rapid technological changes necessitated a change in approach to a more connected and adaptable process (Hekkert et al., 2007).

In a dynamic, non-linear ecosystem, innovation is not a linear process, but rather a result of factors and multiple interactions. Ecosystems are adaptable systems that can vary depending on technological advancement, market demands, and regulatory actions. This is a highly critical factor in the current rapidly changing and risky business environment. The main aspect of the industrial ecosystem is that it is not a uniform notion. There are many ecosystems, and each has a set of unique characteristics and interactions (Teece, 1992).

This is a vital element since contextual issues define the nature of innovation. Cultural frameworks, normative operations, stirring mechanisms, and available resources influence the operation and interaction in these structures. The understanding of the importance of the context of the industrial ecosystem is fundamental for policymakers, business operators, and other stakeholders (Powell et al., 1996). This approach to framing is vital in managing and sustaining vibrant innovation structures (Cooke, 2001). Therefore, the industrial innovation ecosystem is a significant paradigm in the understanding and fostering of innovation. It underscores collaboration, adaptability, and framework as critical drivers of industrial innovation. In the context of the growing global risk business, these ecosystems will be crucial in defining the future of industries.

2.5 THE EVOLUTION OF INDUSTRIAL INNOVATION PERSPECTIVES

Early visions of industrial evolution presented a largely linear and static view of the process. Expression of the view was reflected in a series of movements from research and development to production and then to market introduction. The perception of industrial evolution associated with the works of Schumpeter published in the first part of the 20th century was described as a set of discrete steps or stages linked to one another (Schumpeter, 1934). However, the perception started to change with the understanding of industrial evolution as a highly non-linear process lacking coherence or sequence.

The non-linear perspective of development was introduced by Kline and Rosenberg (1986) based on a concept of a "chain model" of industrial evolution. The model recognized industrial development as a complex phenomenon with feedback between its elements, thus being drastically different from the linear model.

The onset of the information era and the development of digital technologies further influenced the concept of industrial evolution, focusing on network innovations where cooperation and information exchange between participants became key components. The role of networks in the evolutionary process was presented by Powell et al. (1996).

Indeed, the most significant factor determining the industrial process is people. The creativity, knowledge, and skills of the people are essential factors of innovation. In his work, Florida (2002) described the concept of a "creative class" that included a population segment responsible for driving economic growth due to their innovation.

Another key factor influencing industrial process is culture. Organizational or national culture determined by the willingness to take risks, reflecting some experimentalism, and promoting cooperation is likely to enhance innovative evolution. The national cultures theory presented by Hofstede (1980) reflects the impact of national cultures on organizational culture and behavior patterns.

Technology, and especially digital devices and platforms, is another factor that has significantly influenced the landscape of industrial innovation. The speed of technological development itself is an example of such change accelerating, as rendered by Moore's Law (1965). Technology keeps developing, recycling, facilitating faster spins of the wheel for innovators and providing them with both more opportunities and challenges.

Similar to innovation ecosystems, the perspective of innovation ecosystems is a significant creation relevant to our topic. An innovation ecosystem is a complicated network of various actors participating in the innovation process, a network that, when interacting, results in innovation. This view of economy and development enriches, as opposed to possibly replaces, more traditional systems theory, which also emphasizes interaction (Adner & Kapoor, 2010).

Formulas of specialization can partially explain this development: the more complex the technologies and markets become, the more instruments might simultaneously address professional gaps. This makes collaboration and integration factors of critical importance. At the same time, industrial innovation is a multi-level phenomenon that happens at the individual, organizational, and additional levels: the national level and the industry and subindustry levels (Edquist, 1997).

Moreover, innovation is multi-modal: complementing Moore's concepts, different innovations exist similar to the range (Tidd & Bessant, 2011). That is, innovation is not only technological and not only at all levels, dependent but mutually affecting, such as process, organizational, or business model innovation.

Finally, innovation is multi-modal: it occurs between different nodes within the network. Nodes are the organizations or individuals involved in some way; the presence or absence of connections and knowledge flowing variety between them is crucial (Granovetter, 1977).

2.6 ADVANCED CONCEPTS IN INDUSTRIAL INNOVATION ECOSYSTEMS

The shifting landscape of industrial innovation is evident from the appearance of several advanced concepts—from the Quintuple Innovation Helix to Industry 5.0 and Society 5.0. These examples illustrate the reconfiguration of people and technology's role in the innovation ecosystem, stressing an integrated, human-centered approach (Carayannis et al., 2024).

The Quintuple Innovation Helix (QIH) (Carayannis et al., 2012; Carayannis & Rakhmatullin, 2014) is a framework that underscores the interconnection and collaborative nature of the innovation process among five primary actors—government, academia, industry, civil society, and individuals. It expands the Triple Helix model, which covers the relationship between government, academia, and industry, and the Quadruple Helix model (Carayannis & Campbell, 2009; Carayannis & Campbell, 2010, 2012), which adds the public to the innovation process.

In the QIH framework, individuals are crucial. Their knowledge, competencies, creativity, and proactiveness are key elements driving the innovation process and its results. Entrepreneurs, researchers, scientists, mentors, educators, and consumers and users of innovative goods and services all have distinct roles in the framework from change-makers that foster synergies to networks to collective intelligence and innovation capacity.

The idea of Industry 5.0 exemplifies the subsequent phase of technological advancement in industrial processing and creation. While its predecessor focused on automation and cyber-physical systems, Industry 5.0 highlights the significance of humanity by prioritizing human–machine interaction, sustainability, and socio-economic considerations. It combines robots and automation with the authors' creativity, critical thinking, and adaptive capabilities to envision an "industry of contrasts" where people and technology fulfill industry's potentialities for sustainability, inclusiveness, and effectiveness.

The concept of Society 5.0, also known as the "Super Smart Society," is a human-centric approach to digital transformation. It is an ideal vision of a future society that uses advanced technologies to solve social problems and maximize the quality of living for people. By incorporating the technological advances of previous societal stages and administering with new tools, Society 5.0 aspires to be a sustainable and inclusive society. Above all, Society 5.0 centers man, modifying recent technological developments specifically on increasing his well-being, happiness, and fulfillment.

The implications for Industry 5.0 and Society 5.0 are as follows. The QIH framework mentions the need for different development and collaboration with innovative initiatives between signatories to address unfulfilled societal challenges. The core idea behind this collaboration is the exchange and transfer of knowledge, with academia having a particular responsibility for research and the development of new technologies. Governments should, in turn, have a role in the broad policymaking that would promote an ecosystem of innovation and ensure that technologies are used ethically and responsibly.

Civil society organizations are also involved in the process, ensuring the promotion of sustainable ideas and equitable access and benefits. The QIH framework also emphasizes the role of individuals as active member participants in the innovation process. In Industry 5.0, people encourage skill development and active participation in the workforce. In Society 5.0, people are similarly empowered, and this allows them to shape their lives, communities, promote social innovation, and achieve personal and social achievement.

2.7 CONCLUSIONS

In conclusion, the background of industrial innovation and technological dynamics studies the role and influence of technology in establishing a new industry and restructuring the economy and society at large. The relations and links between technology and industrial innovation processes stimulate economic development and competition and revolutionize industries with innovative breakthroughs.

The appearance of technological advances and especially disruptive and discontinuous innovation has facilitated changes in industries and helped create new business models and consumer behavior. Such kinds of innovations have even "destroyed some industries" and built new ones, changed everything, including how consumers behave and producers work.

Industry 4.0 has changed industry development and production, integrating digital progress into production. Smart factories have started with innovative thinking and functioning, allowing machines and systems to acclimatize themselves to the environment and create complicated decisions. Digital innovation in a production-related sense has changed industry's fabric and stimulated more connectivity and application and structure over originality and simplicity and shifted people's focus into a facilitating solution. This transformation has also forced people to focus on creating new business areas and adding value and emphasis on complexity and focus on creating a solve-facet approach, simplicity, and newness.

The industrial innovation ecosystem's concept perceives a turn time in innovation and stimulates development as a new one. It has stimulated all impact scenarios and promotes involvement and a network of stakeholders who interact in their production and participate in industries, research and development, and government agencies. It expounds the interactions and developments of sectors to prepare the innovation for the interactive and performance-oriented place, emphasizing the importance of interaction and adaptability, and to see an interested seduction and developments.

Industrial innovation paradigms have morphed from linear and static models to prepared, non-linear, and networked ones. The growing realization that innovation is a non-linear, non-directional cycle reliant on a variety of dimensions and variables has fueled this transformation. Network innovations are being prioritized, and cooperation and communication between different stakeholders are critical. People, culture, technology, and innovation ecosystems are now essential to the conversation regarding industrial innovation. The multi-level and multi-modal nature of innovation is evident in this approach, underscoring its complexity and interdependence.

More sophisticated concepts such as the Quintuple Innovation Helix, Industry 5.0 and Society 5.0 are now working to redefine the collaboration of people and technology. The QIH model shows how several critical stakeholders may help facilitate the process, while Industry 5.0 learns from and attracts more directly from human–machine collaboration and sustainability. Society 5.0 piques our interest in how technology can enhance and transform our daily lives in a meaningful and productive way. To summarize, this part of the book illustrates that the field in which we are operating is rapidly trying to get to grips with digital labor, complicated innovative ecosystems, and advanced concepts. The future centerpieces of industrial evolution will be technology and human-centered approaches that promote teamwork and adaptability. To achieve our objectives, it is critical to keep up with the transformations that are occurring and to be strategic in aligning ourselves.

REFERENCES

Adam, L., Assaker, R., Hébert, P., Lietaer, O., & Mathieu, S. (2017). *Additive Manufacturing Simulation Solution As Enabler For Confident Lightweight Automotive Design*. SPE Automotives.

Adner, R., & Kapoor, R. (2010). Value creation in innovation ecosystems: How the structure of technological interdependence affects firm performance in new technology generations. *Strategic Management Journal*, 31(3), 306–333. DOI: 10.1002/smj.821

Agrawal, A., Gans, J., & Goldfarb, A. (2018). *Prediction Machines: The Simple Economics of Artificial Intelligence.* Boston, MA: Harvard Business Review Press.

Al-Fuqaha, A., Guizani, M., Mohammadi, M., Aledhari, M., & Ayyash, M. (2015). Internet of things: A survey on enabling technologies, protocols, and applications. *IEEE Communications Surveys & Tutorials*, 17(4), 2347–2376. DOI: 10.1109/COMST.2015.2444095

Alpaydin, E. (2016). *Machine learning: The new AI.* Cambridge, MA: MIT Press.

Anderson, P., & Tushman, M. L. (1990). Technological discontinuities and dominant designs: A cyclical model of technological change. *Administrative Science Quarterly*, 35(4), 604–633. DOI: 10.2307/2393511

Arthur, W. B. (2009). *The Nature of Technology: What It Is and How It Evolves.* New York, NY: Free Press.

Ashton, K. (2009). That 'internet of things' thing. *RFID Journal.* DOI: 10.1109/JPROC.2009.2021077

Atzori, L., Iera, A., & Morabito, G. (2010). The internet of things: A survey. *Computer Networks*, 54(15), 2787–2805. DOI: 10.1016/j.comnet.2010.05.010

Baines, T., Lightfoot, H., Benedettini, O., & Kay, J. M. (2009). The servitization of manufacturing: A review of literature and reflection on future challenges. *Journal of Manufacturing Technology Management*, 20(5), 547–567. DOI: 10.1108/17410380910960984

Borgia, E. (2014). The Internet of Things vision: Key features, applications and open issues. *Computer Communications*, 54, 1–31. DOI: 10.1016/j.comcom.2014.09.008

Bower, J. L., & Christensen, C. M. (1995). Disruptive technologies: Catching the wave. *Harvard Business Review*, 73(1), 43–53.

Brettel, M., Friederichsen, N., Keller, M., & Rosenberg, M. (2014). How virtualization, decentralization and network building change the manufacturing landscape: An Industry 4.0 perspective. *International Journal of Mechanical, Industrial Science and Engineering*, 8(1), 37–44.

Brynjolfsson, E., & McAfee, A. (2014). *The Second Machine Age: Work, Progress, and Prosperity in a Time of Brilliant Technologies.* New York, NY: W. W. Norton & Company. DOI: 10.5555/2651320

Bughin, J., Hazan, E., Ramaswamy, S., Chui, M., Allas, T., Dahlström, P., Henke, N., & Trench, M. (2017). *Artificial Intelligence: The Next Digital Frontier?* McKinsey Global Institute.

Bughin, J., et al. (2018). *Skill Shift: Automation and the Future of the Workforce.* McKinsey Global Institute. DOI: 10.1007/s12599-018-0554-4

Carayannis, E. G., Barth, T. D., & Campbell, D. F. (2012) The Quintuple Helix innovation model: global warming as a challenge and driver for innovation. *Journal of Innovation and Entrepreneurship*, 1(2). DOI: 10.1186/2192-5372-1-2

Carayannis, E. G., Kostis, P. C., & Kafka, K. I., & Valvi, T. (2024) Towards Industry 6.0 and techno-centric vs human-centric smart balancing: The journey from Industry and Society 4.0 towards Industry and Society 5.0 and beyond. In G. Meramveliotakis & M. Manioudis (Eds.), *Sustainable Development, Political Economy and Institutions: A Pluralistic Approach.* Routledge.

Carayannis, E. G., & Campbell, D. F. J. (2009). Mode 3 and Quadruple Helix: Toward a 21st Century Fractal Innovation Ecosystem. *International Journal of Technology Management*, 46, 201–234. https://doi.org/10.1504/IJTM.2009.023374

Carayannis, E. G., & Campbell, D. F. J. (2010). Triple Helix, Quadruple Helix and Quintuple Helix and How Do Knowledge, Innovation and the Environment Relate to Each Other?: A Proposed Framework for a Trans-disciplinary Analysis of Sustainable Development and Social Ecology. *International Journal of Social Ecology and Sustainable Development (IJSESD)*, 1(1), 41–69. https://econpapers.repec.org/article/iggjsesd0/v_3a1_3ay_3a2010_3ai_3a1_3ap_3a41-69.htm

Carayannis, E. G., & Campbell, D. F. J. (2012). Mode 3 knowledge production in quadruple helix innovation systems. 21st-century democracy, innovation, and entrepreneurship for development. *Springer Briefs in Business*, 63–69. https://doi.org/10.1007/978-1-4614-2062-0

Carayannis, E. G., & Rakhmatullin, R. (2014). The quadruple/quintuple innovation helixes and smart specialization strategies for sustainable and inclusive growth in Europe and beyond. *Journal of the Knowledge Economy*, 5, 212–239. https://doi.org/10.1007/s13132-014-0185-8.

Christensen, C. M. (1997). *The Innovator's Dilemma: When New Technologies Cause Great Firms to Fail.* Boston, MA: Harvard Business School Press. DOI: 10.15358/9783800642816

Christensen, C. M., & Bower, J. L. (1996). Customer power, strategic investment, and the failure of leading firms. *Strategic Management Journal*, 17(3), 197–218.

Christidis, K., & Devetsikiotis, M. (2016). Blockchains and smart contracts for the internet of things. *IEEE Access.* DOI: 10.1109/ACCESS.2016.2566339

Cooke, P. (2001). Regional innovation systems, clusters, and the knowledge economy. *Industrial and Corporate Change*, 10(4), 945–974. DOI: 10.1093/icc/10.4.945

Davenport, T. H., & Ronanki, R. (2018). Artificial intelligence for the real world. *Harvard Business Review*, 96(1), 108–116.

De Filippi, P., & Wright, A. (2018). *Blockchain and the Law: The Rule of Code.* Harvard University Press. DOI: 10.4159/9780674985913

Downes, L., & Nunes, P. (2013). Big bang disruption. *Harvard Business Review*, 91(3), 44–56.

Edquist, C. (1997). Systems of innovation approaches – Their emergence and characteristics. In *Systems of Innovation: Technologies, Institutions and Organizations* (pp. 1–35). London: Routledge.

Euchner, J. (2023). Democratizing innovation. *Research-Technology Management*, 66(4), 9–10. DOI: 10.1080/08956308.2023.2212584

Florida, R. (2002). *The Rise of the Creative Class.* Basic Books.

Ford, M. (2015). *Rise of the Robots: Technology and the Threat of a Jobless Future.* Basic Books. DOI: 10.5555/2813886

Francis L. D., & Woodcock, M. (2024). *Untangling the Relationship between Innovation and Agility.* IntechOpen. DOI: 10.5772/intechopen.112557

Fursov, K., & Linton, J. (2022). Social innovation: Integrating product and user innovation. *Technological Forecasting and Social Change*, 174. DOI: 10.1016/j.techfore.2021.121224.

Gereffi, G., Humphrey, J., & Sturgeon, T. (2005). The governance of global value chains. *Review of International Political Economy*, 12(1), 78–104. DOI: 10.1080/09692290500049805

Gobble, M. M. (2014). Charting the innovation ecosystem. *Research-Technology Management*, 57(4), 55–59. DOI: 10.5437/08956308X5704004

Goodfellow, I., Bengio, Y., & Courville, A. (2016). *Deep Learning.* Cambridge, MA: MIT Press. DOI: 10.5555/3086952

Granovetter, M. (1977). The strength of weak ties. *American Journal of Sociology*, 78(6), 1360–1380. DOI: 10.1086/225469

Grech, A., & Camilleri, A. F. (2017). Blockchain in education. *JRC Science for Policy Report.* DOI: 10.2760/60649

Green, R., & Newman, P. (2017). Citizen utilities: The emerging power paradigm. *Energy Policy*, 105, 283–293.
Gubbi, J., Buyya, R., Marusic, S., & Palaniswami, M. (2013). Internet of Things (IoT): A vision, architectural elements, and future directions. *Future Generation Computer Systems*, 29(7), 1645–1660. DOI: 10.1016/j.future.2013.01.010
Hekkert, M. P., Suurs, R. A. A., Negro, S. O., Kuhlmann, S., & Smits, R. E. H. M. (2007). Functions of innovation systems: A new approach for analysing technological change. *Technological Forecasting and Social Change*, 74(4), 413–432. DOI: 10.1016/j.techfore.2006.03.002
Hilty, L. M., et al. (2006). The relevance of information and communication technologies for environmental sustainability – A prospective simulation study. *Environmental Modelling & Software*. https://doi.org/10.1016/j.envsoft.2006.05.007
Hirschberg, J., & Manning, C. D. (2015). Advances in natural language processing. *Science*, 349(6245), 261–266. DOI: 10.1126/science.aaa8685
Hofstede, G. (1980). *Culture's Consequences: International Differences in Work-Related Values*. Sage Publications.
Iansiti, M., & Lakhani, K. R. (2020). *Competing in the Age of AI: Strategy and Leadership When Algorithms and Networks Run the World*. Boston, MA: Harvard Business Review Press. DOI: 10.1007/978-3-030-46140-9
Jackson, D. J. (2011). *What Is an Innovation Ecosystem?* National Science Foundation.
Jordan, M. I., & Mitchell, T. M. (2015). Machine learning: Trends, perspectives, and prospects. *Science*, 349(6245), 255–260. DOI: 10.1126/science.aaa8415
Kagermann, H., Wahlster, W., & Helbig, J. (2013). *Recommendations for Implementing the Strategic Initiative INDUSTRIE 4.0*. Final report of the Industrie 4.0 Working Group.
Katz, R. (2015). *The Impact of Broadband on the Economy: Research to Date and Policy Issues*. Telecommunication Development Sector, ITU.
Kline, S. J., & Rosenberg, N. (1986). An overview of innovation. In *The Positive Sum Strategy: Harnessing Technology for Economic Growth* (pp. 275–305). National Academy Press.
Kostis, P. C. (2021). Culture, innovation and economic development. *Journal of Innovation and Entrepreneurship*. DOI: 10.1186/s13731-021-00163–7.
Kostis, P. C., Kafka, K. I., & Petrakis, P. E. (2018) Cultural change and innovation performance. *Journal of Business Research*, 88, 306–313.
Krebs, H. I., & Volpe, B. T. (2015). Rehabilitation robotics. In *Springer Handbook of Robotics* (pp. 1685–1728). Springer.
Lasi, H., Fettke, P., Kemper, H. G., Feld, T., & Hoffmann, M. (2014). Industry 4.0. *Business & Information Systems Engineering*, 6(4), 239–242. DOI: 10.1007/s12599-014-0334-y
LeCun, Y., Bengio, Y., & Hinton, G. (2015). Deep learning. *Nature*, 521(7553), 436–444. DOI: 10.1038/nature14539
Lin, P., Abney, K., & Bekey, G. A. (Eds.). (2012). *Robot Ethics: The Ethical and Social Implications of Robotics*. MIT Press.
Malerba, F. (2002). Sectoral systems of innovation and production. *Research Policy*, 31(2), 247–264. DOI: 10.1016/S0048-7333(01)00139-1
Manyika, J., Chui, M., Bughin, J., Dobbs, R., Bisson, P., & Marrs, A. (2013). *Disruptive Technologies: Advances that will Transform Life, Business, and the Global Economy*. McKinsey Global Institute.
Marjani, M., et al. (2017). *Big IoT Data Analytics: Architecture, Opportunities, and Open Research Challenges*. IEEE Access.

Marr, B. (2016). *Big Data in Practice: How 45 Successful Companies Used Big Data Analytics to Deliver Extraordinary Results*. Chichester, UK: Wiley. DOI: 10.1002/9781119278825

Mazzucato, M. (2013). *The Entrepreneurial State: Debunking Public vs. Private Sector Myths*. Anthem Press.

McAfee, A., & Brynjolfsson, E. (2012). Big data: The management revolution. *Harvard Business Review*, 90(10), 60–68.

Moore, G. E. (1965). Cramming more components onto integrated circuits. *Electronics Magazine*, 38(8), 114–117.

Nandakumar, N., & Raja, T. (2019). Experimental investigation of mechanical behavior in 3D printed PLA triply periodic minimal surface structure for orthopedics. DOI: 10.20902/ijctr.2019.130122

Neely, A. (2008). Exploring the financial consequences of the servitization of manufacturing. *Operations Management Research*, 1(2), 103–118. DOI: 10.1007/s12063-009-0015-5

Nelson, R. R. (1993). *National Innovation Systems: A Comparative Analysis*. Oxford University Press.

Nidumolu, R., Prahalad, C. K., & Rangaswami, M. R. (2013). Why sustainability is now the key driver of innovation. *IEEE Engineering Management Review*. DOI: 10.1109/EMR.2013.6601104.

Perez, C. (2002). *Technological Revolutions and Financial Capital: The Dynamics of Bubbles and Golden Ages*. Cheltenham, UK: Edward Elgar. DOI: 10.4337/9781781005323

Perez, C. (2010). Technological revolutions and techno-economic paradigms. *Cambridge Journal of Economics*. DOI: 10.1093/cje/bep051

Petrakis, P. E., Kostis, P. C., & Valsamis, D. G. (2015, July) Innovation and competitiveness: Culture as a long-term strategic instrument during the European Great Recession. *Journal of Business Research*, 68(7), 1436–1438.

Porter, M. E. (1998). *Clusters and the New Economics of Competition*. Harvard Business Review.

Porter, M. E., & Heppelmann, J. E. (2014). How smart, connected products are transforming competition. *Harvard Business Review*, 92(11), 64–88.

Powell, W. W., Koput, K. W., & Smith-Doerr, L. (1996). Interorganizational collaboration and the locus of innovation: Networks of learning in biotechnology. *Administrative Science Quarterly*, 41(1), 116–145. DOI: 10.2307/2393988

Reyna, A., et al. (2018). On blockchain and its integration with IoT. Challenges and opportunities. *Future Generation Computer Systems*. DOI: 10.1016/j.future.2018.05.046

Rifkin, J. (2014). *The Zero Marginal Cost Society: The Internet of Things, the Collaborative Commons, and the Eclipse of Capitalism*. New York, NY: Palgrave Macmillan.

Roman, R., et al. (2013). On the features and challenges of security and privacy in distributed internet of things. *Computer Networks*. DOI: 10.1016/j.comnet.2012.12.018

Russell, S., & Norvig, P. (2016). *Artificial Intelligence: A Modern Approach* (3rd ed.). Upper Saddle River, NJ: Prentice Hall.

Rüßmann, M., Lorenz, M., Gerbert, P., Waldner, M., Justus, J., Engel, P., & Harnisch, M. (2015). *Industry 4.0: The Future of Productivity and Growth in Manufacturing Industries*. Boston Consulting Group.

Saxenian, A. (1994). *Regional Advantage: Culture and Competition in Silicon Valley and Route 128*. Harvard University Press.
Schumpeter, J. A. (1934). *The Theory of Economic Development*. Harvard University Press.
Schwab, K. (2017). *The Fourth Industrial Revolution*. Geneva, Switzerland: World Economic Forum.
Schwartz, D., Youngs, N., & Britto, A. (2014). *The Ripple Protocol Consensus Algorithm*. Ripple Labs Inc.
Serrano, D., et al. (2009). *Nanotechnology for Sustainable Energy*. Renewable and Sustainable Energy Reviews.
Shafi, M., et al. (2017). 5G: A tutorial overview of standards, trials, challenges, deployment, and practice. *IEEE Journal on Selected Areas in Communications*. DOI: 10.1109/JSAC.2017.2692307
Shahid, N. and Sheikh, N. (2021) Impact of big data on innovation, competitive advantage, productivity, and decision making: Literature review. *Open Journal of Business and Management*, 9, 586–617. doi: 10.4236/ojbm.2021.92032.
Siciliano, B., & Khatib, O. (Eds.). (2016). *Springer Handbook of Robotics*. Springer. DOI: 10.1007/978-3-319-32552-1
Surmen, H. K., Ortes, F., & Arslan, Y. (2023). Fundamentals of 3D printing and its applications in biomedical engineering. DOI: 10.1007/978-981-15-5424-7_2
Taylor, R. H., Menciassi, A., Fichtinger, G., Fiorini, P., & Dario, P. (2016). Medical robotics and computer-integrated surgery. In *Springer Handbook of Robotics* (pp. 1657–1684). Springer. DOI: 10.1007/978-3-319-32552-1_63
Teece, D. J. (1992). Competition, cooperation, and innovation: Organizational arrangements for regimes of rapid technological progress. *Journal of Economic Behavior & Organization*, 18(1), 1–25. DOI: 10.1016/0167-2681(92)90050-L
Tian, F. (2017). An agri-food supply chain traceability system for China based on RFID & blockchain technology. Conference on Service Systems and Service Management. 10.1109/ICSSSM.2016.7538424
Tidd, J., & Bessant, J. (2011). *Managing Innovation: Integrating Technological, Market and Organizational Change*. John Wiley & Sons.
Tushman, M. L., & Anderson, P. (1986). Technological discontinuities and organizational environments. *Administrative Science Quarterly*, 31(3), 439–465. DOI: 10.2307/2392832
Utterback, J. M. (1994). *Mastering the Dynamics of Innovation*. Boston, MA: Harvard Business School Press.
Vandermerwe, S., & Rada, J. (1988). Servitization of business: Adding value by adding services. *European Management Journal*, 6(4), 314–324. DOI: 10.1016/0263-2373(88)90033-3
Venkatesh, V., et al. (2012). Consumer acceptance and use of information technology: Extending the unified theory of acceptance and use of technology. *MIS Quarterly*, 36(1), 157–178.
Wang, J., et al. (2018). Deep learning for smart manufacturing: Methods and applications. *Journal of Manufacturing Systems*. DOI: 10.1016/j.jmsy.2018.01.003
Wang, R. Y., & Strong, D. M. (1996). Beyond accuracy: What data quality means to data consumers. *Journal of Management Information Systems*. DOI: 10.1080/07421222.1996.11518099
Westerman, G., Bonnet, D., & McAfee, A. (2014). *Leading Digital: Turning Technology into Business Transformation*. Boston, MA: Harvard Business Review Press.

Yeung, K. (2017). Hypernudge: Big Data as a mode of regulation by design. *Information, Communication & Society*. DOI: 10.1080/1369118X.2016.1186713

Zhang, L., Zhang, L., & Du, B. (2016). Deep learning for remote sensing data: A technical tutorial on the state of the art. *IEEE Geoscience and Remote Sensing Magazine,* 4(2), 22–40. DOI: 10.1109/MGRS.2016.2540798

3. Measuring industrial innovation

Elias G. Carayannis and Pantelis C. Kostis

3.1 INTRODUCTION

Measuring industrial innovation is paramount for assessing and driving economic development in the modern industrial field. This chapter investigates the history, significance, and methods of measuring industrial innovation, uncovering conventional metrics and innovative approaches that reflect modern industries' enticing nature. The issue of industrial innovation measurement is critical for firms and stakeholders as it helps to generate relevant insights for strategic planning, investing, and policymaking. Ultimately, innovation measurement is enforced and applied to assess the efficiency of industries and their potential to influence international market trends (Khachaturyan & Klicheva, 2022).

Measurement-related perspectives have shifted dramatically throughout history. Initially focused on outcomes like patents and research and development expenditures, the evolution concept expanded to incorporate a broader spectrum of innovation activities. This gradual process has allowed for discovering innovation's multi-factorial character and generative factors, transcending tradition as a primary metric (Rovere et al., 2020).

In the following sections, induction frames, such as research and development (R&D) expenditures, patent analysis, publications, and the role in assessing industrial innovation, will be explored. The limitations and challenges concerning this perspective will also be presented, including a lack of holistic representation, a time factor, and geographic and sectoral biases. Furthermore, new generation induction frames, whose principle is the M4 Framework integrating innovative methodologies, such as semantics and big data analytics, will also be introduced. These perspectives offer a broader, more complex lens on industrial innovation, reflecting modern technological advancements and industrial dynamics.

This chapter provides a robust insight into the methodologies and challenges of measuring industrial innovation used to present the induction frames and other challenges. It serves as a gateway for expanding the traditional measurement of modern industrial innovation and covers complementary and traditional perspectives.

3.2 TRADITIONAL INNOVATION INDICATORS

Traditional indicators of industrial innovation have long been the cornerstone of measurement and understanding of the innovative progress and impact on industries. These indicators may provide a structure and encompass many aspects of an innovative landscape. This section of the chapter defines traditional indicators of innovation and explains their importance in measuring industrial innovation processes. Types of traditional indicators will be discussed with their meaning, including R&D expenditure, patent analysis, publications and citations, and technology lifecycle analysis. It is important to understand that while these indicators are valuable for providing different sides of the innovative process, they also have many limitations, such as the incomplete picture of innovation, time lag, and location and settlement biases. By discussing the strengths and limitations of the traditional indicators of innovation, this section aims to provide a broader perspective on the use of these metrics in the framework of measurement of industrial innovation.

3.2.1 Definition and Importance

Traditional innovation indicators have always been essential in identifying and interpreting industrial innovation dynamics. Observed from a quantitative perspective, these indicators help define factors of an industry's or branch's innovative activity and output and include such measurements as R&D expenditure and patents, publications, and citations (Babko-Malaya et al., 2015). Indicators like those above provide a more granular look at the industry's innovation processes.

As the name implies, the indicator's domestic expenditure on R&D reflects the financial resources organizations invest in developing new products, services, or processes. This indicator directly reflects the amount of resources used to innovate and is often used as a researcher's measure of investment within the industry or branch.

Patents allow one to judge the intellectual copyright and technological development generated by industrial activity. A patent innovation is, legally speaking, a unique corporate development asset or technology for further development. Thus, this indicator helps explain the industrial contribution to technology-related intellectual property and technological progress (Babko-Malaya et al., 2015).

The number of publications and citations in scientific and technical journals helps measure the number of scientific publications and the dissemination of the path of the technology spreading within the scientific community. Unlike bibliographic synthesis, this indicator helps measure the scholars' influence and "voice" (Ogliastri et al., 2019).

Lifecycle technology assesses technology development and market entry from inception to obsolescence. This measurement is essential for facilitating decisions about technology entry, maturity, and potential as an investment.

However, traditional measurements have disadvantages. They often leave out several aspects of innovation. For instance, some branches, mainly those in which industrial development is more "intangible" and poorly understood, less developed, have fewer patent opportunities and are understudied. Additionally, some indicators are time-lagged to the point of showing the results of work that has been completed in the distant past (Ogliastri et al., 2019).

Finally, one must select the necessary indicators according to the industry's current dynamics, technologies, science, and expenditures. The focus is not only on developing a deep understanding of basic indicators, but it is also important to develop new, more sensitive instruments over time (Babko-Malaya et al., 2015).

3.2.2 Types of Traditional Indicators

Research and development expenditure indicates a country's or an organization's commitment to innovation and technological development. According to Griliches (1990), it strongly predicts future economic growth and productivity. Hall et al. (2010) support this statement by indicating R&D spending with the development of new products or processes. Thus, R&D spending can be viewed as a measure of innovation investment and a developmental indicator for research activities' intensity and focus.

Patent analysis is another important instrument of technological assessment. Archibugi and Pianta (1996) explained that a patent is a legal document that helps protect intellectual property and, at the same time, is a suitable indicator of technological advancement and competitiveness. This argument was supported by Lanjouw and Schankerman (2004), who claimed that the volume of patent applications and grants could indicate regional or sectoral innovation capability. Thus, this method provides a clearer picture of development trends and research directions.

The volume of publications and citations remains one of the most traditional methods for assessing scientific and academic research output. King (2004) pointed out the importance of publication in science as a measure of scientific influence and productivity. Citation count was used to assess research papers' success and relevance. Moed (2005) opposed the idea that it always serves as a measure of citations and an account for community response.

Technology Lifecycle Analysis is, perhaps, the most important, as lifecycle analysis explains the stages of technology development and adoption. Ford and Ryan (1981) regarded this model to understand technology in its stages of development, maturity, and decline. At the same time, Tushman and Anderson (1986) explained how technology evolution leads to industry transformation, emergence, and re-emergence.

3.2.3 Limitations and Challenges

While the mentioned traditional indicators provide meaningful data about innovation, they give only a partial view of the issue. More specifically, as Bozeman et al. (2002) argue, most existing R&D investment is expenditure-based and including patent analysis indicators only considers the formal and mostly visible part of innovation, thus leaving aside the informal and especially process innovations. Additionally, other authors pointed out that this concern can extend to socio-economic sectors. Godin (2002) stated that the focus on R&D indicators can greatly underestimate innovation levels in those areas.

Despite these limitations, such traditional indicators have weaknesses that hinder quick and potentially accurate measurements. First, measurement lag is an issue with most existing metrics. As Jaffe and Trajtenberg (2002) claim, patents arising from R&D expenditures don't tend to be filed until several years after the R&D takes place, and once filed, patents must be approved, which can take years. Second, there is a geographic and industrial bias, as the fact sometimes blurs our understanding since the innovation fields differ—for instance, what is a technological innovation in one country might be an organizational innovation in another (Hall et al., 2005).

Another problem of such indicators is an excessive focus on quantitativeness, as Rothwell and Zegveld (1985) argue that the emphasis has been too much on quantity rather than on quality and more heavily on application against the complete addressable market and export potential than against social and environmental acceptability. Another problem is that it is difficult to measure incremental innovation using the traditional approach; for instance, Tidd and Bessant (2011) refer to this as it can be difficult to detect substantial innovation in the face of major companies at the forefront of a given market. Quite similarly, Granstrand (1999) criticized the current approach of measurement of innovation with a focus on patents as it creates a bias regarding technology licensing.

3.3 NEW GENERATION INNOVATION MEASURES AND INDICATORS

In the world of ever-accelerating technological progress and transformative innovation, traditional innovation measures increasingly appear deficient in reflecting the full range of innovation that happens in our day and age. As a result, there has been a need to turn toward new generation innovation measures and indicators that would be able to offer a more thorough, evolving, and correct picture of innovative activities.

This entails acknowledging the complexity, interconnectedness, and multilevel nature of innovation in the digital era, where developments occur at an unprecedented speed and influence various sectors and areas of life. Indeed, the advent of new generation measures is conditioned by the need to understand and quantify the innovation in digitalizing life and work, user and open innovations, and integration of the Internet of Things (IoT) and the Internet of Everything (IoE). Such indicators are not limited to merely counting the number of patents or level of R&D expenditure but rather focus on innovation's impact, spread, and network effects.

Moreover, they are designed to use big data analytics and real-time data analysis to provide more adequate and relevant statistics for policymaking and strategic planning. In this context, predictive analytics in innovation becomes crucial for relevant stakeholders, allowing them to forecast developments and be prepared for future challenges and opportunities. Therefore, introducing new generation measures into the innovation landscape signifies a significant step in understanding what happens behind progress and how it can be achieved and sustained in a world of complexity and interaction.

3.3.1 Introduction to the M4 Framework

Elias G. Carayannis's M4 Framework, as a summary, embodies a big step forward in the matter of measuring innovation. As Carayannis and Campbell (2009) state, the main novelty of this model is the multidimensional understanding of innovation, as an innately complex phenomenon that is influenced by many elements within the innovation ecosystem. Unlike other models that are concerned primarily with included quantitative indicators such as R&D spending or the number of patents created, the M4 Framework also includes socio-psychological and technological indicators in order to give a fuller picture of innovation.

The key point of Carayannis and Campbell is the highlighting of "Meta-Techno-Economic Networks," which are necessary to examine all innovative processes. This concept accentuates not only the interconnectedness of diverse fields of human endeavor but also how that interconnectedness defines new sectors. This way, the M4 Framework is more than a devised economic indicator; it is also a profound sociological and technological inquiry that enables a more comprehensive approach to how innovations come to be and then evolve into full sectors.

The M4 Framework also includes semantics and big data in defining indicators. According to Carayannis and Provance (2012), combining semantic analysis with big data should enable the processing of large amounts of data and the creation of new knowledge based on complex interrelations and hidden patterns. According to Carayannis and Provance (2012), semanticists are concerned primarily with meaning, not only with form. That is why big data analytics is important, as the form must be measured and assessed, but only semantics will uncover meaningful patterns within a dataset. This aspect is particularly important in the digital age with growing support.

Despite its advantages, the M4 measurement framework has several limitations or difficulties. The foremost challenge is integrating and analyzing data from various sources. This requires the availability of tools and methodology and professional integrators in several fields. However, the complication of integrating data provides the potential for more substantiated and informed indicator metrics.

Another challenge is ensuring the usability of the data. In contrast to other branches of science where the data is usable and final, collected data in innovation fields may not be useful in improving a theory or product that retracts a new novelty level. Hence, the M4 Framework must have a continuous data collection and analysis mechanism to ensure its usability.

In terms of implication, the M4 Framework has far-reaching implications for policy and strategy. The framework provides a more extended view of the innovation environment and the various relationships in the sector. This will allow policymakers to make an informed decision and create appropriate policies. Understanding the main variables or interests, such as how they interplay and recommendations for intervention, will empower policymakers to ensure the overall development of the innovation ecosystem.

Thus, the M4 Framework enables policymakers to focus on the major policies that drive innovation and understand which aspects to concentrate investment on. The proposed model also facilitates shaping policies that address specific categories of innovation challenges.

3.3.2 Advanced Metrics and Measurements

The IoT/IoE ecosystems are major advances in measuring innovation. Essentially, IoT/IoE ecosystems, as mentioned by Ziouvelou et al. (2017), transform the business in terms of how we appreciate and evaluate innovation through crowd-sourced information in critical domains. These ecosystems utilize user-owned gadgets, including mobile and wearable devices, to identify and evaluate phenomena, resulting in a multidimensional data collection and investigation approach. Speaking of these phenomena, Javed et al. (2020) discuss the IoT's role in creating open innovation ecosystems, especially in smart cities, by removing the importance of interoperability and security in these systems.

Indeed, the digitalization of life and business has implications for the environment in which humans function. Many aspects of this digital conversion have resulted in the need for novel, revised, and appraised metrics. As we transition toward more digital processes in agriculture and manufacturing, consumer outputs and processes, including digital technologies, must be evaluated using novel metrics.

User innovation and open innovation metrics are more important than ever in comprehending the vast environment of innovation. Discussing Agriculture 4.0, Silva et al. (2023) describe the part open innovation plays in this novel age and emphasize that the IoT is an essential technology. Additionally, they call for more understanding and advanced capabilities. Li et al. (2023) relate technological developments, including the IoT and machine learning, to autonomous methods and sustainability. They also call for open-source software (OSS) to encourage independent invention.

3.3.3 Management and Monitoring of Innovation

The use of real-time data analysis is an increasingly important factor in innovation management and control. Real-time data analysis for innovation management will help organizations stay sensitive to market dynamics and technological changes. This is critical in an ever-changing business environment, where today is critical to the success of organizations. This enables managers to maintain a constant data flow and use it to make informed decisions. Additionally, real-time data analysis significantly improves the ability to monitor innovative initiatives. New products, services, and ways of doing business can be quickly exchanged and prioritized based on the immediate data available to managers.

Predictive analysis predicts future trends and helps drive efficiency in managing innovation and making informed decisions. Adebiyi (2023) studies predictive analytics of effectiveness in assessment and gives possibilities such as financial reporting, fraud and risk identification, and real-time policy decisions. This can analyze historical data and modeling to predict future events, making key organizational functions more accurate and reliable. It allows management to engage with opportunities and risks rather than just opportunities.

In terms of innovation, predictive analysis can use data to predict and change market trends and consumer choices. In the process, it changes technology and other primary factors. Additionally, predictive analysis can contribute to strategies to manage and lead patient-centered schemes following a better platform of the industry structure. Real-time data analysis and predictive analysis have strong policy implications. Management can use data to develop and prioritize appropriate strategies. This can help ensure appropriate investment is made in viable projects. In addition, it has been used for monitoring and evaluation. This model has been designed to study decision-making patterns that are offered to improve overall performance. Real-time data analysis and predictive analysis are not the only forms of field operation. This is the increase of the strategic harmonization of the sound of orientation within the material framework. This is done according to the vertical technologies shaping the provision of the information it demands.

3.4 MEASURING INNOVATION ECOSYSTEMS PERFORMANCE

Performance of innovation ecosystems is a fundamental aspect in the dynamic world of technological and economic development. With the integration of multiple actors, including firms, government, and academia, innovation ecosystems are highly dedicated to ensuring that any country's growth and competitiveness in the global market are sustainable. This shall focus on the definitions and qualities of innovation ecosystems and components as well as the various stakeholders' relationships. This section shall also focus on the performance measures comprising the various methods such as network analysis and economic impact that provide a baseline for understanding the performance mechanisms. The section shall use various case studies and examples to focus on the performance of some of the successful ecosystems and provide lessons that can be learned and best practices that can be emulated.

3.4.1 Understanding Innovation Ecosystems

Innovation ecosystems are multidimensional networks that combine different actors, including firms, government organizations, and higher education institutions, to promote innovation and economic development. Prokop et al. (2019) argue the importance of innovation ecosystems that enable firms to innovate, especially in ICT. While conducting their study, the authors conclude that components such as information resources and the ability to cooperate are the most important. It is also evident that an actor driven by knowledge creation collaborates with the funding body and the overall knowledge user to form an ecosystem.

Hailu and Chebo (2021) explain the role of industrial parks in establishing an entrepreneurial ecosystem to help small manufacturing firms, emphasizing the importance of available infrastructure. Segers (2017) also pays attention to the role and interaction of different actors and to the engagement in strategic alliances and open innovation practices. The author claims that conduct externalities support the governance of policies at the regional level. The synergy between the conceptual expectations defines this interaction and the role of each actor. They also rely on firms determined by practical market needs and the possibility of commercializing results and funding governed by policy and academics that conduct basic research. Political implications and public policy are essential aspects of the feasibility of these actions. Prokop et al. (2019) explored the impact of public policy and political implications on the outcomes of innovations in European ICT firms.

Nature-standing institutions are expected to conduct basic research and generate the essential knowledge based on which innovation implementation occurs. Data and commercial feasibility are the primary challenges facing this organization. They conduct the research and outline its possible applications.

3.4.2 Performance Measurement Approaches

Network analysis is another essential way of measuring the performance of an innovation ecosystem. It involves assessing the structure and relationships of various ecosystem elements such as firms, universities, and government agencies. The measure seeks to ascertain how these elements interact and cooperate in innovation development.

Zhou et al. (2022) applied social network analysis to ascertain the impact of high-speed rail on regional green innovation performance. They found that certain network actors, such as transportation network connectivity and network centrality, influence innovation outcomes in the region.

Byrne et al. (2021) applied network capital to the various linkage categories in an innovation ecosystem. They also developed the network visualization approach V-LINC, which indicates the cluster's economic influence and network diversity, underscoring the need to measure innovation network inputs and outputs.

Another vital way to ascertain the performance of an innovation ecosystem is through economic impact analysis. The measure involves assessing the direct economic contribution of innovation activities through job creation, value-added revenue, and growth in the entire generation in each region or industry.

Noja et al. (2022) applied advanced econometric techniques to assess how energy innovations and environmental performance influence economic sustainability in EU development. Takala et al. (2023) discussed the impacts and regional innovation ecosystem indicators supporting sustainable development. They also emphasized that one needs to have a varied and comparison needs-based data review methodology when assessing the impact of regional innovation policy and Smart Specialisation Strategy on the economy of the European Union.

The measure also involves assessing the Return on Investment ROI of the innovation efforts and funds in the sector. The measure helps policymakers know if they are getting value for their money invested in innovation. The economic impact assessment doesn't just assess the direct economic benefit of the innovation but also the broad socio-economic benefits such as quality of life, environmental friendliness, and social justice. A comprehensive performance measure of an innovation ecosystem should also contain the economic impact assessment and the network analysis. Network analysis focuses on the structural and relational aspects, while the economic impact assessment measures the interconnectedness between the elements.

The two measures are valuable in offering information to policymakers, the business community, and academia on the various contributions that the innovation ecosystem makes to economic development.

3.5 CONCLUSIONS

The above analysis of the measurement of industrial innovation highlights the importance of measuring economic growth and industrial competitiveness. Generally, with the dynamism of the industrial landscape throughout history to the modern era, innovation measurement has had to keep pace with and reflect the current developments. This ideal chapter extensively addressed the different measurement dimensions concerning measuring industrial innovation.

Several traditional indicators, such as R&D expenditure, patent applications, and publications, have laid the foundation for measuring industrial innovation. On the one hand, these indicators provide measurable and real measures that show what the industrial players have done to enhance innovation.

However, given some of the limitations of these indicators, including biases and lags, it is important to consider more aspects of measurement. New-generation indicators, such as the M4 Framework for industry, are great milestones that have advanced the science of measuring innovation. These measures have advanced technologies and methodologies, such as big data and semantics, that show the industry's combined and more advanced phenomenon, including the market aspect. The Meta–Techno–Economic Networks, as covered by the M4 Framework, are evidence of the industry's interrelatedness and interconnectedness. The chapter also presented how innovation ecosystems can also be measured. The measure included network analysis and economic impact, which measures how active parts of a network are and how other players rely on one another.

Measurement of industrial innovation is a complex task that should combine existing and innovative methodologies. Traditional indicators laid the foundation for measurement and constructing the understanding of industrial development, while new-generation indicators provide a complete picture of innovation development. At the same time, one of the important conditions for the strategic development of the industry and regulatory policy is the efficient management and control of indicators using real-time analysis and artificial intelligence monitoring.

Meanwhile, as industries develop, the measurement methods will also change to ensure an accurate reflection of the dynamics of industrial development and support steps to ensure sustainable economic development. Thus, several future industrial innovation measurement trends can be identified, which would depend on new technologies and constant changes in global markets and focus on sustainable development and social responsibility.

Firstly, artificial intelligence (AI), machine learning technologies, and blockchain will expand. These technologies support large data volumes, make predictions, and provide reliable and transparent records. This approach helps to modernize measurement methodologies in terms of analyzing indicators in real time.

Secondly, measuring indicators will increasingly focus on assessing the environmental and social impact. Such sustainability indicators, ethical behavior, and social responsibility will be considered no less important than financial and technological ones. It also reflects the current business trends, where companies are held accountable for environmental and social responsibility.

Thirdly, the measurement of innovations will be increasingly characterized by individualizing indicators for each industry. Thus, to assess the efficiency and rationality of development, they will use metrics for a more detailed comparison and clarity to identify problems and prospects for development.

Finally, with the increasing trend toward open and collaborative innovation, there will be a new need for metrics to better measure the value of partnerships, knowledge sharing, and co-creation across sectors. Overall, the future of industrial innovation measurement will be more integrated, holistic, and responsible. It will utilize new technologies to enable more meaningful insights, consider sustainability and social impact measures, and reflect the nature of industries and regions. As the industrial innovation landscape shifts over time, these trends will help shape the development of more and better innovation metrics.

REFERENCES

Adebiyi, O. O. (2023). *Exploring the Impact of Predictive Analytics on Accounting and Auditing Expertise: A Regression Analysis of LinkedIn Survey Data. Asian Journal of Economics, Business and Accounting*, 23(22), 286–305. https://ssrn.com/abstract=4626506

Archibugi, D., & Pianta, M. (1996). Measuring technological change through patents and innovation surveys. *Technovation*, 16(9), 451–468. https://doi.org/10.1016/0166-4972(96)00031-4

Babko-Malaya, O., Seidel, A., Hunter, D., HandUber, J., Torrelli, M., & Barlos, F. (2015). Forecasting technology emergence from metadata and language of scientific publications and patents. *International Society for Scientometrics and Infometrics*. https://www.issi-society.org/proceedings/issi_2015/0340.pdf

Bozeman, B., Dietz, J. S., & Gaughan, M. (2002). Scientific and technical human capital: An alternative model for research evaluation. *International Journal of Technology Management*, 24(2–3), 716–740. https://doi.org/10.1504/IJTM.2001.002988

Byrne, E., Doyle, E., & Hobbs, J. (2021). Network diversity, distance and economic impact in a cluster: Visualising linkages and assessing network capital. *Competitiveness Review*, 31, 5.

Carayannis, E. G., & Campbell, D. F. J. (2009). 'Mode 3' and 'Quadruple Helix': Toward a 21st century fractal innovation ecosystem. *International Journal of Technology Management*, 46(3–4), 201–234.

Carayannis, E. G., & Provance (2012). *Mode 3 Knowledge Production in Quadruple Helix Innovation Systems, 21st-Century Democracy, Innovation.* and Entrepreneuership for Development.

Ford, D., & Ryan, C. (1981). Taking technology to market. *Harvard Business Review*, 59(2), 117–126.

Godin, B. (2002). The rise of innovation surveys: Measuring a fuzzy concept. *Research Policy*, 31(2), 109–123.

Granstrand, O. (1999). *The Economics and Management of Intellectual Property: Towards Intellectual Capitalism*. Edward Elgar Publishing.

Griliches, Z. (1990). Patent statistics as economic indicators: A survey. *Journal of Economic Literature*, 28(4), 1661–1707. https://doi.org/10.3386/w3301

Hailu, T., & Chebo, A. (2021). The role of industrial parks entrepreneurial ecosystem in strengthening ventures' capability: Evidence from Ethiopian small manufacturing enterprises. *Research Square*. https://doi.org/10.21203/rs.3.rs-1049854/v1

Hall, B. H., Jaffe, A. B., & Trajtenberg, M. (2005). Market value and patent citations. *RAND Journal of Economics*, 36(1), 16–38. https://www.jstor.org/stable/1593752

Hall, B. H., Lotti, F., & Mairesse, J. (2010). Innovation and productivity in SMEs: Empirical evidence for Italy. *Small Business Economics*, 34(3), 225–242. https://doi.org/10.1007/s11187-009-9184-8

Jaffe, A. B., & Trajtenberg, M. (2002). *Patents, Citations, and Innovations: A Window on the Knowledge Economy*. MIT Press.

Javed, A., Kubler, S., Malhi, A., Nurminen, A., Robert, J., & Främling, K. (2020). *bIoTope: Building an IoT Open Innovation Ecosystem for Smart Cities*. https://doi.org/10.1109/ACCESS.2020.3041326

Khachaturyan, M., & Klicheva, E. (2022). Factors of innovation management transformation in digital innovation ecosystems of Russian companies. *International Journal of E-Government Research*, 18(4), 1–16. https://dx.doi.org/10.4018/ijegr.315603

King, D. A. (2004). The scientific impact of nations. *Nature*, 430(6997), 311–316. https://doi.org/10.1038/430311a

Lanjouw, J. O., & Schankerman, M. (2004). Patent quality and research productivity: Measuring innovation with multiple indicators. *The Economic Journal*, 114(495), 441–465. https://doi.org/10.1111/j.1468-0297.2004.00216.x

Li, T., Zhu, J., Luo, J., Yi, C., & Zhu, B. (2023). Breaking triopoly to achieve sustainable smart digital infrastructure based on open-source diffusion using government–platform–user evolutionary game. *Sustainability*, 15(19), 14412. https://doi.org/10.3390/su151914412

Moed, H. F. (2005). *Citation Analysis in Research Evaluation*. Dordrecht: Springer.

Noja, G., Cristea, M., Panait, M., Trif, S.-M., & Ponea, C. Ş. (2022). The impact of energy innovations and environmental performance on the sustainable development of the EU countries in a globalized digital economy. *Frontiers in Environmental Science,* 10, 934404. https://doi.org/10.3389/fenvs.2022.934404

Ogliastri, E., Pamplona, J. B., & Villegas, M. G. (2019). Management and innovation in Latin America: Introduction. *Gestão & Regionalidade*, 35, 105.

Prokop, V., Stejskal, J., & Hájek, F. (2019). Ways to boost firms' innovation within innovation ecosystems: Case of European ICT firms. Proceedings of the 1st International Conference on IT, Communication and Technology for Better Life ICT4BL - Volume 1, 22–28, 2019. Bangkok, Thailand.

Rothwell, R., & Zegveld, W. (1985). *Reindustrialization and Technology*. Longman.

Rovere, R. L. L., Santos, G. de O., & Vasconcellos, B. L. X. (2020). Challenges for the measurement of innovation ecosystems and entrepreneurial ecosystems in Brazil. *Revista de Empreendedorismo e Gestão de Pequenas Empresas*, 10(1), 1971. https://dx.doi.org/10.14211/regepe.v10i1.1971

Segers, J. (2017). *The Interplay of Regional Systems of Innovation, Strategic Alliances and Open Innovation*. Thèse présentée en vue de l'obtention du grade de Docteur en Sciences Economiques et de Gestion

Silva, F. T., Baierle, I. C., Corrêa, R. G. F., Sellitto, M., Peres, F. A. P., & Kipper, L. M. (2023). Open innovation in agribusiness: Barriers and challenges in the transition to agriculture 4.0. *Sustainability*. 2023; 15(11):8562. https://doi.org/10.3390/su15118562

Takala, M., Tukiainen, T., Salminen, V., Sarkkinen, J. (2023). Impacts and indicators of regional innovation ecosystems supporting sustainable development. In V. Salminen (Ed.), *Human factors, business management and society* (Vol. 97). AHFE Open Access. AHFE (2023). International Conference. AHFE Open Access, vol. 97. AHFE International, USA. http://doi.org/10.54941/ahfe1003881

Tidd, J., & Bessant, J. (2011). *Managing Innovation: Integrating Technological, Market and Organizational Change*. John Wiley & Sons.

Tushman, M. L., & Anderson, P. (1986). Technological discontinuities and organizational environments. *Administrative Science Quarterly*, 31(3), 439–465. https://doi.org/10.2307/2392832

Zhou, Y., Fan, Q.-M., & Tao, C. (2022). The impact of high-speed rail on regional green innovation performance—Based on the dual perspective of high-speed rail opening and high-speed rail network. *Polish Journal of Environmental Studies,* 31(6). https://doi.org/10.15244/pjoes/155961

Ziouvelou, X., Alexandrou, P., Angelopoulos, C., Evangelatos, O., Fernandes, J., Loumis, N., McGroarty, F., Nikoletseas, S., Rankov, A., Raptis, T. P., Ståhlbröst, A., & Ziegler, S. (2017). Crowd-driven IoT/IoE ecosystems: A multidimensional approach. Proceedings of the 2017 European Conference on the Internet of Things (ECIOT).

4. The political dynamics of industrial innovation

Elias G. Carayannis and Pantelis C. Kostis

4.1 INTRODUCTION

This chapter discusses the complex and often overlooked relationship between politics and industrial innovation. The interaction of key areas of technology and politics has historically significantly shaped technological development. It is still an exceptionally responsive predictor of industrial change. The correlation between the two components is critical knowledge, and the goal is to understand how industrial innovation affects global policy holistically.

One key to understanding this aspect is the commentary on how crucial politics is in innovation. Political decisions, such as the government's allocation of funds for research and development to distant trade activity, have a massive effect on the direction and pace of technological development. The politically astute nation builds stronger innovation platforms, placing fewer obstacles to technological advancement, from policy to dynamic conditions.

This chapter also examines the global dynamics that influence industrial innovation. The world is becoming more aligned, and political, geo-technological, and geo-economic frontiers are crucial for the growth of innovation.

Global patterns are a crucial element. These are not only a rivalry to provide technology but also a necessity and issue many applicants fail to understand head-on. The chapter discusses geo-strategic dynamics, offering examples from specific studies that demonstrate the impact of strategy on presentations that are close to the human race

The role of technology in global politics will also propose examples of all technologies that have influenced the world power struggle. Examining the economic consequences of rare-dimensional shows in this part may be important. Advances in technology and policy and industry, foreign policy design, and industrial innovation. It assumes that policy creates a landscape, and these factors need to be focused on. The latter should not be examined with one factor pulled out of that aspect.

The chapter introduces a study of the implementation of sustainable behavior policy, the global sector's situation, and the final moment in the conclusion based on examples. Should technological advances be driven by economic development or counterbalanced by environmental protection?

4.2 GLOBAL-LEVEL DYNAMICS

This section addresses how industrial innovation in the current century influences and is influenced by global dynamics. It is structured into four broad, independent but interconnected spheres: Geo-Strategic Dynamics, Geo-Technological Dynamics, Geo-Economic Dynamics, and Geo-Political Dynamics. Each of these dimensions presents a different perspective through which the complexity of global patterns and industrial innovation can be discerned. These include the strategic competencies and aspirations of nations that respond to technological changes, the impact of the disruptors in innovation on global politics and economies, and the balance of power strategies. Ultimately, the section attempts to interrogate the webs of relationships and shaping influences characterizing the topography of global innovation in the current century.

4.2.1 Geo-Strategic Dynamics

Geo-Strategic Dynamics form the basis for analyzing the global innovation landscape, including the strategic decisions leading nations make and their actions in response to technological advancement. In this way, these dynamics determine the course and progress of innovation, influencing economic advancements, the national political and military system, and the global military-political balance. Thus, innovations are strategic not purely when a breakthrough is reached in technology but due to the degree of dependence on these designs and the geo-political dimensions of strategies to achieve these designs. Strategic innovations are crucial in forming national economies and reacting to global integration processes.

According to Shelomentsev et al. (2021) one of the critical tasks of strategic innovation in that area remains the implementation of the processes of new product creation in Global Value Chains (GVCs). As part of these factors, they determine the effectiveness of the functioning of enterprises and the national economy in general, the improvement of which is one of the main ways to ensure further economic growth and competitiveness of countries, which addresses the logical system between the technological and socio-economic regimes.

The classic example of the hot race was the space race, which took place during the Cold War between the Soviet Union and the United States. After these achievements, a man was sent into outer space, and the first Earth satellite was launched—our planet's first spacecraft. Leading nations are constantly negotiating their status, role, and power through the prism of scientific-technical progress.

Another classic example of hot politics is the Internet, which was initially a project financed by the US Department of Defense. The transformation of the Internet from a communication network for military purposes into an information-sharing structure for the whole world demonstrates how strategic innovations can overcome the initial goal and form global socio-economic relations.

Another good example of how politics is related to strategic goods such as oil, gas, and petroleum goods and the Arctic region. Kozmenko and Kozmenko (2022) analyzed how petroleum and oil influence countries' national budgets and politics and provide the basis for hot politics.

Another aspect of strategic innovation is the transformation of geo-political dynamics. Karkazis (2019) analyzed how Turkey developed its position as one of the large geo-political powers in Southern Europe based on its strategic properties of European investments and which developments are occurring due to Turkey's growing power in the region.

4.2.2 Geo-Technological Dynamics

Geo-Technological Dynamics are used to denote the impact of technology on global politics and presents the strategic decisions pursued by different nations. On the one hand, it focuses on advancing technology's ability to change politics in different countries and even the international power landscape. On the other hand, this concept can address technology's role in politics, especially its impact on developing nations and military strategies.

The most critical cases of geo-technological dynamics are technology and energy politics. Bajrektarević (2012) is concerned with the geopolitics of technology in the hydrocarbon status quo and addresses the strategic focus of oil and energy leverage in politics. This example shows that specific technological advancements in energy production and consumption can change the balance of power; the spread of technology focused on political geography.

Straccamore et al. (2023) demonstrate how geography and borders impact the dissemination of technological innovation. Although their study reveals that political geography has an almost negligible effect, the overall spread of technology has led to a new global patenting ecosystem and distinct technological innovation pathways.

Cheung (2010) focuses on the changing power and, therefore, Chinese technology power and even notes the differences in a significant rise as a military power through technology.

4.2.3 Geo-Economic Dynamics

As the term implies, geo-economic dynamics lay in the economic dimensions of global innovations and their effects on international trade, industry, and economic strategy. In national and international cases, it is essential to view how technological improvement contributes to economic expansion while forming trading alliances and economics-focused policies in one or another country.

The present shape of the world economy, with its fast restructuring due to the industries of Industry 4.0, globalization, and the toughening rivalry with many states, is a bright illustration of innovation's value in one's economic growth. According to WIPO (2021), the issue of innovation as the foundation on which industrialization is based is particularly important for developing countries such as Ukraine. It is one of the most effective means of diversifying the economy, eliminating structural distinctions, and advancing into a new international division of labor sectors. Hence, it is okay to consider how innovations can contribute to economic evolution and support one when trading on the global stage.

The world financial situation revolutionized notably after the 2008 slump. Srivastava et al. (2016) discussed the legacy and possibilities such a period provided from the global recession to the recovery period. This research indicates how technology may stimulate international trade, industry, and life to foster sustainable economic evolution.

The financial relationship between the United States and China also deserves attention as a compelling case. Muhammad et al. (2023) critically analyzed the pros and cons of this country's relationship as trading partners, focusing on exchange disparities, pricing, and currency control. This examination reveals how technological and economic components influence the connection between two states and the whole planet.

Rzayev et al. (2020) investigated the geo-institutional character of GVCs, focusing on the value-added measurements and ending with consumption in different markets of the Azerbaijani economy is one of the components of geo-economic dynamics that need consideration. This analysis indicates how one's connection with GVCs may determine economic evolution and national mean.

4.2.4 Geo-Political Dynamics

Geo-political dynamics refer to the influence of political power and decision-making on global innovation. This concept assesses the impact of political strategies, international relations, and policy decisions on creating a particular landscape in which technological advancement and innovation occur. The role of politics in the innovation process constitutes multiple dimensions, including federal spending and national regulation, popular international collaboration or competition, and other aspects.

The current impact of the COVID-19 pandemic on the global world order is a good example of this dynamic. According to Zorko and Lučev (2021), a practical examination of geo-political and geo-economic consequences found three types of geo-political games: the game of labeling and non-movement, the game of racing with vaccines, and the game of the securitization of the pandemic. This example demonstrates how geo-political dynamics include shifts in political power that affect innovation strategies.

Other examples include the US–China rivalry that has disrupted global governance and has led to the decoupling of value chains. Vertinsky et al. (2023) suggest that the disengagement process's rates and costs will be so unbearable that the world will return to inertia from square one. The authors offer an alternative approach, claiming that the US and China are too closely linked to decouple fully. They also suggest investigating the influence of emerging middle powers on global and regional governance.

Moreover, Öniş and Kutlay (2016) study Turkey's geo-political power, concluding that the existing arguments regarding emerging middle powers' limited influence require more examination.

Lastly, geography plays a significant role in geo-political dynamics, particularly in local innovation systems. Miao (2020) explores the typology of such systems, using the example of the Optics Valley in China. The scholar concludes that Local Innovation Systems (LIS) analysis should include the local articulation of similar regional and national systems.

4.3 CONVERGENCE OF INDUSTRIAL AND INNOVATION POLICIES

Industrial and innovation policies are rapidly changing landscapes developed in a way in which the flat and circular geometry shifts and reforms itself. This section identifies this development's historical patterns and contemporary flow, including how the convergence of the two policy aspects influences the economic and technology breakpoints. Similarly, the section also explores the convergence's effectivity in national and global dimensions and answers some of the questions in terms of adaptation of the related dynamics to shape the newly formed approach. Overall, the section provides the reader with an insight of the blend of industry and innovation-centered growth dimensions and allows better understanding of the roots of this underlying and most effective change in policy approach that will determine the future response to the key development and economic issues.

4.3.1 The Blurring Lines between Industrial and Innovation Policies

The border between industrial and innovation policies has become increasingly blurred in the past several decades. The described phenomena could be explained by the understanding that innovation is a key driver of industrial competitiveness and is thus closely related to national and international economic performance.

The textbook by Cirera et al. (2020) is a comprehensive reading that covers innovation policy from the perspective of developing and developed economies. With a focus on their growth strategies, the study finds a fair amount of evidence that increased innovation-focused activities enhance firms' productivity and thus countries' competitiveness. Additionally, the example of Singapore presented in the work of Goh (2006) clearly shows the evolution of the industrial policy-making system toward the support of innovation.

Another case study is represented by the work of Grabas and Nützenadel (2013), who provide a historical overview of industrial policy in Europe associated with the post-World War II era, showing that national traditions and the country's economic system are crucial to shaping these policies. The work also shows that industrial policies have been successful in contributing to the economic growth of the countries discussed and their integrated innovation strategies.

Finally, a study by Yan et al. (2021) shows how green innovation in the manufacturing industry in China illustrates various characteristics of this efficiency across industries. This work is especially relevant because it demonstrates the necessity to integrate innovation policies and the industrial system to promote sustainable development. Overall, the trend combined with other phenomena discussed in this chapter indicates that industrial and innovation policies are interrelated and should be integrated.

4.3.2 Impact on National and International Levels

The convergence of industrial and innovation policies has profound implications at national and international levels. The integration impacts policy formulation and implementation at the national scale. The policy orientation affects how the country orients its economic development, enhances technological development, and promotes an ecological agenda. Several countries have already embraced the convergence, and the results manifest in advances across their aspects of economics and technology. At the international level, the convergence has influenced some of the policies and legal frameworks embraced by different states.

For example, climate change initiatives target city and regional development. According to Kociuba and Wajs (2021), top-down analysis of the policies reveals that the top nation-states implemented them through devolution to local authorities. Such a scenario manifests in developing environments that meet the needs of existing and future generations. The aspects of globalization also offer transformations within public implementation and formulation.

Gunggut (2009) analyzed how globalization necessitated the development of policies that lead to forest management. The study highlights the interplay of global and national interests leading to the same goals. External reference pricing is another instance that has impacted more than one country internationally. Fontrier et al. (2019) conducted a pooled study on the Enterprise Resource Planning's (ERP) effect on different countries. The study synthesized the benefits and costs associated with the policy, considering that the benefits are often allied to the policy. Powers (2020) presents the situation in Jordan, where national and transnational issues have influenced each other. The case study explains how issues may intertwine in the future. These case studies highlight the benefits and costs associated with policy convergence at the national and international levels.

4.4 THE ROLE OF SUSTAINABLE POLICIES

The prominently-discussed thematic quest of sustainability's critical engagement with industrial innovation is examined in this section. Sustainability is defined and considered in the implications of the term in the context of technological and industrial development, and the vital necessity of sustainable policies' development is explained for ensuring long-term economic and environmental stability. Moreover, this section tackles various examples of innovation policies that embrace sustainability principles, including existing renewable energy technology, sustainable or green manufacturing principles, and the circular economy concept. The barriers and opportunities associated with these examples and the balance between economic development and environmental impact are explored. Furthermore, this section examines future trends in sustainable policymaking to argue how the policies can be effectively enacted to support the development of sustainable and resilient industrial systems.

4.4.1 Sustainability in the Context of Industrial Innovation

The described approach to sustainability in industrial innovation is a complete reorientation to include environmental and social components in the industrial process and technological advances. It is relevant for solving global environmental problems and providing future economic prospects and social development. Thus, sustainability consideration in innovation policies is becoming more of a necessity, given the goal of ensuring resilient and sustainable industrial growth.

Fan et al. (2021) explain why corporate governance sustainability should be provided through organizational innovation. They emphasize that organizational innovation that affects sustainability for companies striving to promote Industry 4.0 generation is obtained through a customer-oriented approach and organizational culture as well as leadership style. It is important to focus on the role of sustainability in the innovation processes of the new industrial momentum.

Bigliardi and Filippelli (2022) insist on the necessity of different knowledge and skills for embedding sustainability into innovation. They support that companies should exploit external knowledge and technologies to succeed in embedding sustainability into their innovation. Among many concerns on this topic, Zhang et al. (2021) focused on discussing the unsatisfactory results of industrial green innovation to note the need to balance achievement transformation and scientific research and development. Finally, Carcillo (2011) elucidates the issues described from the perspective of developing economies. Thus, the overview of existing literature on these issues shows the challenging and perspective side of industrial innovation with sustainability.

4.4.2 Examples of Sustainable Innovation Policies

Renewable technologies are the first in line when it comes to sustainable innovation. These types of technologies, including solar, wind, hydroelectric, and geo-thermal power, are based on abandoning traditional energy reliant on fossil fuels for low-carbon modifications. Renewables aim to balance gas emissions, fight climate change, and decrease dependence on non-renewables. Due to the need for carbon-free solutions, renewables are highly popular among governments and industries today. Solar panels and wind turbines have become commonplace in urban and country areas while creating energy storage, advanced battery systems, and smart grids ensure the satisfaction of energy needs isolated by renewable costing.

Eventually, renewables cause the appearance of new industries and workplaces. This tendency benefits not only the planet but also the economy. Eventually, platforms and companies that work on active engagement with renewables head for the developments of the new global market, and their countries become the leaders of this competition. Green manufacturing is the change in the industrial production processes for the benefit of the Earth. Green processes and technologies cover the whole range of ecological manufacturing, from minimizing emissions and waste through changing materials to more ecological ones and using energy-efficient facilities.

The basic strategies of greening manufacturing lie in implementing cleaner production, starting with choosing less harmful materials and wastes and minimizing the last through recycling and utilization. Moreover, the approach to energy also matters. Companies should start using energy-efficient or low-emissions equipment and optimize the energy consumption for production. Green manufacturing harms the environment less and costs less in the long run. The circular economy is an economic technique designed to develop businesses and the economy and benefit the environment.

Overall, the principles of a circular economy include design with longevity, renewability, reuse, repairability, and recycling, which limit the waste and usage of resources. The model needs absolute refurbishment of design, purchase, and recycling chains along with consumer behavior and form of organization to be applied. For example, companies may switch to a product-as-a-service strategy, giving a consumer their treatment appliance but fully owning it. This forces companies to not produce waste and use long-lasting components as they must pay for their fault.

4.4.3 Challenges and Opportunities

One of the primary challenges in implementing sustainable innovation policies is the balance between economic interest and environmental concern. The two needs appear to be opposing sides of a seesaw, considering that promoting the former diminishes the second. Nevertheless, the planet's long-term sustainability follows this perspective, and complex tradeoffs are required. Considering the necessity to address environmental issues such as climate change, pollution, and resource depletion, and the essentiality of economic growth to promote job creation, enhanced living standards, and a nation's development aspiration, the traditional business models attached to profit maximization must be transformed.

A unique opportunity in this situation represents the development of green industries and sustainable solutions that maintain the levels of economic growth but diminish the environmental footprint. Renewable energy companies stimulate emission reduction and create new job prospects. Green manufacturing and the circular economy led to reduced costs and the expansion of the potential markets; simultaneously, industry's demand for natural resources and the waste generated decreased. The integration of governments in this process is pivotal. State regulations that benefit green investments, green taxation generating revenues to fund the innovation, and the ban on harmful practices must be imposed. Nevertheless, such measures should not undermine entrepreneurial freedom or impose excessive costs to limit financial opportunities depending on industry locations.

Concern for the future suggests that the development of sustainability policy will include more consideration of all factors. Investing in the research and development of the technologies is a key focus. Besides renewable energy production and green manufacturing, agriculture, transportation, and waste management demand innovative interventions. Awareness-raising is essential, considering that most of the public has insufficient knowledge about environmental concerns. Transborder cooperation and alignment of various sector requirements and preferences are essential to developing integrated strategies. Considering the global issue, international cooperation is essential for resolving climate change. The legal framework is required to promote the switch from traditional to sustainable business models. Carbon pricing, subsidies for green technologies, and waste and pollution are already seen in international markets. The models must remain non-intrusive and equal for all parties concerned to prevent shortages or the congestion of legal requirements depending on the market size or restriction and costs depending on the production location or type. Finally, given that the clients change, the policies must be flexible and adapt, although the predefined path must remain sustainable. The initiatives must support low-carbon projects, develop proven environmentally friendly and sustainable technologies, and cooperate with stakeholders and various international markets.

4.5 CONCLUSIONS

The chapter's focus on the intricate relationship between politics and industrial innovation highlights their interactions as dynamic and complex processes that profoundly impact the trajectory of technological development.

Political decisions, including funding for research and development and the nature of a given nation or region's international trade policies, among other similar matters, play a decisive role in determining the direction, and sometimes even the pace, of innovation. Every political environment can either support such an outcome by fostering an environment where innovation thrives or disrupt it by placing barriers to its progress.

In shedding light on the global-level dynamic, the chapter explained the various facets of the four geos: strategic, technological, economic, and political factors that either influence or are influenced by industrial innovations. The subject is more than just a contest for supremacy over technology but also one of cooperation, including shared challenges where different actors try to make progress. The strategic positioning of nations in the global innovation landscape, the role of technology in geopolitics, and the economic implications of global innovations were some of the major categories under review.

The emergence of a single set of industrial innovation policies and innovation policies, the latter increasingly tending to integrate the former as a key part of their activities, is increasingly blurring the lines between the two pivotal areas and, in the process, reshaping the industrial and economic landscapes, both at the national and international levels.

Additionally, industrial innovation has been considered critical for sustainable policies. Policymakers must integrate sustainability into their innovation policies because it is critical for the economy and the environment. That will help to address global environmental problems, making the economy more sustainable and life more comfortable for all. Some examples provided for sustainable policies include green energy technologies, the principles of green manufacturing, and the circular economy. The chapter also expected that consideration be given to new directions in sustainable policymaking, such as the balance between economic growth and sustainable development. Consequently, the chapter offered a comprehensive understanding of politics in industrial innovation. Each subtopic is key to the broader understanding of the subject and presents key opportunities and challenges in engineering.

REFERENCES

Bajrektarević, A. 2012. "Geopolitics of Technology and the Hydrocarbon Status Quo." *Geopolitics, History, and International Relations* 4 (1): 128–142.

Bigliardi, B., and S. Filippelli. 2022. "Sustainability and Open Innovation: Main Themes and Research Trajectories." *Sustainability* 14 (11): 6763. https://doi.org/10.3390/su14116763.

Carcillo, J. 2011. *Developing Economies: Innovation, Investment and Sustainability.* New York: Nova Science Publishers. 2012. Print.

Cheung, T. 2010. *The Changing Dynamics Behind China's Rise as a Military Technological Power.* SITC Policy Briefs, 2010(Policy Brief 16). Retrieved from https://escholarship.org/uc/item/0366d670

Cirera, X., J. Frias, J. Hill, and Y. Li. 2020. "A Practitioner's Guide to Innovation Policy." https://doi.org/10.1596/33269.

Fan, Y.-J., S.-f. Liu, D. Luh, and P.-S. Teng. 2021. "Corporate Sustainability: Impact Factors on Organizational Innovation in the Industrial Area." *Sustainability* 13 (4): 1979. https://doi.org/10.3390/SU13041979.

Fontrier, A.-M., J. Gill, and P. Kanavos. 2019. "International Impact of External Reference Pricing: Should National Policy-Makers Care?" *The European Journal of Health Economics* 20 (8): 1137–1149. https://doi.org/10.1007/s10198-019-01083-w.

Goh, A. L. S. 2006. "Evolution of Industrial Policy-making in Support of Innovation: The Case of Singapore." *International Journal of Innovation and Learning.* https://doi.org/10.1504/IJIL.2006.008183.

Grabas, C., and A. Nützenadel. 2013. "Industrial Policies in Europe in Historical Perspective." WWWforEurope Working Paper No. 15, WIFO Studies, WIFO, number 46867, February.

Gunggut, H. 2009. "Globalization and Its Impact on Public Policy Formulation and Implementation: Case Study of Forest Conservation in Sabah." https://eprints.ums.edu.my/id/eprint/19744/1/Globalization%20and%20its%20impact.pdf

Karkazis, J. 2019. “The Regional Geo-economic Dynamics of Turkey in the Context of Europe: 2000–2014 the Emergence of Turkey as One of the Leading Geo-economic Powers of Europe.” *Journal of World Economic Research* 8 (2): 11. https://doi.org/10.11648/J.JWER.20190802.11.

Kociuba, D., and K. Wajs. 2021. “Impact of the Implementation of EU, National and Local Policies and Legislation on the Transition Towards Eco-cities in Poland.” https://doi.org/10.2478/bog-2021-0026.

Kozmenko, S., and A. Kozmenko. 2022. “The Arctic Geo-Economy: Mobility of Strategic Oil Resources at the End of Globalization.” *Arctic and North* 49: 33–47.

Miao, J. T. 2020. “Definition and Typologies of Local Innovation Systems: A Case Study of Optics Valley in Central China.” *Regional Studies, Regional Science* 7 (1): 1–16. https://doi.org/10.1080/23792949.2019.1672572.

Muhammad, A., M. E. Elton Mike, M. B. Idris, A. A. Ishaq, and B. Osaretin. 2023. “The Geo-economics of U.S.-China Financial Relations: Challenges and Opportunities in a Global Context.” *Journal of Economics, Commerce and Accounting* 2 (3). https://doi.org/10.56556/jescae.v2i3.558.

Öniş, Z., and M. Kutlay. 2016. “The Dynamics of Emerging Middle-Power Influence in Regional and Global Governance: The Paradoxical Case of Turkey.” *Australian Journal of International Affairs* 70 (4): 343–362. https://doi.org/10.1080/10357718.2016.1183586.

Powers, C. 2020. “How Neoliberalism Comes to Town: Policy Convergence, (Under) Development, and Jordanian Economics under King Abdullah.” *Middle East Critique* 29 (3): 261–280. https://doi.org/10.1163/18763375-01202002.

Rzayev, A., F. Dilavarov, and G. Ibrahimova. 2020. “Geo-economic Character of GVC in the Global Reproductive Process System.” Proceedings of the 3rd International Conference Spatial Development of Territories. https://dx.doi.org/10.2991/aebmr.k.210710.009.

Shelomentsev, A., K. S. Goncharova, I. Stepnov, J. Kovalchuk, D. Lan, and R. S. Golov. 2021. “Strategic Innovation as a Factor of Adaptation of National Economies to the Development of Global Value Chains.” *Sustainability* 13 (17): 9765. https://doi.org/10.3390/su13179765.

Srivastava, D., P. Chugan, N. C. Soni, and N. Patel. 2016. “Macro and Micro Dynamics for Empowering Trade, Industry and Society.” Excel India Publishers, New Delhi for Institute of Management, Nirma University, Ahmedabad.

Straccamore, M., V. Loreto, and P. Gravino. 2023. “The Geography of Technological Innovation Dynamics.” *Scientific Reports* 11: 48342. https://doi.org/10.1038/s41598-023-48342-8.

Vertinsky, I., Y. Kuang, D. Zhou, and V. Cui. 2023. “The Political Economy and Dynamics of Bifurcated World Governance and the Decoupling of Value Chains: An Alternative Perspective.” *Journal of International Business Studies*. https://doi.org/10.1057/s41267-023-00597-z.

WIPO. 2021. *Global Innovation Index 2020: Who Will Finance Innovations*. WIPO.

Yan, Y., J. Li, and Y. Xu. 2021. “Research on Industry Difference and Convergence of Green Innovation Efficiency of Manufacturing Industry in China Based on Super-SBM and Convergence Models.” *Mathematical Problems in Engineering*. https://doi.org/10.1155/2021/4013468.

Zhang, L., P. Liu, and H. Tarbert. 2021. “Analysis on Spatio-temporal Characteristics and Influencing Factors of Industrial Green Innovation Efficiency—From the

Perspective of Innovation Value Chain." *Preprints* 2021: 2021110485. https://doi.org/10.20944/preprints202111.0485.v1
Zorko, M., and J. Lučev. 2021. "Geographical Patterns and Geo-Economic Reasoning of the Pandemic Consequences: Old Geopolitical 'Games' in the Post-COVID Global Order." *Socijalna Istraživanja* 59. https://doi.org/10.5673/SIP.59.0.4.

5. The innovation ecosystems of robust, resilient, and competitive societal models

Elias G. Carayannis and Pantelis C. Kostis

5.1 INTRODUCTION

Innovation ecosystems are dynamic systems and comprise multiple actors like companies, higher education institutions, government, and others (Carayannis, 2013). These ecosystems seek to drive innovation through interactions and knowledge-based sharing among these ecosystem participants. The concept of an innovation ecosystem relates to the concept that innovation is a collaborative process, and as such is enriched through the interaction between several parties (Carayannis & Campbell, 2009).

An innovation ecosystem can be compared to a natural ecosystem, where different organisms interact with each other and the environment to create a stable ecosystem (Campbell & Carayannis, 2007). Likewise, an innovation ecosystem can be defined as the space in which these different actors' interactions enable the conception and diffusion of new ideas, new products, and new services. When this happens, clusters and networks of actors often emerge which increase the innovative outputs of the involved actors. Accordingly, innovation ecosystems have been found to be facilitated by digital platforms and services through networks sharing information, resources, and best practices (Carayannis et al., 2021).

For an innovation ecosystem to work effectively, it must possess traits that enable it to adapt in a rapidly changing environment. Three obvious qualities are robustness, resilience, and competitiveness (Carayannis et al., 2025). (a) Robustness describes the ecosystem's strength to withstand shocks and stresses while delivering its basic functions. The robustness helps keep the ecosystem humming along even during bad economic times or other roadblocks. (b) Resilience focuses on the capacity to adapt after a disruption. It shows the potential for adjustment. It describes what is essential in a world that is progressing both with technical advances and market trends. (c) Competitiveness is a measure of the ability of the innovation ecosystem to attract and allocate talent and investment. A competitive world fosters an environment conducive to innovation. Over the long run, competition makes the ecosystem attractive to both new entrants and incumbents, driving continued innovation and economic growth.

It is the mix of robustness, resilience, and competition that forms the solid foundation of an innovation ecosystem. These characteristics enable the ecosystem to sustain its innovative activities, adapt itself to new conditions, and be at the cutting edge of technological and economic growth. In this way, innovation ecosystems can reinforce the general development and competitiveness of regions and countries (Carayannis, Canestrino et al., 2024).

In this chapter, an emphasis is placed on the interplay of individuals, culture, and technology in an innovation ecosystem, doing a comparative work on the Nordic and US models to understand what kind of conditions innovation ecosystems have to fulfill in order to reach robustness, resilience, and be competitive.

5.2 PEOPLE, CULTURE, AND TECHNOLOGY COMPLEX DYNAMICS

5.2.1 The Role of Human Capital in Innovation

Human capital, which is the sum of an individual's knowledge, skills, and abilities, is a key driver in innovation (Demircioglu et al., 2024). Human capital development is realized through ongoing skill training, which will result in the labor force maintaining a continued capacity for adapting to new technologies and methods. One needs to learn new skills not only very quickly, but also to apply them. Ongoing training initiatives ensure that employees remain up to date on new technologies and industry trends. It is well-documented that properly trained staff are more effective and efficient in their work, taking advantage of new tools and new technologies to increase speed, quality, and productivity. Moreover, a versatile workforce will probably be more likely to develop creative ideas and solutions. Training across functions can encourage creative thinking.

Human capital development can be realized by different means. Formal education provides formal instruction, providing education in knowledge and skills for a broad array of professions. On-the-job training contributes practical experience so the employee can apply theoretical lessons to real situations that develop analytic capacity (Bauernschuster et al., 2009). Workshops, seminars, and even certification courses provided for job training keep the employee current in the industry while learning new skills. Additionally, the guidance and support of more seasoned employees in the form of mentorship and coaching can help less experienced employees develop their skills and advance their careers.

As the foundation of human capital formation, education plays a significant role in innovation (Bonesso et al., 2020). People who are being educated can receive the understanding that participation in the innovation hub is required. This development is within the responsibility of educational institutions. In the current knowledge societies, universities and research institutions are the motors of innovation, creating pioneering research that results in new technologies and scientific discoveries. They graduate students who join the workforce with recent knowledge and abilities, ready to work in innovation. Collaborations between universities and industry help to transfer knowledge and technology that drive innovation. Such partnerships may lead to research results being commercialized and new products and services being created.

Examples of educational models that enable innovation are experiential learning programs with work placements where students have the opportunity to apply their theoretical knowledge to real-world examples and are better prepared for innovation roles (Lee et al., 2010). Interdisciplinary learning helps students learn in other disciplines, leading them to view the world from multiple perspectives and solve problems through varied means, which is important for innovation. The bottom line is that the importance of knowledge and the ability to use human capital through education and training pave the way for innovation and staying competitive in an incredibly fast-paced, technology-based world.

5.2.2 Cultural Influences on Innovation

Culture plays a critical role in the way innovation is seen and adapted in a society and its organizations (Kostis, 2021). National culture—the shared values, beliefs, and norms of a society—also influences attitudes to risk, entrepreneurship, and collaboration—all necessary foundations for innovation (Kostis et al., 2018). In some communities, there is a greater propensity toward risk-taking and entrepreneurial spirit, which can create a more diverse and dynamic innovation ecosystem (Petrakis et al., 2015). Readily apparent innovations, for example, spread more easily in societies that tolerate risk and new behaviors, while fear of risk discourages new investments (Petrakis et al., 2016).

Another consideration in innovation is the influence of organizational culture, which is a system of shared assumptions, values, and behavioral norms that govern the way people do things in a company. Companies that encourage a culture of transparency, innovation, and learning are more prone or able to clear out a space where new ideas can grow. In such a culture, employees are encouraged to venture out of their comfort zone and take on new approaches. Conversely, institutions that rely on rigid authority and traditional methods may suppress inventiveness and prohibit creativity (Kafka et al., 2022; Kafka & Kostis, 2024).

Multicultural collaboration, the process of bringing people from different cultures together, can have a major impact on creativity (Petrakis & Kostis, 2014). When different cultures come together, they bring different perspectives, different ways of seeing the world, different ways of solving problems. This diversity of experience can result in more creative solutions and greater overall creativity in the process of innovation (Bakas et al., 2020).

However, leading cross-cultural teams necessitates understanding differences in culture and putting in place inclusive measures. Communication is key to make sure all team members feel appreciated and understood irrespective of their culture. Conflict and misunderstandings due to cultural differences may be minimized by cultural competence training and the development of transparent, inclusive, and non-threatening communication practices.

Cross-cultural collaboration not only stimulates innovation, but it can also speed up the movement of new ideas across countries and lead to economic development and growth (Petrakis & Kostis, 2013; Kafka & Kostis, 2021; Kostis, 2024). In-country teams can share new and old information and adapt breakthrough ideas to meet the specific preferences of customers in a new market. This may help accelerate and diffuse the adoption of new technologies and new practices.

5.2.3 Technological Advancements and Human Interaction

The dynamic between humans and technology is central to today's innovation ecosystems. Advances in technology are ever changing the way people work, talk, and relate, and these changes mean new possibilities and obstacles. The interface between man and machine also plays a key role in determining how effectively these technologies can be exploited for innovation (Carayannis, Kostis, Kafka et al., 2024).

The human–technology interface includes the design and usability of technological tools and systems. We must recognize user-friendly design as the way to fully leverage these technologies to be productive and innovative. Technology that users can easily access and use allows them to work on solving problems creatively, not dealing with overly complicated technology. This simplicity of use can increase task and process productivity, increasing innovation.

The human–technology interaction relates also to the infusion of complex technology into daily practices. Devices make human abilities superhuman, ushering in tools to do things that were once unimaginable or prohibitively labor-intensive. For example, through artificial intelligence (AI) data analytics we can get insights that lead to strategic decision-making, and robotics can take over most repetitive work, leaving human workers more time to be creative and strategic. Incorporation of these technologies into workflows is required to obtain their full benefits and promote innovation.

Adaptation to technical transformation is also essential for human–technology interaction. Whether it be new apps, devices, networks, or systems, both people and companies need to constantly change to keep up. This transition includes, but is not limited to, learning new technical equipment and the ability to take advantage of new technologies. Since technology is always changing, companies have to help their employees be lifelong learners and keep up with those changes.

Transitioning effectively to new technology is rarely just a matter of training and is also a change of attitude and way of doing things. People must be encouraged to embrace change. Processes must be simple to use. That can be done through extensive training programs, mentorship, and creating an environment that supports new ideas and innovation.

Moreover, companies have to be forward-looking in finding and introducing new ideas to upgrade their innovation capacity. This requires keeping up the speed with the latest technology advancements, investing in research and development (R&D) to develop new technologies, and building relationships with technology companies and academia. In doing so, they can position themselves to harness the benefits of new technology and incorporate such technology into their innovation strategies.

5.2.4 Complexity and Innovation Ecosystems

Innovative ecosystems are by their very nature complex systems composed of many interacting parts and stakeholders, such as firms, universities, labs, governments, etc. The appropriate management of this complexity is key to creating a dynamic and productive innovation climate (Liu et al., 2024). Lessons learned from how to address complexity and case studies of complex innovation ecosystems offer useful learnings on how to address these challenges (Petrakis & Kafka, 2018).

Approaches to manage complexity in innovation ecosystems usually include whole-system and adaptive approaches. One very powerful approach is systems thinking, trying to understand and act based on the interdependencies between the player and the ecosystem. An ecosystem-level perspective allows stakeholders to locate leverage points and foresee ripple effects when the ground shifts. Such a strategy aids in developing interventions that strengthen the general performance and robustness of the ecosystem.

Another approach is to promote good communication and cooperation between ecosystem members. Open and transparent communication pathways are fundamental to sharing information, resources, experiences, and best practices. Connected and coordinated collaboration tools and platforms can make these situations less uncertain. It is also important to develop the trust and understanding among users to promote cooperation and minimize friction (Petrakis & Kostis, 2015).

The ability to be flexible to meet complexity is a necessity (Zheng & Cai, 2022). The time requirement should be able to adapt to technological changes, market conditions and regulatory environments by itself. This calls for a culture of continuous learning, experimentation, and agility. This can help foster an appetite for change within ecosystem organizations and individuals, and to see challenges as sources of economic development and innovation.

Good governance and public policy also contribute to the handling of complexity (Oliver & Rittblat, 2023). Equally, policies that encourage innovation (for example investment in R&D, tax initiatives, infrastructure development) may help to provide ground upon which ecosystem activities can occur. A good governance structure is also important to keep a coherent, efficient ecosystem.

Examples of nuanced innovation systems are useful to illustrate how such approaches can function in practice. One among thousands of such examples is, of course, Silicon Valley, which illustrates how complexity can be effectively managed through intelligent systems thinking, good networks, and an innovative culture. At the heart of Silicon Valley's success is its dense web of tech companies, venture capital firms, research institutions, and skilled workers that interact dynamically to produce innovation. The open and collaborative nature of the area, combined with large public and private investment, has produced an environment where new ideas can be quickly developed and scaled.

Another case in point is the entrepreneurial ecosystem in Shenzhen, China. In a couple of decades, Shenzhen has gone from a small fishing village to a global technology hub. This change has been empowered by forward government policies, significant infrastructure investment, and a strong focus on education and people development. Shenzhen's environment promotes the collaboration of officials, corporates, and colleges, which helps the adaptation and the technology evolution. The city's concentration of high-technology industries, including electronics, telecommunications, and pharmaceuticals, has led to a highly concentrated, modern, and innovative urban region.

Another useful model should be sought in the Nordic countries of Europe. Notably, Nordic innovation ecosystems have a reputation for strong public–private partnerships and a focus on sustainability and social welfare. Sweden, Finland, and Denmark are just some examples of countries that seem to have got a good handle on navigating innovation based on a culture deeply embedded in trust, equality, and cooperation. These are environments that have strong governmental backing, educated populations, and community-driven innovation. There has been an emphasis on sustainable and inclusive growth that is resulting in the emergence of technologies and business models that deal with economic and social issues.

5.2.5 Social Dynamics and Innovation

Social aspects are a critical issue to help the development of innovation ecosystems. These ecosystems affect the process of innovation due to the interconnections between organizations and communities (Audretsch et al., 2022). There are two social dynamics relevant particularly to innovation: social networks and social capital.

Social networks represent the pattern of relationships and connections between people and organizations (Molina-Morales & Martínez-Fernández, 2010). Such networks enable movement of information, resources, and ideas, which in turn fuel innovation. In a system of innovation, social networks may appear in the form of professional alliances, industry clusters, academic collaboration, or even informal networks of colleagues. The benefits of successful social networks are numerous:

1. Social networks provide a platform to propagate information and share knowledge. Through association, creative actors learn the ways of the greatest other actors in terms of ideas, technologies, and good ideas of working that might otherwise be missed. This knowledge sharing expedites the innovation process, saving time and resources on gaining the necessary knowledge.
2. Innovation can often benefit from available resources including financial, equipment, and skill-related resources. Social networks enable network participants to spread news about resources and help innovators source support. For instance, a startup could use its contacts to locate investors or partners to supply the required capital and expertise.
3. Social networking also provides opportunities for collaboration between people and organizations with different skills and interests. Joint ventures usually yield more creative end products when varied worldviews and competencies are merged to address complex issues. The networks also serve to create trust and understanding of others' perspectives, which are critical to effective collaboration.

Another interesting dimension of social dynamics concerns the influence of social capital on innovation processes (Heusler et al., 2025). Social capital is the value that is generated by networks, or the whole of social contacts; it is the positive outcome of a network. High social capital can facilitate the innovation trajectory in a variety of ways:

1. Social capital induces trust and cooperation within networks. Trusting parties are more likely to offer and share information, resources, and support. This trust lowers perceived collaboration risks and promotes more open and effective communication. This makes innovation projects more likely to be successful
2. Mutual aid in high social capital networks is likely to be repaid at a later time. This culture of reciprocity guarantees that provision is there for making innovation feasible. For instance, one established entrepreneur might train a beginner, who could then provide insights or connections down the road.
3. Social capital enhances the community spirit among members of the innovation ecosystem and reinforces the shared sense of belonging. Invested community members drive participation in and support of innovation efforts, financially or emotionally speaking. This kind of collective action amplifies a positive feedback process in which successful innovation activities work to reinforce the community and its social capacity.

Success stories of the positive effects of social networks and social capital on innovation can be found in many of the world's highly successful innovation ecosystems. Regions such as Silicon Valley thrive on their dense and interactive social networks, where entrepreneurs, investors, engineers, and academics meet and communicate over time. This dense network culture, along with strong social capital, has contributed to making Silicon Valley the world capital of technological innovation.

In the same way, the Nordic countries enjoy a strong social capital and well-established networks around their innovation ecosystems. The spirit of solidarity and high level of trust among these societies helps in active cooperation and full systems sharing and ends up in creative products that address economic as well as societal issues.

5.3 NORDIC MODELS VS. US MODELS

5.3.1 A Comparison of Nordic and US Modes of Innovation

There are as many types of innovation around the world as our different cultural, economic, and historical backgrounds allow. The Nordic and US innovation models, especially, are two entirely different ways to create innovation, both with advantages and drawbacks. This knowledge of traits and their temporal evolution sheds light on how divergent environments have the potential to sculpt innovation systems.

Collaboration, inclusivity, and sustainability are all key to the Nordic innovation model (Stiglitz, 2015). One of the highlights of this model has been the public–private partnerships. Governments in the Nordic region, with prominent roles played in Sweden, Finland, Denmark, and Norway, are highly proactive in providing funding, setting policy frameworks, and developing infrastructure to drive innovation. Many of these collaboratives aim at tackling societal challenges such as healthcare, the environment, or social security, and thus mirror the Nordic ambition to drive a well-functioning and sustainable growth.

Equally important in the Nordic model is the focus on equality and trust (Cooke, 2016). A culture of trust and equality favors direct communication and cooperation between public authorities, private companies, and academic organizations. Such a collective space is required for the sharing of expertise and competing on who can come up with the best solution. Secondly, the Nordic model invests heavily in education and lifelong learning, which is vital to having a workforce well-equipped with the right skills for innovation.

The US model of innovation is, by comparison, much more market-driven and entrepreneurially focused (Atkinson, 2014). Silicon Valley, being the home of US innovation, is the epitome of this model, with its high density of tech companies, investors, and talent. The case of the US model shifts the emphasis to the speed of commercialization and scalability, changing the market and economy in a big way.

Key features of the US innovation model are risk tolerance and a supportive environment for entrepreneurs. Venture funding and angel investors feed start-ups crucial capital, letting them test and grow at high speed. Facilitated by a favorable legal and regulatory climate for entrepreneurship, the United States is an attractive market for entrepreneurs overall. While this allows multiple business models to thrive, it also means that the US is a fertile field for innovation, since companies must continually innovate so as not to be left behind.

The historical evolution of both models is described to understand how their genetic characteristics have originated. The Nordic innovation model can be traced back to the social democratic traditions that focus on the welfare state, social equity, and collective action. After World War II, the Nordic countries spent on creating extensive welfare systems and strong public institutions to create fertile ground for collaborative innovation. The emphasis was on education and research, and this level of investment in universities and research organizations helped develop the culture of lifelong learning and innovation (Kostis & Kafka, 2022).

The innovation style in the United States developed in a capitalist, free-market context. In the post-war period, technology exploded in a variety of fields that were a result of direct government support as well as private sector initiatives (Simons & Walls, 2015). Of course, Silicon Valley, formed in the late 20th century, was a significant development as a global center for tech and entrepreneurship, presenting a mix of academic excellence, venture capital, risk-taking, and disruption.

As distinct as they are, both the Nordic and US models have demonstrated the capacity to generate innovation in their own contexts. The Nordic model has a unique focus on how social and environmental concerns can be worked into the innovation process, in support of sustainable and inclusive growth. The US is a role model for fostering high-impact, scalable innovation through its vibrant entrepreneurial ecosystem and strong focus on the marketplace.

5.3.2 Government Policies and Support

Innovation ecosystems are influenced and promoted directly by government policy and support. The government's proper role in innovation is providing a favorable environment for research and development, offering financial support, or shaping regulations to give incentives to innovate without hurting the public. The Nordic and US models are examples of different ways of government orientation toward innovation.

The role of the government in managing innovation is high in the Nordic countries (Cooke, 2016). The Nordic governments invest heavily in education and research to provide universities with the resources necessary to pursue leading-edge research in new technologies. Public investment in research and development is large, and in many cases larger than private investment. Part of this support is direct, via grants and subsidies, and part indirect, with tax incentives and accompanying infrastructure (Stiglitz, 2015).

A focus on public–private collaboration is key to the Nordic approach (Isaksen, 1997). Governments work in close partnership with private corporations, universities, and research organizations to stimulate innovation. These stakeholder collaborations have a specific focus on societal "grand" challenges, for example, in areas of healthcare, environment, and social justice.

What is more, the Nordic policy agenda is heavily influenced by sustainability and corporate social responsibility principles (Cooke, 2016). Policy mechanisms for pulling innovation toward social welfare and environmental sustainability are developed. This is illustrated by the strong embrace of green technologies and practices in different sectors in the Nordic nations. The role of government in establishing such ambitious environmental goals and incentivizing sustainable innovation has been crucial in this success.

By comparison, the US government's approach to innovation is more dispersed and market-led (Keller & Block, 2013). The federal and state governments are not surprisingly the largest funders of research and development through agencies such as the National Science Foundation (NSF) and the National Institutes of Health (NIH), but they also count on the private sector. The American model also incentivizes competition and entrepreneurship and provides significant support for startups and high-risk innovation initiatives through venture capital.

There are lots of models for how governments and individuals should do this, but in the US, government support generally takes the form of competitive grants, contracts, and tax incentives designed to jump-start private sector investment in innovation (Block et al., 2020). For instance, the Small Business Innovation Research (SBIR) and Small Business Technology Transfer (STTR) programs provide essential support for small businesses conducting cutting-edge research. The US government promotes innovation by protecting the innovations that individuals and businesses create with strong intellectual property protections, the promise that patent holders and companies will be able to control how their inventions are used and be compensated from the usage of their inventions.

5.3.3 Corporate Culture and Organizational Structure

Organizational structure and corporate culture are essential to the determination of innovation capacity of organizations across different ecosystems. The corporate culture contrasts between Nordic and American models reflect incompatible styles of cultivating creativity, cooperation, and flexibility. Also, the organizational structures can help or hinder the innovation process, depending on how they are established and employed.

Traditionally, the culture in Nordic industry has been based on trust, equality, and cooperation (Stiglitz, 2015). These cultural norms foster a sense of appreciation and enable employees to participate in the innovation process. Nordic companies tend to be based on the principles of work–life balance, employee well-being, and involving everyone in decisions. Such an inclusive culture promotes the free flow of information and ideas, necessary for creativity and innovation. Individuals are frequently entrusted with great freedom, enabling them to experiment with new ideas and to act on opportunities.

Business processes in Nordic organizations are often characterized as "flat" and "decentralized" (Cooke, 2016). This lack of vertical structure means that it is easier for decisions and information to flow between the different tiers of the business. Decentralized structures allow teams to make decisions locally and be responsive to change and opportunity. Cross-functional teams are everywhere and combine diverse skills and points of view to address complex challenges. Such a collaborative way of working accelerates the innovation process and helps find solutions that are more encompassing and that take multiple facets of a challenge into account.

US corporate culture, on the other hand, tends to be more competitive and independent (Mowery, 1992). The stress is on performance, outcome, and entrepreneurship. Risk-taking is not discouraged, innovation is rewarded, but this culture can be much more hierarchical and competitive. Though such a competitive culture can drive high innovation, it can also cause stress and low cooperation if not handled properly.

US companies tend to have hierarchical structures, though many forward-thinking companies, especially within the tech industry, take on more fluid and dynamic structures (Atkinson, 2014). Hierarchy inhibits freedom and causes a delay in decision-making; it kills creativity (Breznitz & Cowhey, 2012): every idea must travel through all layers of management. But many US firms are evolving toward more agile and flexible organizations to raise their performance on innovation. These structures promote effective collaboration between departments that are quick to adapt to market changes.

The influence of these corporate cultures and organizational structures on innovation cannot be understated (Katz, 2016). A flat and decentralized makeup of a company gives it the flexibility and ability to respond immediately to address new challenges and take advantage of new opportunities in the market. The open culture means a broad mix of ideas and perspectives are considered, which is crucial for more creative solutions.

In the US, hyper competition is not only well-entrenched but also a way of life. Although hierarchical structures might hinder innovation, the move toward more dynamic and easily changeable organizational models limits these problems. Firms that achieve the right balance of competitive desires and cooperative actions can attain incredible levels of innovation and market success.

5.3.4 Collaboration and Networking

Collaboration and networking are important for thriving innovation ecosystems as they leverage the transfer of ideas, resources, and competencies. The Nordic and US models have identified collaboration and networking as key elements of their strategies but adopt means to pursue these that are molded by their different cultural and institutional conditions.

What makes the Nordic model great is that it focuses heavily on trust, equality, and cooperation to motivate a working environment that encourages innovation (Hilson 2008). Nordic models are based on highly collaborative efforts as they usually base most of their efforts on large public–private partnerships where government, industry, and universities closely collaborate on research and development projects. Such partnerships are usually enabled, in part, by government policies and funding initiatives to facilitate innovation and sustainability (Cooke, 2016). The focus on social well-being and inclusive growth also leads the Nordics' innovation ecosystems to give preference to projects that have wide societal benefits.

The network of the Nordic model is also seen as being relatively dense and potent (Stiglitz, 2015). Innovation centers, clusters, and incubators are catalysts for connecting startups with larger organizations and research (Isaksen, 1997). These networks facilitate knowledge sharing, mentoring, and collaboration to stimulate the development and commercialization of new technologies. Conferences, workshops, hackathons, and culture-building activities are crucial characteristics of the Nordic innovation culture.

The US model of innovation, on the other hand, can be more market-oriented and business-oriented with a high value placed on competitiveness and entrepreneurship (Mowery, 1992). Execution in the US is more focused on strategic deals and partnerships between private companies and venture capital (VC). Such joint ventures are motivated by the desire for a high competitive advantage (Atkinson, 2014). There are public–private partnerships, but usually the private sector leads innovation.

The US innovation system is renowned for its flourishing networking infrastructure; this is especially true for numerous technology hotspots, such as Silicon Valley (Katz, 2016). These are places where large numbers of tech companies, investors, and skilled workers are packed together, and the result is a highly fertile laboratory for innovation. While networking is the most effective method for landing a job in the US, the plethora of industry associations, professional networks, and business accelerators ensure the work will not be painful. These communities are key to the success of startups in terms of funding, mentorship, and access to the market. The highly competitive nature of the innovation ecosystem in the United States also means that network building is commonly aimed at establishing high-impact connections with potential for rapid scaling and commercialization.

Notwithstanding their dissimilarities, Nordic and US patterns share an awareness of the significance of networks and partnerships for innovation. In both dimensions, strong networks allocated information, resources, and support flow facilitate the creation and spread of new technologies. Public–private or private–private partnerships allow the sharing of resources, risks, and complementary strengths.

5.4 THE FUTURE OF INNOVATION ECOSYSTEMS

Innovation is ever changing, shaped by new trends and increased focus on global cooperation. The marketplaces that build around innovation ecosystems must adopt new approaches, technologies, and collaborations to stay competitive and expand in a sustainable manner (Carayannis, Kostis, Dincer et al., 2024). Investigating the new trends that are currently influencing the future of innovation ecosystems and global cooperation as a key condition for innovation development is very important.

One of the more crucial of these new trends is the trend toward the full digitalization of all areas of life and work (Kaputa et al., 2022). Technologies such as AI, the Internet of Things (IoT), and blockchain are disrupting industries by enabling new business models, increasing efficiency, and providing personalized experiences to consumers. These technologies are at the heart of the fourth industrial revolution-based on the fusion of physical, digital, and biological domains. Innovation ecosystems should adjust to develop technology expertise and encourage its cross-utilization beyond segments.

A further tendency is the increasing focus on sustainability and the circular economy (Kremmydas & Kostis, 2024). With environmental considerations taking on ever greater urgency, innovation ecosystems around the world are putting emphasis on processes and technologies that shrink waste and save materials while improving sustainability (Carayannis, Grigoroudis et al., 2024). Green technologies, renewable energy solutions, and sustainable manufacturing processes are expected to rank high in future innovation.

Democratizing innovation is also a trend; more people can access tools and platforms to contribute to the process of innovation (Qureshi, 2020). With open-source platforms and online collaboration tools, smaller players can innovate without major capital expenditure. This democratization is opening the door to a wider range of potential innovators, supporting a more inclusive innovation environment.

In addition, social innovation which uses novel solutions to meet social needs, is taking on a greater profile. It is about using technology and out-of-the-box thinking to solve social problems. Social innovation stresses the importance of working across sectors, as well as involving communities in the innovation process to produce solutions that are both effective and equitable (Jareh, 2025).

Moreover, global collaboration is necessary to drive innovation forward. Challenges for the world currently are complex, including climate change, pandemics, economic disparity, among others, and they necessitate collective action and sharing of resources and intelligence on a global level (Kostis & Kafka, 2023). The creation of international research partnerships is an important element of collaboration worldwide. Cross-border collaborations (Carayannis et al., 2023) of universities, research institutes, and companies are being established to undertake joint R&D. Such partnerships facilitate the exchange of expertise, resources, and best practices, and so are likely to produce a more resilient and creative output.

International cooperation is also about establishing international innovation networks and clusters (Chen et al., 2021). These networks are networks of innovation hubs across different countries, which can exchange ideas, talent, and investment. Involving oneself in such networks, innovation ecosystems gain access to world markets, receive various knowledge, and scale the innovation more quickly.

Moreover, international cooperation can be a tool in bridging the digital divide and in facilitating a more equitable distribution of the benefits derived from innovation (Ingram, 2021). Advanced innovation ecosystems can contribute to the development of local capabilities and inclusive growth through the transfer of technology and knowledge with emerging economies. One such response is the role of technology transfer and international development projects.

5.5 CONCLUSIONS

This chapter has offered a thorough analysis of the Nordic and US innovation ecosystems, based on their different, as well as similar, setups and dilemmas. Are both models acknowledging the significance of education and skill building for the life course of an individual? The Nordic emphasis on inclusive and lifelong learning complements the US emphasis on professional and entrepreneurial education to create diverse and flexible resource bases. National and corporate cultures have substantial influence on innovation. The Nordic model's focus on trust, equality, and cooperation differs significantly from the US model's competitive and individualistic culture, but they surely prove effective for the purpose of innovation in their respective environments. Innovation relies on efficient human–technology interfaces, as well as on the possibility of adjusting to new technologies. The two models are based on modern technologies, but their implementation and instantiation are different.

Community is key for both focus areas, but in different ways. The latter particularly differs from the European one on account of better public sector support and good citizen participation in the Nordic model; a breadth and depth in its venture capital environment and strategic collaborations in the American model. Innovation is fostered by state sponsorship. The sustainability and inclusiveness character of the Nordic model stems from strong public investment and a demanding regulatory framework, while the erection speed of the US model is based on a more market-oriented setup and encouraging regulation. Innovation strategies are critical to embed sustainability for long-term success. Both models show successful strategies, with that of the Nordics emphasizing environmental sustainability, while the US is harnessing market forces for green innovation.

Typical problems include the challenge of meeting technology demand, and of providing access to innovation resources fairly. Cross-learning between the models may help stimulate innovation globally. In today's environment, global cooperation and connections are key to driving innovation. Collective action can help to solve global problems, speed up technological progress, and ensure that everyone shares in the dividends of growth.

From the perspective of legislators, it is decisive to set good frameworks for innovations in terms of funding, infrastructure, and regulations. Public–private partnerships and sustainable practices can foster long-term growth in policies. Taking steps to bridge socio-economic differences and providing equal access to education, resources, and opportunities are the key to nurturing a broad innovation ecosystem. For such collaborative work, there is a need to facilitate global collaboration by encouraging international research partnerships and innovation networks that mitigate global challenges and build on international knowledge.

Industry leaders should invest in lifelong learning and skills upgrading for their staff to remain technologically current and to be agents of innovation. Fostering an organizational culture based on the simultaneous pursuit of competition and collaboration can inspire people to be creative and have open lines of communication between and among teams. Moreover, driving innovation to solve environmental and social challenges and remain competitive.

Academia should work interdisciplinary, integrating fields that bring knowledge together in new and unified ways. Collaborating with industry and government allows the flow of academic knowledge and technology that can be applied in the real world. Contribution to international cooperation by engaging in multinational research and knowledge transfer contributes to the mutual objective of promoting innovation.

Finally, the Nordic and US innovation models provide key lessons on how to develop strong, resilient, and competitive innovation ecosystems. By leveraging this learning and collaborating across sectors and geographies, policymakers, business leaders, and scholars can improve their innovation strategies to foster global development in the rapidly changing world.

REFERENCES

Atkinson, R.D. (2014). *Understanding the US National Innovation System*. ITIF, June.

Audretsch, D.B., Eichler, G.M., & Schwarz, E.J. (2022). Emerging Needs of Social Innovators and Social Innovation Ecosystems. *International Entrepreneurship and Management Journal*, 18, 217–254. https://doi.org/10.1007/s11365-021-00789-9

Bakas, D., Kostis, P.C., & Petrakis, P.E. (2020). Culture and Labor Productivity: An Empirical Investigation. *Economic Modelling*, 85, 233–243. https://doi.org/10.1016/j.econmod.2019.05.020.

Bauernschuster, S., Falck, O., & Heblich, S. (2009). Training and Innovation. *Journal of Human Capital*, 3(4), 323–353. https://doi.org/10.1086/653713.

Block, F., Keller, M.R., & Negoita, M. (2020). Network Failure and the Evolution of the US Innovation System. *Journal of Industry, Competition and Trade*, 20(2), 235–247.

Bonesso, S., Gerli, F., Pizzi, C., & Boyatzis, R.E. (2020). The Role of Intangible Human Capital in Innovation Diversification: Linking Behavioral Competencies With Different Types of Innovation. *Industrial and Corporate Change*, 29(3), 661–681. https://doi.org/10.1093/icc/dtz062.

Breznitz, D., & Cowhey, P. (2012). America's Two Systems of Innovation: Innovation for Production in Fostering US Growth. *Innovations: Technology, Governance, Globalization*, 7(3), 127–154.

Campbell, D., & Carayannis, E.G. (2007). A "Mode 3" Systems Approach for Knowledge Creation, Diffusion and Use: Towards a Twenty-First-Century Fractal Innovation Ecosystem. In E. G. Carayannis, & C. Ziemnowicz (Eds.), *Rediscovering Schumpeter. Creative Destruction Evolving into "Mode 3"*. Palgrave Macmillan.

Carayannis, E.G. (2013). The Innovation Ecosystem. In *The Innovation Union in Europe* (pp. 3–41). Edward Elgar Publishing.

Carayannis, E.G., & Campbell, S.F.J. (2009). 'Mode 3' and 'Quadruple Helix': Toward a 21st Century Fractal Innovation Ecosystem. *International Journal of Technology Management*, 46(3–4). https://doi.org/10.1504/IJTM.2009.023374

Carayannis, E.G., Canestrino, R., & Magliocca, P. (2024). From the Dark Side of Industry 4.0 to Society 5.0: Looking "Beyond the Box" to Developing Human-Centric Innovation Ecosystems. *IEEE Transactions on Engineering Management*, 71, 6695–6711. https://doi.org/10.1109/TEM.2023.3239552.

Carayannis, E.G., Grigoroudis, V., Kostis, P.C., Kafka, K.I., & Valvi, T. (2024). Integrated Framework for Sustainable and Inclusive Development Through Circular Efficacious Entrepreneurship and Innovation Ecosystems. In J.J. Ferreira, M. Klodsten, & D. Urbano (Eds.), *Circular Entrepreneurship Ecosystems: Theory and Practice*. Edward Elgar. https://doi.org/10.4337/9781035318247.00011.

Carayannis, E.G., Grigoroudis, E., Stamati, D., & Valvi, T. (2021). Social Business Model Innovation: A Quadruple/Quintuple Helix-Based Social Innovation Ecosystem. *IEEE Transactions on Engineering Management,* 68(1), 235–248. https://doi.org/10.1109/TEM.2019.2914408.

Carayannis, E.G., Kostis, P.C., Dincer, H., & Yuksel, S. (2023). Quality Function Deployment-Oriented Strategic Outlook to Sustainable Energy Policies Based on Quintuple Innovation Helix. *Journal of the Knowledge Economy*. https://doi.org/10.1007/s13132-023-01394-7.

Carayannis, E.G., Kostis, P.C., Dincer, H., & Yuksel, S. (2024). Economic Impacts of Integrating Strategic Innovation in Environmental Policy-Making for Sustainable Energy Investments. *Journal of the Knowledge Economy*. https://doi.org/10.1007/s13132-024-01981-2.

Carayannis, E.G., Kostis, P.C., Kafka, K.I., & Valvi, T. (2024). Towards Industry 6.0 and Techno-Centric vs Human-Centric Smart Balancing: The Journey From Industry and Society 4.0 Towards Industry and Society 5.0 and Beyond. In G. Meramveliotakis & M. Manioudis (Eds.), *Sustainable Development, Political Economy and Institutions: A Pluralistic Approach*. Routledge.https://doi.org/https://doi.org/10.4324/9781003349402-10.

Carayannis, E.G., Kafka, K.I., Kostis, P.C., & Valvi, T. (2025). Robust, Resilient and Remunerative (R3) SMEs Ecosystems in the Quintuple Helix Plus Context: Industry 5.0, Society 5.0 and AI Modalities Challenges and Opportunities for Theory, Policy and Practice. In V. Aranitou, M. Manioudis, & A. Aggelakis (Eds.), *Small and Medium-Sized Enterprises (SMEs) and Growth: A Wide-View Analytical Perspective*. Palgrave Macmillan. https://doi.org/10.1007/978-3-031-74554-6_8.

Chen, Y., Li, J., & Li, R. (2021). Cluster Internationalization: Qualitative Review, Theoretical Direction, and the Rise of Emerging Markets' Themes. *Sustainability*, 13(19), 10514. https://doi.org/10.3390/su131910514

Cooke, P. (2016). Nordic Innovation Models: Why Is Norway Different? *Norsk Geografisk Tidsskrift – Norwegian Journal of Geography*, 70(3), 190–201. https://doi.org/10.1080/00291951.2016.1157120
Demircioglu, M.A., Audretsch, D.B., & Link, A.N. (2024). Innovation in Public Organizations: The Role of Human Capital. *Public Management Review*, 1–26. https://doi.org/10.1080/14719037.2024.2381073
Heusler, A.H., Foutz, N.Z., Spann, M., et al. (2025). The Idea Marketplace: Diversity, Social Capital, and Innovation. *Journal of the Academy of Marketing Science*, 53, 150–171. https://doi.org/10.1007/s11747-024-01045-6
Hilson, M. (2008). *The Nordic Model: Scandinavia Since 1945*. London: Reaktion Books.
Ingram, G. (2021). *Bridging the Global Digital Divide: A Platform to Advance Digital Development in Low- and Middle-Income Countries*. Brookings.
Isaksen, I. (1997). Regional Clusters and Competitiveness: The Norwegian Case. *European Planning Studies*, 5, 65–76. https://doi.org/10.1080/09654319708720384
Jareh, A. (2025). Sustainable Social Innovation as a Solution for Systemic Change and Resilience. *Sustainability*, 17(4), 1583. https://doi.org/10.3390/su17041583
Kafka, K.I., & Kostis, P.C. (2021). Post-materialism and economic growth: Cultural backlash, 1981–2019. *Journal of Comparative Economics*, 49(4), 901–917. https://doi.org/10.1016/j.jce.2021.04.001.
Kafka, K.I., & Kostis, P.C. (2024). Unravelling the Innovation Puzzle: The Interplay between Uncertainty, Economic Institutions, and Innovation Outcomes in Advanced and Developing Economies. *Journal of Technological Forecasting and Social Change*, 198. https://doi.org/10.1016/j.techfore.2023.123027.
Kafka, K.I., Kostis, P.C., & Petrakis, P.E. (2022). Institutional Effects on Innovation and the Requirements for Structural Reforms. *Journal of the Knowledge Economy*, 13, 211–235. https://doi.org/10.1007/s13132-020-00705–6.
Kaputa, V., Loučanová, E., & Tejerina-Gaite, F.A. (2022). Digital Transformation in Higher Education Institutions as a Driver of Social-Oriented Innovations. In C. Păunescu, K.L. Lepik, & N. Spencer (Eds.), *Social Innovation in Higher Education*. Springer. https://doi.org/10.1007/978-3-030-84044-0_4
Katz, J.S. (2016). What Is a Complex Innovation System? *PLoS One*, 11(6), e0156150.
Keller, M.R., & Block, F. (2013). Explaining the Transformation in the US Innovation System: The Impact of a Small Government Program. *Socio-Economic Review*, 11(4), 629–656.
Kostis, P.C. (2021) Culture, Innovation and Economic Development. *Journal of Innovation and Entrepreneurship*. https://doi.org/10.1186/s13731-021-00163-7.
Kostis, P.C. (2024). Cultural Background as a Crucial Factor for Sustainable Development. In G. Meramveliotakis & M. Manioudis (Eds.), *Sustainable Development, Political Economy and Institutions: A Pluralistic Approach*. Routledge. https://doi.org/10.4324/9781003349402-13.
Kostis, P.C., & Kafka, K.I. (2022). The European Experience in Lifelong Learning and the Restructuring of the Economy. In P.E. Petrakis (Ed.), *Human Capital and Production Structure in the Greek Economy: Knowledge, Abilities, Skills* (Chapter 8). Palgrave Macmillan. https://doi.org/10.1007/978-3-031-04938-5_9.
Kostis, P.C., & Kafka, K.I. (2023) Examining the Interplay of Climate Change, Cultural Dynamics, and Sustainable Development: A Global Perspective, *Sustainability*, 15(18), 13652. https://doi.org/10.3390/su151813652.
Kostis, P.C., Kafka, K.I., & Petrakis, P.E. (2018). Cultural Change and Innovation Performance. *Journal of Business Research*, 88, 306–313.

Kremmydas, C., & Kostis, P.C. (2024). Advancing Sustainability: Green Product Satisfaction, Circularity and Sustainable Development. *International Journal of Social Ecology and Sustainable Development (IJSESD)*, 15, 1. https://doi.org/10.4018/IJSESD.335037.

Lee, S.Y., Florida, R., & Gates, G. (2010). Innovation, Human Capital, and Creativity. *International Review of Public Administration*, 14(3), 13–24. https://doi.org/10.1080/12294659.2010.10805158.

Liu, Z., Li, Z., Zhang, Y., Mutukumira, A.N., Feng, Y., Cui, Y., Wang, S., Wang, J., & Wang, S. (2024). Comparing Business, Innovation, and Platform Ecosystems: A Systematic Review of the Literature. *Biomimetics*, 9(4), 216. https://doi.org/10.3390/biomimetics9040216

Molina-morales, F.X., & Martínez-fernández, M.T. (2010). Social Networks: Effects of Social Capital on Firm Innovation. *Journal of Small Business Management*, 48(2), 258–279. https://doi.org/10.1111/j.1540-627X.2010.00294.x

Mowery, D.C. (1992). The US National Innovation System: Origins and Prospects for Change. *Research Policy*, 21(2), 125–144.

Oliver, A.L., & Rittblat, R. (2023). Facilitating Innovation for Complex Societal Challenges: Creating Communities and Innovation Ecosystems for SDG Goal of Forming Partnerships. *Sustainability*, 15(12), 9666. https://doi.org/10.3390/su15129666

Petrakis, P.E., & Kafka, K.I. (2018). Sustainable Entrepreneurial Activity Within Complex Economic Systems. In H. Emmert-Streib & M. Dehmer (Eds.), *Entrepreneurial Complexity*. Taylor & Francis Group.

Petrakis, P.E., & Kostis, P.C. (2013). Economic Growth and Cultural Change. *Journal of Behavioral and Experimental Economics* (formerly *The Journal of Socio-Economics*), 47, 147–157.

Petrakis, P.E., & Kostis, P.C. (2014). Medium Term Effects of Culture, Transactions and Institutions on Opportunity Entrepreneurship. *Journal of Innovation and Entrepreneurship*, 3, 11.

Petrakis, P.E., & Kostis, P.C. (2015). The Role of Knowledge and Trust in SMEs. *Journal of the Knowledge Economy*, 6(1), 105–124.

Petrakis, P.E., Kostis, P.C., & Kafka, K.I. (2016). Secular Stagnation, Faltering Innovation, and High Uncertainty: New-Era Entrepreneurship Appraisal Using Knowledge-Based Thinking. *Journal of Business Research*, 69(5), 1909–1913.

Petrakis, P.E., Kostis, P.C., & Valsamis, D.G. (2015). Innovation and Competitiveness: Culture as a Long-Term Strategic Instrument During the European Great Recession. *Journal of Business Research*, 68(7), 1436–1438.

Qureshi, Z. (2020). *Democratizing Innovation: Putting Technology to Work for Inclusive Growth*. Brookings.

Simons, K.L., & Walls, J.L. (2015). USA's National Innovation System. *Wiley Encyclopedia of Management*, 1–32.

Stiglitz, J. (2015). Leaders and Followers: Perspectives on the Nordic Model and the Economics of Innovation. *Journal of Public Economics*, 127, 3–16.

Zheng, X., & Cai, Y. (2022). Transforming Innovation Systems into Innovation Ecosystems: The Role of Public Policy. *Sustainability*, 14(12), 7520. https://doi.org/10.3390/su14127520

PART II

Enabling technologies, risks, and decision-making

6. Cybersecurity: The backbone of industrial innovation excellence

Sokratis Katsikas

6.1 INTRODUCTION

Cybersecurity plays a pivotal role in shaping the future of industrial innovation by ensuring the security, reliability, and integrity of critical systems. In an era driven by digital transformation, industries increasingly rely on advanced technologies such as artificial intelligence (AI), automation, and cloud computing to push the boundaries of innovation. However, with these advancements come heightened cyber risks that can jeopardize intellectual property, operational efficiency, and stakeholder trust.

This chapter explores the critical relationship between cybersecurity and industrial innovation, highlighting how security measures protect intellectual property, enable technological advancements, and ensure operational resilience. As industries move toward implementing the Industry 4.0 paradigm (Xu et al., 2021), cybersecurity provides stability and safeguards against unauthorized access. Compliance with cybersecurity regulations is essential for protecting sensitive data, mitigating legal risks, and fostering trust among customers, investors, and regulatory bodies. Businesses that maintain strong security practices enhance their credibility and drive technological progress. Cybersecurity innovation plays a vital role in advancing industrial security through improvements in threat detection and mitigation. AI-driven analytics, quantum-resistant cryptography, and blockchain-based authentication enhance resilience while supporting the adoption of cutting-edge technologies. Additionally, cybersecurity facilitates secure collaboration, enabling industries to exchange ideas, protect proprietary data, and build global partnerships without fear of cyber threats. A strong cybersecurity foundation ensures that businesses can innovate safely and sustainably, driving industrial growth while maintaining security and efficiency.

The Centres for Research-based Innovation (SFI) scheme is a Norwegian initiative managed by the Research Council of Norway, designed to strengthen industrial innovation through long-term research collaborations between research and development (R&D)-intensive companies, leading research institutions, and the public sector. It fosters industry-oriented research clusters, supports researcher training, and promotes global competitiveness. SFI centers are temporary research entities hosted by Norwegian research organizations, responsible for scientific, administrative, and financial management. The scheme requires active industry participation, with each center having at least three user partners (private companies or public sector entities), to ensure research findings are translated into practical innovations. These centers also play a key role in education, collaborating with accredited universities to enhance researcher training and knowledge transfer. They function within their host institution, without separate legal status, governed by a board. Leadership is provided by a director, appointed with scientific and administrative autonomy. Funding follows a co-investment model, where user partners must contribute at least 50% of the Research Council's annual support. Contributions include cash funding, staff allocations, and essential infrastructure. By fostering innovation, industry partnerships, and global research collaboration, the SFI scheme reinforces Norway's leadership in science and technology, ensuring a sustainable and competitive research ecosystem.

The Norwegian Centre for Cybersecurity in Critical Sectors (NORCICS) is a center under the SFI scheme. Hosted by the Norwegian University of Science and Technology (NTNU), NORCICS fosters collaboration between public and private sector partners to advance cybersecurity research and industry innovation. Since its launch in 2020, NORCICS has aligned with Norway's National Cybersecurity Strategy (Norwegian Ministeries, 2019), focusing on secure digital transformation of the industry, infrastructure resilience, cybercrime prevention, and research-based education. The center addresses cyber risks such as IT/OT integration, Internet of Things (IoT) security, and AI-driven automation risks, ensuring national digital sovereignty and a more resilient society with the objectives of:

- strengthening strategic alliances between industry, government, and research institutions;
- expanding international cybersecurity collaboration and knowledge exchange;
- delivering pioneering research and validating innovative cybersecurity solutions; and
- training highly skilled cybersecurity professionals to support national security.

NORCICS follows the Open Innovation 2.0 (OI2) paradigm and methodology (Curley & Salmelin, 2017) that supports open innovation following the Quadruple Helix approach (Carayannis & Campbell, 2009) to accelerate the transfer of research and innovation results to regional growth and employs the Technology Transfer model of Gorschek et al. (2006), as adapted and shown in Figure 6.1 (Briand et al., 2012), enabling industry user partners to shape research roadmaps. It focuses on developing operational cybersecurity technologies, raising awareness, and facilitating knowledge transfer to businesses. Following a midway evaluation by the Research Council of Norway, NORCICS was recognized for excellent performance, securing continued funding until 2028. Its final three-year phase will refine innovation strategies, research priorities, and long-term sustainability, ensuring Norway's leadership in cybersecurity resilience and digital transformation.

The remainder of this chapter is structured as follows: In Section 6.2 we discuss the multifaceted relationship between cybersecurity and industrial innovation. In Section 6.3 we present the Norwegian SFI scheme and in Section 6.4 we focus on the case study of the Norwegian Centre for Cybersecurity in Critical Sectors (NORCICS). Finally, Section 6.5 summarizes our conclusions.

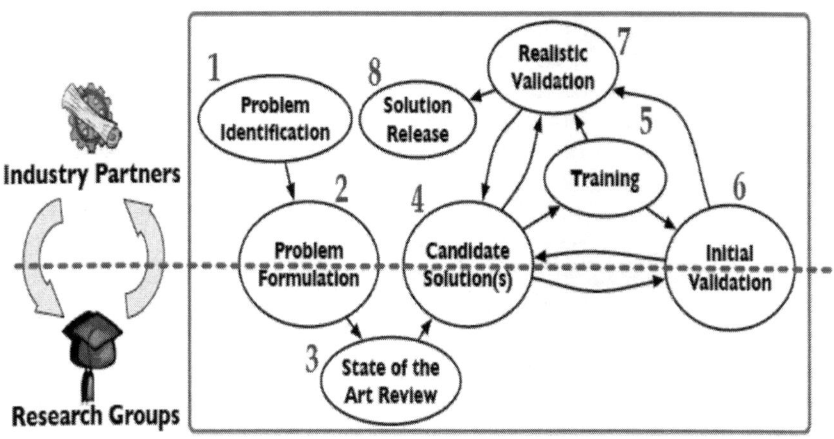

Source: Briand et al., 2012.

Figure 6.1 *The NORCICS research-based innovation approach*

6.2 CYBERSECURITY AND INDUSTRIAL INNOVATION: HOW ARE THE TWO INTERCONNECTED?

Cybersecurity and industrial innovation are deeply interconnected, as cybersecurity serves as a foundation for secure digital transformation, operational resilience, and trust within industries. As organizations adopt emerging technologies, they unlock new opportunities for efficiency and progress. However, these advancements also introduce cyber risks that, if unaddressed, can compromise intellectual property, disrupt operations, and weaken stakeholder confidence. In this section, we discuss key connections between cybersecurity and industrial innovation.

6.2.1 Protecting Intellectual Property

In today's fast-paced and highly competitive business landscape, industries thrive on continuous innovation. From cutting-edge technological advancements to proprietary designs and unique business strategies, intellectual property serves as a key asset that differentiates companies from their rivals. Cybersecurity plays a crucial role in safeguarding this valuable information from malicious actors who seek to exploit or steal trade secrets for financial gain, competitive advantage, or even geopolitical influence. Without adequate security measures, businesses risk losing their competitive edge, facing legal challenges, or suffering financial losses due to intellectual property theft. Implementing robust cybersecurity measures helps prevent unauthorized access, data breaches, and insider threats. These precautions not only protect sensitive company data but also foster an environment where innovation can flourish without fear of external interference. Additionally, securing intellectual property enhances trust among stakeholders, investors, and customers by demonstrating commitment to data protection and ethical business practices. In turn, this strengthens brand reputation and encourages continued innovation within the industry.

6.2.2 Enabling Digital Transformation: The Role of Cybersecurity in Advancing Innovation

Smart technologies drive efficiency, automation, and data-driven decision-making, but they also introduce new vulnerabilities that cyber threats can exploit. Cybersecurity acts as a safeguard, ensuring that interconnected systems remain resilient against attacks, unauthorized access, and data breaches. A secure digital ecosystem enables industries to embrace innovation without fear of disruption. Organizations can confidently implement cutting-edge technologies, optimize operations, and explore new business models while maintaining stability and reliability. By fortifying networks, securing data exchanges, and implementing threat detection mechanisms, companies can ensure business continuity and protect valuable assets.

Additionally, cybersecurity fosters trust among stakeholders, customers, and regulatory bodies. When digital transformation is backed by strong security measures, businesses not only meet compliance requirements but also demonstrate their commitment to responsible technological adoption. This trust accelerates collaboration and encourages the development of groundbreaking solutions that shape the future of industries. By prioritizing cybersecurity, industries unlock the full potential of digital transformation while minimizing risks, enhancing efficiency, and driving sustainable innovation in a rapidly evolving technological landscape.

6.2.3 Enhancing Operational Resilience: Strengthening Industries against Cyber Threats

In an increasingly digital and interconnected world, industries face a constant threat from cyberattacks that can disrupt operations, compromise sensitive data, and result in financial losses. Cybersecurity measures play a critical role in ensuring that businesses can withstand, respond to, and recover from these cyber threats while maintaining operational continuity. By implementing proactive security strategies, organizations can safeguard their digital infrastructure against disruptions.

Operational resilience is not just about preventing cyberattacks but also about minimizing downtime and ensuring a swift recovery in the event of an incident. Businesses that invest in strong cybersecurity frameworks, including regular security audits and employee training, develop a robust defense system that enables them to resume normal operations with minimal impact. This level of preparedness reduces vulnerabilities, prevents costly delays, and protects vital assets, allowing organizations to remain agile in the face of evolving cyber threats.

The confidence that comes with enhanced cybersecurity resilience encourages industries to embrace emerging technologies and innovative processes without hesitation. Businesses can push forward with digital transformation knowing that their security infrastructure is capable of mitigating potential risks. A resilient cybersecurity posture not only protects operations but also fosters a culture of trust, adaptability, and technological progress across industries.

6.2.4 Building Trust with Stakeholders: Strengthening Relationships through Cybersecurity

In today's interconnected digital landscape, trust is more than just a business advantage; it is a necessity for sustained success. Strong cybersecurity practices serve as a powerful indicator of a company's commitment to safety, reliability, and ethical responsibility, fostering confidence among key stakeholders, including customers, business partners, and regulatory authorities.

Customers expect their personal data to be protected when interacting with companies. By implementing robust cybersecurity measures, businesses reassure customers that their information remains secure, strengthening brand loyalty and encouraging repeat engagement.

Business partners and suppliers also rely on secure digital environments to facilitate collaboration and maintain smooth operations. A company with rigorous cybersecurity measures minimizes the risk of cyber threats disrupting supply chains, financial transactions, and shared digital platforms. This level of cybersecurity preparedness fosters trust and reliability, making organizations attractive partners for long-term alliances and strategic initiatives.

Regulatory bodies play a crucial role in enforcing cybersecurity compliance across industries. Companies that proactively adhere to cybersecurity regulations and best practices not only avoid penalties but also demonstrate their commitment to responsible digital governance. By maintaining transparency in cybersecurity policies and actively addressing emerging threats, businesses position themselves as trusted industry leaders, earning the confidence of regulators and reinforcing their reputation in the market.

Ultimately, trust is the foundation of successful innovation and collaboration. When stakeholders feel secure with a company's cybersecurity measures, they are more willing to invest, collaborate, and explore new technological advancements together.

6.2.5 Supporting Regulatory Compliance: Ensuring Innovation within Legal Frameworks

As industries embrace digital transformation, the need to comply with cybersecurity regulations and standards has become increasingly critical. Governments and regulatory bodies around the world establish strict cybersecurity guidelines to protect sensitive data, prevent cyber threats, and ensure that industries operate within legal boundaries. By adhering to these regulations, businesses can confidently innovate while maintaining compliance with established legal frameworks.

Regulatory compliance is not just about avoiding penalties; it also serves as a safeguard against financial and reputational risks. Failure to meet cybersecurity standards can lead to data breaches, intellectual property theft, and operational disruptions, all of which can severely impact an organization's credibility and profitability. By integrating robust cybersecurity practices, industries can minimize vulnerabilities and strengthen their security posture.

Additionally, compliance enhances the trust and credibility of industrial innovations. Businesses must demonstrate commitment to security and ethical data handling. Compliance with cybersecurity regulations reassures customers, investors, and partners that an organization prioritizes data protection and operates with integrity. This trust fosters stronger industry relationships, encourages collaboration, and drives market adoption of emerging technologies.

Meeting regulatory requirements also provides organizations with a competitive edge. Companies that proactively align with evolving cybersecurity standards position themselves as industry leaders, gaining access to new business opportunities, funding sources, and global markets. By embedding cybersecurity into innovation strategies, businesses can seamlessly navigate regulatory landscapes while driving technological advancements in a secure and responsible manner.

6.2.6 Driving Innovation in Cybersecurity Itself: Advancing Security to Empower Industries

As cyber threats evolve in complexity and sophistication, the demand for advanced cybersecurity solutions has become a driving force behind innovation in the field. The need to stay ahead of cybercriminals, protect sensitive data, and safeguard digital infrastructures pushes industries to develop cutting-edge security technologies that continuously adapt to emerging challenges.

Cybersecurity advancements do more than just protect digital assets; they fuel broader industrial innovation by creating a secure foundation for new and emerging technologies. Industries can confidently adopt new and emerging disruptive technologies without the fear of cyber threats compromising their progress. As cybersecurity continues to advance, industries gain the freedom to innovate, explore new frontiers, and drive technological evolution with greater security and resilience.

6.2.7 Facilitating Collaboration: Strengthening Innovation through Secure Connectivity

In today's interconnected digital landscape, industries rely on seamless collaboration to drive innovation and achieve technological breakthroughs. Whether working on joint research initiatives, sharing critical data, or co-developing cutting-edge solutions, businesses must operate within secure digital environments to protect sensitive information and intellectual property. Cybersecurity plays a pivotal role in enabling this collaboration by safeguarding networks, systems, and data exchanges against cyber threats, unauthorized access, and leaks.

Robust cybersecurity measures allow organizations to confidently engage in collaborative innovation without the fear of cyberattacks or data breaches disrupting their progress. These security frameworks ensure that proprietary ideas, research findings, and technological advancements remain protected, fostering a culture of trust among industry partners.

When industries can exchange ideas and share resources without hesitation, the pace of technological progress accelerates significantly. Secure digital ecosystems encourage global collaboration, bringing together experts from different sectors and geographical regions to push the boundaries of innovation. Whether in fields like artificial intelligence, biotechnology, or smart manufacturing, the ability to work together securely leads to transformative advancements that shape the future.

Additionally, cybersecurity-driven collaboration extends beyond corporations; it supports academic institutions, research organizations, and start-ups in contributing to industry-wide innovation. By ensuring secure data sharing and research integrity, cybersecurity strengthens partnerships that drive scientific discoveries, technological improvements, and economic growth.

6.2.8 Safeguarding Critical Systems: Strengthening Security for Industrial Operations

Modern industries depend on highly interconnected digital infrastructures to drive efficiency, automation, and productivity. From smart manufacturing systems and IoT devices to automated supply chains and cloud-based operations, these technologies enable seamless workflows, data-driven decision-making, and real-time monitoring.

Cybersecurity plays a crucial role in ensuring the security and resilience of these critical systems. Advanced security measures allow industries to identify and neutralize cyber threats before they escalate. Machine learning-powered threat analysis, intrusion detection systems, and continuous network monitoring help organizations proactively defend against cyberattacks, safeguarding their infrastructure from malicious actors. Encryption technologies are also essential in protecting industrial data integrity. Whether securing proprietary designs, confidential business strategies, or operational processes, encryption ensures that information remains unreadable to unauthorized entities. Secure communication protocols further prevent data interception, reinforcing the confidentiality and reliability of digital operations. Additionally, access controls and multi-factor authentication mechanisms play a vital role in preventing unauthorized entry into industrial systems. By restricting access to only authorized personnel and implementing strong authentication protocols, organizations mitigate the risk of cyber intrusions that could lead to system manipulation, data theft, or operational disruptions.

Ensuring cybersecurity within industrial ecosystems enables companies to confidently adopt emerging technologies without compromising stability or safety. Businesses can seamlessly integrate new and emerging disruptive technologies while maintaining operational integrity. A strong cybersecurity framework not only enhances efficiency but also fosters innovation by providing a secure foundation for technological advancements.

Ultimately, cybersecurity is not just a protective measure, it is an enabler of industrial innovation. A strong cybersecurity foundation empowers businesses to explore new frontiers in technology, minimize the accordant risks, enhance efficiency, safeguard their operational resilience, maintain business continuity, prevent legal or ethical complications, foster collaboration, and drive sustainable progress in a digital-first world.

6.3 THE SFI SCHEME

The Centre for Research-based Innovation (SFI) scheme in Norway is a national initiative managed and endorsed by the Research Council of Norway, aimed at strengthening industrial innovation through strategic research collaborations (The Research Council of Norway, 2025). It provides critical funding to designated centers, fostering long-term partnerships between R&D-intensive companies, leading research institutions, and, in some cases, the public sector. The SFI scheme plays a vital role in supporting Norwegian businesses, offering access to highly skilled researchers through training partnerships with accredited universities. It emphasizes effective collaboration among partners, ensuring research outcomes drive business development, sustainable innovation, and long-term value creation.

The scheme is designed to:

1. facilitate sustained cooperation between innovation-driven companies and top-tier research groups;
2. develop industry-oriented research clusters, enhancing Norway's international competitiveness; and
3. support researcher training and knowledge transfer, addressing areas with high potential for value creation.

Each SFI center is a temporary research entity, hosted by a Norwegian research organization known as the host institution. The host institution:

- serves as the formal applicant and project owner for funding;
- manages scientific, administrative, and financial aspects of the center's operations;
- provides essential infrastructure and supplies a significant portion of the scientific personnel; and
- ensures the long-term management of research investments beyond the funding period.

Although SFI centers do not operate as separate legal entities, they function as integral components of their host institutions. Once the Research Council funding ends, the host institution remains responsible for overseeing and utilizing the research investments. Through its strategic focus on innovation, the SFI scheme reinforces Norway's position in global research, technology, and industry leadership.

6.3.1 Collaboration Framework

The SFI scheme mandates active participation from private companies and allows involvement from public entities, collectively referred to as user partners. Each center has at least three user partners, including businesses, which contribute to funding, governance, and research activities. User partners play a crucial role in translating research findings into practical innovations. Beyond mandatory partners, centers can collaborate with other research institutions, referred to as research partners, to enhance scientific expertise and drive innovation. International user and research partners may also participate, ensuring alignment with the SFI scheme's objectives.

The SFI consortium is a collaborative network consisting of the host institution, user partners, and research partners affiliated with an SFI center. These participants, collectively referred to as consortium participants, are responsible for contributing research efforts and financial resources in line with the center's funding and cost plan, aiming to achieve the outcomes outlined in the project description. To ensure flexibility, the SFI scheme permits adjustments to the consortium's composition over time. If a participant wishes to withdraw, they must provide at least six months' notice. In cases where a withdrawal reduces funding or removes essential expertise, the center's board must take steps to secure the necessary resources to ensure the objectives in the project description are met. If key conditions for the center's establishment are no longer met or are significantly altered, the Research Council reserves the right to terminate the contract with the host institution.

The host institution is tasked with developing a formal consortium agreement that defines the structure, operational framework, and collaborative processes within the consortium. This agreement governs the rights and responsibilities of each participant, ensuring clarity and accountability in areas such as resource allocation in line with the funding plan; procedures for joining or withdrawing from the consortium; employer responsibilities and liability considerations; and ownership, utilization rights, licensing, and confidentiality of project outcomes.

The SFI scheme adheres to the Research Council's General Terms and Conditions for R&D Projects (The Research Council of Norway, 2021), which govern ownership rights; utilization and licensing; publication of project results; and confidentiality agreements. The consortium agreement further regulates these areas in alignment with the general terms and conditions.

An SFI center typically consists of research groups working at the same site, which refers to teams located within the same building complex. However, the SFI scheme also supports the formation of "virtual" centers, where research groups collaborate remotely across different locations. Whether physical or virtual, every SFI center must have centralized administration ensuring unified governance; a cohesive research plan aligned with the project description and effective communication systems and mechanisms for staff exchange across different segments.

The center is structured around highly capable researchers with proven expertise. Staff members may engage with the center on a part-time basis, allowing them to continue roles at collaborating institutions and enterprises, including teaching, contract research, and other professional activities. The host institution and consortium partners must collectively determine employment responsibilities, as the center itself cannot act as an employer. A strong emphasis is placed on researcher training in areas vital for innovation and value creation. The center facilitates training for master's and doctoral students, as well as postdoctoral research fellows, and encourages these researchers to conduct part of their work with user partners, fostering industry collaboration. The center must actively promote gender equality in hiring and strive to attract top-tier national and international researchers. It also supports staff exchange programs among consortium and international partners, fostering cross-institutional expertise sharing.

6.3.2 Governance, Management, and Administration

While integrated into the host institution, the SFI center operates independently, guided by its own governing board. Its organizational model aligns with the host institution's framework, ensuring effective interaction with consortium partners. To optimize efficiency, the host institution must provide strong leadership with significant scientific and administrative autonomy; a robust administrative support system; and infrastructure that enables smooth coordination across research teams.

The board of an SFI center is composed of representatives from the host institution, user partners, and research partners within the consortium. To ensure the center maintains a strong user-driven focus, representatives from the user partners must hold the majority of board seats. The board's primary responsibility is to oversee the execution of the center's mission and ensure that the research activities outlined in the project description are completed within the approved budget and timeline. Additionally, the board must promote effective collaboration between the center, the host institution, and consortium partners, while ensuring the host institution retains significant influence over strategic cooperation and operational decisions.

The center is led by a director, who may be supported by a management group. This director, acting as the project manager, must possess a strong research background, demonstrated expertise in research leadership, and effective team-building skills. The director is granted scientific and administrative autonomy, particularly regarding staff recruitment. The host institution, in consultation with consortium partners, is responsible for appointing the director and management team.

To ensure smooth operation, clear governance guidelines must be established, including the board's authority, rules regarding board representation, and the director's mandate. The board is prohibited from making decisions that infringe upon the host institution's responsibilities.

6.3.3 Funding and Financial Structure

The funding model is based on co-investment, where resources are provided jointly by the Research Council and the SFI consortium. The user partners' financial commitment serves as a key indicator of the center's relevance to industry needs. The SFI scheme mandates that private companies and other user partners contribute at least 50% of the Research Council's annual funding. If a partner withdrawal results in private companies and other user partners contributing less than 50% of the Research Council's annual funding, the Research Council may reduce the SFI grant amount. Additional contributions from the host institution and research organizations can further strengthen the center's strategic foundation. Consortium participants may provide funding in multiple forms, including direct financial contributions, staff allocations, and essential research infrastructure. The host institution's budgetary contributions may encompass payroll and social security costs, operational expenses, and equipment depreciation, all in accordance with the Research Council's project cost regulations.

6.3.4 Operational Duration and Closure

The Research Council funds SFI centers for up to eight years from their establishment. Approximately 3.5 years after a center is established, a midterm evaluation is conducted by the Research Council under a common framework, by a panel of international experts. The evaluation examines the scientific achievements of the center relative to the original project description; the impact of research findings on innovation, value creation, and long-term research focus among consortium partners; and the plans for the potential final three-year period of operation. The Research Council assesses the center's administrative framework, and these findings, together with the evaluation panel's report and recommendations, determine whether the center receives continued funding for the remaining eight-year term or faces termination after five years.

Upon termination (after either five or eight years) the Research Council funding ends, and the center ceases to be part of the SFI scheme. If unforeseen circumstances alter the conditions upon which a center was founded, or if the center can no longer operate according to its original principles, the Research Council reserves the right to terminate its contract with the host institution. This includes revoking funding and removing SFI status. When closing a center, the host institution and its partners must ensure that personnel considerations are addressed; especially ensuring that master's students and research fellows can complete their academic programs. They must also take responsibility for ensuring the continuation and management of research investments beyond the period of Research Council funding.

6.4 THE NORWEGIAN CENTRE FOR CYBERSECURITY IN CRITICAL SECTORS[1]

The Norwegian Centre for Cybersecurity in Critical Sectors (NORCICS) is a research-based innovation center under Norway's SFI scheme, with an initial budget of approximately NOK220 million. It is the only research center focusing on cybersecurity that is funded by the Research Council of Norway. Hosted at NTNU, under the Department of Information Security and Communication Technology, NORCICS facilitates collaboration between public and private sector partners to advance cybersecurity research and industry innovation. The center's work is closely connected to the department's Center for Cybersecurity and Information Security—a public–private and civilian–military cooperation with more than 80 partners. NORCICS builds upon these

1 https://www.ntnu.edu/norcics

relationships to provide a center focused on innovation-driven research in cybersecurity of the Critical Sectors.

Since its launch in 2020, NORCICS has focused on secure digital transformation, infrastructure resilience, and cybercrime prevention, aligning with Norway's National Cybersecurity Strategy. It addresses key cybersecurity challenges, including IT/OT integration vulnerabilities, IoT security, and AI-driven automation risks, ensuring national digital sovereignty and the security of Critical Sectors.

6.4.1 Background and Need for NORCICS

The National Cybersecurity Strategy for Norway recognizes the growing risks linked to the rapid digitalization of society. NORCICS contributes directly to all five strategic goals outlined in the strategy, namely (Norwegian Ministeries, 2019):

1. Norwegian companies digitalize in a secure and trustworthy manner and are able to protect themselves against cyber incidents.
2. Critical societal functions are supported by a robust and reliable digital infrastructure.
3. Improved cybersecurity competence is aligned with the needs of society.
4. Society has improved ability to detect and handle cyberattacks.
5. The police have strengthened their ability to prevent and combat cybercrime.

This ensures that organizations within Critical Sectors can safely embrace digital transformation. Critical Sectors encompass industries essential to national security, public health, economic stability, and societal safety.

The National Strategy for Cyber Security Competence (Departementene, 2019) calls for a long-term build-up of cybersecurity competence, encompassing national capacity in the fields of research, development, education, and measures designed to raise awareness in the business community and among the public. It sets as a goal "to provide attractive and competent research environments who attract good researchers and doctoral candidates." NORCICS is one such environment in the area of cybersecurity for the Critical Sectors and educates more than 18 PhD students and more than 7 postdoctoral researchers, competent in the cybersecurity needs of society.

The primary research objective of NORCICS is to develop innovative cybersecurity solutions to address the needs of a highly dynamic ecosystem of socio-technical cyber-physical systems in Critical Sectors. Critical Sectors are sectors which are critical to the nation and whose incapacitation or destruction will have a debilitating impact on national security, economy, public health, or safety. The continuous evolution of Critical Sectors introduces new risks and dependencies. Increasing interconnectivity across sectors, jurisdictions, and national borders compounds cybersecurity threats, creating greater risks for digital sovereignty and autonomy. Thus, proactive cybersecurity measures are essential—not just for economic and societal protection, but also to preserve Norway's national digital sovereignty.

NORCICS seeks to establish a safer, more resilient Norwegian society through advanced cybersecurity solutions. Over the long term, its work will:

1. strengthen strategic alliances between industry, government, and research institutions;
2. expand international collaboration in cybersecurity research and development;
3. deliver groundbreaking research, while validating and demonstrating innovative cybersecurity solutions to drive industry progress; and
4. train high-level cybersecurity professionals, ensuring Norway remains at the forefront of digital security expertise.

Through cutting-edge research, collaboration, and workforce development, NORCICS reinforces Norway's cybersecurity posture, helping Critical Sectors adapt to emerging threats while driving sustainable innovation.

6.4.2 NORCICS Vision and Objectives

Norway is one of the most digitalized countries in the world, and the National Digitalisation Strategy 2024–2030 (Norwegian Ministry of Digitalisation and Public Governance, 2024) is laying the foundation for the country to become the global leader. NORCICS's vision is to contribute to making Norway the most securely digitalized country in the world by improving the cybersecurity and resilience of its Critical Sectors through supporting research-based innovation.

NORCICS's primary objective is to enhance the capability of private and public sector stakeholders to respond to the current and future cybersecurity risks by developing, validating, and operationalizing innovative technologies within a cyber-physical security ecosystem that includes highly trained research personnel.

The following secondary objectives lead to the achievement of the primary objective:

- To create new knowledge that will improve our understanding of the dynamics and interdependencies among Critical Sectors and of cyberattacks against Cyber-Physical Systems.
- To develop, test, and validate in an industrially relevant environment novel, advanced, and innovative methods for preventing cyberattacks against industrial control systems in Critical Sectors.
- To demonstrate in an industrially relevant environment efficient cybersecurity solutions for industrial control systems in Critical Sectors;
- To develop novel methods and tools for cybersecurity training and awareness improvement.
- To effectively transfer the knowledge created within NORCICS among its user partners and other Norwegian businesses and stakeholders.

6.4.3 The NORCICS Consortium

The NORCICS consortium has been put together following several criteria including skills balance, complementarity of expertise, manageability, and sector coverage. It comprises academic and research partners, organizations that can act as multipliers, industrial stakeholders, and end users. Its composition has been carefully designed so that the combination of the individual skills of its members will enable NORCICS to achieve its objectives.

The consortium members have complementary expertise that collectively covers the areas of fundamental research. The NORCICS research partners are SINTEF Energi, SINTEF Digital, SINTEF Manufacturing, Norsk Regnesentral, and the University of Agder. The NORCICS user partners can broadly be classified in three groups:

- A group of businesses/organizations with activity in diverse Critical Sectors—Group 1 (Elvia, Norsk Hydro, Kongsberg Gruppen, Yara International, Sykehuset Innlandet HF, Equinor).
- A group of cybersecurity and/or operational technology providers—Group 2 (Mnemonic, NC Spectrum, Siemens, Diri).
- A group of organizations dedicated to striving toward a safer society, to raising awareness, and to providing advice to Norwegian citizens and enterprises concerning cyber threats, vulnerabilities, and information security—Group 3 (Oslo Police District, Aiba).

6.4.4 The NORCICS Approach to Research and Innovation

6.4.4.1 Research

NORCICS adopts a holistic, comprehensive, and systemic approach to cybersecurity, as illustrated in Figure 6.2. This methodology integrates people, processes, and technology to safeguard Critical Sectors, aligning with the core cybersecurity functions of the NIST Cybersecurity Framework 2.0 (National Institute of Standards and Technology, 2024): govern, identify, protect, detect, respond, and recover. Furthermore, cybersecurity is embedded throughout the entire lifecycle of a product or project, beginning with secure design and extending to safe disposal. Within NORCICS, cybersecurity research leads to the development of reusable methods and tools applicable across various infrastructures. These innovations encompass a broad range of cybersecurity concepts and are rigorously validated through multiple demonstrators across different Critical Sectors.

Created by the Joint Research Centre (JRC), the European Commission's science and knowledge service provides a visual representation of cybersecurity research. Each point in the three-dimensional space represents a research area within cybersecurity. With reference to Figure 6.2, the research within NORCICS addresses all three components of the triplets and focuses on the research domains of: Theoretical Foundations; Network and Distributed Systems; Human Aspects; Education and Training; and Data Security and Privacy, as applied to the application domains: Critical Infrastructures; Industrial Control Systems; and Internet of Things, within the sectorial domains of: Energy; Health; Manufacturing and Supply Chain; and Public Safety.

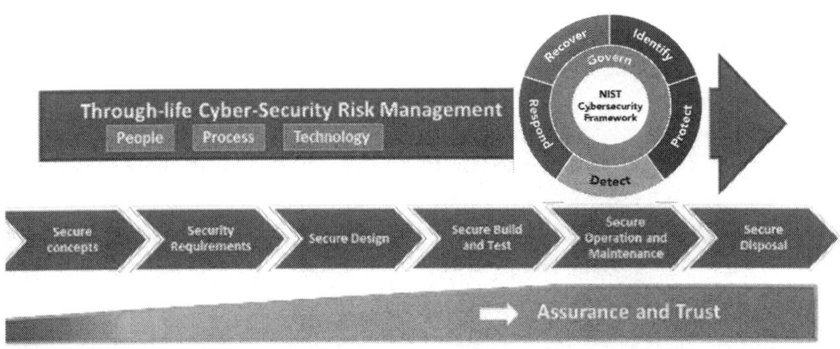

Source: Author's own illustration.

Figure 6.2 Holistic approach to cybersecurity

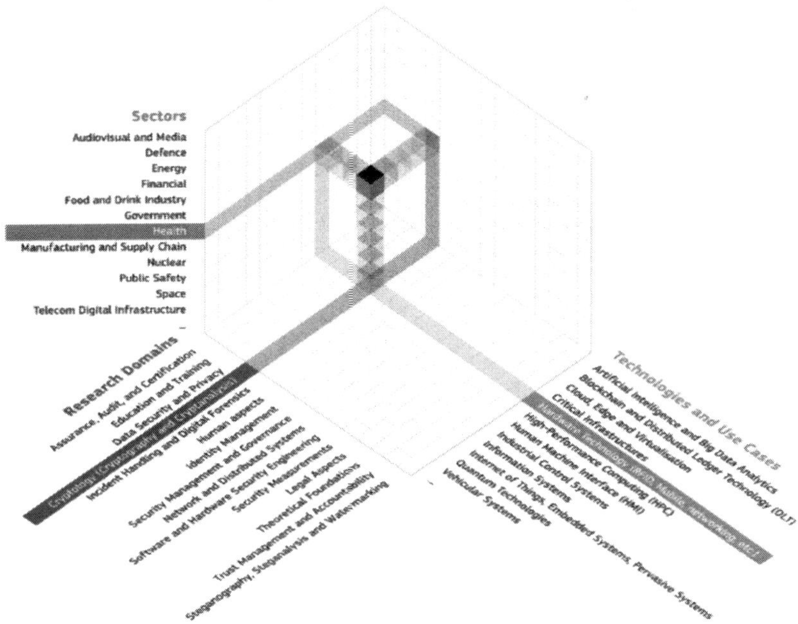

Source: Author's own illustration.

Figure 6.3 *Cybersecurity research*

As shown in Figure 6.4, the work within NORCICS is organized in six work packages, three of which are dedicated to research activities. These are:

- **Work Package 2—Foundations:** WP2 is dedicated to the design and analysis of tools and methods that are necessary to understand the security of critical systems and infrastructures, particularly when confronted by advanced adversaries. These activities range from understanding high-level dependencies and resulting vulnerabilities that may also be exploitable by sophisticated adversaries to more in-depth analytical methods for protocols and interactions found in cyber-physical systems, particularly with real-time systems.
- **Work Package 3—Technologies, applications, and services:** WP3 drives forward research on the technologies, applications, and services essential for securing and enhancing the resilience of critical infrastructures. By focusing on key areas such as 5G, data analytics, IT/OT integration, and human factors, WP3 lays the groundwork for more secure, adaptive

systems vital for the future of Critical Sectors. As progress continues, WP3 will remain at the cutting edge of developing solutions that will address the evolving cybersecurity challenges of tomorrow.

- **Work Package 4—Demonstration environments:** This work package is responsible for testing and demonstrating the solutions and foundations developed in NORCICS, both in laboratory and real-world environments, in collaboration with user partners for validation and verification. The demonstrators are being developed in four sectors: Cyber-Physical Electricity Systems, Industry 4.0, Distributed Healthcare, and Smart Districts.

The remaining three workpackages in Figure 6.4 are support workpackages, aiming at managing the NORCICS project (WP6), disseminating its results (WP5), and managing the innovation produced within NORCICS (WP1).

In addition to the structural organization of the research work as described above, the research within NORCICS, guided by the user partners' strategic innovation priorities, is organized into four Focus Areas (FAs), as shown in Figure 6.4. Each FA addresses a range of cybersecurity challenges that arise in the process of digital transformation in Critical Sectors. Specifically, research in FA1 (titled "IT&OT integration") addresses such challenges arising because of the integration of Information Technology (IT) and Operational Technology (OT) systems. Research in FA2 (titled "5G") addresses challenges with the secure exploitation, usage, and security of 5G and other communication

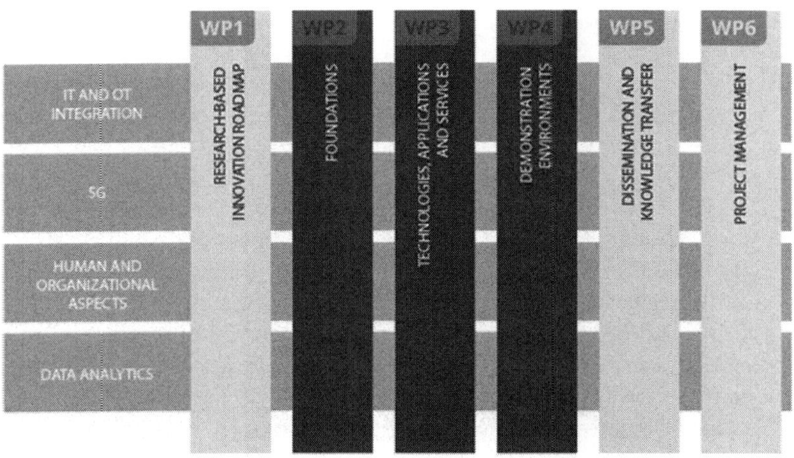

Source: Author's own illustration.

Figure 6.4 *NORCICS work organization*

technologies; cryptographic approaches are also included here. Research in FA3 (titled "Human and organizational aspects") addresses non-technological challenges, to ensure the holistic approach to cybersecurity that NORCICS follows. Research in FA4 (titled "Data analytics") is concerned with the efficient leveraging of data analytics to address cybersecurity challenges in the digital transformation process.

6.4.4.2 Innovation

NORCICS follows the Research Council of Norway definition of innovation: "Innovation is new or significantly improved goods, services, processes, organizational forms, or making models that are adopted to achieve value creation and or societal benefit" (Norges Forskningråd, 2011).

NTNU and SINTEF have jointly developed guidelines on how to improve the SFI centers' contribution to innovation (Størkersen et al., 2023). These guidelines are the basis of how NORCICS views and works with innovation. As discussed in Section 6.4.2, the NORCICS user partners can be broadly classified into three groups. Leveraging the research on cybersecurity in NORCICS for innovation and value creation takes on different forms for each of these groups. Whereas for Group 2 the research within NORCICS is an opportunity to innovate by improving their services and/or starting new ones, for Group 1 cybersecurity research is seen as an enabler of innovation in their own business domain, by supporting the improvement of their cybersecurity posture thereby enhancing their competitiveness, rather than as an opportunity, by itself, to innovate in their own domain. For Group 3, innovation is seen as improving the quality and trustworthiness of the services they already offer to society at large and/or offering new ones. Nevertheless, the value created by bringing together into the same ecosystem organizations from diverse domains and business sectors is acknowledged by all the NORCICS partners.

The core of the NORCICS innovation potential is at its partner organizations. This potential is fostered by:

- Building partners' understanding of how research is key to making significant improvements in their own organization.
- Demonstrating how research results can be used by user partners to improve a process or product within their own organization. One example of this is the uptake of a gamified approach to cybersecurity awareness developed within NORCICS, that is being taken up by a user partner to improve the awareness-building process for their employees.
- Fostering networking of partners for collaboration on research tasks and exchanging experiences and facilitating the undertaking of collaborative research.
- Disseminating the research results to the partners and society.

- Connecting PhD work to partners' challenges, for example, via MSc theses.
- Developing innovation understanding among PhD candidates.

NORCICS uses several instruments to create value for its partners:

- **Industry Partner Workshops—hosted by partners:** Three times a year NORCICS arranges partner workshops; nine such workshops have been organized since NORCICS started operating, with 45 participants on average. The aim of these workshops is to allow partners to discuss their ongoing cybersecurity challenges and connect these to the center's research. Two of the workshops each year are hosted by a partner, preferably at their premises. The host organization, in collaboration with the center management, sets the agenda to highlight their thematic interests. The third partner workshop each year is a joint conference between NORCICS and the NTNU CCIS. The partner workshops have resulted in increased partner maturity toward research and innovation; trust among partners to collaborate and share information and knowledge; definition of new research tasks based on partners' research interests; spin-off workshops between groups of partners on specific subject matter; and partner participation in adjacent forums, for example, the Norwegian Ecosystem for Secure IT-OT Integration (NESIOT) (Anon., 2025).
- **One-to-one partner meetings:** The NORCICS management has annual one-on-one partner meetings with each partner in the consortium. The aim is to identify how ongoing tasks or new tasks are relevant to the partner's strategic priorities, increase partner engagement, and secure the partner's participation in the center.
- **PhD workshop for innovation:** NORCICS, in collaboration with the NTNU Department of Information Security and Communication Technology, arranged a workshop for PhD students on how to identify the innovation potential from their PhD research. The workshop gave the PhD students the opportunity to reflect on the innovation potential of their own research, in addition to attending lectures on the innovation process, including how they can get support from local innovation consultants and the NTNU Technology Transfer services.
- **Industrial PhDs and partner innovation:** NORCICS has ten industrial/public affiliated PhDs in collaboration with industry/government partners. These candidates are engaged in research highly relevant and closely related to NORCICS tasks. The main supervisors of these candidates are NORCICS researchers, and members of staff of industrial/government partners serve as co-supervisors. All these PhDs are supported by both

the Research Council of Norway and their employer or by their employer alone.

- **PhD and postdoctoral researchers' engagement with partners for innovation:** In addition to the natural link between PhD research and innovation within partners that the industrial PhDs provide, other NORCICS PhD candidates and postdoctoral researchers have engaged with user partners for innovation.
- **Start-up partners for entrepreneurial insight:** In 2023, two start-up companies, AiBA and Diri, joined NORCICS. Having start-ups in the consortium gives industrial partners and PhD and other researchers insight into how they go from research and an idea to a start-up. The start-up partners benefit from their participation in NORCICS by getting access to researchers and subject matter experts that increase their credibility toward investors and collaboration partners. Additionally, one new start-up (SeCore), based in part on research performed within NORCICS, has been created.

As innovation occurs in collaboration with others, NORCICS is a partner in a larger ecosystem comprising:

- The Center for Cyber and Information Security (CCIS), NTNU.[2] Many NORCICS researchers are participating in research activities in both NORCICS and CCIS.
- Two catapult centers: Manufacturing Technologies (Raufoss)[3] working with issues toward the manufacturing industry and Industry 4.0. DigiCat (Ålesund)[4] and the Norwegian Cyber Range (Gjøvik),[5] for cybersecurity companies.
- Digital Innlandet[6] and Norwegian Cybersecurity Cluster,[7] to increase cybersecurity knowledge toward SMEs.
- NTNU Technology Transfer AS,[8] for supporting researchers' ideas and innovation potential.

---

2 https://www.ntnu.edu/ccis/center-for-cyber-and-information-security
3 https://raufossindustripark.no/katapulten-2
4 https://www.digicat.no/digicat
5 https://www.ntnu.edu/ncr
6 https://www.digitalinnlandet.no/
7 https://www.cybersecuritycluster.no/om
8 https://www.ntnutto.no/

- Vaager Innovasjon,[9] SIVA financial innovation center,[10] for generating ideas and supporting other cybersecurity start-ups.
- An MSc program in Industrial Innovation and Digital Security[11] was established in 2021 at NTNU in Gjøvik, as a result of NORCIS and the collaboration between the Department of Information Security and Communication Technology and the Department of Industrial Economics and Technology Management at Gjøvik.

Other innovations achieved through the research performed in NORCICS include patent applications, testbeds, pilots and testing projects, demonstration projects, start-ups, new methods, and models.

Focusing on the innovation potential of the research performed within NORCICS, we conclude that several of the expected research outcomes have already been achieved and most of the remaining ones are addressed in tasks currently underway. However, the uptake of such research results by the user partners is still limited; this is mostly due to the inherent latency of research uptake into practice, particularly when processes rather than products are targeted for innovation. When it comes to value creation, the work within NORCICS has already achieved or is justifiably expected to achieve in its remaining lifetime, all the expected value-creating results.

6.4.5 How NORCICS Is Governed and Managed

The governance and management bodies of NORCICS are the General Assembly, the Board, the Director, and the Scientific Management Team. This structure is depicted in Figure 6.5.

- **General Assembly:** The General Assembly consists of one delegate from each partner. It is responsible for setting the strategic directions of the center; for approving the plans to implement the strategy; and for assessing the results. It meets once a year.
- **Board:** The Board is the formal decision-making body of NORCICS. The Board is chaired by the Dean of the NTNU Faculty of Information Technology and Electrical Engineering. Representatives of the following partners, selected according to their extent of participation in the project and on sector representativeness, make up the Board: Elvia AS, Norsk Hydro ASA, Equinor ASA, Mnemonic AS, Oslo Police District, NTNU,

---

9 https://vaager.com/
10 https://siva.no/english/
11 https://www.ntnu.no/studier/miids

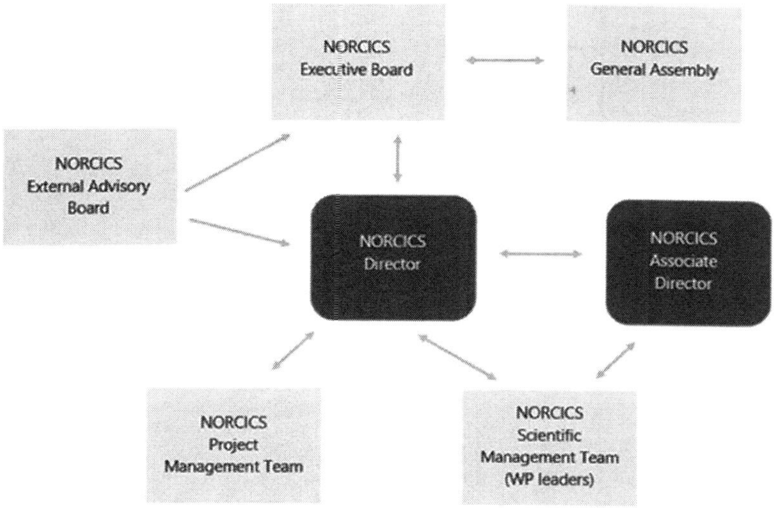

Source: Author's own illustration.

Figure 6.5 The NORCICS governance and management structure

SINTEF Energi, Kongsberg Gruppen ASA. The Board is responsible for the overall management of the project. Board members are delegated the necessary authority to make decisions binding the partner they represent. The Board meets every four months to monitor and direct the progress of the project.

- **Center Director:** The center director is responsible for the overall project coordination and management. He reports to the Board; he has overall responsibility for the project; he is responsible for implementing the decisions of the Board; he is implementing the technical directions and strategies of the project; and he is the contact point of the project with the Research Council of Norway. In his duties, he is assisted by the associate director. The administrative coordinator of NORCICS completes the NORCICS management team.
- **Scientific Management Team:** The coordination, planning, and monitoring of the research and development work in the project is performed by the NORCICS Scientific Management Team, which includes the WP leaders and is chaired by the Director. The Scientific Management Team meets weekly. The responsibility for the planning, execution, and monitoring of the work within the research activities lies with the WP Leaders. The

Extended Scientific Management Team, in which the Focus Area Leaders also participate, meets monthly.

- **External Advisory Board:** The research and development work in the project is supported by an international External Advisory Board (EAB), consisting of leading scientists in the fields of interest to the project, representatives of the Norwegian industry, and policymakers. The EAB provides external quality assurance to NORCICS; it is convened once every year during the annual NORCICS workshop.

6.4.6 International Cooperation

Several internationally highly reputed centers active in the field of cybersecurity collaborate with NORCICS. The selection of international collaborators has been made based on the complementarity of expertise; geographical coverage; the strategic importance of a long-lasting alliance; and existing strong collaboration relationships with NORCICS partners. International collaboration is important to ensure that Norwegian partners are up to date with international developments in the field and to multiply the spread of new knowledge and innovation. It is also expected to play an important role in the innovation process by allowing Norwegian industry to gain access to a broader pool of resources and knowledge. International cooperation also provides opportunities for the exchange of visiting researchers and PhD candidates; for joint supervision of PhD theses, following the model of the Innovative Training Networks (ITN) of the Marie Curie Actions for collaborative PhD education; and for adjunct professorships to international faculty.

NORCICS actively pursues the enlargement of the initial pool of international collaborators, including through its initiation of and participation in consortia to apply for projects funded by the European Commission. The following universities are currently collaborating with NORCICS:

- Michigan Technological University, USA
- George Washington University, USA
- University of Florida, Nelms Institute for the Connected World, USA
- US Military Academy, USA
- University of Guelph, Canada
- Polytechnique Montréal, Canada
- New York University Abu Dhabi, UAE
- Technische Universität München, Germany
- Universität Passau, Germany
- Technische Universität Hamburg, Germany
- Danmarks Tekniske Universitet, Denmark

- Singapore University of Technology and Design, Singapore
- Telecom SudParis, France
- Università degli Studi di Cagliari, Italy
- Universidad de Málaga, Spain
- Indian Institute of Technology Kanpur, India

6.4.7 What NORCICS Has Achieved to Date

On October 1, 2024, NORCICS celebrated four years of operation. In the same year, the Research Council of Norway (RCN) commenced the midterm evaluation of NORCICS, as they do with all SFIs. The purpose of this evaluation is to review the progress made against plans, assess achievements, and evaluate the continuing relevance of objectives and research methodologies. It also aims to examine plans for the remaining four years under RCN funding and the center's sustainability beyond that period.

The first phase of the process is the self-evaluation, which includes a survey among the NORCICS partners to assess the work performed within the center and the benefits they derive from their participation. This phase also involves compiling a Self-Evaluation Report, structured along six "success criteria," namely: Research Activity; Innovation and Value Creation; Internationalization; Researcher Training and Recruitment; Partners and Funding; and Organization. Additionally, the External Advisory Board was invited to evaluate NORCICS's performance over the past four years. All these forms of self-assessment concluded that NORCICS has performed well and has achieved significant research results that bring value to its partners and to Norway. Some highlights of the achievements follow.

Research in NORCICS has led to the publication of over 150 scientific works, demonstrating its significant contributions to the cybersecurity field. Several major breakthroughs have been achieved, advancing knowledge and practical applications in critical cybersecurity domains. NORCICS remains firmly aligned with its primary and secondary research objectives, showing excellence and impact in its ongoing studies. However, further efforts are required to fully realize certain secondary objectives, particularly in developing novel methodologies and tools to enhance cybersecurity training and awareness. Strengthening initiatives in this domain will ensure broader industry adoption and improved cybersecurity preparedness.

The center actively engages in collaborative efforts with international research groups, clusters, and organizations, facilitating the internationalization of both the Norwegian research and business sectors. For illustration, NORCICS has established cooperation with 25 EU projects through the European Cluster for Securing Critical Infrastructures, alongside forming partnerships with 20 entities in the European Knowledge Hub and Policy

Testbed for Critical Infrastructure Protection. Moreover, the NORCICS partners actively engage in standardization bodies, notably CENELEC TC 65X on systems and elements used for industrial process measurement, control, and automation, in addition to esteemed international organizations, such as the European Cyber Security Organization (ECSO) and the European Union Agency for Cybersecurity (ENISA). NORCICS is not represented in these organizations; rather, the results, experiences, and processes carried out within these bodies are effectively communicated and disseminated within NORCICS through the center's communication activities, and vice versa.

Furthermore, the center actively strives to co-organize, host, support, and participate in an increasing number of international academic conferences. NORCICS researchers regularly partake in the program committees of well-established, highly esteemed international conferences, and the center's director until recently chaired the Steering Committee of the ESORICS Conferences. Additionally, NORCICS researchers also serve as editors for several international scientific journals and as guest editors of special issues in such journals.

NORCICS has performed quite well when it comes to following its plans and achieving its objectives with respect to international cooperation; however, physical international mobility has been limited. This is primarily because the nature of cybersecurity research carried out in the center does not, to date, lend itself to extensive use of laboratory facilities. Accordingly, remote collaboration is usually preferred over the physical presence of researchers at the center's premises. Such physical mobility is expected to increase in the coming years, as the NORCICS demonstrators and testbeds evolve.

The center directly supports and recruits PhD candidates and postdoctoral researchers; in addition, several PhD candidates not directly funded by the center are active in the center's research. In addition, academic staff involve MSc students in the center's research activities with 70 students having undertaken research topics related to NORCICS tasks between fall 2023 and spring 2025.

The training of doctoral researchers is across several institutions, with the bulk of PhD candidates being trained at NTNU (with the University of Agder also training candidates) and specifically in the PhD program in information security and communication technology (PHISCT). The program includes research-specific elements but also transferable skills. Thus, so far, 11 candidates are supported by the center budget at NTNU and one at the University of Agder; in addition, 12 more students work on projects supported by the center but are otherwise funded. More than half (16 out of 24) of the candidates were Norwegian nationals, and 8 of the 24 were female (~33%), both above the reference averages of the overall PhD program at the NTNU Department of Information Security and Communication Technology and comparing favorably nationally. It is worth mentioning, specifically due to the traditional male dominance in the field that NORCICS operates in, that as of October 2024, the gender balance of the NORCICS funded PhDs is 50% female (6/12). The emphasis on national recruitment is significant not only in the interest of providing a national talent pool but also given the constraints on overseas recruitment owing to national security and export control compliance requirements.

PhD candidates are typically involved not only with their research in the center but also the corresponding research group providing an "academic home" within the department organizing meetings and seminars including modules on research methods and specialization areas. Candidates are also encouraged to participate in winter and summer schools and conferences both to deepen their academic profile and also to strengthen their personal networks; the latter is also supported by meetings with and secondments to industrial and public sector partners.

Recruitment of postdoctoral researchers has been limited to four positions directly supported by the center for two or three years, giving opportunities not only for deepening their research profile but also further activities in support of a competitive placement for their future career. These include networking actions such as seminars and conferences, but also individual mentoring to provide a pathway to establish an independent research agenda as well as the opportunity to observe and participate in teaching and grant-writing activities. In one case, this has already been successful in the direct hire of a candidate for a permanent academic position.

NORCICS research results inform the educational offering of the academic partners at all levels, thereby raising the quality of formal education at these institutions. Furthermore, EVU (continuing education) business-oriented courses have been developed and delivered by NORCICS researchers that utilize NORCICS research results. The NORCICS director sits on the Steering Committee of the Nemonoor European Digital Innovation Hub (EDIH) that offers AI and cybersecurity business-oriented courses to Norwegian businesses. A direct result of the cooperation within NORCICS of researchers in the NTNU IIK and IØT departments is the establishment of a new MSc study program, titled Master of Industrial Innovation and Digital Security (MIIDS). The program is developing well, and two cohorts of students have already graduated. The number of applicants for the study program is increasing and, with an increased quality of education and more marketing efforts, the student numbers are expected to increase. The research within NORCICS T3.15 has, among others, resulted in developing a 7.5 ECTS MSc course on Hardware Security in Embedded Systems. The course is being offered for the first time in the fall 2024 semester.

We conclude that the plans have been followed, and the achievement of the accordant objectives is well on track.

6.4.8 Looking Ahead

As always, there is room for improvement. The midterm evaluation panel recommended the following (NORCICS Underway Assessment Panel, 2025):

- The center could benefit from an expansion into additional Critical Sectors (for example, telecommunications, water management, maritime). Consider adding more user partners to enhance the center's capabilities.
- Generalization of research results. Demonstrate universal validity by evaluating the research results within and across various Critical Sectors. In this regard, supply chain security could serve as an effective example.
- So far, the needs of user partners have primarily driven and influenced research tasks. Consider also taking the opposite approach, by initiating your own research tasks and sharing your findings with the companies to their benefit.
- To foster inter-task cooperation, install a regular weekly PhD seminar in which every PhD student must present on a six-month basis. The seminar should be publication-oriented with the goal of finding common research interests among the PhDs leading to joint publications.
- Invest in innovative methods to enhance cybersecurity training and awareness. There is significant potential in cyber ranges, both in collaboration with user partners and for the benefit of students in Master's programs. Explore opportunities for joint activities with the Norwegian national cyber range.
- Reschedule the planned workshop for the continuation of NORCICS after RCN funding to 2026.
- While the center already shows commitment in terms of gender equality policies, as well as Equity, Diversity, and Inclusion (EDI) principles, additional measures could be introduced to further enhance inclusivity and improve gender balance at senior levels.
- Engage with relevant policymakers and politicians (through the head of department, dean, etc.), as well as the Chamber of Commerce and similar business organizations (via user partners), and NTNU alumni to raise awareness about the benefits of joining NORCICS. Their support could help expand into additional Critical Sectors and attract more user partners. Support from partner organizations SINTEF and NTNU CCIS may also be valuable in this effort.

6.5 CONCLUSIONS

This chapter underscored the critical role of cybersecurity in industrial innovation, particularly in safeguarding intellectual property, ensuring operational resilience, and supporting digital transformation. Through the SFI scheme and the case study of the SFI Norwegian Centre for Cybersecurity in Critical Sectors (NORCICS), research-driven solutions are fostering cybersecurity advancements, strengthening global partnerships, and enabling industry collaboration. Cybersecurity is essential for industrial innovation, providing protection against cyber threats while enabling technological advancements.

The SFI scheme fosters research collaboration, driving innovation in Norwegian industries through structured partnerships between academia, industry, and government. Research-driven cybersecurity innovation accelerates business growth, strengthens critical infrastructure, and reinforces Norway's leadership in digital security.

NORCICS plays a pivotal role in cybersecurity research, supporting strategic alliances, enhancing cybersecurity resilience, and training skilled professionals. As NORCICS prepares for its final three-year phase, the focus remains on ensuring sustainable cybersecurity progress by bridging academic research with industry applications, fostering global collaboration, and reinforcing Norway's cybersecurity resilience. Future priorities include expanding industry partnerships, increasing cybersecurity training, improving knowledge transfer, and refining research methodologies.

REFERENCES

Briand, L., Falessi, D., Nejati, S., Sabetzadeh, M., & Yue, T. (2012). Research-based innovation: A tale of three projects in model-driven engineering. In R. B. France, J. Kazmeier, R. Breu, & A. C. (Eds.), *Model driven engineering languages and systems. 15th international conference, MODELS 2012, Innsbruck, Austria, September 30 – October 5, 2012, proceedings* (pp. 793–809). Berlin, Heidelberg: Springer Berlin Heidelberg.

Carayannis, E. G., & Campbell, D. F (2009). 'Mode 3' and 'Quadruple Helix': Toward a 21st century fractal innovation ecosystem. *International Journal of Technology Management*, 46(3–4), 201–234.

Curley, M., & Salmelin, B. (2017). *Open innovation 2.0: The new mode of digital innovation for prosperity and sustainability*. Cham, Switzerland: Springer Nature.

Departementene. (2019, January 30). *Nasjonal strategi for digital sikkerhetskompetanse*. Retrieved from https://www.regjeringen.no/contentassets/8ed748d37e504a46987 4ce936551b4f8/nasjonal-strategi-for-digital-sikkerhetskompetanse.pdf

Gorschek, T., Garre, P., Larsson, S , & Wohlin, C. (2006). A model for technology transfer in practice. *IEEE Software*, 23(6), 88–95.

National Institute of Standards and Technology. (2024, February 26). *The NIST cybersecurity framework (CSF) 2.0*. Retrieved from https://nvlpubs.nist.gov/nistpubs/CSWP/NIST.CSWP.29.pdf

NORCICS Underway Assessment Panel. (2025). *Panel's report: NORCICS SFI Norwegian Centre for Cybersecurity in Critical Sectors.* Retrieved from https://www.ntnu.edu/documents/1294734959/0/SFI+NORCICS_mideval.pdf/ee1bf85e-9972-b99d-5a81-90b663b191e6?t=1744619139801

Norges Forskningråd. (2011, June 14). Innovasjon Forskningsrådets strategi 2011–2014. *Innovasjon.* Retrieved from https://www.forskningsradet.no/siteassets/publikasjoner/1253970499777.pdf

Norwegian Ecosystem for Secure IT-OT Integration (NESIOT). (2025). *SFI Norwegian C Xentre for Cybersecurity in Critical Sectors (NORCICS).* Retrieved from https://www.ntnu.edu/norcics/it-ot-integration-nesiot

Norwegian Ministeries. (2019). *National cyber security strategy for Norway.* Retrieved from https://www.regjeringen.no/contentassets/c57a0733652f47688294934ffd93fc53/national-cyber-security-strategy-for-norway.pdf

Norwegian Ministry of Digitalisation and Public Governance. (2024). The digital Norway of the future: National digitalisation strategy 2024–2030. *Government.no.* Retrieved from https://www.regjeringen.no/contentassets/c499c3b6c93740bd989c43d886f65924/en-gb/pdfs/digitaliseringsstrategi_eng.pdf

Størkersen, K., Langseth, M., Wærnes, A., Måsøy, S.-E., Sletta, H., & Ragnhild, . . . (2023). *Hvordan styrke SFI-enes bidrag til innovasjon? Råd og anbefalinger.* NTNU Open. Retrieved from https://ntnuopen.ntnu.no/ntnu-xmlui/bitstream/handle/11250/3126685/SFI_Rapport_B5_30.08.pdf?sequence=1&isAllowed=y

The Research Council of Norway. (2021, January 1). *General terms and conditions for R&D contracts.* General Terms and Conditions for R&D Contracts. Retrieved from https://www.forskningsradet.no/siteassets/generelle-krav-og-vilkar-for-foi-prosjekter/generelle-vilkar-01012021-eng-ny.pdf

The Research Council of Norway. (2025). *Centre for research-based innovation – SFI V – Phase 2.* Retrieved from https://www.forskningsradet.no/en/call-for-proposals/2025/centre-for-research-based-innovation-sfi-v-phase-2/

Xu, X., Lu, Y., Vogel-Heuser, B., & Wang, L. (2021). Industry 4.0 and Industry 5.0—inception, conception and perception. *Journal of Manufacturing Systems,* 61, 530–535. https://doi.org/10.1016/j.jmsy.2021.10.006.

7. Cybersecurity, privacy, and safety in industrial innovation

Elias G. Carayannis and Nikos R. Zotas

7.1 THE EVOLUTION OF CYBERSECURITY IN INDUSTRIAL INNOVATION

Cybersecurity has evolved significantly alongside industrial development, reflecting the increasing digitalization and interconnectivity of industrial systems. In earlier industrial eras, security primarily focused on physical safeguards, such as securing facilities and protecting machinery from theft or sabotage. However, the advent of digital technologies introduced new vulnerabilities, necessitating a shift toward digital protection measures.

7.1.1 Historical Perspective

The emergence of computer systems in industrial environments during the late 20th century marked the first wave of cyber vulnerabilities. Early industrial networks were largely isolated, with limited exposure to external threats. However, as industries began adopting Supervisory Control and Data Acquisition (SCADA) systems and networked environments to monitor and control processes, vulnerabilities became more apparent (Lipovsky, 2017).

Malicious actors quickly recognized opportunities to exploit weak security measures in these systems. SCADA systems, originally designed with a focus on reliability rather than security, often lacked robust authentication and encryption mechanisms (Constantin, 2014). This made them susceptible to unauthorized access, manipulation, and disruption (Pliatsios et al., 2020).

7.1.2 Digitalization and Cloud Computing

The rise of cloud computing and digitally interconnected systems brought unparalleled efficiency, scalability, and flexibility to industrial operations. Cloud technologies allowed industries to store, process, and analyze vast

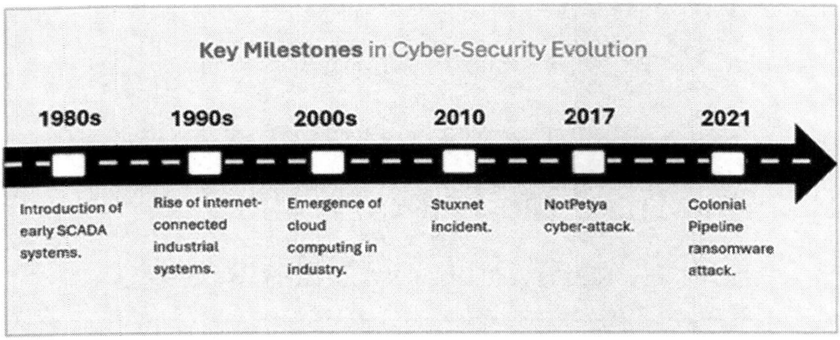

Source: Author's own illustration.

Figure 7.1 Timeline of key milestones in cybersecurity evolution

amounts of data in real time, enabling predictive maintenance, streamlined workflows, and data-driven decision-making (Goud, 2024).

However, these advancements also introduced significant cyber risks (Varnado & Matthew, 2024):

- Data breaches: unauthorized access to sensitive industrial data.
- Ransomware attacks: malicious software encrypting data and demanding ransom payments.
- Industrial espionage: theft of proprietary technologies and intellectual property.

Industries that failed to implement adequate cybersecurity measures became vulnerable to financial losses, reputational damage, and operational disruptions (Dawood et al., 2023).

7.1.3 Critical Infrastructure as a Target

In today's digital age, industrial systems are considered critical infrastructure, encompassing sectors such as energy, transportation, manufacturing, and healthcare. These systems are essential for societal functioning, making them attractive targets for cybercriminals and state-sponsored attacks.

The infamous Stuxnet worm serves as a watershed moment in the history of industrial cybersecurity. Discovered in 2010, Stuxnet targeted Iran's nuclear program, demonstrating how malware could physically damage industrial equipment through cyber means. This attack underscored the devastating potential of cyber threats in industrial settings (Gregersen, 2024).

Modern cyberattacks on critical infrastructure include:

- Colonial Pipeline Ransomware Attack (2021): Disrupted fuel supplies across the eastern United States, causing economic and logistical turmoil (Easterly & Fanning, 2023).
- NotPetya Malware (2017): Targeted industrial systems worldwide, causing billions of dollars in damage (Greenberg, 2018).
- SolarWinds Supply Chain Attack (2020): Compromised software used by industrial and government systems globally (Jena 2024).

7.1.4 The Shift to Proactive Cybersecurity Measures

As industrial systems become increasingly interconnected, traditional reactive security measures are proving inadequate. Organizations are now adopting proactive strategies to safeguard their operations:

- Threat Intelligence Platforms: These systems enable real-time monitoring and detection of potential threats, allowing organizations to anticipate and mitigate cyber risks before they materialize. By analyzing data from various sources, threat intelligence platforms provide actionable insights to strengthen security postures (Alqudhaibi et al., 2023).
- Zero-Trust Architecture: This security model operates on the principle of "never trust, always verify," requiring continuous authentication and monitoring for every access attempt, regardless of its origin. Implementing Zero-Trust Architecture ensures that both internal and external threats are addressed, enhancing overall security (PWC, 2020).
- Security by Design: Integrating security measures during the system development phase ensures that industrial applications are built with robust defenses from the outset. This approach minimizes vulnerabilities and reduces the need for costly retrofits or patches after deployment (Malik, 2024).

7.1.5 Case Examples

1. **Stuxnet:** Stuxnet was a sophisticated cyberattack specifically designed to sabotage Iran's nuclear enrichment facilities. The malware targeted programmable logic controllers (PLCs) used to control industrial centrifuges. By manipulating system behavior while showing normal operational data to operators, Stuxnet caused physical damage to the centrifuges without

immediate detection. This attack highlighted the potential of cyber tools as weapons of cyber warfare, showcasing a new era of digital conflict (Kushner, 2024).

2. **Colonial Pipeline Ransomware Attack:** In 2021, a ransomware attack on the Colonial Pipeline disrupted fuel supplies across the US East Coast. Hackers exploited a compromised password to gain access to the network. The attack resulted in widespread fuel shortages, financial losses, and significant disruption to critical infrastructure. The Colonial Pipeline incident emphasized the vulnerabilities within industrial systems and the cascading effects of cyber breaches (Beerman et al., 2023).
3. **German Steel Mill Attack:** In 2014, a cyberattack targeted a German steel mill, causing significant physical damage to a blast furnace. Hackers gained access through a phishing email, infiltrating the mill's control systems. The attackers manipulated industrial controls, causing equipment failures that led to operational disruptions and physical damage. This incident underscored the direct correlation between cyber vulnerabilities and physical safety risks (MST, 2021).

Table 7.1a Comparison of security measures—pre-digital era (before 1980s), physical security

Key technologies	Common threats	Characteristics
Surveillance Cameras	Theft	Focused on securing physical premises and assets
Physical Locks and Barriers	Sabotage	Minimal reliance on digital technologies
Guard Patrols	Unauthorized Physical Access	Security breaches were primarily physical in nature

Table 7.1b Comparison of security measures—early digital era (1980s–2000s), network security

Key tech	Common threats	Characteristics
Firewalls	Malware	Introduction of basic digital networks
Antivirus Software	Viruses	Use of Supervisory Control and Data Acquisition (SCADA) systems
Intrusion Detection Systems (IDS)	Data Breaches	Vulnerabilities due to lack of encryption and limited authentication protocols
Network Segmentation	Unauthorized Access	Increased dependency on IT infrastructure

Table 7.1c Comparison of security measures—modern industrial digital era (2010s–present), cyber-resilience

Key tech	Common threats	Characteristics
Zero-Trust Architecture	Ransomware	Integration of IoT, AI, and Big Data
Threat Intelligence Platforms	Industrial Espionage	Real-time threat monitoring and advanced analytics
Blockchain for Data Integrity	Intellectual Property Theft	Automated incident response and predictive threat intelligence
End-to-End Encryption	Supply Chain Vulnerabilities	Focus on proactive security and risk mitigation
Cloud Security Solutions	Phishing Attacks	Enhanced compliance with international regulations (e.g., GDPR, NIST)

7.1.6 Cybersecurity as an Enabler of Innovation

Despite these challenges, effective cybersecurity measures are now viewed as enablers of innovation rather than obstacles. Industries that prioritize cyber-resilience can:

- safeguard intellectual property;
- build trust with partners and customers;
- ensure uninterrupted operations.

As industries continue to adopt smart manufacturing, autonomous factories, and Internet of Things (IoT) ecosystems, the role of cybersecurity will only grow in importance. Organizations must remain vigilant, adaptive, and forward-thinking to address evolving cyber threats and harness the full potential of industrial innovation (Deloitte, 2019).

7.2 PRIVACY CHALLENGES IN THE DIGITAL INDUSTRIAL LANDSCAPE

In an era dominated by digital transformation, industries are increasingly reliant on data-driven technologies such as Big Data analytics, Artificial Intelligence (AI), and the Internet of Things (IoT). These tools have redefined operational efficiency, predictive maintenance, and resource optimization. However, this digital revolution comes with significant privacy challenges. The sheer volume and sensitivity of data being generated, collected, and analyzed creates vulnerabilities that industries must address (Tertulino et al., 2024).

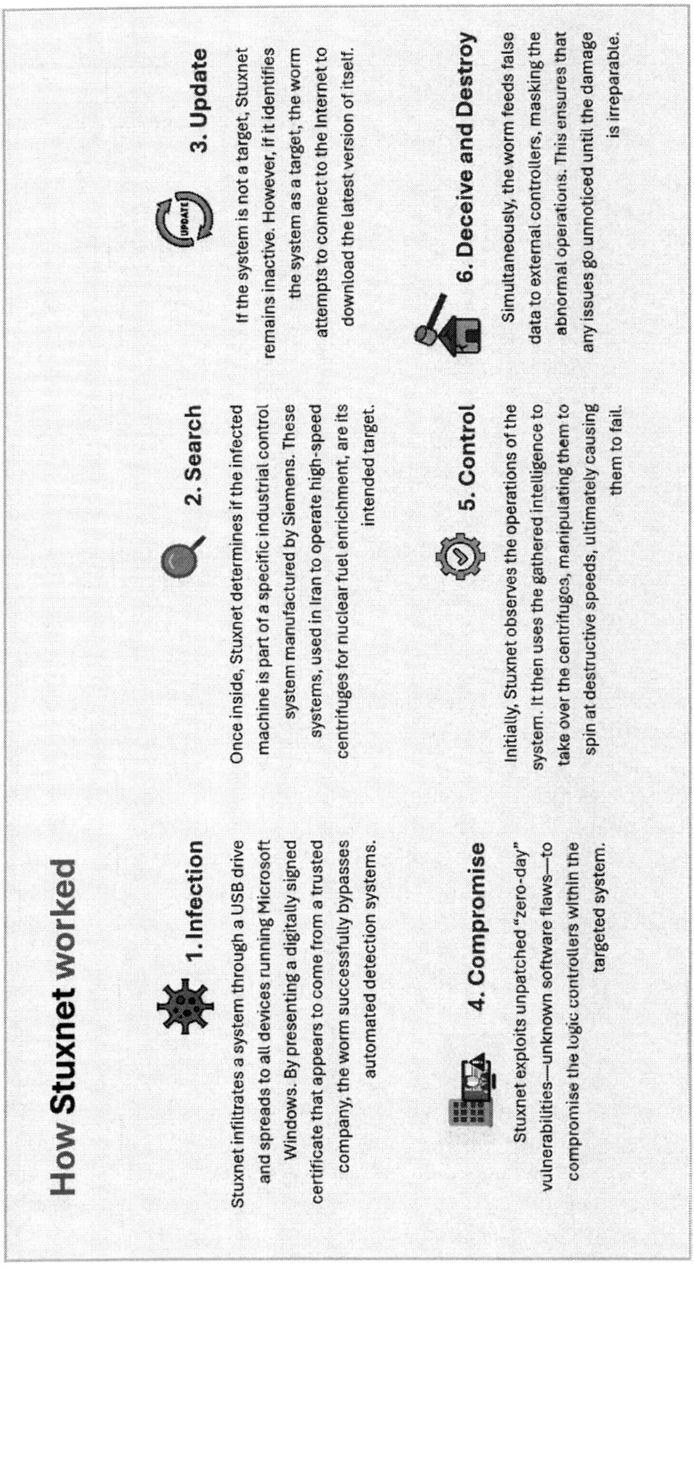

Source: Author's own illustration based on L-Dopa.

Figure 7.2 *How Stuxnet worked*

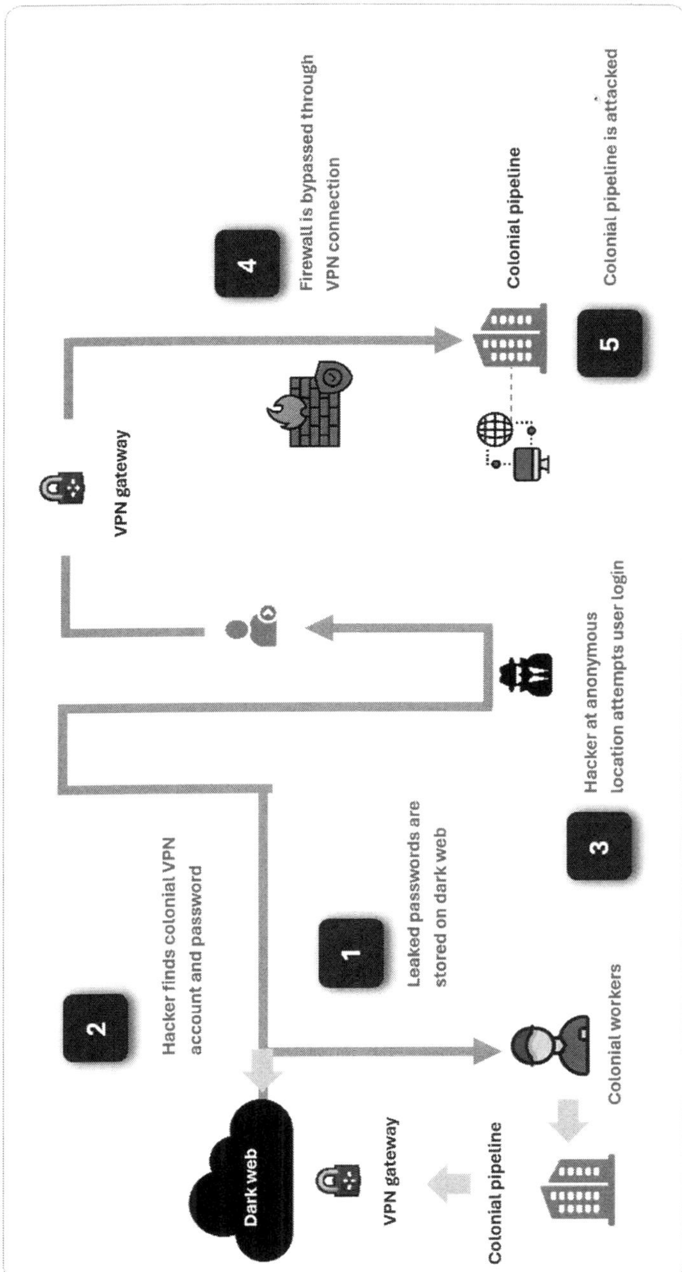

Source: Author's own illustration based on Beerman et al., 2023.

Figure 7.3 Colonial pipeline ransomware attack

Source: Author's own illustration based on Dover Microsystems.

Figure 7.4 Overview of German steel mill attack

From regulatory compliance to ethical dilemmas, privacy concerns are deeply intertwined with industrial innovation. The consequences of poor data governance extend beyond financial penalties, impacting organizational trust, reputation, and long-term sustainability. This chapter explores the multi-faceted challenges of privacy in the digital industrial landscape, analyzing key legal frameworks, ethical considerations, and practical approaches to building resilient data privacy structures (Sharghivand & Derakhshan, 2021).

7.2.1 Data-Driven Industries: The Role of Big Data and IoT

The integration of Big Data analytics and IoT technologies has revolutionized industrial operations, enabling predictive maintenance, streamlined supply chains, and cost efficiencies. Industries can now monitor processes in real-time, reduce equipment downtime, and optimize resource allocation. These advancements, however, are deeply reliant on the collection and processing of vast amounts of personal and operational data.

IoT devices continuously collect data from machinery, logistics systems, and workplace environments. This data ranges from operational efficiency metrics to sensitive employee information. However, the vast volume and variety of data introduce significant risks. Cloud-based storage solutions, while scalable and accessible, are susceptible to cyberattacks, data leaks, and misconfigurations that can compromise confidentiality and integrity (Maayan, 2024).

Another critical concern is the reliance on third-party vendors for data processing and analysis. Outsourcing these functions often involves sharing sensitive data with external partners, raising questions about data ownership, trust, and regulatory compliance (Boeckl et al., 2019).

To address these risks, industries must establish robust data governance frameworks, focusing on secure data collection, ethical usage, and compliance with privacy standards. Data privacy should be a built-in feature of all digital industrial systems rather than an afterthought (Sharma, 2024).

7.2.2 Legal Frameworks and Global Privacy Regulations

In an era of globalized digital infrastructure, legal frameworks play a pivotal role in defining the boundaries of data usage and privacy compliance. Governments and international bodies have introduced stringent regulations to ensure transparency, accountability, and data security (Bansal, 2024).

The General Data Protection Regulation (GDPR), enforced by the European Union, has become the gold standard for data privacy. It mandates transparency in data collection, explicit user consent, and the right to have personal data deleted. Non-compliance with GDPR can result in fines reaching millions of euros.

In the United States, the California Consumer Privacy Act (CCPA) grants individuals the right to know what data is collected about them, how it is used, and the ability to opt out of data sales. Similarly, other regions and industries have their own privacy frameworks, such as HIPAA for healthcare and PCI DSS for financial transactions.

However, compliance with these regulations is not merely about avoiding penalties. Organizations that demonstrate strong adherence to data privacy standards gain a competitive advantage by building trust with stakeholders, clients, and employees. Industries must invest in legal expertise and implement data privacy strategies that align with both global and regional regulations.

7.2.3 The Paradox of Innovation vs. Privacy

Innovation and privacy are often seen as conflicting priorities. While data-driven technologies like AI and machine learning offer unparalleled opportunities for industrial growth, they are heavily dependent on access to vast datasets. Privacy regulations, on the other hand, impose restrictions on how this data can be collected, stored, and utilized (Kuzmenko, 2023). For example, AI-driven predictive maintenance relies on detailed operational datasets, which may include proprietary or sensitive information. Similarly, safety improvements driven by machine learning algorithms require data on employee activities, raising concerns about surveillance and consent.

At the same time, excessive employee monitoring can create a culture of mistrust and reduce workplace morale. Companies must carefully evaluate where to draw the line between necessary oversight and intrusive surveillance. Industries must adopt a principled approach to data usage. Transparency in how data is collected and used, meaningful consent from stakeholders, and responsible AI development practices are essential for balancing innovation with privacy (Thu, 2025).

7.2.4 Case Studies of Privacy Violations

Privacy violations in industrial and digital ecosystems have led to significant financial, ethical, and operational consequences. Below are some key real-world examples that highlight the risks associated with poor data governance and misuse of personal and operational data.

These cases illustrate the far-reaching consequences of privacy violations, including financial penalties, legal battles, and loss of trust. They emphasize the importance of robust privacy frameworks, ongoing compliance efforts, and ethical accountability.

Table 7.2 Global privacy regulations comparison table

-	GDPR[1] (General Data Protection Regulation)	CCPA[2] (California Consumer Privacy Act)	HIPAA[3] (Health Insurance Portability and Accountability Act)	PIPEDA[4] (Personal Information Protection and Electronic Documents Act)	LGPD[5] (Lei Geral de Proteção de Dados)
Region	European Union	California, USA	USA (Nationwide)	Canada	Brazil
Scope	Organizations processing EU residents' personal data, regardless of the company's physical location.	Businesses operating in California meeting revenue or data volume thresholds.	Healthcare providers, insurance companies, and third-party health service providers.	Private-sector organizations handling personal data during commercial activities.	Organizations processing personal data of individuals in Brazil.
Key Provisions	Explicit consent for data collection, the right to be forgotten, mandatory breach notification.	Data transparency, opt-out options, right to deletion.	Protection of health information, restricted sharing without consent, breach notification.	Consent requirements, data accuracy, and security safeguards.	User consent, mandatory data protection officers, breach reporting.
Penalties	Fines up to €20 million or 4% of global annual turnover.	Up to $7,500 per intentional violation.	Fines up to $1.5 million per year per violation.	Fines up to C$100,000 per violation.	Fines up to 2% of annual revenue, capped at 50 million Brazilian reais.
Rights	Access, rectification, erasure, portability, objection.	Right to know, right to delete, right to opt-out of sale.	Right to access, amend, and obtain an account of disclosures.	Access, correction, and the right to challenge compliance.	Access, correction, deletion, portability.

-	GDPR[1] (General Data Protection Regulation)	CCPA[2] (California Consumer Privacy Act)	HIPAA[3] (Health Insurance Portability and Accountability Act)	PIPEDA[4] (Personal Information Protection and Electronic Documents Act)	LGPD[5] (Lei Geral de Proteção de Dados)
Enforcement	European Data Protection Board (EDPB).	California Attorney General.	US Department of Health and Human Services (HHS).	Office of the Privacy Commissioner of Canada (OPC).	National Data Protection Authority (ANPD).
Exemptions	Certain national security and defense data processing.	Certain business-to-business (B2B) transactions and employee data.	Research data under anonymized conditions.	Government data and data collected for journalistic, artistic, or literary purposes.	Public safety, national defense, and journalistic purposes.[6]

Notes: 1. GDPR: Regulation (EU) 2016/679 of the European Parliament and of the Council of 27 April 27, 2016 on the protection of natural persons with regard to the processing of personal data and on the free movement of such data, and repealing Directive 95/46/EC (General Data Protection Regulation). (Source.)
2. CCPA: The California Consumer Privacy Act of 2018 (CCPA) gives consumers more control over the personal information that businesses collect about them, and the CCPA regulations provide guidance on how to implement the law. (Source.)
3. HIPAA: The Health Insurance Portability and Accountability Act of 1996 (HIPAA or the Kennedy–Kassebaum Act) is a United States Act of Congress enacted by the 104th United States Congress and signed into law by President Bill Clinton on August 21, 1996. (Source.)
4. PIPEDA: The Personal Information Protection and Electronic Documents Act (PIPEDA) sets the ground rules for how private-sector organizations collect, use, and disclose personal information in the course of for-profit, commercial activities across Canada. PIPEDA also applies to the personal information of employees of federally-regulated businesses. (Source.)
5. LGPD: Brazilian General Data Protection Law (Source)
6. The details provided in this table are accurate at the time of writing. Privacy regulations, legal interpretations, and case outcomes are subject to change. Readers are advised to refer to the latest official sources and regulatory updates for the most current information.

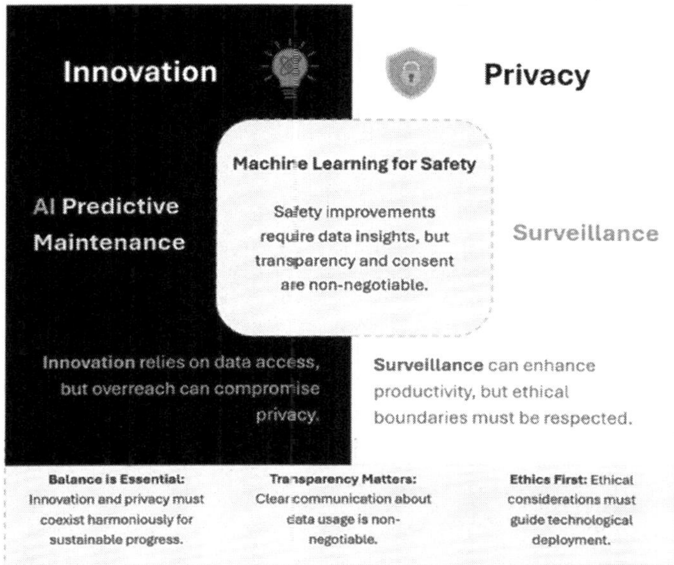

Source: Author's own illustration.

Figure 7.5 The privacy paradox: balancing innovation and privacy

7.2.5 Ethical Challenges in Balancing Privacy and Innovation

Privacy extends beyond being a legal requirement; it is a fundamental ethical obligation that industries must uphold to protect individuals, employees, and society. As industries increasingly rely on data-driven innovation, the challenge lies in balancing technological progress with the safeguarding of fundamental rights. This requires a critical evaluation of how data practices affect individuals and communities. Organizations must ensure fairness in algorithms, prevent discrimination, and foster inclusive outcomes. Predictive AI tools, for example, can inadvertently perpetuate biases if they are trained on incomplete or skewed datasets, leading to harmful outcomes that erode trust in technology and the organizations deploying it (Patel, 2024).

Transparency is a cornerstone of ethical data management. Employees, stakeholders, and consumers must clearly understand how their data is collected, stored, processed, and used. This requires accessible communication that avoids overly technical jargon or complex legal language. In large industrial ecosystems, consent must move beyond mere checkbox agreements

Table 7.3 Well-known case studies of privacy violations

Case Study	Description	Key Violation	Outcome
TikTok's Alleged Violations of Children's Privacy (Ng & Sisco, 2024)	Lawsuit for violating COPPA by collecting personal data from users under 13 without parental consent.	Children's privacy violation	Lawsuit filed by US Department of Justice
LinkedIn's GDPR Breach (The Associated Press, 2024)	Fined €310 million for processing personal data for targeted advertising without a lawful basis.	GDPR breach	€310 million fine imposed
Fortescue's Surveillance Scandal (Hyland, 2024)	Hired private investigators to surveil former employees and their families, raising ethical concerns.	Unethical surveillance	Public backlash and reputational damage
Facebook's Beacon Program (TechRepublic Staff, 2020)	Tracked users' activities on third-party websites without explicit consent, leading to a lawsuit.	Unauthorized data collection	Class-action lawsuit and program shutdown
Google's Safari Tracking Incident (Arthur, 2012)	Bypassed privacy settings in Safari browser to place tracking cookies without user consent.	Bypassing user privacy settings	$22.5 million FTC fine

to become a meaningful and informed process, empowering individuals to make deliberate choices about their data. Organizations must also adopt robust accountability mechanisms to address any misuse or mishandling of data swiftly and transparently. Proactive governance structures, such as internal ethics committees, can provide effective oversight. These committees, composed of diverse stakeholders including data scientists, legal experts, ethicists, and community representatives, should monitor data practices, review datasets for bias, and evaluate ethical risks associated with new technologies (Bibi, 2024).

Ethical data management must be integrated into the innovation process itself. Privacy-by-design and ethics-by-design frameworks ensure that fairness, transparency, and accountability are embedded from the earliest stages of product development. By doing so, organizations can align technological progress with the protection of human rights. This approach not only mitigates ethical risks but also fosters trust, enhancing the organization's reputation and strengthening relationships with employees, customers, and communities. Ethical stewardship of data is not just a moral imperative; it is a strategic advantage that enables sustainable growth in an increasingly data-driven world. By committing to these principles, industries can harness the potential of innovation while respecting the rights and dignity of all stakeholders (AI Guardian, 2024).

7.2.6 Building a Resilient Data Privacy Framework

A resilient data privacy framework is more than a technical construct—it is a strategic cornerstone that fosters long-term growth, ensures regulatory compliance, and builds trust with stakeholders. In today's data-driven world, a robust framework is essential for protecting sensitive information while enabling organizations to innovate responsibly. Building such a framework requires a comprehensive approach that integrates technical safeguards, organizational policies, and cultural change.

At the heart of a resilient data privacy framework is the principle of data minimization. Organizations should collect only the data necessary for specific, clearly defined operational purposes. Excessive data collection not only increases the risk of breaches but also creates unnecessary complexity in compliance efforts. By limiting data collection to what is truly essential, businesses can reduce vulnerabilities and maintain a more streamlined, efficient data handling process (Khan, 2021).

Encryption protocols are a critical layer of defense, safeguarding data both at rest and in transit. Advanced encryption technologies, combined with regularly updated security keys, ensure that data remains protected even if it is intercepted or accessed without authorization. Encryption should be applied to all sensitive information, including personal identifiers, financial records, and operational data, making it inaccessible to unauthorized users (Sargiotis, 2024).

Access controls play an equally vital role in maintaining data security. Implementing strict, role-based access policies ensures that individuals within the organization can only access the information necessary for their job functions. Multi-factor authentication (MFA) and activity logging further enhance security by verifying user identities and monitoring for suspicious behavior. Regularly reviewing and updating access permissions can prevent privilege creep and reduce insider threats (Hall, 2024).

To maintain the integrity of the framework, continuous audits are essential. Regular assessments of data handling practices, security measures, and compliance protocols help identify vulnerabilities and address them before they become critical issues. These audits should be proactive, utilizing tools such as penetration testing, vulnerability scanning, and third-party reviews to provide a comprehensive evaluation of the organization's privacy defenses (Badman, 2024).

Beyond technical measures, employee education is a foundational element of a resilient privacy framework. Fostering a culture of data privacy awareness ensures that every employee understands the importance of protecting sensitive information and their role in upholding organizational policies. Training programs, regular updates on emerging threats, and clear communication of best practices can help embed privacy consciousness into the organizational ethos (Emtrain, 2024).

Finally, cross-functional collaboration is crucial to the success of a data privacy framework. Privacy challenges are multi-faceted, requiring coordinated efforts from IT, legal, compliance, and operational teams. By fostering collaboration across these disciplines, organizations can create integrated solutions that address technical, legal, and strategic aspects of data privacy. This alignment ensures that privacy initiatives are not siloed but are instead a shared responsibility throughout the organization.

Building a resilient data privacy framework is a dynamic process that requires ongoing investment, adaptation, and commitment. As data volumes grow and threats evolve, organizations must remain proactive in enhancing

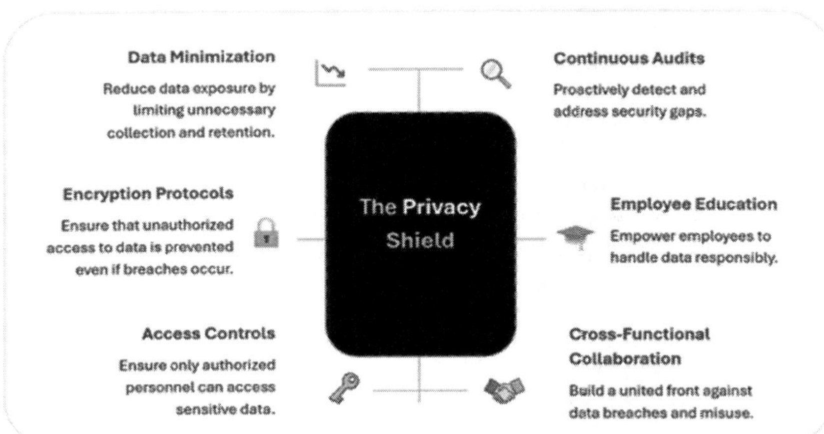

Source: Author's own illustration.

Figure 7.6 *The privacy shield: a visual representation of data privacy resilience*

their privacy practices. By prioritizing these key components, businesses can protect sensitive information, maintain trust, and position themselves for sustainable success in an increasingly interconnected world (Ieremchuk & Iaskova, 2024).

7.3 SAFETY IMPLICATIONS OF CYBERSECURITY IN INDUSTRIAL SYSTEMS

The integration of digital technologies has transformed traditional manufacturing and operational processes. Smart grids, autonomous factories, and industrial IoT (IIoT) systems have become cornerstones of industrial innovation. While these advancements offer unparalleled efficiency, productivity, and scalability, they also expose industrial systems to significant cybersecurity risks (Nankya et al., 2023). Cyberattacks targeting critical infrastructure are no longer isolated incidents; they have evolved into sophisticated threats capable of causing operational disruptions, financial loss, and even endangering human lives. The Colonial Pipeline ransomware attack serves as a stark example of how a single breach can create cascading consequences across multiple sectors. In this section, we will explore the evolving concept of safety in industrial systems, the role of cybersecurity in safeguarding industrial networks, the growing necessity for robust cyber defenses, and key lessons learned from real-world incidents (Bouhdada & Ayala, 2024).

7.3.1 Defining Safety in Industrial Innovation: From Physical Safety to Digital Safety

Traditionally, safety in industrial systems focused on physical security: preventing machinery malfunctions, reducing workplace hazards, and mitigating environmental damage. However, the digital transformation brought by Industry 4.0 has introduced a new dimension of safety—digital safety. This includes protecting the integrity, availability, and confidentiality of data and systems (Shilenge & Telukdarie, 2022).

The convergence of operational technology (OT) and information technology (IT) has created deeply interconnected systems where digital vulnerabilities can have physical consequences. For example, a cyberattack on an industrial control system (ICS) could disrupt critical processes, trigger equipment malfunctions, or even lead to hazardous conditions for workers (Guess, 2022).

Moreover, modern industrial environments rely on advanced technologies like AI-powered analytics, IoT devices, and cloud-based platforms. Each of these technologies brings increased efficiency but also expands the potential attack surface for cybercriminals. Weak authentication, unpatched vulnerabilities, and misconfigured systems create openings for malicious actors to exploit.

Ensuring safety in industrial innovation now requires a holistic approach, addressing both physical and digital aspects of security. This includes safeguarding intellectual property, employee data privacy, and maintaining system resilience in the face of increasing cyber threats (Sangkhro & Agrawal, 2023).

7.3.2 Role of Cybersecurity in Ensuring the Safety of Connected Industrial Systems

Modern industrial systems depend heavily on interconnected devices, sensors, and automated control systems. These systems generate, exchange, and analyze vast amounts of real-time data, enabling smarter decision-making and enhanced operational efficiency. However, these benefits come with significant vulnerabilities (Pochmara & Świetlicka, 2024). For example, autonomous factories depend on sensors, control systems, and robotics for seamless production. A cyberattack targeting these systems could manipulate machinery, causing equipment failures, production delays, or even physical harm to workers. Similarly, smart grids rely on digital systems for load balancing, power distribution, and outage management. A breach in these systems could lead to widespread power failures, disrupting businesses and daily life.

Cybersecurity in industrial systems involves implementing robust security measures such as network segmentation, multi-factor authentication, and end-to-end encryption. Industrial operators must also adopt proactive threat detection tools, such as AI-powered security monitoring systems, to identify and neutralize threats before they can cause damage. Moreover, collaboration is essential between IT professionals, engineers, and safety managers to ensure comprehensive protection across all layers of the industrial system. Cybersecurity is no longer an isolated IT function but an integral part of operational safety, requiring cross-functional coordination (Amos, 2024).

7.3.3 The Growing Need for Cybersecurity to Ensure Operational Safety

As industrial systems become increasingly intertwined with digital technologies, the potential consequences of cyberattacks grow more severe, transcending data breaches to directly impact physical operations, safety, and organizational stability. Cyber threats in industrial systems are no longer isolated to IT departments but have expanded into core operational environments, making cybersecurity a fundamental pillar of operational safety (Dal Molin, 2024).

Table 7.4 The pivotal role of cybersecurity in protecting connected industrial environments

Role of Cybersecurity	Description
Preventing Unauthorized Access	Ensuring robust access control mechanisms to protect industrial control systems from unauthorized entry.
Data Integrity and Confidentiality	Safeguarding industrial data from manipulation, tampering, or theft.
Real-Time Threat Monitoring	Utilizing AI-driven security solutions to monitor networks continuously for anomalies and threats.
System Resilience	Ensuring systems can recover quickly after a cyberattack or failure.
Zero-Trust Security Models	Ensuring systems can recover quickly after a cyberattack or failure.

The key cyber threats to industrial systems include:

1. **Ransomware Attacks:** These attacks involve malicious software encrypting critical systems or data, effectively halting operations until a ransom is paid. For example, a ransomware attack on a manufacturing plant could disrupt production lines, delay deliveries, and result in substantial financial losses and reputational damage.
2. **Industrial Sabotage:** Attackers may manipulate control systems to cause deliberate physical harm. For instance, changing temperature controls in chemical plants or overloading systems in power grids can lead to catastrophic failures, endangering workers and surrounding communities.
3. **Espionage:** Cyber espionage targets proprietary designs, trade secrets, and sensitive operational data. Competitors or malicious state actors might exploit stolen information to gain a competitive advantage or cause strategic harm.
4. **Supply Chain Attacks:** Many industrial systems rely on third-party vendors for software, hardware, and maintenance services. Attackers exploit vulnerabilities in these supply chains to gain access to the primary systems, sometimes remaining undetected for extended periods.

These threats are no longer hypothetical—they represent real, documented risks with far-reaching consequences. For example, a ransomware attack on an oil refinery's digital control system could disrupt fuel supplies to an entire region, impacting transportation, logistics, and public services.

Table 7.5 Real-world consequences of cybersecurity failures

Consequences	Description
Operational Disruption	Cyberattacks can halt manufacturing processes, delay shipments, and cause inventory shortages, directly affecting revenue and operational timelines.
Physical Safety Risks	Manipulating industrial control systems can lead to physical hazards, including explosions, chemical leaks, and fires, endangering lives and the environment.
Financial Damage	The cost of operational downtime, coupled with ransom payments and legal liabilities, can cripple organizations financially.
Reputational Damage	Trust in an organization's ability to safeguard critical systems is vital. A publicized cyberattack can erode trust and lead to long-term reputational harm.

These consequences highlight the need for cybersecurity measures to be treated with the same urgency as traditional safety protocols in industrial environments.

7.3.3.1 Proactive measures to enhance cybersecurity in industrial systems

To address these growing threats, organizations must transition from reactive to proactive cybersecurity strategies. This requires a multi-faceted approach that integrates people, technology, and processes (Alqudhaibi et al., 2025).

1. **Regular Vulnerability Assessments:** Routine security audits and vulnerability scans help identify weaknesses in industrial systems, enabling organizations to address security gaps before they are exploited.
2. **Employee Cybersecurity Training:** Human error remains one of the leading causes of cybersecurity breaches. Comprehensive training programs can raise awareness about phishing, social engineering, and secure password practices, reducing the risk of inadvertent security lapses.
3. **Incident Response Plans:** Preparing for worst-case scenarios is critical. Detailed incident response plans ensure that organizations can act swiftly and efficiently in the event of a cyberattack, minimizing downtime and mitigating damage.
4. **Network Segmentation:** Isolating critical systems from less secure networks reduces the risk of lateral movement by attackers, containing breaches and limiting damage.

5. **Adoption of International Cybersecurity Standards:** Frameworks such as the National Institute of Standards and Technology (NIST) Cybersecurity Framework and IEC 62443 provide internationally recognized best practices for securing industrial control systems. These standards offer guidelines on risk assessment, incident management, and continuous monitoring to safeguard digital assets effectively.
6. **Advanced Threat Detection Systems:** Leveraging AI-driven monitoring tools and real-time analytics can help identify unusual patterns or anomalies in industrial networks, allowing quick intervention before threats escalate.
7. **Collaboration Across Stakeholders:** Governments, regulatory bodies, private companies, and cybersecurity experts must collaborate to share intelligence, develop threat response protocols, and establish industry-wide security standards.

7.3.4 Case Study: Colonial Pipeline Ransomware Attack

The Colonial Pipeline ransomware attack in 2021 remains one of the most impactful examples of the consequences of cyberattacks on industrial systems. As a major supplier of fuel to the eastern United States, Colonial Pipeline played a critical role in maintaining energy security and economic stability. However, a ransomware attack brought the entire operation to a halt.

The attackers, identified as the DarkSide group, infiltrated Colonial Pipeline's IT systems, encrypting crucial files and demanding a ransom for their release. Although the breach primarily targeted digital infrastructure, the

Source: Author's own illustration.

Figure 7.7 The role of leadership in cybersecurity initiatives

Table 7.6 Key takeaways from the case study of colonial pipeline ransomware attack

Key Takeaways	Description
Point of Entry	Attackers exploited a compromised VPN password to gain access to Colonial Pipeline's systems.
Operational Shutdown	The company preemptively shut down operations to contain the threat, leading to fuel shortages across several states.
Economic Impact	The incident caused financial losses, increased fuel prices, and widespread panic buying.
Regulatory Fallout	The breach triggered heightened cybersecurity regulations for critical infrastructure operators.

consequences extended into the physical world. Fuel shortages caused panic buying, logistical disruptions, and price hikes, demonstrating how digital vulnerabilities can have tangible real-world effects.

The Colonial Pipeline attack underscores the importance of having a robust cybersecurity infrastructure in place. Measures such as secure authentication systems, regular software updates, employee training, and incident response plans are essential to preventing similar incidents.

Furthermore, this case highlights the need for stronger public–private partnerships to address cyber threats. Governments and private sector stakeholders must collaborate to share threat intelligence, develop industry-wide security standards, and implement policies that mandate strong cybersecurity practices.

The convergence of physical and digital safety in industrial systems demands a new paradigm in safety management. Cybersecurity is no longer optional but a fundamental pillar of industrial safety. Organizations must adopt a holistic approach that integrates technology, processes, and people to build secure and resilient systems. Only through collaboration, innovation, and proactive risk management can industries navigate the complex cybersecurity landscape and ensure both operational continuity and safety in the digital age.

7.4 KEY CYBERSECURITY THREATS TO INDUSTRIAL INNOVATION

Digital technologies such as the IoT, AI, cloud computing, and automation drive unprecedented innovation. However, these advancements also expose industrial systems to a wide range of cybersecurity threats. Cyberattacks have the potential to disrupt operations, compromise sensitive data, and cause significant financial and reputational damage. This section explores the key cybersecurity threats facing industrial innovation, provides real-world examples, and highlights industry-specific vulnerabilities. (Torkington, 2024)

7.4.1 Overview of Key Cybersecurity Threats

As industrial systems become increasingly digital and interconnected, they face growing risks from cyber threats. These threats, including ransomware, industrial espionage, intellectual property theft, supply chain vulnerabilities, and IoT security gaps, pose significant challenges to operational stability and innovation. Cyberattacks can disrupt production, steal sensitive data, and cause cascading effects across supply chains, leading to financial losses and reputational damage. Addressing these vulnerabilities is crucial to ensuring resilience, protecting intellectual assets, and sustaining innovation in modern industrial environments (Gordon, 2024).

1. **Ransomware:** Ransomware remains one of the most pervasive and damaging threats to industrial systems. Attackers use malicious software to encrypt critical files and demand ransom payments in exchange for decryption keys. Industrial environments, particularly those reliant on automated production lines and connected machinery, are prime targets because any disruption can result in significant financial losses. Ransomware attacks not only disrupt production but also create cascading effects across supply chains, impacting stakeholders and customers (Sobers, 2024).
2. **Industrial Espionage:** Industrial espionage involves cybercriminals or state-sponsored actors infiltrating industrial systems to steal trade secrets, proprietary designs, or research and development data. In innovation-driven industries, the theft of sensitive intellectual property can undermine years of investment and research. Industrial espionage not only damages competitiveness but can also erode investor and customer confidence (Zhurer, 2024).
3. **Intellectual Property Theft:** Closely related to industrial espionage, intellectual property (IP) theft focuses on stealing patents, designs, formulas, or copyrighted technology. IP theft can result in counterfeit products flooding the market, diluting brand value, and reducing an organization's competitive edge. IP theft stifles innovation by diminishing the incentive for companies to invest in research and development (R&D) and undermines the economic potential of breakthrough technologies (Brook, 2024).
4. **Supply Chain Vulnerabilities:** Modern industrial systems rely heavily on third-party vendors, software suppliers, and hardware manufacturers. These dependencies create vulnerabilities, as attackers can exploit

weaknesses in the supply chain to gain access to primary systems. Supply chain attacks are particularly dangerous because they can remain undetected for extended periods, giving attackers ample time to cause significant damage (Sharma et al., 2021).

5. **IoT Vulnerabilities in Industrial Ecosystems:** The adoption of Industrial IoT (IIoT) devices has revolutionized industrial systems by enabling real-time monitoring, automation, and predictive maintenance. However, IoT devices often lack robust security measures, making them vulnerable to unauthorized access and exploitation. IoT vulnerabilities can serve as entry points for larger attacks, allowing cybercriminals to move laterally across networks and access critical systems (Mourtzis et al., 2019).

7.4.2 Disruption of Innovation Processes by Cyber Threats

Cyberattacks do not merely disrupt day-to-day operations; they pose a significant threat to innovation processes across industrial sectors. The following are key ways cybersecurity threats hinder industrial innovation:

Example: In 2017, Merck & Co., a global pharmaceutical company, experienced a significant ransomware attack that disrupted its worldwide operations. The attack, attributed to the NotPetya ransomware, led to halted production, affecting the company's ability to fulfill orders for certain products in various

Table 7.7 Key ways that cybersecurity threats hinder industrial innovation

Key Ways	Description
Operational Downtime	Ransomware attacks or system compromises can halt entire production lines, delaying product launches and stalling innovation cycles.
Loss of Intellectual Property	Stolen patents, designs, or formulas can nullify years of research and development, reducing the incentive to innovate.
Financial Drain	Resources diverted to recover from cyberattacks or pay ransom demands reduce budgets allocated for research, development, and innovation.
Trust Erosion	Breaches can damage the trust of customers, partners, and stakeholders, creating long-term barriers to collaboration and investment in innovative projects.
Regulatory Hurdles	In the aftermath of a cyberattack, companies may face increased scrutiny and regulatory requirements, slowing down innovation timelines.

markets. Merck reported that the incident caused substantial financial losses, with estimates of over $300 million in the third quarter of 2017 alone (Vijayan, 2017).

7.4.2.1 Industry-specific cybersecurity threats

Different industries face unique cybersecurity challenges based on their operational structures, reliance on digital technologies, and data sensitivity. Below are key industry-specific threats:

To mitigate these threats, industrial organizations must:

Cybersecurity is no longer just about defense—it's about enabling secure and resilient innovation. As industries continue to digitize, building robust cyber defenses will be critical to fostering a culture of innovation and safeguarding technological advancements from malicious threats (Safitra et al., 2023).

7.5 THE ROLE OF CYBERSECURITY IN ENABLING INDUSTRIAL INNOVATION

Industrial innovation is the engine driving progress in today's interconnected and rapidly transforming world. Digital advancements such as the IIoT, cloud-based platforms, AI, and automation have redefined how industries operate, collaborate, and compete. However, these innovations come with new challenges, particularly in safeguarding critical assets, proprietary technologies, and operational continuity. Cybersecurity has emerged as not just a protective measure but a vital enabler of industrial innovation. By fostering trust, securing IP, supporting digital transformation, and facilitating technology adoption, cybersecurity ensures industries can innovate confidently and sustainably (Moeti, 2024).

7.5.1 Building Trust in Industrial Ecosystems

Trust is the foundation of any successful industrial ecosystem. As organizations embrace connected networks, share sensitive data, and collaborate globally, the assurance of security becomes critical. Cybersecurity enables trust by ensuring data confidentiality, integrity, and availability while protecting operational environments from disruption.

Industrial ecosystems rely on extensive partnerships—spanning suppliers, manufacturers, customers, and regulators. Cybersecurity reinforces these relationships by safeguarding shared platforms and communication channels. Organizations can share sensitive information and leverage collaborative technologies without fear of exposure or manipulation (Parthasarathy, 2024).

Table 7.8 Key industry-specific threats came from cybersecurity challenges

Industry	Primary Threats	Impact	Example
Manufacturing	Ransomware, IoT vulnerabilities, industrial sabotage.	Downtime in production lines, compromised product quality, and significant financial losses.	A ransomware attack on a major automobile manufacturing plant halted operations for weeks, causing substantial delays in vehicle deliveries.
Energy Sector	Industrial sabotage, ransomware, espionage.	Power outages, disruption of essential services, and economic instability.	The 2015 cyberattack on Ukraine's power grid resulted in prolonged blackouts affecting thousands of residents.
Healthcare	Ransomware, intellectual property theft, IoT vulnerabilities.	Delayed patient care, compromised medical device security, and theft of sensitive patient data.	Cyberattacks on connected medical devices have led to vulnerabilities where attackers could manipulate life-saving equipment.
Chemical and Petrochemical Industries	Industrial sabotage, supply chain attacks, ransomware.	Chemical spills, explosions, environmental damage, and worker safety risks.	Hackers targeting temperature control systems in chemical plants risk creating hazardous conditions.
Logistics and Supply Chain	Supply chain attacks, ransomware, IoT vulnerabilities.	Delayed shipments, loss of inventory, and customer dissatisfaction.	Cyberattacks on logistics platforms have disrupted global supply chains, causing delays and increased costs.

The presence of a secure ecosystem encourages the adoption of innovative solutions, fostering greater collaboration and paving the way for shared advancements across industries.

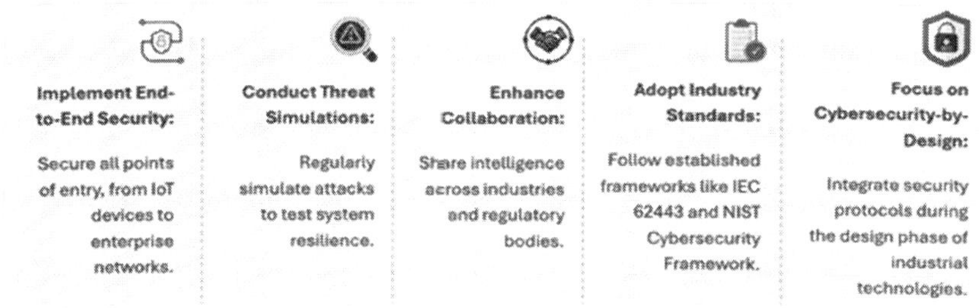

Source: Author's own illustration.

Figure 7.8 Addressing cybersecurity threats in industrial innovation

Table 7.9 Key contributions of cybersecurity to trust

Key Contributions	Description
Data Integrity	Guarantees that shared data remains accurate and tamper-proof, enabling informed decision-making.
Operational Reliability	Prevents interruptions in industrial processes, ensuring continuity and stable partnerships.
Transparency	Strengthens trust among stakeholders by demonstrating commitment to robust security measures.

7.5.2 Safeguarding Intellectual Property and Proprietary Technologies

Intellectual property (IP) is the lifeblood of innovation. It includes patents, research, designs, and technologies that give organizations their competitive edge. The growing sophistication of cyber threats has made IP theft one of the most pressing concerns for industries, especially those heavily invested in R&D (Decybr, 2023).

Cybersecurity plays a critical role in protecting IP against espionage, theft, and unauthorized access. Measures such as encryption, access control, and secure data-sharing protocols create a protective shield around proprietary information, ensuring it remains confidential and unaltered.

By safeguarding IP, cybersecurity ensures that investments in innovation yield returns, bolstering an organization's ability to remain competitive in a global market (CCCS, 2024).

Table 7.10 *Key elements of cybersecurity in IP protection*

Key Elements	Description
Controlled Access	Limits who can view or manipulate sensitive information, ensuring only authorized personnel have access.
End-to-End Encryption	Protects data during storage and transmission, preventing unauthorized interception.
Proactive Monitoring	Identifies and neutralizes potential breaches before they escalate into significant risks.

Table 7.11 *Core cybersecurity contributions to digital transformation*

Core Contributions	Description
Cloud Security	Protects sensitive data and workloads in cloud environments through multi-layered defenses and compliance with global standards.
IIoT Protection	Secures connected devices that monitor, control, and automate industrial processes, preventing unauthorized access and sabotage.
Zero-Trust Architecture	Enforces strict access controls, requiring continuous verification of users and devices to prevent breaches.

7.5.3 Enabling Digital Transformation in Industrial Systems

Digital transformation has become synonymous with industrial progress, allowing organizations to harness the power of real-time data, advanced analytics, and interconnected systems. Cloud-based manufacturing, digital twins, and IIoT devices have revolutionized industries, offering unprecedented efficiency and scalability. However, these advancements have also expanded the attack surface, introducing vulnerabilities that can jeopardize operations (Raimundo & Rosário, 2022).

Cybersecurity serves as the backbone of digital transformation, mitigating risks while enabling seamless integration of new technologies. It ensures that critical systems remain operational and protected from malicious actors.

By embedding security into digital transformation initiatives, organizations can confidently adopt technologies that optimize operations, reduce costs, and unlock new opportunities.

7.5.4 Driving Innovation Adoption through Cybersecurity

The adoption of disruptive technologies often requires organizations to venture into uncharted territories. Cybersecurity provides the confidence necessary for leadership to pursue bold innovations without fear of catastrophic risks. By mitigating the threats associated with technological adoption, cybersecurity fosters an environment conducive to exploration and experimentation (Möller, 2023).

Industries with strong cybersecurity frameworks are better positioned to lead in their respective fields, setting the stage for sustained technological progress.

7.5.5 Integrating Cybersecurity into Innovation Frameworks

For cybersecurity to truly enable industrial innovation, it must be seamlessly integrated into the organization's broader innovation strategy. This integration requires alignment between leadership, operations, IT, and R&D teams to create a unified approach to managing risks (Kapletia et al., 2014).

Integrating cybersecurity into every phase of the innovation lifecycle not only reduces risks but also enhances the efficiency and effectiveness of technological deployment.

7.5.5.1 The long-term value of cybersecurity investments

Investing in cybersecurity is no longer a discretionary expense; it is a strategic imperative that drives resilience, fosters growth, and ensures sustainability in a dynamic and increasingly competitive industrial landscape. Robust cybersecurity frameworks do more than protect against immediate threats—they create

Source: Author's own illustration.

Figure 7.9 *How cybersecurity enables innovation adoption*

Source: Author's own illustration.

Figure 7.10 Strategies for effective cybersecurity integration

a foundation for sustained innovation, operational continuity, and market leadership. A detailed analysis of the key benefits highlights how cybersecurity investments translate into tangible value for organizations (Parker, 2024).

Cybersecurity investments extend far beyond risk mitigation—they underpin business continuity, foster market confidence, and create the conditions necessary for sustained innovation. By prioritizing cybersecurity, organizations gain resilience against immediate threats while positioning themselves for long-term success in an ever-changing industrial landscape (Ferraioli, 2022). As industries become more interconnected and technology-dependent, cybersecurity will remain a cornerstone of sustainable growth, enabling organizations to thrive in the face of uncertainty and complexity (Forbes, 2024).

7.6 STRATEGIES FOR INTEGRATING CYBERSECURITY IN INDUSTRIAL INNOVATION

The integration of cybersecurity into industrial innovation is no longer optional; it is an essential aspect of creating resilient, efficient, and sustainable systems. As industrial ecosystems grow increasingly connected and reliant on advanced technologies like IoT, AI, and big data, the need for robust cybersecurity measures intensifies. This chapter outlines strategies for embedding security into industrial processes, explores best practices, and highlights the role of global standards and cooperation.

Table 7.12 The long-term values of cybersecurity investments

Key Area	Impact	Examples
Business Continuity	Ensures uninterrupted operations, minimizing downtime and mitigating risks.	• Industrial control systems remain operational during ransomware attacks. • Supply chains unaffected by breaches.
Operational Resilience	Strengthens ability to recover quickly from cyber incidents, ensuring consistent workflows.	• Robust incident response plans. • Quick recovery from Distributed Denial of Service (DDoS) attacks on manufacturing systems.
Innovation Stability	Protects R&D processes from disruptions, enabling steady development of new products.	• Secure collaboration platforms for global research teams. • Stable production cycles.
Market Advantage	Builds trust with stakeholders, enhancing reputation and customer loyalty.	• Trusted brand image attracts new customers. • Preferred partner for secure supply chains.
Customer Trust	Reassures customers their data is secure, fostering long-term loyalty.	• Strong data encryption policies. • Transparent handling of cybersecurity protocols.
Partnership Opportunities	Attracts collaborators and suppliers who prioritize secure operations.	• Joint ventures with high-security standards. • Participation in secure industrial ecosystems.
Brand Equity	Enhances market positioning by demonstrating robust cybersecurity capabilities.	• Recognition for regulatory compliance. • Favorable press coverage for security investments.
Future Preparedness	Equips organizations to handle evolving threats and meet new regulations with agility.	• Threat intelligence systems detect advanced cyber threats. • Compliance with GDPR, NIST, and other standards.
Regulatory Compliance	Avoids penalties and ensures smooth operations across global markets.	• Adherence to ISO/IEC 27001. • Meeting industry-specific cybersecurity frameworks like IEC 62443.

Key Area	Impact	Examples
Long-Term Resilience	Builds a proactive approach to address uncertainties, from geopolitical risks to technology shifts.	• Preparedness for AI-driven cyberattacks. • Ability to pivot quickly during supply chain disruptions.
Innovation Enablement	Creates a secure foundation for adopting new technologies and fostering creativity.	• Secure cloud environments for data analytics. • Safe integration of IIoT devices in smart factories.
Resource Optimization	Reduces costs associated with breaches, freeing up budgets for innovation.	• Fewer payouts for ransomware demands. • Reduced downtime costs from cyber incidents.
Technology Adoption	Accelerates the implementation of advanced solutions, driving competitive edge.	• Deployment of digital twins. • Adoption of predictive maintenance systems using IIoT.
Risk-Tolerant Culture	Encourages experimentation by mitigating fears of catastrophic failures.	• Pilot projects for AI integration. • Exploration of blockchain for secure traceability.
Integrated Ecosystems	Enhances security across interconnected systems, enabling seamless collaboration.	• Unified cybersecurity standards across partners. • Secure data sharing in aerospace or defense sectors.
Sustainability	Supports responsible innovation while reducing risks to critical infrastructure.	• Protection of renewable energy grids. • Secured water treatment facilities

7.6.1 Security-by-Design Approach in Industrial Processes and Systems

Where cyber threats pose significant risks, the security-by-design methodology has become a cornerstone of effective cybersecurity strategies. This proactive approach embeds security measures into industrial systems from the very beginning of the design and development process, rather than addressing vulnerabilities reactively after deployment. By integrating security at the inception stage, industries can build robust and resilient systems capable of withstanding evolving cyber threats.

At its core, the security-by-design methodology is governed by several key principles. One of the most critical is the incorporation of encryption protocols for both communication and data storage. In industrial environments, sensitive information flows continuously between systems and devices, such as sensors, controllers, and operational hubs. Encryption protocols like AES-256 for data storage and Transport Layer Security (TLS) for data transmission ensure that even if data is intercepted, it remains inaccessible to unauthorized actors. This layer of protection is particularly vital for safeguarding proprietary operational data and personal information in connected ecosystems (Woods, 2018).

Another foundational principle is ensuring the interoperability and security of system components. Industrial ecosystems often comprise a wide variety of components sourced from different vendors, including sensors, industrial control systems, and software platforms. Ensuring these components can seamlessly integrate while maintaining robust security is essential. Adopting standards such as IEC 62443 and using secure APIs can facilitate this interoperability, enabling industrial systems to operate cohesively without compromising security (Costa, 2021).

Access control mechanisms form another vital layer of security. These mechanisms must be embedded at every level of the system to limit unauthorized access. Role-based access control (RBAC) ensures that personnel have access only to the specific functions they need, while multi-factor authentication (MFA) adds an additional layer of protection. Together, these measures help mitigate risks associated with insider threats and external breaches, which can compromise critical industrial operations (Lindemulder & Kosinski, 2024).

Source: Author's own illustration.

Figure 7.11 *The main benefits from the security-by-design approach in industrial processes and systems*

The benefits of adopting a security-by-design approach are significant and far-reaching. Firstly, it reduces costs associated with post-deployment fixes. Retrofitting security measures into existing systems can be a complex and expensive undertaking, especially in large-scale industrial setups. By incorporating security from the outset, industries can avoid these challenges, reducing both costs and operational disruptions.

Secondly, systems designed with security as a core principle tend to be more reliable, fostering greater trust among stakeholders, including customers, partners, and regulators. Demonstrating a commitment to robust security practices builds confidence in the safety and reliability of industrial systems, an increasingly important factor in today's cyber-aware world.

Finally, the approach minimizes downtime caused by cyber incidents. Security-by-design addresses vulnerabilities before they can be exploited, reducing the likelihood of attacks and ensuring uninterrupted operations. This is particularly critical for industries like energy, manufacturing, and healthcare, where disruptions can have severe economic and social consequences (Inspira, 2024).

Real-world examples illustrate the practical application of this approach. Autonomous factories, for instance, rely on IoT devices, robotics, and AI to optimize production. By integrating real-time threat detection algorithms during the design phase, these systems can monitor network traffic for irregularities, identify potential threats, and take preventive actions before malicious activities escalate. Similarly, smart grids, which depend on seamless communication between substations, meters, and control systems, use secure protocols like DNP3-SA to authenticate devices and encrypt data exchanges. This ensures that critical infrastructure remains protected against unauthorized access and tampering.

Beyond technical measures, adopting a security-by-design approach requires a cultural shift within organizations. Collaboration among developers, engineers, and security experts is crucial to ensure that security considerations are prioritized throughout the system lifecycle. Training and awareness programs for design teams play an essential role in fostering this proactive mindset, ensuring that security becomes an integral part of the development process rather than an afterthought (Fluchs et al., 2022).

In conclusion, the security-by-design methodology is indispensable for modern industrial innovation. By embedding security measures at the earliest stages of development, industries can create systems that are not only secure but also efficient and trustworthy. As cyber threats continue to evolve, adopting a security-by-design approach will be critical to achieving operational resilience, protecting critical assets, and ensuring the long-term success of industrial ecosystems.

7.6.2 Best Practices for Integrating Cybersecurity into Industrial Innovation Frameworks

The integration of cybersecurity into industrial innovation frameworks is vital to safeguarding operations against the growing complexity of cyber threats. Adaptive strategies ensure that industrial systems remain resilient, secure, and efficient. Three core practices—risk assessments, cyber-resilience measures, and incident response planning—are essential for achieving this goal.

7.6.2.1 Risk assessments

Risk assessments form the foundation of an effective cybersecurity strategy. They identify vulnerabilities in industrial systems and provide insights into potential threats. Comprehensive assessments involve tools like vulnerability scanning, penetration testing, and system audits. These methods uncover weaknesses in networks, software, and hardware, helping organizations stay ahead of emerging risks (Gale, 2023).

A crucial component of risk assessments is the development of a risk matrix, which categorizes threats based on their likelihood and potential impact. This prioritization enables organizations to focus resources on mitigating the most critical vulnerabilities. For example, high-impact threats, such as ransomware targeting OT, require immediate attention, while lower-impact risks can be addressed in subsequent phases (Industry Risk, 2019).

7.6.2.2 Cyber-resilience

Cyber-resilience ensures that industrial systems can maintain critical functions even in the face of cyber incidents. Redundancy is a key element, enabling systems to continue operating by switching to backup processes or infrastructure if primary systems are compromised (Kim, 2017).

To strengthen resilience, organizations should implement anomaly detection systems powered by AI. These systems monitor network activity and flag irregular behaviors that may indicate a cyberattack. By detecting potential threats early, organizations can respond swiftly to mitigate damage (Wai & Lee, 2023).

Micro-segmentation is another critical practice. It divides networks into smaller segments, limiting the lateral movement of attackers within a system. For instance, if a cyber intruder gains access to one segment, micro-segmentation prevents them from easily infiltrating other parts of the network, thus containing the breach.

Training response teams to handle these scenarios is equally important. Simulated attack exercises help teams refine their response skills and prepare for real-world threats. Additionally, recovery plans should include regular backups and restoration testing to ensure that systems can be quickly restored to operational status without data loss or prolonged downtime (Hyseni, 2024).

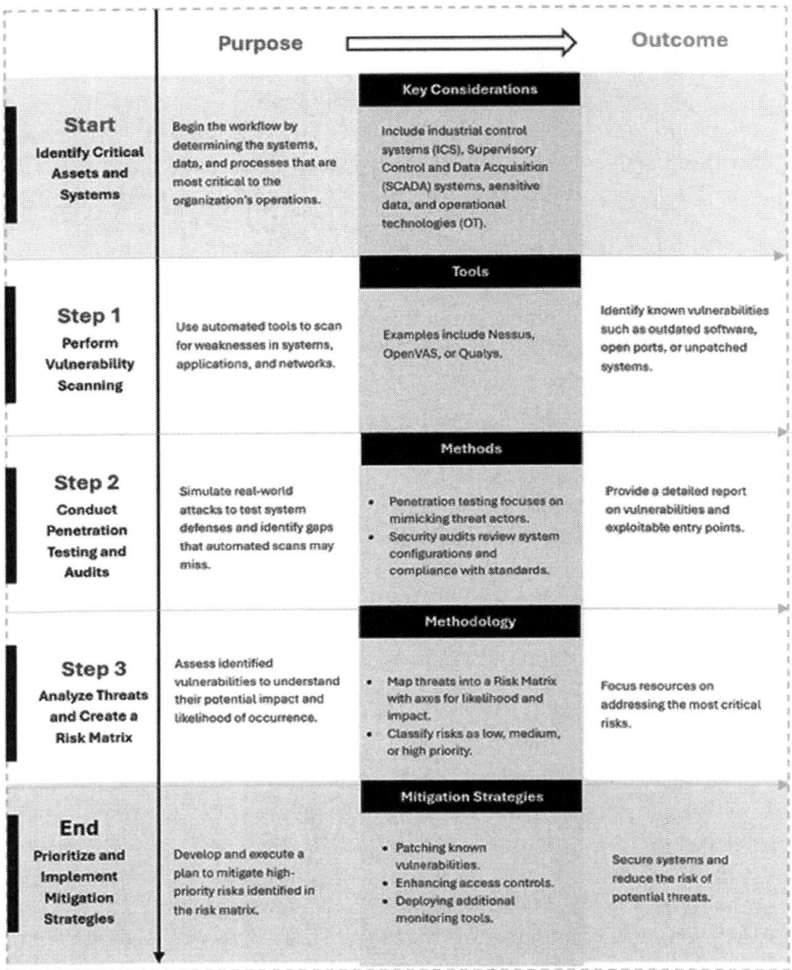

Source: Author's own illustration

Figure 7.12 Risk assessment workflow flowchart

7.6.3 Role of Government, Industry Standards, and International Cooperation in Cybersecurity

The role of governments, industry standards, and international cooperation in enhancing cybersecurity is indispensable in a world where cyber threats

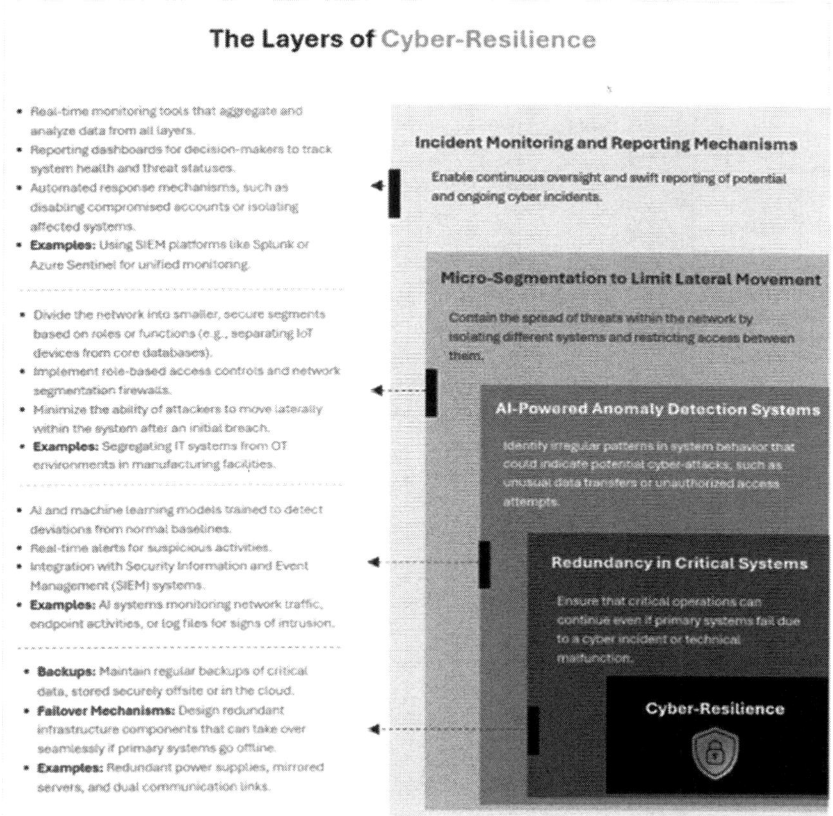

Source: Author's own illustration

Figure 7.13 *Cyber-resilience diagram*

are increasingly complex and borderless. Each entity contributes uniquely to creating a secure digital and industrial ecosystem by enforcing regulations, setting benchmarks, and fostering collaboration (Fadia et al., 2020).

7.6.3.1 Government initiatives

Governments around the world are at the forefront of enforcing cybersecurity regulations to protect critical infrastructure and industries. They develop policies and mandates to ensure organizations implement robust cybersecurity measures that align with national security priorities.

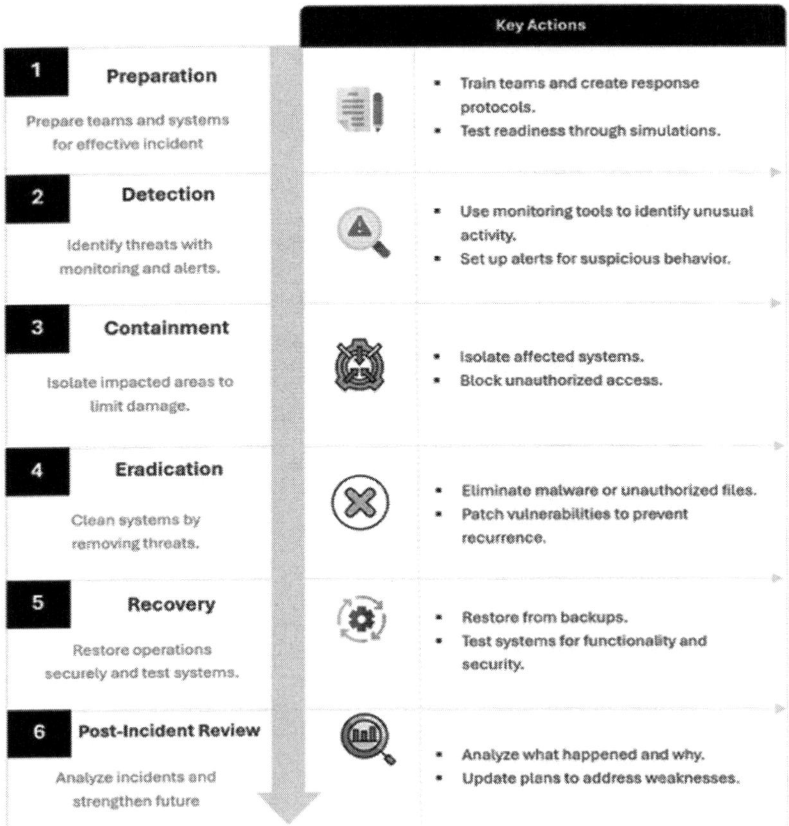

Source: Author's own illustration

Figure 7.14 *Phases of an incident response plan*

1. **Cybersecurity Maturity Model Certification (CMMC):** A US initiative for defense contractors, the CMMC ensures that companies meet specific cybersecurity requirements to safeguard sensitive information within the Department of Defense supply chain. This model combines various cybersecurity standards, including NIST and ISO, to create a unified compliance framework, with levels ranging from basic to advanced security (DoD CIO).
2. **The EU Cybersecurity Act:** The European Union has introduced the Cybersecurity Act to establish a framework for certifying secure digital

Table 7.13a The role of government initiatives in cybersecurity

Initiatives/Standards	Purpose	Examples
Cybersecurity Maturity Model Certification (CMMC)	Ensures defense contractors meet cybersecurity standards to protect sensitive supply chain information.	US Department of Defense requiring CMMC certification for contractors.
EU Cybersecurity Act	Creates a certification framework for secure digital systems to build trust in connected technologies.	Certification of IoT devices in manufacturing under the EU framework.

Table 7.13b The role of industry standards in cybersecurity

Initiatives/Standards	Purpose	Examples
ISO 27001 (Information Security Management)	Provides a structured framework for protecting information and managing security risks.	A global manufacturer implementing ISO 27001 to secure proprietary designs and sensitive data.
NIST Cybersecurity Framework (CSF)	Guides organizations in identifying, protecting, detecting, responding, and recovering from cybersecurity threats.	US energy providers adopting NIST CSF for OT systems.
IEC 62443 (Cybersecurity for Industrial Automation and Control Systems)	Ensures the security of control systems in industrial environments.	Industrial automation companies implementing IEC 62443 to secure SCADA systems.

Table 7.13c The role of international cooperation in cybersecurity

Initiatives/Standards	Purpose	Examples
Global Forum on Cyber Expertise (GFCE)	Fosters global collaboration on cybersecurity capacity building and knowledge sharing.	Cross-border training initiatives led by GFCE members in Europe and Asia.
Public–Private Partnerships (PPPs)	Enhances cybersecurity by fostering collaboration between governments and private organizations.	Collaboration between national security agencies and technology firms to develop real-time threat detection tools.
Global Standards Alignment	Harmonizes cybersecurity standards across borders to protect international supply chains.	Multinational companies aligning GDPR and ISO 27001 for compliance and operational security.

systems. The Act emphasizes creating trust through the certification of systems, products, and processes, ensuring that they meet high-security standards. It is especially critical for IoT devices and other connected technologies in industrial ecosystems (EUR-Lex).

These initiatives serve as benchmarks, compelling organizations to prioritize cybersecurity as part of their operational strategies and protect sensitive information from evolving threats.

7.6.3.2 Industry standards

Industry standards are crucial in setting universally accepted benchmarks for managing cybersecurity risks. They provide organizations with structured frameworks to address vulnerabilities and enhance system security.

1. **ISO 27001 (Information Security Management):** This international standard outlines a framework for establishing, implementing, maintaining, and improving information security management systems (ISMS). It focuses on risk assessments, access control, and continuous monitoring, ensuring that industrial organizations protect their assets and sensitive data (ISO Standards, 2022).
2. **NIST Cybersecurity Framework (CSF):** Developed by the US National Institute of Standards and Technology, the NIST CSF is widely used across industries to manage and reduce cybersecurity risks. It provides a flexible structure based on five core functions: Identify, Protect, Detect, Respond, and Recover. This adaptability makes it suitable for organizations of varying sizes and sectors (NIST Cybersecurity Framework).
3. **IEC 62443 (Cybersecurity for Industrial Automation and Control Systems):** Designed specifically for industrial environments, IEC 62443 addresses the unique challenges faced by OT systems. It includes guidelines for securing control systems, ensuring that industrial operations remain safe and resilient against cyber threats (ISA).

Adopting these standards allows organizations to demonstrate a commitment to best practices while aligning with regulatory and operational expectations.

7.6.3.3 International cooperation

Cyber threats transcend national boundaries, necessitating collaboration among nations, industries, and organizations. International cooperation fosters knowledge sharing, resource pooling, and joint action against cyber adversaries (UNODC, n.d.).

1. **Cross-Border Initiatives:** Programs like the Global Forum on Cyber Expertise (GFCE) bring together governments, international organizations,

and private entities to enhance global cybersecurity capacity. These initiatives focus on sharing best practices, developing training programs, and building a unified approach to tackling cyber risks.

2. **Public–Private Partnerships (PPPs):** Governments and private sectors collaborate to develop secure industrial ecosystems. For example, collaborations between tech companies and national security agencies help design advanced threat intelligence platforms. PPPs are instrumental in addressing supply chain vulnerabilities by creating shared databases of trusted suppliers and vendors.
3. **Global Standards Alignment:** Efforts to harmonize standards across borders ensure that international supply chains are uniformly protected. This includes aligning regional frameworks like GDPR with global standards such as ISO 27001.

The combined efforts of governments, industry standards bodies, and international coalitions form the backbone of a resilient cybersecurity landscape. By enforcing regulations, providing structured guidelines, and fostering cross-border collaboration, these entities empower organizations to mitigate cyber risks effectively. In an interconnected industrial world, where vulnerabilities in one region can impact systems globally, these cooperative measures are essential for safeguarding innovation and ensuring operational security.

7.6.4 Case Examples of Successful Integration of Cybersecurity in Industries

The integration of robust cybersecurity measures has been critical in transforming industries, safeguarding operations, and fostering innovation. These case studies from the automotive, energy, and manufacturing sectors demonstrate how effective implementation of cybersecurity strategies can lead to enhanced safety, efficiency, and trust.

7.6.4.1 The automotive sector: over-the-air updates by Tesla

Tesla has set a benchmark for cybersecurity in the automotive industry through its over-the-air (OTA) update system. This system allows Tesla vehicles to receive software updates remotely, ensuring that cybersecurity patches and system improvements are deployed promptly across its fleet (Rambus Press, 2022). Tesla's OTA updates address vulnerabilities and enhance system features without requiring physical intervention. For instance, a security flaw discovered in the vehicle's software can be mitigated within hours through a remote update. This has two impacts:

1. **Enhanced Vehicle Safety:** the ability to respond quickly to vulnerabilities reduces the risk of cyberattacks on connected vehicle systems, such as infotainment or autonomous driving modules.

2. **Increased Customer Trust:** Tesla's proactive approach to cybersecurity builds confidence among customers, assuring them that their vehicles remain secure and updated with the latest technologies.

This integration exemplifies how continuous updates and real-time security measures can protect critical systems in increasingly connected vehicles, setting a precedent for the automotive industry.

7.6.4.2 The energy sector: NERC-CIP standards for critical infrastructure protection

In the energy sector, the North American Electric Reliability Corporation Critical Infrastructure Protection (NERC-CIP) standards have become a cornerstone for safeguarding critical power infrastructure (Awati & Cole, 2022). NERC-CIP mandates energy providers to implement strict cybersecurity measures, including access controls, continuous monitoring, and incident response plans. These standards are designed to protect power grids, substations, and other critical infrastructure from cyber threats. This has two impacts:

1. **Reduced Vulnerabilities:** Energy providers adhering to NERC-CIP standards have significantly improved the resilience of their operations, reducing risks from cyberattacks that could disrupt electricity supply.
2. **Operational Continuity:** By ensuring compliance, energy companies minimize the likelihood of widespread outages caused by targeted attacks, such as malware or ransomware incidents.

Through these standards, the energy sector has demonstrated the importance of regulatory frameworks in creating a unified approach to cybersecurity, ensuring the reliability and safety of critical services.

7.6.4.3 The manufacturing sector: Siemens's industrial cybersecurity integration

Siemens has pioneered cybersecurity in the manufacturing sector by embedding industrial security solutions within its Totally Integrated Automation (TIA) Portal. This platform integrates cybersecurity measures at the heart of manufacturing processes, providing comprehensive protection for automated production lines (Schott, 2022). The TIA Portal includes features such as secure communication protocols, user authentication, and automated monitoring tools to detect and respond to cyber threats in real time. This has two impacts:

1. **Protected Production Lines:** By securing control systems and automation processes, Siemens has mitigated risks of operational disruptions caused by cyber incidents, such as unauthorized access or malware.

2. **Increased Operational Efficiency:** The proactive detection and prevention of cybersecurity threats reduce downtime and ensure smooth production workflows.

Siemens's approach highlights the necessity of integrating cybersecurity directly into industrial systems, offering manufacturers a blueprint for securing their operations while maintaining productivity and innovation.

7.7 FUTURE DIRECTIONS AND EMERGING TRENDS IN CYBERSECURITY AND PRIVACY

As industries become more interconnected and reliant on advanced technologies, the landscape of cybersecurity and privacy continues to evolve. Emerging technologies, new paradigms, and shifting industrial priorities are reshaping how organizations approach security and privacy. This section explores the future of cybersecurity and privacy, focusing on technological advancements, the role of Industry 5.0, and evolving frameworks.

7.7.1 Emerging Technologies in Cybersecurity

The landscape of cybersecurity is undergoing rapid transformation with the advent of advanced technologies like AI, blockchain, and quantum computing. These technologies are reshaping how organizations protect their systems, data, and infrastructure from evolving cyber threats (EC-Council University, 2024).

7.7.1.1 Artificial intelligence (AI): revolutionizing threat detection

AI is revolutionizing cybersecurity by enabling systems to detect, predict, and respond to threats in real time. Its ability to analyze vast datasets, recognize patterns, and identify anomalies makes it a critical tool for mitigating cyber risks.

Table 7.14 The impact and the future of AI in cybersecurity

Applications	Advantages	Future Potential
AI is used in threat intelligence platforms, Security Information and Event Management (SIEM) systems, and Endpoint Detection and Response (EDR) tools. These systems can detect irregularities such as unusual login patterns or unexpected data transfers.	AI enhances detection accuracy, reduces false positives, and automates repetitive security tasks, allowing human analysts to focus on strategic issues.	AI's predictive analytics could preemptively identify vulnerabilities, preventing attacks before they occur.

Table 7.15 The impact and the future of blockchain in cybersecurity

Applications	Advantages	Future Potential
Blockchain is widely used for securing IoT ecosystems, managing digital identities, and ensuring data authenticity in supply chains.	By eliminating single points of failure, blockchain reduces the risk of data breaches. It also provides an immutable audit trail, which enhances trust in multi-party transactions.	Blockchain's integration with AI could create new paradigms for secure communication and real-time fraud detection.

7.7.1.2 Blockchain: enhancing data security

Blockchain technology, with its decentralized and tamper-proof nature, is becoming an essential tool in cybersecurity. Its distributed ledger system ensures data integrity, transparency, and resilience against unauthorized modifications.

7.7.1.3 Quantum computing: the next frontier

Quantum computing poses both opportunities and challenges for cybersecurity. Its computational power can solve complex problems that are currently infeasible for traditional computers, but it also threatens existing encryption methods.

7.7.2 Impact of Industry 5.0 on Cybersecurity, Privacy, and Safety

Industry 5.0 marks a transformative shift in industrial innovation, emphasizing the integration of human creativity with advanced technologies such as AI, robotics, and the IoT. Unlike its predecessor, which focused on automation and

Table 7.16 The impact and the future of quantum computing in cybersecurity

Opportunities	Risks	Future Potential
Developing quantum-resistant cryptographic algorithms to secure sensitive data.	Quantum computers could render current encryption techniques, like RSA and ECC, obsolete.	Organizations are investing in post-quantum cryptography to safeguard data against quantum-based attacks.

efficiency, Industry 5.0 centers on human-centric principles, sustainability, and resilience. This shift has profound implications for cybersecurity, privacy, and safety, requiring organizations to address new challenges in an interconnected and rapidly evolving landscape.

One of the most significant changes introduced by Industry 5.0 is the seamless collaboration between humans and intelligent machines. This interaction leverages the strengths of both parties, with machines providing precision and speed while humans contribute creativity and decision-making. However, this increased collaboration also introduces vulnerabilities. Interfaces such as collaborative robots (cobots) and augmented reality systems can become targets for cyberattacks. For instance, a breach in a cobot's programming could lead to unsafe movements, posing risks to workers and disrupting operations. Protecting these systems demands robust encryption, real-time threat detection, and secure communication protocols. Advanced authentication methods, such as biometrics, are becoming essential to ensure only authorized personnel can access critical systems (Abishek et al., 2023).

In addition to enhancing collaboration, Industry 5.0 places a strong emphasis on building resilient and sustainable systems, particularly in critical sectors such as energy, water, and transportation. As industrial processes become increasingly digitized and interconnected, the potential impact of cyberattacks on these infrastructures grows. Cyber-resilience strategies are evolving to prioritize redundancy, continuity, and swift recovery from disruptions. Ensuring operational stability is vital, as even minor breaches can lead to significant societal and economic consequences. Sustainability efforts in Industry 5.0 also require ethical data usage. Predictive maintenance systems, for example, rely on vast datasets to optimize resources, but ensuring the privacy of this data is crucial to prevent exploitation or misuse. Privacy frameworks must evolve to incorporate ethical principles and comply with regulations like GDPR, while emerging decentralized models, such as blockchain, offer promising solutions for secure and transparent data management (Adel & Alani, 2024).

Industry 5.0 underscores the convergence of cybersecurity, privacy, and safety. Organizations must adopt holistic approaches that integrate robust data protection measures with safety protocols to address the complexities of this new paradigm. Ethical considerations must guide the development and implementation of these systems, ensuring that technological progress respects individual and industrial privacy. By fostering proactive measures, such as continuous monitoring, predictive analytics, and rapid incident response capabilities, organizations can mitigate risks and secure the resilience of critical infrastructures. In doing so, Industry 5.0 not only enhances industrial capabilities but also ensures a sustainable, secure, and human-centric future (Boubaker, 2023).

7.7.3 New Paradigms in Cybersecurity

As the cyber threat landscape evolves, organizations are adopting innovative paradigms to address vulnerabilities and enhance resilience. Among these, Zero-Trust Architecture and Digital Twins for Industrial Safety stand out as transformative approaches, redefining traditional cybersecurity models to meet the demands of modern industrial systems.

7.7.3.1 Zero-trust architecture: a fundamental shift in security

The zero-trust model challenges the traditional perimeter-based security approach by operating on the principle of "never trust, always verify." It assumes that threats can originate both inside and outside an organization's network, making continuous authentication and real-time monitoring essential for every access attempt, regardless of its origin (SANS Cyber Defense, 2023).

7.7.3.1.1 Implementation in industrial systems

Industries are shifting away from traditional security models that focus on fortifying the perimeter. Instead, they are adopting zero-trust environments that provide comprehensive protection against insider threats, such as compromised employee credentials, and external threats, like phishing attacks. For example, in a manufacturing plant, access to OT systems is controlled through zero-trust principles. Workers accessing machinery through IoT interfaces must authenticate themselves at multiple checkpoints, while AI-powered monitoring tools continuously evaluate their activities for anomalies.

7.7.3.2 Digital twins for industrial safety: bridging the physical and virtual worlds

Digital twins are virtual replicas of physical assets, systems, or processes. By mirroring real-world operations in a digital environment, digital twins provide an advanced platform for real-time monitoring, predictive maintenance, and cybersecurity threat simulations (Varghese et al., 2022).

7.7.3.2.1 Case example

In a smart factory, digital twins can replicate the operation of an assembly line. By simulating a ransomware attack that locks down machinery, the organization can evaluate how such an attack would disrupt production and test their response protocols. This proactive approach enables the development of robust mitigation strategies without impacting actual operations.

Table 7.17 Impact of Industry 5.0 on cybersecurity, privacy, and safety

Category	Key Focus	Implications	Examples
Human–Machine Collaboration	Seamless integration of humans and machines, e.g., cobots and AR systems.	Requires robust security for interfaces to ensure safety and prevent cyberattacks.	Securing AR systems for industrial training.
Cyber-Resilience	Ensuring operational continuity during cyberattacks.	Redundancy, incident response plans, and threat detection are critical.	Resilient energy grids protecting against cyber disruptions.
Sustainability and Privacy	Ethical use of data for sustainable practices, e.g., predictive maintenance.	Privacy frameworks must ensure compliance with GDPR and ethical data usage.	Anonymizing IoT data for predictive maintenance in factories.
Privacy Framework Evolution	Adapting frameworks to decentralized data models, e.g., blockchain.	Secures sensitive data with transparency and accountability.	Blockchain for ensuring supply chain data integrity.
Physical and Digital Safety	Protecting human–machine interactions and operational systems.	Security measures must address both physical and cyber risks.	Preventing unauthorized cobot access in factories.
Holistic Security Frameworks	Unifying cybersecurity, privacy, and safety strategies.	Proactive monitoring and rapid response ensure resilience.	Monitoring IoT devices in smart factories.
Ethical Considerations	Respecting privacy, transparency, and fairness in industrial applications.	Ensures privacy-aligned technological progress and compliance with standards.	Developing AI tools that respect confidentiality and minimize bias.

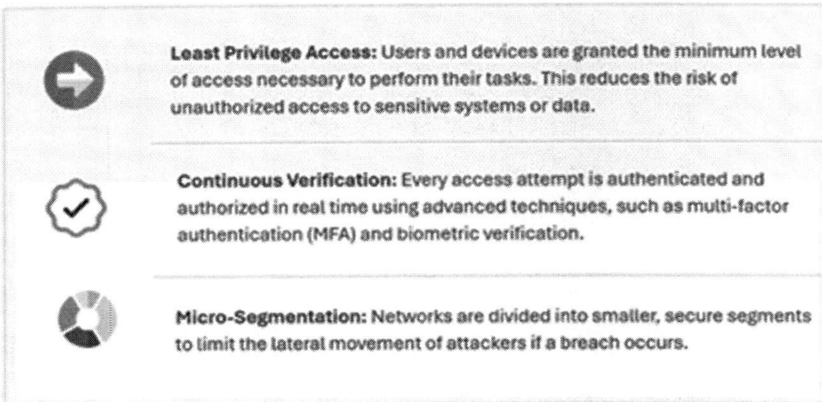

Source: Author's own illustration.

Figure 7.15 The core principles of the zero-trust model

Source: Author's own illustration.

Figure 7.16 The benefits of zero trust in industrial systems

The adoption of zero-trust architecture and digital twins for industrial safety represents a significant advancement in cybersecurity. By moving beyond traditional security models, these paradigms enable organizations to address complex threats while maintaining operational efficiency and safety. Together, they form a critical foundation for building resilient industrial systems capable of thriving in an increasingly interconnected and vulnerable digital landscape.

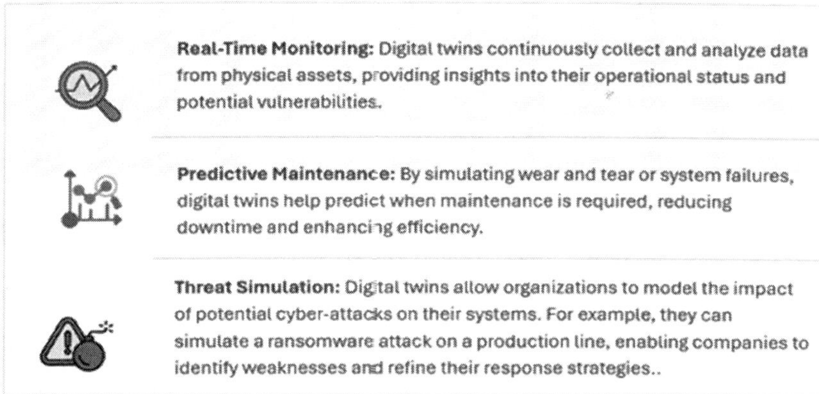

Source: Author's own illustration.

Figure 7.17 The key applications of digital twins for industrial safety

Source: Author's own illustration.

Figure 7.18 The benefits of digital twins for industrial safety

7.8 CONCLUSION

The rapid advancements in industrial technologies, driven by Industry 4.0 and 5.0, have transformed the global industrial landscape, bringing unprecedented opportunities for efficiency, productivity, and innovation. However, this transformation has also introduced a host of challenges, particularly in the realms of cybersecurity, privacy, and safety. Addressing these challenges is not only essential for protecting critical industrial systems but also for ensuring the long-term sustainability and resilience of industrial innovation.

Throughout this chapter, we explored the evolving cybersecurity landscape, the impact of emerging technologies, and the paradigm shifts required to protect industrial systems in an increasingly interconnected world. The integration of advanced tools such as AI, blockchain, and quantum computing has revolutionized cybersecurity practices, enabling real-time threat detection, secure data management, and predictive resilience against future threats. At the same time, concepts such as zero-trust architecture and digital twins have redefined how organizations approach security and operational safety, bridging the gap between the physical and digital domains.

A recurring theme is the critical interdependence of cybersecurity, privacy, and safety. In an age where industrial systems rely on vast amounts of data and human–machine collaboration, safeguarding privacy is just as important as protecting physical and digital assets. Privacy frameworks must evolve to address ethical concerns and comply with global regulations, ensuring transparency and accountability in data usage. Simultaneously, safety measures must expand beyond traditional physical considerations to include digital risks, as breaches can have catastrophic consequences for both human life and industrial operations.

As we look to the future, the integration of cybersecurity, privacy, and safety must be a foundational priority for policymakers, industry leaders, and technology innovators. Governments play a pivotal role by enforcing regulations that mandate robust security practices and foster international collaboration to combat cyber threats that transcend borders. Industry standards, such as ISO 27001 and IEC 62443, provide critical frameworks for organizations to develop resilient systems, while initiatives like the Global Forum on Cyber Expertise (GFCE) promote global knowledge sharing and capacity building.

To ensure sustainable industrial innovation, organizations must adopt a proactive and holistic approach to cybersecurity. This includes implementing advanced technologies, fostering a culture of security awareness, and continuously updating practices to address emerging threats. Investments in research and development, cross-sector collaboration, and workforce training are vital to staying ahead of the evolving threat landscape.

The future of industrial innovation depends on the ability to balance technological progress with robust protections for security, privacy, and safety. By adopting forward-thinking policies and strategies, industries can not only mitigate risks but also unlock new opportunities for growth, ensuring that innovation remains sustainable, resilient, and human-centric. As we embrace the possibilities of Industry 5.0 and beyond, safeguarding the foundations of cybersecurity, privacy, and safety will be essential for building a secure and prosperous industrial future.

REFERENCES

Abishek, B. A., T. Kavyashree, R. Jayalakshmi, S. Tharunkumar, and R. Raffik. "Collaborative Robots and Cyber Security in Industry 5.0." 2023 2nd International Conference on Advancements in Electrical, Electronics, Communication, Computing and Automation (ICAECA), Coimbatore, India, 2023, pp. 1–6. https://doi.org/10.1109/ICAECA56562.2023.10200319.

Adel, A., and N. HS Alani. "Human-Centric Collaboration and Industry 5.0 Framework in Smart Cities and Communities: Fostering Sustainable Development Goals 3, 4, 9, and 11 in Society 5.0." *Smart Cities* 7, no. 4 (2024): 1723–1775. https://doi.org/10.3390/smartcities7040068.

AI Guardian. "The Pivotal Role of an AI Ethics Committee: Navigating AI Dilemmas." *AI Guardian*, 2024. https://www.aiguardianapp.com/ai-ethics-committee.

Alqudhaibi, A., M. Albarrak, A. Aloseel, S. Jagtap, and K. Salonitis. "Cybersecurity Threats in Critical Infrastructure for Industry 4.0: A Proactive Approach Based on Attacker Motivations." *Sensors* 23, no. 9 (2023): 4539. https://doi.org/10.3390/s23094539.

Alqudhaibi, Adel, Majed Albarrak, Sandeep Jagtap, Nikki Williams, and Konstantinos Salonitis. "Securing Industry 4.0: Assessing Cybersecurity Challenges and Proposing Strategies for Manufacturing Management." *Cyber Security and Applications* 3 (2025). https://doi.org/10.1016/j.csa.2024.100067.

Amos, Zac. *Why Collaboration Is Essential for Cybersecurity Teams*. International Society of Automation (ISA), 2024.

Arthur, Charles. "Google to Pay Record $22.5m Fine to FTC over Safari Tracking." *The Guardian*, August 9, 2012. https://www.theguardian.com/technology/2012/aug/09/google-record-fine-ftc-safari.

Awati, Rahul, and AwatiBen Cole. "North American Electric Reliability Corporation Critical Infrastructure Protection (NERC CIP)." *TechTarget*, 2022. https://www.techtarget.com/searchsecurity/definition/North-American-Electric-Reliability-Corporation-Critical-Infrastructure-Protection-NERC-CIP.

Badman, Annie. "Data Data Protection Strategy: Key Components and Best Practices." *IBM*. 2024. https://www.ibm.com/think/insights/data-protection-strategy?.

Bansal, Anshu. "GDPR vs. HIPAA vs. CCPA vs. PCI: Compliance Differences." *CloudDefense.AI*. 2024. https://www.clouddefense.ai/gdpr-vs-hipaa-vs-ccpa-vs-pci/?.

Beerman, J., D. Berent, Z. Falter, and S. Bhunia. "A Review of Colonial Pipeline Ransomware Attack." IEEE/ACM 23rd International Symposium on Cluster, Cloud and Internet Computing Workshops (CCGridW), Bangalore, India, 2023, pp. 8–15. https://doi.org/10.1109/CCGridW59191.2023.00017.

Bibi, Palwasha. "Establishing Transparency and Accountability in AI: Ethical Standards for Data Governance and Automated Systems." 2024. https://doi.org/10.13140/RG.2.2.25599.83366.

Boeckl, Katie, et al. *Considerations for Managing Internet of Things (IoT) Cybersecurity and Privacy Risks*. NIST (National Institute of Standards and Technology, 2019. https://doi.org/10.6028/NIST.IR.8228.

Boubaker, Khobeib Ben. "Industry 5.0: Where Does Cybersecurity Fit In?" *Stormshield*. 2023. https://www.stormshield.com/news/industry-5-0-where-does-cybersecurity-fit-in/?.

Bouhdada, Jalal, and Marco Ayala. *Securing Industrial Control Systems and Safety Instrumented Systems: A Practical Guide for Safeguarding Mission and Safety Critical Systems.* IEEE Books, 2024. https://ieeexplore.ieee.org/servlet/opac?bknumber=10769223.

Brook, Chris. "IP Theft: Definition and Examples." *Fortra Digital Guardian*, 2024. https://www.digitalguardian.com/blog/ip-theft-definition-and-examples.

CCCS. *Security Considerations for Research and Development Organizations* (ITSAP.00.130). Government of Canada, 2024. https://www.cyber.gc.ca/en/guidance/security-considerations-research-and-development-itsap00130?.

Constantin, Lucian. "New Havex Malware Variants Target Industrial Control System and SCADA Users." *PCWorld,* 2014. https://www.pcworld.com/article/439993/new-havex-malware-variants-target-industrial-control-system-and-scada-users.html?.

Costa, Felipe Sabino. *A Practical Approach to Adopting the IEC 62443 Standards.* ISA – Global Cybersecurity Alliance, 2021.

Dal Molin, Patrícia. "Cyberattack on Industrial Systems: A Growing Threat." *Lumiun Blog,* 2024. https://www.lumiun.com/blog/en/cyberattack-on-industrial-systems-is-a-growing-threat/.

Dawood, M., S. Tu, C. Xiao, H. Alasmary, M. Waqas, and S. U. Rehman. "Cyberattacks and Security of Cloud Computing: A Complete Guideline." *Symmetry* 15, no. 11 (2023): 1981. https://doi.org/10.3390/sym15111981.

Decybr. "Protecting Intellectual Property: Cybersecurity for Research and Development." *Decybr,* 2023. https://decybr.com/protecting-intellectual-property-cybersecurity-for-research-and-development/?.

Deloite. "Cybersecurity for Smart Factories: Tools for Managing Cyber Threats to Manufacturing." *Deloitte Insights,* 2019. https://www2.deloitte.com/content/dam/Deloitte/us/Documents/energy-resources/cybersecurity-for-smart-factories-mfg.pdf.

DoD CIO. *Chief Information Officer, U.S. Department of Defense.* DoD CIO, n.d.

Easterly, Jen, and Tom Fanning. "The Attack on Colonial Pipeline: What We've Learned & What We've Done Over the Past Two Years." *Cybersecurity & Infrastructure Security Agency "CISA",* 2023. https://www.cisa.gov/news-events/news/attack-colonial-pipeline-what-weve-learned-what-weve-done-over-past-two-years?.

EC-Council University. *Staying Ahead of the Curve: Emerging Cybersecurity Technologies.* EC-Council University, 2024.

Emtrain. "The Importance of Data Privacy Training for Employees." *Emtrain*, 2024. https://emtrain.com/blog/code-of-conduct/data-privacy-training-for-employees/?.

EUR-Lex. *The EU Cybersecurity Act.* EUR-Lex, n.d. https://eur-lex.europa.eu/legal-content/EN/TXT/?uri=legissum:4398780.

Fadia, Ankit, Mahir Nayfeh, and John Noble. *How Governments Can Combat Intensifying Cybersecurity Risks.* McKinsey & Company, 2020. https://www.mckinsey.com/industries/public-sector/our-insights/follow-the-leaders-how-governments-can-combat-intensifying-cybersecurity-risks.

Ferraioli, James. *Megatrends: Opportunities on the front lines of Cybersecurity.* Morgan Stanley, 2022.

Fluchs, S., E. Tasten, M. Mertens, A. Horch, R. Drath, and A. Fay. "Security by Design Integration Mechanisms for Industrial Control Systems." IECON 2022 – 48th Annual Conference of the IEEE Industrial Electronics Society, Brussels, Belgium, 2022, pp. 1–6. https://doi.org/10.1109/IECON49645.2022.9968406.

Forbes. "Return on Investment of Cybersecurity: Making the Business Case." *Forbes Technology Council*, 2024. https://councils.forbes.com/blog/roi-of-cybersecurity.

Gale, Tim. "Cybersecurity Risk Assessment Strategies in Industrial Control Systems." *AIChE*, 2023. https://www.aiche.org/resources/publications/cep/2023/december/cybersecurity-risk-assessment-strategies-industrial-control-systems?.

Gordon, Jonathon. "The Evolving Threat Landscape – From Ransomware to State-Sponsored Espionage." *Industrial Cyber*, 2024. https://industrialcyber.co/analysis/the-evolving-threat-landscape-from-ransomware-to-state-sponsored-espionage/?.

Goud, Naveen. "The Rising Threat of Cloud Ransomware: A Global Concern for Businesses of All Sizes." *Cybersecurity Insiders*, 2024. https://www.cybersecurity-insiders.com/the-rising-threat-of-cloud-ransomware-a-global-concern-for-businesses-of-all-sizes/?.

Greenberg, Andy. "The Untold Story of NotPetya, the Most Devastating Cyberattack in History." *Wired*, 2018. https://www.wired.com/story/notpetya-cyberattack-ukraine-russia-code-crashed-the-world/.

Gregersen, Erik. "Stuxnet." *Britannica*, 2024. https://www.britannica.com/technology/Stuxnet?.

Guess, Gary. "The Rise of IT/OT Convergence in Industry 4.0." *engineering.com*, 2022. https://www.engineering.com/the-rise-of-it-ot-convergence-in-industry-4-0/?.

Hall, Aaron. *Legal Compliance and Data Protection in Employee Data Privacy*. Aaron Hall Attorney, 2024.

Hyland, Anne. "Fortescue Spies Sifted through Personal Mail of Ex-Staff, Followed Family Members to Kmart: Court Told." *The Age*, 2024. https://www.theage.com.au/business/companies/fortescue-seeks-to-suppress-600-page-document-detailing-spying-on-ex-staff-20240710-p5jsiu.html.

Hyseni, Vlerë. "A Comprehensive Guide to Cybersecurity Incident Response Plan." *Pecb*, 2024. https://pecb.com/article/a-comprehensive-guide-to-cybersecurity-incident-response-plan.

Ieremchuk, Oleksandr, and Daria Iaskova. "Building a Resilient Data Management Strategy: Key Steps and Best Practices." Trinetix. 2024. https://www.trinetix.com/insights/building-a-resilient-data-management-strategy-key-steps-and-best-practices?.

Industry Risk. *Risk Assessment Matrix*. Industry Risk, 2019. https://industryrisk.com.au/risk-assessment-matrix/?.

Inspira. *Importance of Security-by-Design for IT and OT Systems in Building a Security Resilient Framework*. Inspira Eenterprise, 2024. https://inspiraenterprise.com/importance-of-security-by-design-for-it-and-ot-systems-in-building-a-security-resilient-framework/?.

ISA. *ISA/IEC 62443 Series of Standards*. ISA, n.d.

ISO Standards. *ISO/IEC 27001:2022*. ISO Standards, 2022. https://www.iso.org/standard/27001.

Jena, Baivab Kumar. "SolarWinds Attack And All The Details You Need To Know About It." *Simplilearn*, 2024. https://www.simplilearn.com/tutorials/cryptography-tutorial/all-about-solarwinds-attack.

Kapletia, Dharm, Massimo Felici, and Nick Wainwright. "An Integrated Framework for Innovation Management in Cyber Security and Privacy. Communications in Computer and Information Science." *Communications in Computer and Information Science* 470 (2024): 135–147, DOI:10.1007/978-3-319-12574-9_12.

Khan, Mohammed. "Data Minimization—A Practical Approach." *ISACA*, 2021. https://www.isaca.org/resources/news-and-trends/industry-news/2021/data-minimization-a-practical-approach?.

Kim, C. "Keynote Speaker 1: Cyber-resilient ICS through Diversified Redundancy and Intrusion Detection." 2017 12th International Conference for Internet Technology and Secured Transactions (ICITST), Cambridge, UK, pp. 15–15. 2017. https://doi.org/10.23919/ICITST.2017.8356331.

Kushner, David. "The Real Story of Stuxnet." *IEEE Spectrum*, 2024. https://spectrum.ieee.org/the-real-story-of-stuxnet.

Kuzmenko, Valentin. "Data Privacy Paradox: Balancing Innovation with Protection in the Age of AI." *Hyperight*, 2023. https://hyperight.com/data-privacy-paradox-balancing-innovation-with-protection-in-age-of-ai/.

Lindemulder, Gregg, and Matt Kosinski. *What Is Role-based Access Control (RBAC)?* IBM, 2024. https://www.ibm.com/think/topics/rbac.

Lipovsky, Robert. "Seven Years after Stuxnet: Industrial Systems Security Once Again in the Spotlight." 2017. https://www.welivesecurity.com/2017/06/16/seven-years-stuxnet-industrial-systems-security-spotlight/?" (welivesecurity).

Maayan, Gilad David. "10 Risks of IoT Data Management." *The Data Administration Newsletter*, 2024. https://tdan.com/10-risks-of-iot-data-management/32157?.

Malik, Vaibhav. *Secure by Design: Implementing Zero Trust Principles in Cloud-Native Architectures.* Cloud Security Alliance, 2024. https://cloudsecurityalliance.org/blog/2024/10/03/secure-by-design-implementing-zero-trust-principles-in-cloud-native-architectures?.

Moeti, Michael. *The Impact of Cybersecurity on Industrial Operations Caused by Digital Transformation from Industry 4.0 to Industry 5.0.* 2024. https://doi.org/10.5772/intechopen.114961.

Möller, D.P.F. "Cybersecurity in Digital Transformation." In: *Guide to Cybersecurity in Digital Transformation." Advances in Information Security*, vol 103. Springer, 2023. https://doi.org/10.1007/978-3-031-26845-8_1.

Mourtzis, Dimitris, Konstantinos Angelopoulos, and Vasilios Zogopoulos. "Mapping Vulnerabilities in the Industrial Internet of Things Landscape." *Procedia CIRP* 84 (2019): 265–270. https://doi.org/10.1016/j.procir.2019.04.201.

MST. *Cyber Case Study: Hack at Steel Mill Causes Physical Damage.* MST Insurance Solutions, 2021.

Nankya, M., R. Chataut, and R. Akl. "Securing Industrial Control Systems: Components, Cyber Threats, and Machine Learning-Driven Defense Strategies." *Sensors* 23, no. 21 (2023): 8840. https://doi.org/10.3390/s23218840.

Ng, Alfred, and Josh Sisco. "Justice Department Sues TikTok over Alleged Kids' Privacy Violations." *POLITICO*, 2024. https://www.politico.com/news/2024/08/02/doj-sues-tiktok-00172483?.

NIST Cybersecurity Framework. *Cybersecurity Framework,* n.d. https://www.nist.gov/cyberframework.

Parker, Samantha. "The Strategic Value of Treating Cybersecurity as an Investment." *Agileblue,* 2024. https://agileblue.com/the-strategic-value-of-treating-cybersecurity-as-an-investment/.

Parthasarathy, Sriraman. "Building Trust in Digital Strategy: A Key to Competitive Advantage and Long-Term Success." *CXOToday*, 2024. https://cxotoday.com/interviews/building-trust-in-digital-strategy-a-key-to-competitive-advantage-and-long-term-success/.

Patel, Mayur. "The Ethics of AI Addressing Bias, Privacy, and Accountability in Machine Learning." *cloudthat*, 2024. https://www.cloudthat.com/resources/blog/the-ethics-of-ai-addressing-bias-privacy-and-accountability-in-machine-learning?.

Pliatsios, D., P. Sarigiannidis, T. Lagkas, and A. G. Sarigiannidis. "A Survey on SCADA Systems: Secure Protocols, Incidents, Threats and Tactics." *IEEE Communications Surveys & Tutorials* 22, no. 3 (2020): 1942–1976. https://doi.org/10.1109/COMST.2020.2987688.

Pochmara, J., and A. Świetlicka. "Cybersecurity of Industrial Systems —A 2023 Report." *Electronics*, 13 (2024): 1191. https://doi.org/10.3390/electronics13071191.

PWC. "Zero Trust Architecture: A Paradigm Shift in Cybersecurity and Privacy." 2020. https://www.pwc.ch/en/publications/2020/ch-pwc-zero-trust-architecture-a-paradigm-shift.pdf?.

Raimundo, R. J., and A. T. Rosário. "Cybersecurity in the Internet of Things in Industrial Management." *Applied Sciences* 12, no. 3 (2022): 1598. https://doi.org/10.3390/app12031598.

Rambus Press. "What Is OTA in Automotive? Over the Air Updates Explained." *Rambus*, 2022. https://www.rambus.com/blogs/ota-updates-explained/.

Safitra, M. F., M. Lubis, and H. Fakhrurroja. "Counterattacking Cyber Threats: A Framework for the Future of Cybersecurity." *Sustainability* 15, no. 18 (2023): 13369. https://doi.org/10.3390/su151813369.

Sangkhro, R., and A. K. Agrawal. "Cybersecurity in Industrial Control Systems: A Review of the Current Trends and Challenges." 10th International Conference on Computing for Sustainable Global Development (INDIACom), New Delhi, India, pp. 355–359, 2023.

SANS Cyber Defense. *What Is Zero Trust Architecture?* SANS, 2023. https://www.sans.org/blog/what-is-zero-trust-architecture/?.

Sargiotis, D. "Data Security and Privacy: Protecting Sensitive Information." In *Data Governance*. Springer, 2024. https://doi.org/10.1007/978-3-031-67268-2_6.

Schott, Stephan. "TIA Portal for Improved Cyber Security in an Industrial Setting // TIA Portal für mehr Cybersicherheit im Industriellen Umfeld." *Siemens*, 2022. https://blog.siemens.com/2022/01/tia-portal-for-improved-cyber-security-in-an-industrial-setting-tia-portal-fur-mehr-cybersicherheit-im-industriellen-umfeld/?.

Sharghivand, N., and F. Derakhshan. "Data Security and Privacy in Industrial IoT." In *AI-Enabled Threat Detection and Security Analysis for Industrial IoT*, edited by H. Karimipour and F. Derakhshan. Springer, 2021. https://doi.org/10.1007/978-3-030-76613-9_3.

Sharma, Deepshikha. "Top 10 Data Governance Best Practices for the Manufacturing Industry." *ScikiQ*, 2024. https://Top 10 Data Governance Best Practices for the Manufacturing Industry.com/blog/top-10-data-governance-best-practices-for-manufacturing-industry/?.

Sharma, S. K., P. R Srivastava, and A Kumar. "Supply chain vulnerability assessment for manufacturing industry." *Annals of Operations Research* 326 (2021): 653–683. https://doi.org/10.1007/s10479-021-04155–4.

Shilenge, M. C., and A. Telukdarie. "Optimization of Operational and Information Technology Integration Towards Industry 4.0." IEEE 31st International Symposium on Industrial Electronics (ISIE), Anchorage, AK, USA, 2022, pp. 1076–1081, 2022. https://doi.org/10.1109/ISIE51582.2022.9831605.

Sobers, Rob. "Ransomware Statistics, Data, Trends, and Facts." *Varonis*, 2024. https://www.varonis.com/blog/ransomware-statistics.

TechRepublic Staff. "Facebook Data Privacy Scandal: A Cheat Sheet." *TechRepublic*, 2020. https://www.techrepublic.com/article/facebook-data-privacy-scandal-a-cheat-sheet/.

Tertulino, R., N. Ivaki, and H. Morais. "Design a Software Reference Architecture to Enhance Privacy and Security in Electronic Health Records." *IEEE Access* 12 (2024): 112157–112179. https://doi.org/10.1109/ACCESS.2024.3441751.

The Associated Press. "LinkedIn Hit with 310 Million Euro Fine for Data Privacy Violations from Irish Watchdog." *The Associated Press*, October 24, 2024.

Thu, Ha Dao. "AI and Data Privacy: Balancing Innovation with Security." *Smartdev*, 2025. https://smartdev.com/ai-and-data-privacy-balancing-innovation-with-security/.

Torkington, Simon. "5 Cybersecurity Risks Posed by Emerging Technology – and How We Can Defend Against Them." *WEF (World Economic Forum)*, 2024. https://www.weforum.org/stories/2024/10/cyber-resilience-emerging-technology-ai-cybersecurity/.

UNODC. *International Cooperation on Cybersecurity Matters*. UNODC, n.d.

Varghese, Seba Anna, Alireza Dehlaghi Ghadim, Ali Balador, Zahra Alimadadi, and Panos Papadimitratos. "Digital Twin-based Intrusion Detection for Industrial Control Systems." *arxiv*, 2022. https://doi.org/10.48550/arXiv.2207.09999.

Varnado, Lauren, and Richardson Matthew. "Navigating cybersecurity and corporate espionage risks to the oil and gas industry." *Reuters*, 2024. https://www.reuters.com/legal/legalindustry/navigating-cybersecurity-corporate-espionage-risks-oil-gas-industry-2024-12-20/?.

Vijayan, Jai. "Ransomware Attack on Merck Caused Widespread Disruption to Operations." *Dark Reading*, 2017. https://www.darkreading.com/cyberattacks-data-breaches/ransomware-attack-on-merck-caused-widespread-disruption-to-operations?.

Wai, E., and C. K. M. Lee. "Seamless Industry 4.0 Integration: A Multilayered Cyber-Security Framework for Resilient SCADA Deployments in CPPS." *Applied Sciences* 13, no. 21 (2023): 12008. https://doi.org/10.3390/app132112008.

Woods, Eoin. "Secure by Design – Security Design Principles for the Working Architect." *slideshare*, 2018. https://www.slideshare.net/slideshow/secure-by-design-security-design-principles-for-the-working-architect-124478440/124478440?.

Zhurer, Yevhen. "Industrial & Corporate Espionage: What Is It? Cases & Best Prevention Practices." *Syteca*, 2024. https://www.syteca.com/en/blog/prevent-industrial-espionage.

8. Industrial network innovation and industrial chains

Elias G. Carayannis and Nikos R. Zotas

8.1 INTRODUCTION

Industrial networks are interconnected systems of organizations collaborating to achieve shared goals by leveraging their unique strengths and resources. These networks, alongside industrial chains that represent the flow of goods, services, and information from raw materials to end consumers, play a pivotal role in structuring industrial activity and fostering innovation. By pooling resources, sharing expertise, and co-developing solutions, industrial networks create opportunities for technological advancements, process optimization, and market expansion. Collaboration within these systems enhances competitiveness by streamlining operations, minimizing inefficiencies, and enabling rapid adaptation to market demands. This environment of shared goals and mutual reliance fosters continuous improvement, driving industries toward sustainable growth and resilience.

Globalization and digitalization have significantly influenced industrial networks and chains, reshaping their structures and operations. Globalization has expanded the reach of networks, integrating diverse economies and providing access to broader resources, talent, and markets. While this interconnectedness has unlocked new opportunities, it has also introduced complexities and vulnerabilities, such as geopolitical risks and global supply chain disruptions. Digitalization, on the other hand, has revolutionized these systems by enabling real-time data sharing, advanced analytics, and seamless communication. Technologies like the Internet of Things (IoT), big data, and artificial intelligence (AI) have enhanced visibility, enabling proactive management and fostering more agile, responsive networks capable of adapting to changing conditions.

The evolution from linear value chains to dynamic ecosystems marks a fundamental transformation in industrial systems. Traditional supply chains, characterized by rigid, sequential processes, are being replaced by decentralized, interconnected ecosystems that prioritize adaptability and collaboration. Industry 4.0 technologies, including blockchain and cyber-physical systems, have been instrumental in this shift. These technologies promote transparency, trust, and integration of physical and digital processes, resulting in networks that are more resilient and capable of responding to uncertainties.

This shift has also redefined the role of industrial networks and chains. No longer limited to the efficient flow of resources, they have become key enablers of innovation and competitiveness in the global economy. By fostering collaboration and leveraging advanced technologies, these networks contribute to developing new products, improving processes, and creating sustainable practices that align with the demands of an increasingly interconnected world.

As industries navigate the complexities of globalization and digital transformation, the significance of industrial networks continues to grow. Their ability to adapt, innovate, and maintain resilience in the face of challenges underscores their pivotal role in shaping the future of industrial activity. These networks are not only a foundation for operational efficiency but also a catalyst for sustained innovation and competitiveness in an ever-changing global landscape.

8.2 HISTORICAL EVOLUTION OF INDUSTRIAL NETWORKS AND SUPPLY CHAINS

The historical evolution of industrial networks and supply chains reflects the profound changes in how industries organize, manage, and adapt their operations to meet the demands of an increasingly complex global economy. From the rigid and linear structures of traditional supply chains to the flexible, interconnected ecosystems of modern industrial networks, this transformation has been driven by technological advancements, shifting market dynamics, and evolving customer expectations. Early models prioritized efficiency through standardized processes and centralized control, often at the expense of flexibility and responsiveness (Whitfield, 2022). Over time, however, the advent of innovations like just-in-time (JIT) manufacturing, lean production, and digital technologies has revolutionized supply chain management, enabling dynamic collaboration and real-time decision-making. These changes have not only enhanced operational efficiency but have also fostered innovation and resilience across industries. This section delves into the transition from traditional supply chains to modern industrial networks, exploring the technological milestones that have shaped this evolution. Through case studies from sectors like automotive and electronics, it highlights how industries have adapted their network structures to leverage emerging opportunities and address global challenges, showcasing the critical role of supply chain transformation in sustaining competitiveness in today's fast-changing environment (Krykavskyy & Stasiuk, 2022).

8.2.1 Early Models: Traditional Supply Chains vs. Modern Industrial Networks

The evolution from traditional supply chains to modern industrial networks marks a fundamental shift in how industries manage the flow of goods, services, and information. Traditional supply chains, which dominated the industrial landscape for much of the 20th century, were characterized by linear, hierarchical structures where each entity—suppliers, manufacturers, distributors, and retailers—functioned as distinct, isolated units. Communication between these entities was often limited to immediate upstream or downstream partners, creating silos and reducing overall visibility across the chain. These systems operated on standardized processes designed to optimize efficiency and minimize costs, often through mass production and inventory-driven strategies like the Economic Order Quantity (EOQ) model.

While effective in stable environments with predictable demand, traditional supply chains were inherently rigid and ill-equipped to handle disruptions. Long lead times, high inventory levels, and centralized decision-making processes limited their ability to adapt to sudden changes in market conditions or supply constraints. Additionally, these supply chains focused primarily on cost efficiency rather than fostering innovation or responding to dynamic consumer needs (EPA, 2024).

Modern industrial networks have emerged as a response to the limitations of traditional supply chains, driven by globalization, technological advancements, and shifting market demands. Unlike their predecessors, modern networks are decentralized, interconnected ecosystems that emphasize collaboration, flexibility, and real-time responsiveness. Advances in technology have played a pivotal role in this transition. For example, just-in-time (JIT) manufacturing eliminated the need for excessive inventory by aligning production schedules with real-time demand. Lean production methods further enhanced efficiency by eliminating waste and streamlining processes.

The rise of digital technologies such as the IoT, AI, and big data analytics has been transformative for modern industrial networks. These technologies enable real-time communication and data sharing across all stakeholders, enhancing visibility and decision-making capabilities. Blockchain technology adds another layer of transparency and trust, particularly in managing complex, multi-tiered supply chains. Modern networks also prioritize collaboration, with stakeholders engaging in strategic partnerships, co-creation, and knowledge sharing to foster innovation and resilience.

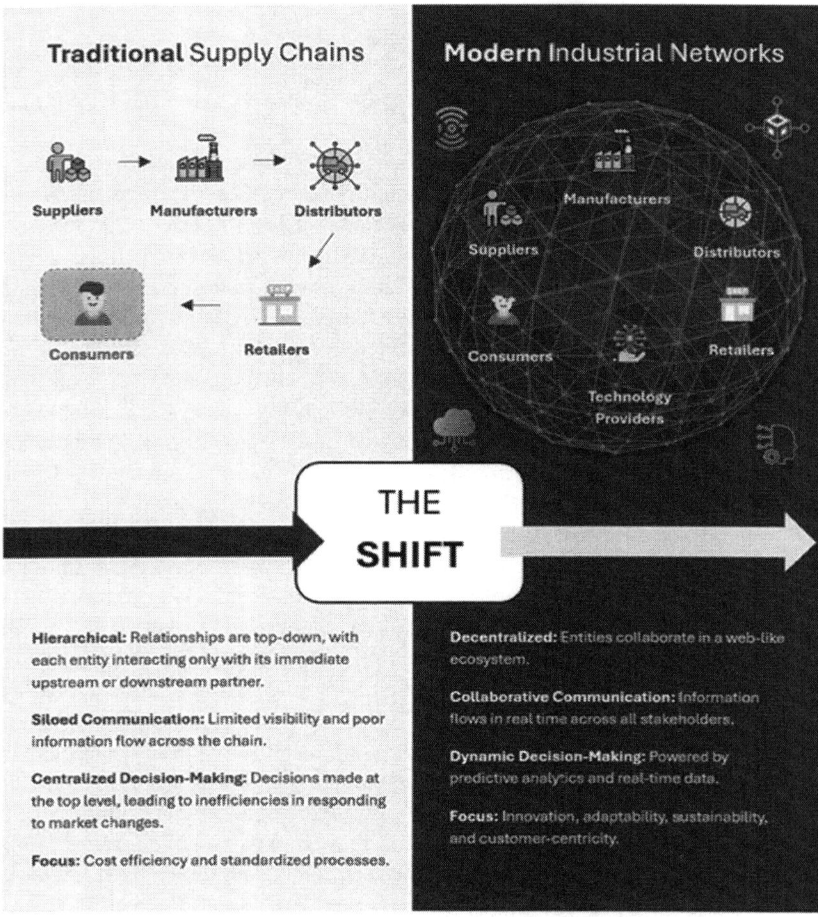

Source: Author's own illustration.

Figure 8.1 *Timeline of key milestones in cybersecurity evolution*

The shift to modern networks reflects a broader change in priorities, where adaptability, sustainability, and customer-centricity take precedence over cost alone. By leveraging technology and fostering collaboration, these networks have redefined the industrial landscape, enabling industries to navigate the complexities of globalization and respond proactively to market challenges. This transformation underscores the critical role of modern industrial networks in driving competitiveness and innovation in the global economy (Laage-Hellman et al., 2021).

8.2.2 The Transformation of Industrial Chains through Technological Advancements

The transformation of industrial chains has been driven by significant technological advancements that have revolutionized the way businesses manage production, operations, and supply chains. Among the most influential developments are JIT manufacturing and lean production, both of which have redefined efficiency, adaptability, and competitiveness in modern industries.

Just-in-time manufacturing, first popularized by Toyota in the mid-20th century, revolutionized traditional supply chain practices by aligning production schedules closely with actual demand. Unlike traditional models that relied on large inventories to buffer against uncertainties, JIT focuses on producing and delivering only what is needed, when it is needed, and in the quantities required. This shift dramatically reduced waste, minimized storage costs, and improved operational efficiency. However, JIT also required precise coordination among suppliers, manufacturers, and distributors, emphasizing the importance of reliable communication and real-time data sharing (Raza, 2024).

Lean production further enhanced the transformation of industrial chains by introducing a systematic approach to eliminating waste and optimizing processes. By focusing on value creation and identifying inefficiencies, lean principles helped industries streamline their operations, reduce costs, and improve quality (DeRose, 2024). Techniques such as value stream mapping, *kaizen* (continuous improvement), and the 5S methodology became integral to industrial practices, fostering a culture of efficiency and innovation.

The advent of digital technologies has further accelerated the transformation of industrial chains. IoT devices have enabled real-time tracking of goods and assets, providing unparalleled visibility across supply chains. AI and machine learning have introduced predictive analytics, allowing companies to anticipate demand fluctuations, optimize production schedules, and mitigate potential disruptions. Cloud computing and big data analytics have facilitated seamless collaboration among global stakeholders, enabling data-driven decision-making and improved supply chain agility (Tripathi & Nishad, 2019).

Technological advancements have also paved the way for new paradigms such as cyber-physical systems and digital twins. Cyber-physical systems integrate physical processes with digital intelligence, enhancing operational precision and efficiency. Digital twins—virtual replicas of physical assets—allow companies to simulate scenarios and optimize processes without interrupting actual operations.

These advancements collectively reflect a fundamental shift from rigid, linear supply chains to dynamic, interconnected networks capable of adapting to the complexities of the modern industrial landscape. By leveraging these technologies, industrial chains have become more efficient, resilient, and customer-centric, laying the foundation for sustained innovation and competitiveness in an era of rapid technological change.

8.2.3 Case Studies: Evolution of Network Structures in Automotive and Electronics Industries

The evolution of industrial network structures has been particularly evident in industries like automotive and electronics, where dynamic market demands and technological advancements have necessitated innovative approaches to supply chain management and collaboration. These case studies highlight how these industries have transformed their traditional supply chains into modern, interconnected networks.

1. **Automotive Industry:** Toyota and the Lean Supply Chain Revolution: Toyota's pioneering of the JIT manufacturing system marked a turning point in the automotive industry. Faced with resource constraints in post-war Japan, Toyota developed a highly efficient production system that synchronized manufacturing with real-time demand. This required establishing close relationships with suppliers, which were integrated into Toyota's broader network. By sharing forecasts, production schedules, and quality standards, Toyota created a tightly-knit, collaborative ecosystem (Perry, 2024).

   Over time, other automotive companies adopted Toyota's principles, incorporating lean manufacturing and digital tools to further enhance their supply chains. Today, technologies such as the IoT, AI, and blockchain are used to monitor and manage complex global networks. Companies

Table 8.1 Case studies in automotive and electronics industries

Case Study	Key Innovation	Technology Utilized	Impact
Automotive	JIT and Lean Supply Chain	IoT, AI, Blockchain	Reduced waste, improved efficiency, enhanced resilience
Electronics	Global Network Ecosystem	AI, Big Data, Strategic Partnerships	Enhanced visibility, rapid scaling, and innovation

like Tesla have taken this transformation further by vertically integrating production processes, ensuring greater control and agility in response to disruptions.

2. **Electronics Industry:** Apple and the Global Network Ecosystem: Apple exemplifies the evolution of supply chains into global network ecosystems. The company relies on a highly interconnected and geographically diverse network of suppliers, manufacturers, and logistics providers. Its approach combines centralized design and innovation with decentralized production across regions like Asia and North America.

   Apple's ability to maintain visibility and control over its supply chain is powered by advanced digital tools. The company uses AI and big data analytics to monitor supplier performance, predict potential disruptions, and optimize inventory management. Moreover, Apple's collaboration with strategic partners like Foxconn ensures rapid scaling of production capacity to meet global demand for its products (Seka, 2024).

Both the automotive and electronics industries illustrate the shift from traditional supply chains to collaborative networks. These sectors have embraced digital transformation, leveraging technologies like predictive analytics, cloud computing, and the IoT to enhance visibility and coordination. Furthermore, both industries prioritize sustainability by adopting practices such as circular economy principles and carbon-neutral production.

These case studies underscore the importance of adaptability, innovation, and collaboration in modern industrial networks. As industries face increasing complexity and global challenges, the evolution of network structures continues to play a critical role in driving competitiveness and resilience.

8.3 THEORETICAL FRAMEWORKS OF INDUSTRIAL NETWORKS

Theoretical frameworks provide essential insights into the complexities and strategic significance of industrial networks, which function as dynamic systems shaped by economic, organizational, and relational principles. Key perspectives such as the resource-based view (RBV), network theory, and transaction cost economics explain how organizations leverage resources, form relationships, and manage costs within these networks, offering a foundation for understanding their motivations and success factors (Augusto & Souza, 2015). Complementing these traditional approaches, the Quadruple and Quintuple Innovation Helix models emphasize the importance of multi-actor collaboration, integrating stakeholders such as academia, industry, government, and civil society to drive innovation and sustainability. Central to industrial networks are their core components—nodes, actors, and linkages—whose interactions define network dynamics. Trust, cooperation, and competition among participants are pivotal in shaping performance and resilience. This section explores these theoretical foundations, illustrating how they influence the structure, behavior, and success of modern industrial networks.

8.3.1 Key Theoretical Perspectives: Resource-Based View, Network Theory, and Transaction Cost Economics

The study of industrial networks is deeply rooted in theoretical perspectives that explain their structure, behavior, and strategic importance. Among these, the RBV, network theory, and transaction cost economics provide foundational frameworks for understanding how organizations operate and succeed within interconnected systems.

1. **Resource-Based View (RBV):** The RBV emphasizes the importance of unique resources and capabilities in achieving competitive advantage. Within industrial networks, organizations leverage their specialized assets, such as technological expertise, skilled labor, or proprietary processes, to create value. These resources, when valuable, rare, inimitable, and non-substitutable (VRIN criteria), can provide a sustainable competitive edge. In networked environments, the RBV highlights the role of resource sharing and pooling among participants. For instance, organizations collaborate to access complementary resources, such as knowledge or technology, that they cannot develop independently. This shared approach enables innovation, cost efficiency, and resilience, particularly in industries characterized by rapid technological change or resource constraints.
2. **Network Theory:** Network theory focuses on the structure and dynamics of relationships within a system of interconnected entities. In the context of industrial networks, it examines the roles of nodes (organizations), actors (individuals or groups), and linkages (relationships). The theory posits that the position of an organization within a network—its centrality—significantly influences its power, access to resources, and ability to innovate. For example, organizations occupying central positions in a network can act as hubs, coordinating activities and disseminating information effectively. Conversely, peripheral organizations may face challenges in influencing network dynamics but can exploit niche opportunities. Network theory also explores concepts like network density, clustering, and the strength of ties, emphasizing the balance between strong, stable relationships and weak, flexible connections that foster diversity and innovation.

3. **Transaction Cost Economics (TCE):** TCE examines the costs associated with coordinating and managing exchanges within and between organizations. In industrial networks, TCE helps explain the decision-making processes behind outsourcing, partnerships, and vertical integration. Organizations seek to minimize transaction costs—such as search, negotiation, and enforcement costs—by choosing governance structures that align with the complexity and uncertainty of their transactions. For example, in highly dynamic industries, firms may form alliances or joint ventures to share risks and reduce costs associated with navigating unpredictable markets. TCE also highlights the role of trust and reputation in lowering transaction costs within networks, as reliable partners reduce the need for extensive monitoring and contract enforcement.

Together, these theoretical perspectives offer a comprehensive understanding of industrial networks. The RBV focuses on the internal strengths of organizations, network theory examines the relational dynamics among participants, and TCE provides insights into the economic rationale for forming and managing network relationships. By integrating these frameworks, organizations can better navigate the complexities of industrial networks, leveraging their resources, optimizing their positions within the network, and minimizing costs to achieve strategic goals.

These perspectives are essential for understanding the structure and behavior of modern industrial networks, providing tools for fostering collaboration, enhancing innovation, and driving competitive advantage in an increasingly interconnected world.

8.3.2 The Quadruple and Quintuple Innovation Helix Models and Their Relevance to Industrial Networks

The Quadruple and Quintuple Innovation Helix models provide comprehensive frameworks that emphasize the importance of multi-stakeholder collaboration in driving innovation and sustainability within industrial networks. These models recognize the critical roles of academia, industry, government, civil society, and the natural environment in shaping innovation ecosystems, offering a structured approach to addressing complex challenges and seizing opportunities in a rapidly evolving global economy (Carayannis et al., 2020).

The Quadruple Helix model expands the traditional focus on academia, industry, and government by integrating civil society as a key stakeholder. This inclusion acknowledges the growing influence of societal needs, values, and cultural dynamics in the innovation process. Civil society's involvement ensures that innovations are not only economically viable but also socially relevant and widely accepted. In industrial networks, this model facilitates user-driven innovation by fostering collaboration between diverse participants. For instance, in the healthcare sector, partnerships between research institutions, pharmaceutical companies, government agencies, and patient advocacy groups have enabled the development of personalized medicine and telehealth services that align with patient needs and societal priorities. This approach democratizes innovation, aligning it with the expectations and demands of end-users while promoting broader adoption (Carayannis et al., 2024).

The Quintuple Helix model builds upon this framework by incorporating the natural environment as a fifth dimension, reflecting the increasing emphasis on sustainability in modern industrial practices. The integration of environmental considerations encourages industrial networks to innovate responsibly, aligning with global efforts to address climate change, resource scarcity, and ecological degradation. For example, in the renewable energy sector, collaborations between research organizations, green technology companies, governmental bodies, NGOs, and environmental advocates have led to breakthroughs in solar, wind, and other sustainable energy solutions. By embedding environmental priorities within the innovation process, the Quintuple Helix model supports the development of green technologies, circular economy practices, and ecofriendly supply chains, enhancing the resilience and adaptability of industrial networks (González et al., 2023).

These models are particularly relevant in transitioning from traditional linear value chains to dynamic ecosystems characterized by interdependence and co-creation. Industrial networks that adopt these frameworks are better positioned to foster innovation, manage risks, and achieve sustainable growth. By emphasizing trust, transparency, and shared goals, the Quadruple and Quintuple Helix models enable smoother collaboration among stakeholders, ensuring that innovation remains inclusive and impactful.

As industrial networks face mounting challenges, including climate change, technological disruption, and shifting market dynamics, the principles of these models offer a path forward. They provide a blueprint for creating resilient ecosystems that not only adapt to change but also lead the way in driving meaningful, sustainable innovation in the global economy.

8.3.3 Analysis of Network Dynamics: Nodes, Actors, and Linkages in Industrial Chains

The dynamics of industrial networks are shaped by the interactions among their fundamental components: nodes, actors, and linkages. These elements form the backbone of any industrial network, influencing its structure, behavior, and performance. Understanding how they interact is crucial for analyzing

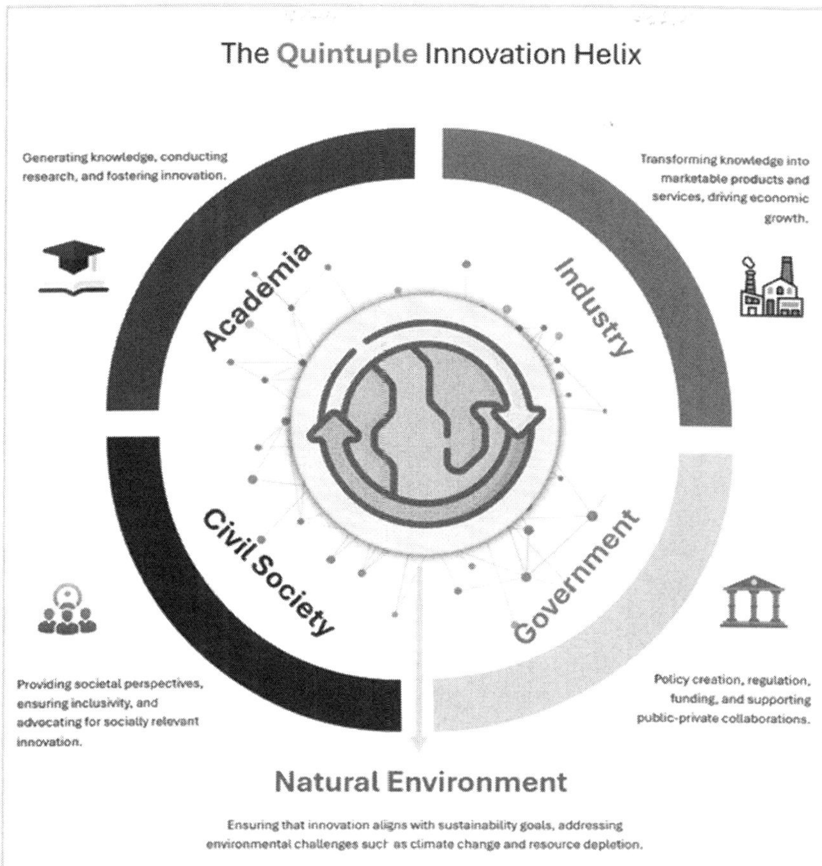

Source: Author's own illustration based on Carayannis, E.G., Barth, T.D. & Campbell, D.F. The Quintuple Helix innovation model: global warming as a challenge and driver for innovation. *J Innov Entrep* 1, 2 (2012). https://doi.org/10.1186/2192-5372-1-2.

Figure 8.2 *Quintuple Innovation Helix*

the flow of resources, information, and value within industrial chains, as well as for fostering collaboration and innovation (Chen et al., 2022).

Nodes represent the key entities within an industrial network, including organizations, institutions, and other stakeholders. Each node brings unique resources, capabilities, and objectives, contributing to the network's overall functionality. In industrial chains, nodes may include raw material suppliers, manufacturers, distributors, retailers, and end consumers. The role and influence of a node depend on its position within the network. Central nodes, often serving as hubs, have a greater impact due to their access to resources, information, and connections. For instance, in the electronics industry, manufacturers like Foxconn act as central nodes, coordinating production for multiple global brands. Peripheral nodes, while less influential, often occupy specialized niches that contribute to the network's diversity and adaptability.

Actors, whether individuals or groups, drive the activities within nodes and determine the strategic direction of the network. They include decision-makers, managers, engineers, and other personnel who play roles in shaping the network's behavior. The relationships among actors, their competencies, and their motivations significantly impact the effectiveness of the network. Collaboration between actors often fosters innovation and problem-solving, particularly in industries where expertise and knowledge sharing are critical. For example, in the automotive sector, collaboration among engineers from different firms has led to advancements in electric vehicle technology and autonomous driving systems (Abrahamsen et al., 2012).

Linkages represent the connections between nodes and actors, facilitating the exchange of resources, information, and value. These connections can be formal, such as contracts and strategic alliances, or informal, such as personal networks and collaborative partnerships. The strength of linkages varies, influencing the flow of information and the degree of trust within the network. Strong linkages, built on trust and reliability, enable seamless collaboration and resilience, while weak linkages, characterized by flexibility and broader outreach, promote innovation and access to diverse opportunities. Balancing strong and weak linkages is critical for maintaining both stability and adaptability in industrial networks (Monticone et al., 2024).

Network dynamics are further influenced by the interplay of trust, cooperation, and competition. Trust strengthens relationships, reduces transaction costs, and facilitates long-term partnerships. Cooperation enhances resource sharing and joint problem-solving, fostering synergies among network participants. Competition, when managed constructively, drives innovation and continuous improvement. Together, these elements shape the behavior and success of industrial networks, enabling them to adapt to changing market conditions and global challenges.

Analyzing nodes, actors, and linkages provides valuable insights into the structure and dynamics of industrial networks, offering strategies for enhancing their efficiency, resilience, and capacity for innovation. This understanding is critical for designing robust networks that can thrive in an increasingly complex and interconnected industrial landscape.

8.3.4 Role of Trust, Cooperation, and Competition in Network Success

Trust, cooperation, and competition are integral to the success of industrial networks, shaping their dynamics, resilience, and ability to innovate. These elements interact to create a balanced environment where participants collaborate effectively while maintaining the drive for continuous improvement and adaptability.

Trust forms the foundation of strong relationships within industrial networks. It reduces uncertainty and transaction costs by fostering transparency, reliability, and confidence among participants. Trust is particularly critical in long-term partnerships, where organizations depend on each other for resource sharing, knowledge exchange, and joint decision-making. For example, in high-tech industries, trust enables seamless collaboration between research institutions and manufacturers, ensuring the successful development of complex innovations. Without trust, networks face increased risks of conflict, inefficiency, and breakdowns in communication (Gausdal et al., 2016).

Cooperation amplifies the benefits of trust by encouraging collective problem-solving and resource pooling. It enables network participants to align their goals, share expertise, and leverage complementary strengths. Effective cooperation fosters synergies that enhance innovation, reduce costs, and improve overall performance. In the automotive sector, alliances between manufacturers and suppliers exemplify how cooperative relationships lead to streamlined production and technological advancements, such as the development of electric vehicles (Liu, 2013).

Competition, though seemingly contradictory, is equally essential for network success. Constructive competition drives organizations to innovate, improve efficiency, and differentiate themselves within the network. It creates a dynamic environment where participants strive to outperform others while adhering to shared objectives. In industrial networks, such competition often coexists with cooperation, exemplified by firms that compete in the marketplace but collaborate on shared infrastructure or research initiatives (Lee & Lee, 2023).

The interplay of trust, cooperation, and competition ensures that industrial networks remain resilient and adaptable. By cultivating trust and fostering cooperative partnerships, while encouraging healthy competition, industrial networks can thrive in an increasingly interconnected and rapidly changing global economy.

8.4 THE IMPACT OF DIGITAL TRANSFORMATION ON INDUSTRIAL NETWORKS

The digital transformation of industrial networks marks a profound shift in how industries operate, innovate, and collaborate. Driven by the advent of Industry 4.0 technologies, industrial networks have transitioned from traditional, linear models to dynamic, interconnected systems that thrive on data, automation, and real-time insights. This transformation is characterized by the integration of advanced technologies such as the IoT, AI, cloud computing, and big data, which have redefined operational efficiency, decision-making, and value creation. Furthermore, innovations like smart manufacturing, cyber-physical systems, and digital twins have enabled industries to optimize processes and predict future trends with remarkable accuracy. The move from centralized to decentralized, data-driven networks has further democratized industrial operations, fostering transparency and resilience through technologies like blockchain (Jwo et al., 2022). These advancements are best understood through case studies in sectors such as aerospace and consumer goods, where digital transformation has revolutionized traditional practices. This section delves into each aspect of digital transformation, exploring its role in reshaping industrial networks and driving innovation (Burrus, 2024).

8.4.1 Role of Industry 4.0 Technologies in Reshaping Industrial Networks

Industry 4.0 technologies are at the heart of the digital transformation reshaping industrial networks. The IoT connects devices and systems across the network, enabling seamless communication and data exchange. IoT sensors embedded in equipment, vehicles, and infrastructure provide real-time updates on performance, enabling predictive maintenance and reducing downtime. For example, manufacturing plants equipped with IoT sensors can automatically adjust production schedules based on real-time demand or equipment conditions, ensuring optimal efficiency.

AI further enhances industrial networks by processing vast amounts of data to uncover patterns, predict outcomes, and optimize operations. AI-driven machine learning models improve demand forecasting, enhance supply chain efficiency, and enable rapid decision-making. In logistics, AI algorithms optimize delivery routes in real time, reducing fuel consumption and delivery times, while in production, AI enhances quality control by identifying defects during manufacturing processes (McKinsey & Company, 2022).

Cloud computing is another cornerstone of Industry 4.0, providing scalable infrastructure for storing and processing large volumes of data. It facilitates

Table 8.2 *Comparison of traditional vs. Industry 4.0-driven industrial networks*

Aspect	Traditional Networks	Industry 4.0 Networks
Communication	Delayed and siloed	Real-time and integrated
Decision-Making	Centralized and reactive	Decentralized and proactive
Data Utilization	Minimal	Comprehensive and predictive
Efficiency	Moderate	High (due to automation and analytics)
Adaptability	Low	High

real-time collaboration among stakeholders, regardless of geographic location, ensuring that all participants in the network have access to up-to-date information. This interconnectedness allows for faster decision-making and greater adaptability to market changes (Epicor, 2024).

Big data analytics unlocks actionable insights from the vast quantities of data generated by IoT devices and other sources. Industries use big data to improve product designs, enhance customer experiences, and optimize resource allocation. For example, in the energy sector, big data analytics enables utilities to forecast energy demand and optimize grid operations, reducing waste and improving sustainability (Ricadela, 2023).

Together, these technologies create a seamless, interconnected ecosystem that prioritizes efficiency, adaptability, and innovation. By integrating Industry 4.0 tools, industrial networks can navigate the complexities of modern markets, remain competitive, and unlock new opportunities for growth.

8.4.2 Smart Manufacturing, Cyber-Physical Systems, and the Integration of Digital Twins

Smart manufacturing represents a paradigm shift in industrial operations, integrating digital technologies into traditional processes to create intelligent systems that improve productivity, reduce waste, and enhance flexibility. A key enabler of smart manufacturing is cyber-physical systems (CPS), which combine physical processes with digital intelligence. CPS allow machines, sensors, and software to communicate and collaborate in real time, enabling automated adjustments to production lines, resource allocation, and quality control (Tao et al., 2019). For example, in automotive manufacturing, CPS systems can detect inefficiencies in assembly lines and reallocate resources to address bottlenecks.

Digital twins, virtual replicas of physical assets or processes, have emerged as a game-changing innovation in industrial networks. Digital twins enable industries to simulate, monitor, and optimize operations without disrupting actual workflows (Hu et al., 2024). For instance, an aerospace company might use a digital twin of an aircraft engine to simulate performance under varying conditions, allowing engineers to identify potential issues and implement improvements before production. This not only reduces costs but also enhances safety and reliability.

Predictive maintenance, enabled by CPS and digital twins, uses data-driven insights to forecast equipment failures before they occur. By addressing potential issues proactively, industries can minimize unplanned downtime, reduce maintenance costs, and extend equipment lifespans. This approach is particularly valuable in sectors like energy and manufacturing, where operational disruptions can be costly and impactful (Lawrence, 2024).

Smart manufacturing, powered by CPS and digital twins, fosters a culture of continuous improvement, sustainability, and innovation. It equips industries with the tools to adapt to changing market demands, optimize resource usage, and maintain a competitive edge in a rapidly evolving global landscape.

8.4.3 The Move from Centralized to Decentralized, Data-Driven Networks

The digital transformation of industrial networks has driven a fundamental shift from centralized control to decentralized, data-driven ecosystems. Traditional networks relied on hierarchical decision-making structures, which limited flexibility and adaptability. In contrast, decentralized networks distribute decision-making authority across multiple nodes, enabling greater agility and resilience.

Blockchain technology has been instrumental in this transition. As a decentralized ledger, blockchain provides a secure and transparent platform for tracking transactions and managing supply chain data. This technology enhances traceability, reduces fraud, and increases accountability (Van Niekerk, 2024). For example, in the food industry, blockchain allows companies to trace products from farm to table, ensuring compliance with safety regulations and enabling rapid responses to recalls.

Edge computing complements blockchain by processing data closer to its source rather than relying on centralized servers. This reduces latency, improves response times, and supports time-sensitive applications like autonomous vehicles, industrial robotics, and smart grids (Siman et al., 2023). Decentralized networks powered by edge computing enable industries to make faster decisions and respond more effectively to local conditions.

The move to decentralized networks also promotes collaboration among stakeholders, fostering innovation and adaptability. By enabling real-time data sharing and transparent communication, these networks create an environment where participants can align their goals, share resources, and innovate collectively. This transition aligns with the principles of Industry 4.0, prioritizing efficiency, transparency, and resilience in global industrial operations.

8.4.4 Case Studies Illustrating Digital Transformation in Key Sectors

The transformative impact of digital technologies on industrial networks is most evident in the aerospace and consumer goods sectors, where companies have leveraged advanced tools to enhance efficiency, resilience, and innovation. By adopting technologies such as digital twins, the IoT, AI, and big data analytics, these industries have not only optimized operations but also redefined customer experiences and product lifecycles.

In the aerospace sector, companies like Boeing and Airbus are at the forefront of digital transformation, utilizing digital twins to revolutionize product development and maintenance. A digital twin is a virtual model of a physical asset, enabling engineers to simulate and analyze performance under various conditions. For instance, before manufacturing an aircraft engine, a digital twin can predict its behavior during different stress levels, temperatures, and altitudes. This allows engineers to detect potential weaknesses and make necessary adjustments, reducing production errors and enhancing safety (Applied CAx, 2023). Furthermore, IoT sensors embedded in aircraft continuously monitor performance during operation, providing real-time data on components such as engines and landing gear. This data enables predictive maintenance, where issues are identified and addressed before they escalate, minimizing

Table 8.3 Benefits of decentralized vs. centralized networks

Criteria	Centralized Networks	Decentralized Networks
Decision-Making	Hierarchical	Distributed
Flexibility	Limited	High
Resilience	Vulnerable to disruptions	Adaptive to disruptions
Technology Utilization	Low	High (Blockchain, Edge Computing)
Collaboration	Restricted	Enhanced (real-time sharing)

Table 8.4 Applications of digital technologies in key sectors

Sector	Technology Used	Impact
Aerospace	Digital Twins, IoT, Big Data	Predictive maintenance, enhanced safety
Consumer Goods	AI, IoT, Big Data, Smart Shelves	Inventory optimization, personalized experience
Consumer Goods	Big Data, IoT, Predictive Analytics	Demand forecasting, reduced waste
Logistics	AI, Blockchain, IoT	Real-time tracking, fraud prevention

downtime and operational costs. The integration of these technologies not only improves efficiency but also ensures that safety and reliability remain paramount in this highly regulated industry.

In the consumer goods sector, companies such as Procter & Gamble have adopted a range of digital tools to streamline their supply chains and enhance customer engagement. By leveraging AI and big data analytics, they can forecast demand with high precision, ensuring that production aligns closely with consumer needs. For example, predictive analytics allows these companies to identify trends in consumer behavior, adjust inventory levels, and optimize distribution networks. This reduces overproduction, minimizes waste, and improves cost efficiency. Additionally, IoT-enabled smart shelves in retail stores provide real-time inventory updates, enabling retailers to restock products efficiently. This technology ensures that consumers have access to the products they need without delays, enhancing the overall shopping experience (DigitalDefynd, 2025).

Beyond operational efficiency, digital transformation in the consumer goods sector fosters greater personalization and responsiveness. By analyzing customer data collected through the IoT and AI systems, companies can create tailored marketing campaigns, product recommendations, and dynamic pricing strategies. This not only boosts customer satisfaction but also strengthens brand loyalty in a competitive marketplace.

These case studies illustrate how digital transformation has enabled industries to transition from reactive to proactive approaches in managing their networks. In aerospace, the focus on real-time data and predictive maintenance enhances safety and efficiency, while in consumer goods, advanced analytics and IoT-driven solutions optimize supply chains and customer experiences. Both sectors exemplify the power of collaboration and innovation in leveraging digital technologies to address contemporary challenges and seize emerging opportunities.

By embracing digital transformation, industries can position themselves for sustained growth and competitiveness in an increasingly interconnected global economy. The lessons from aerospace and consumer goods underscore the importance of adopting advanced technologies, fostering collaboration, and continuously innovating to thrive in a dynamic industrial landscape.

8.5 INNOVATION IN INDUSTRIAL CHAINS: TRENDS AND CHALLENGES

Innovation in industrial chains has undergone significant transformation, influenced by technological advancements, evolving market demands, and the growing need for sustainability. Traditional product-centric models, which focus on maximizing production efficiency, are giving way to service-oriented approaches that prioritize customer value and long-term relationships (Nie et al., 2024). Concurrently, the rise of platform-based business models and innovation ecosystems has revolutionized the way industrial chains operate, fostering collaboration and co-creation. However, as industrial networks evolve, maintaining flexibility, adaptability, and resilience has become increasingly challenging, particularly in the face of global disruptions. To better understand these trends and challenges, examining sectoral innovations in industries such as renewable energy and pharmaceuticals provides valuable insights into how businesses are adapting and thriving (Motyka et al., 2024). This unit explores these transformative shifts and their implications for the future of industrial chains.

8.5.1 Shifts from Traditional Product-Centric Models to Service-Oriented Models (Servitization)

The shift from traditional product-centric models to service-oriented models, known as servitization, represents a major transformation in industrial chains. In traditional models, the primary focus was on manufacturing and delivering physical goods. Companies aimed to optimize production processes, reduce costs, and maximize efficiency. While effective in stable markets, these models often failed to address evolving customer needs for personalized solutions and value-added services (Minaya et al., 2024).

Servitization has redefined the value proposition of industrial chains by integrating services into traditional product offerings. Instead of merely selling products, companies now focus on delivering comprehensive solutions that include maintenance, consulting, and performance monitoring. This shift not only enhances customer satisfaction but also creates long-term revenue streams. For example, in the manufacturing sector, companies like Rolls-Royce have implemented a service-oriented model through their "Power by the Hour" program, where customers pay for engine uptime rather than purchasing the engine outright. This model incentivizes both parties to prioritize efficiency and reliability (Smith, 2013).

The adoption of servitization is driven by advancements in digital technologies such as the IoT and big data analytics. These technologies enable real-time monitoring of products and predictive maintenance, ensuring consistent performance and reducing downtime. Additionally, servitization aligns with the broader trend of sustainability by encouraging resource optimization and extending product lifecycles (Tronvoll et al., 2020).

While servitization offers numerous benefits, it also presents challenges. Transitioning to a service-oriented model requires significant changes in organizational structure, skillsets, and business strategies. Companies must invest in digital infrastructure, build customer-centric capabilities, and adapt to new revenue models. Despite these hurdles, the shift toward servitization is transforming industrial chains, creating opportunities for innovation, customer engagement, and long-term growth.

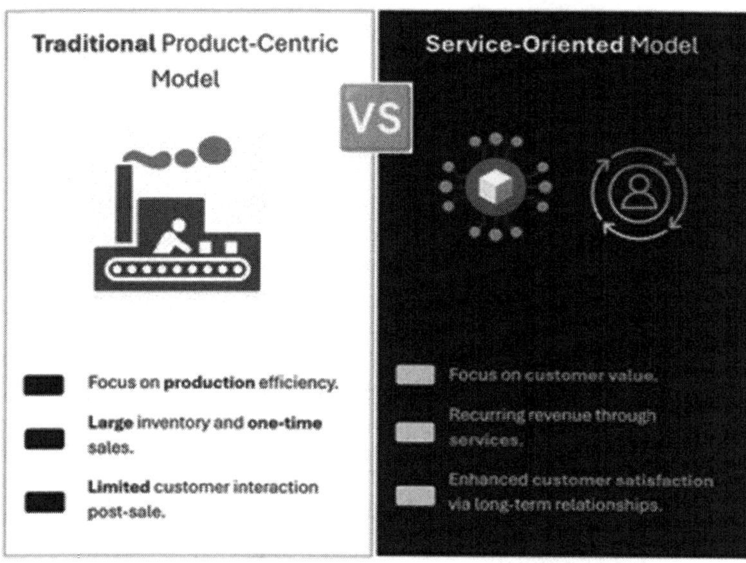

Source: Author's own illustration.

Figure 8.3 *Shifts from product-centric to service-oriented models—servitization*

8.5.2 Emergence of Platform-Based Business Models and Innovation Ecosystems

Platform-based business models and innovation ecosystems have emerged as transformative trends in industrial chains, enabling new forms of collaboration, value creation, and efficiency. Unlike traditional linear supply chains, platform-based models operate as interconnected networks that facilitate interactions among multiple stakeholders, including suppliers, manufacturers, customers, and technology providers (Minz et al., 2024).

Platforms serve as centralized hubs where participants can exchange goods, services, and information. For instance, in the logistics industry, platforms like Alibaba's Cainiao network integrate data from various stakeholders to optimize supply chain operations and enhance delivery efficiency (TLI, 2024). Similarly, in manufacturing, platforms like GE's Predix enable companies to monitor equipment performance, predict maintenance needs, and improve operational efficiency.

Innovation ecosystems, closely tied to platform-based models, bring together diverse actors to co-create solutions and drive technological advancements. These ecosystems thrive on collaboration and knowledge sharing, fostering innovation at an accelerated pace. For example, in the automotive industry, Tesla's ecosystem includes partnerships with suppliers, technology firms, and energy providers, enabling the rapid development of electric vehicles and energy storage solutions (Lähteenmäki & Töyli, 2023).

Digital technologies such as the IoT, AI, and blockchain underpin the success of platform-based models and ecosystems. These technologies provide the infrastructure for real-time communication, data sharing, and transaction transparency, ensuring seamless interactions among participants.

Table 8.5 Comparison of product-centric and service-oriented models

Aspect	Product-Centric Model	Service-Oriented Model (Servitization)
Focus	Manufacturing physical goods	Delivering value-added services
Revenue	One-time product sales	Recurring revenue from services
Customer Interaction	Minimal post-sale	Long-term relationships
Technology Use	Limited	High (IoT, AI, predictive maintenance)
Sustainability	Low	High (resource optimization, lifecycle extension)

While platform-based models offer numerous advantages, they also pose challenges. Coordinating a diverse range of stakeholders requires robust governance structures and trust-building mechanisms. Additionally, issues such as data privacy, cybersecurity, and intellectual property rights need to be addressed to ensure sustainable growth. Despite these challenges, platform-based business models and innovation ecosystems are reshaping industrial chains, unlocking new opportunities for collaboration and growth (Mbanefo & Grobbelaar, 2024).

8.5.3 Challenges of Maintaining Flexibility, Adaptability, and Resilience in Industrial Networks

The increasing complexity of industrial networks, driven by globalization and digital transformation, has amplified the need for flexibility, adaptability, and resilience. These qualities are essential for managing uncertainties, responding to disruptions, and capitalizing on emerging opportunities in dynamic markets.

Flexibility allows industrial networks to adapt quickly to changing conditions, such as fluctuating demand, supply chain disruptions, or regulatory shifts (Fragapane et al., n.d.). For example, during the COVID-19 pandemic, industries that demonstrated flexibility—such as manufacturers pivoting to produce medical equipment—were better equipped to navigate the crisis.

Adaptability, closely linked to flexibility, involves the ability to evolve in response to long-term changes (Szemzo et al., 2022). This requires leveraging digital tools like AI and big data analytics to anticipate market trends and adjust strategies accordingly. For instance, in the retail sector, companies like Amazon use predictive analytics to optimize inventory

Table 8.6 Benefits and challenges of platform-based models

Aspect	Benefits	Challenges
Collaboration	Enhances co-creation and innovation	Requires robust governance mechanisms
Efficiency	Optimizes resource utilization	Coordination among diverse stakeholders
Transparency	Improves data sharing and trust	Data privacy and cybersecurity concerns
Scalability	Enables rapid scaling	High initial investment

and personalize customer experiences, enhancing their adaptability in a competitive landscape.

Resilience focuses on the capacity of industrial networks to withstand and recover from disruptions. Building resilience involves diversifying supply chains, fostering strong relationships with suppliers, and investing in technologies that enhance transparency and traceability (Carayannis et al., 2024). Blockchain technology, for example, enables real-time tracking of goods, reducing vulnerabilities and improving supply chain visibility.

Despite their importance, achieving flexibility, adaptability, and resilience poses challenges. Organizations must balance cost efficiency with the need for agility, invest in digital infrastructure, and cultivate a culture of innovation and collaboration. Addressing these challenges is critical for ensuring the long-term success and sustainability of industrial networks in an unpredictable global environment.

8.5.4 Sectoral Examples of Industrial Chain Innovation: Renewable Energy and Pharmaceuticals

The renewable energy and pharmaceutical sectors exemplify the transformative impact of industrial chain innovation, driven by advanced technologies, collaboration, and a focus on addressing global challenges. These industries have redefined traditional supply chains, creating ecosystems that enhance efficiency, sustainability, and resilience.

In the renewable energy sector, the transition from centralized energy systems to decentralized models and smart grids marks a fundamental shift in how energy is produced, stored, and distributed. Companies like Siemens and Tesla are at the forefront of this transformation, developing integrated solutions that optimize energy usage and reduce reliance on fossil fuels. Tesla, for example, has created a seamless ecosystem by combining solar panels, Powerwall batteries, and electric vehicles (Maradin et al., 2022). These components work together to generate, store, and consume renewable energy efficiently, allowing households and businesses to achieve energy independence while contributing to a greener future.

Smart grids, another critical innovation, leverage IoT and AI technologies to monitor and manage energy flows in real-time. These grids enable utilities to balance supply and demand more effectively, integrate renewable energy sources, and enhance grid resilience against disruptions (Ohanu et al., 2024). This level of innovation requires collaboration across industrial chains, including technology providers, policymakers, and energy regulators, to establish the necessary infrastructure and regulatory frameworks for widespread adoption.

In the pharmaceutical sector, the COVID-19 pandemic underscored the importance of agile and resilient supply chains to meet urgent global health needs. Companies like Pfizer and Moderna demonstrated the power of industrial chain innovation in their rapid development, production, and distribution of COVID-19 vaccines (Agampodi et al., 2024). These firms used AI to accelerate drug discovery processes and optimize vaccine formulation. IoT technologies enabled real-time monitoring of production facilities to ensure quality control and compliance. Furthermore, blockchain solutions were deployed to maintain transparency and traceability in vaccine distribution, reducing risks such as counterfeiting and ensuring that vaccines reached their intended destinations safely and efficiently.

The collaboration within the pharmaceutical industry extended across the entire value chain, involving research institutions for clinical trials, regulatory bodies for expedited approvals, and logistics providers for distribution. For example, cold chain logistics, powered by IoT sensors, ensured that vaccines remained within the required temperature range during transportation, preserving their efficacy.

8.5.5 Key Insights and Lessons Learned

These sectoral examples highlight common themes in industrial chain innovation. Both renewable energy and pharmaceuticals emphasize the integration of advanced digital technologies, such as the IoT, AI, and blockchain, to enhance efficiency, transparency, and collaboration. Additionally, they demonstrate the importance of partnerships and multi-stakeholder cooperation in overcoming complex challenges and achieving shared objectives.

The renewable energy sector showcases how innovation can drive sustainability, addressing global challenges like climate change by transitioning to cleaner energy systems. Meanwhile, the pharmaceutical sector exemplifies the potential of agile, technology-enabled supply chains to respond to urgent global crises and deliver life-saving solutions at scale.

Table 8.7 Technologies transforming renewable energy and pharmaceuticals

Sector	Key Technologies	Impact
Renewable Energy	IoT, AI, Smart Grids	Optimized energy use, increased resilience
Pharmaceuticals	AI, IoT, Blockchain	Accelerated development, supply chain transparency

8.6 NETWORK INNOVATION STRATEGIES AND BEST PRACTICES

Industrial networks thrive on innovation, and fostering this innovation requires a strategic approach that leverages collaboration, shared resources, and dynamic relationships. In an increasingly interconnected and competitive global economy, organizations within industrial networks must adopt strategies that encourage collective problem-solving, knowledge sharing, and the co-creation of value (Maurer & Valkenburg, 2013). Approaches such as open innovation, co-creation and collaboration with partners, and the establishment of innovation hubs and clusters have proven effective in driving creativity and resilience in industrial networks. Alongside these strategies, adopting the best practices for managing relationships, facilitating knowledge exchange, and fostering successful joint ventures is critical for sustaining long-term innovation. This unit explores these strategies and best practices, providing insights into how organizations can build robust and forward-thinking networks.

8.6.1 Open Innovation

Open innovation is a strategy that transcends organizational boundaries, encouraging the exchange of ideas, technologies, and resources between companies and external entities. This approach challenges the traditional notion of self-contained innovation by acknowledging that external contributions can significantly enhance an organization's capacity to innovate (Bertello et al., 2024). Open innovation involves two primary pathways: inbound, where organizations incorporate external ideas, and outbound, where internal innovations are shared or licensed to external partners.

One of the most prominent examples of open innovation is Procter & Gamble's Connect + Develop initiative, which invites external partners, including universities, startups, and individual inventors, to collaborate on projects (Huston & Sakkab, 2006). This model has enabled P&G to accelerate product development cycles, reduce research and development (R&D) costs, and commercialize innovations more effectively. For instance, the successful development of Swiffer products was partly driven by insights gained through external collaborations.

Implementing open innovation requires creating mechanisms to connect with external partners, such as innovation contests, crowdsourcing platforms, and joint research projects. Organizations must also establish clear frameworks for managing intellectual property (IP) and ensuring equitable sharing of benefits among collaborators. This fosters trust and incentivizes participation. A prime example is the pharmaceutical industry, where collaborations between

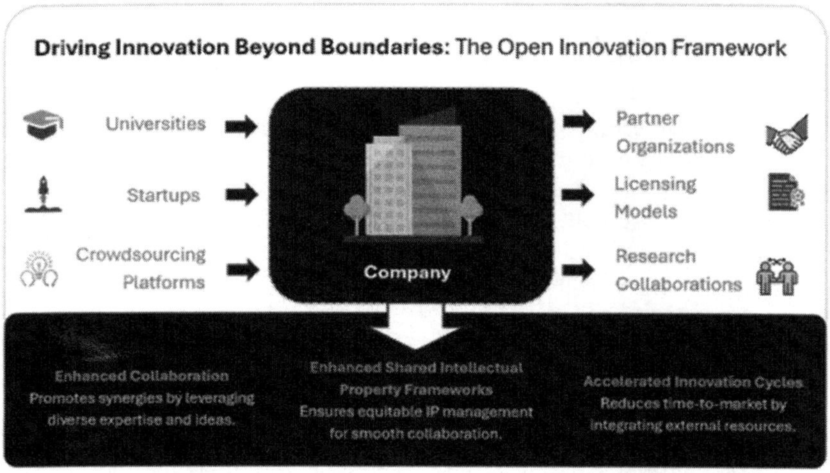

Source: Author's own illustration.

Figure 8.4 Driving innovation beyond boundaries: the open innovation framework

large firms and biotech startups have resulted in groundbreaking treatments by leveraging shared expertise and resources.

While open innovation offers significant benefits, it also presents challenges, including potential IP disputes and integration difficulties. To address these issues, organizations must adopt robust governance structures, define clear partnership agreements, and cultivate a culture that values external contributions. By embracing open innovation, industrial networks can expand their horizons, improve adaptability, and sustain long-term competitiveness (Sánchez-Obando et al., 2024).

8.6.2 Co-Creation and Collaboration with Partners

Co-creation and collaboration involve active participation between network members to design, develop, and implement solutions. This approach leverages the unique expertise, capabilities, and perspectives of different stakeholders, leading to innovative outcomes that no single entity could achieve independently (Klen, 2009). Unlike traditional partnerships, co-creation fosters a sense of shared ownership and responsibility, aligning participants toward common goals.

Table 8.8 Benefits and challenges of open innovation

Aspect	Benefits	Challenges
Innovation Speed	Faster development cycles	Managing IP ownership
Resource Utilization	Access to diverse resources and expertise	Difficulty in integration
Collaboration Potential	Broad partnerships with varied stakeholders	Trust and governance concerns

A notable example is the partnership between Ford and Google, where Ford contributed automotive expertise, and Google brought cutting-edge AI and data analytics (Stach, 2021). This collaboration resulted in innovative connected vehicle technologies, enhancing both vehicle performance and customer experience. Such partnerships exemplify the power of diverse expertise converging to drive innovation.

Effective co-creation requires a foundation of trust, transparency, and shared objectives. Digital collaboration tools, such as Slack, Microsoft Teams, and project management platforms, facilitate real-time communication and coordination among geographically dispersed teams. Regular workshops, brainstorming sessions, and joint strategy meetings further enhance the alignment of goals and foster creativity.

However, co-creation comes with challenges, including managing potential conflicts of interest and bridging cultural differences between organizations. Clear communication, conflict resolution mechanisms, and well-defined partnership agreements are essential to mitigate these risks. Additionally, leadership plays a critical role in aligning stakeholders and ensuring that all parties remain committed to the shared vision (Takahashi & Takahashi, 2022).

By fostering co-creation, industrial networks can unlock synergies, drive innovation, and strengthen relationships, creating an ecosystem that is more adaptable and resilient to market changes

8.6.3 Innovation Hubs and Clusters

Innovation hubs and clusters are concentrated ecosystems where businesses, research institutions, government entities, and startups converge to foster innovation and drive economic growth (Chowdhury et al., 2022). These ecosystems thrive on collaboration, resource sharing, and the exchange of knowledge, creating a fertile ground for experimentation and technological advancement.

Table 8.9 Keys to successful co-creation and collaboration

Key Factor	Description	Example
Trust	Builds strong, reliable relationships	Ford–Google partnership
Clear Objectives	Aligns stakeholders toward shared goals	Tesla's supplier partnerships
Conflict Management	Resolves disputes and maintains progress	Cross-cultural collaboration frameworks
Digital Tools	Enables seamless communication and resource sharing	Slack, Microsoft Teams, collaborative apps

One of the most renowned examples of an innovation cluster is Silicon Valley. This region has become a global epicenter for technological innovation due to its dense concentration of tech companies, venture capital firms, and top-tier research institutions. The success of Silicon Valley lies in its ability to attract top talent, provide ample funding opportunities, and foster a culture of risk-taking and entrepreneurship.

Innovation hubs, such as Berlin's Factory and London's Tech City, provide physical and digital spaces for startups and established companies to collaborate. These hubs offer access to shared resources like research labs, coworking spaces, and funding opportunities, lowering barriers for smaller organizations to innovate. Governments often play a significant role in supporting these hubs by providing grants, tax incentives, and supportive policies (Katz & Wagner, 2014).

Clusters, such as Denmark's renewable energy cluster, demonstrate how geographic proximity and shared industry focus can drive sector-specific advancements. In Denmark, wind turbine manufacturers, policymakers, and research institutions work closely to advance renewable energy solutions, making the country a global leader in this field.

Establishing successful hubs and clusters requires strategic investments in infrastructure, education, and supportive policies. Governments and private investors must create an environment that encourages collaboration, risk-taking, and knowledge sharing (Rangen, 2021). By fostering these ecosystems, industrial networks can remain at the forefront of innovation and respond effectively to emerging challenges.

Table 8.10 Comparison of innovation hubs and clusters

Aspect	Innovation Hubs	Innovation Clusters
Focus	Collaborative spaces for startups and SMEs	Sector-specific geographic concentrations
Support	Access to funding, labs, and mentorship	Government policies and industry support
Examples	Berlin's Factory, London's Tech City	Denmark's renewable energy cluster

8.6.4 Best Practices for Managing Network Relationships, Knowledge Sharing, and Joint Ventures

Managing relationships, facilitating knowledge sharing, and executing joint ventures are critical components of industrial network success. Strong relationships built on trust, transparency, and mutual benefit ensure seamless collaboration and long-term stability. Open and frequent communication, combined with a shared commitment to goals, is essential for maintaining these relationships.

Knowledge sharing is another cornerstone of network innovation. Effective mechanisms for sharing insights, best practices, and technological advancements enable all participants to benefit from the collective expertise within the network (Wulf & Butel, 2017). Tools like cloud-based knowledge management systems, data-sharing platforms, and innovation databases ensure that valuable information is accessible to all stakeholders. For instance, in the pharmaceutical industry, initiatives like open-access research platforms have accelerated drug development by pooling data from multiple sources.

Joint ventures, which involve collaborative efforts between organizations to achieve shared objectives, require meticulous planning and execution (Aschenbroich & Dintelman, 2023). Successful joint ventures begin with clearly defined roles, responsibilities, and resource allocation. For example, the Boeing–Tata Advanced Systems joint venture combines aerospace manufacturing expertise and advanced engineering capabilities, resulting in innovative solutions for the global aerospace industry.

To ensure success, best practices for joint ventures include conducting regular performance evaluations, establishing mechanisms for conflict resolution, and maintaining flexibility to adapt to changing circumstances. Cultivating a culture of innovation and collaboration across the network further enhances the likelihood of success.

Table 8.11 Components of a thriving industrial network

Aspect	Key Components	Examples
Relationships	Trust, transparency, and mutual goals	Boeing–Tata Advanced Systems
Knowledge Sharing	Cloud-based tools, data-sharing platforms	Open-access pharmaceutical research
Joint Ventures	Shared resources and responsibilities	Joint manufacturing initiatives

By adopting these best practices, industrial networks can optimize relationships, facilitate knowledge sharing, and execute joint ventures effectively, creating an environment where innovation thrives, and participants achieve mutual success.

8.7 INDUSTRIAL CHAINS IN A GLOBALIZED ECONOMY: RISKS AND OPPORTUNITIES

The globalization of industrial chains has transformed the way businesses operate, enabling access to new markets, cost efficiencies, and diverse talent pools. This interconnectedness has significantly increased the scale and complexity of supply chains, fostering innovation and growth (Finegan, 2019). However, it also exposes networks to heightened risks, including geopolitical shifts, trade wars, and supply chain disruptions such as those experienced during the COVID-19 pandemic and semiconductor shortages. Multinational corporations and cross-border collaborations play pivotal roles in shaping the global industrial landscape, driving both opportunities and challenges. To navigate this environment effectively, industrial networks must adopt strategies that mitigate risks while enhancing resilience. This unit explores the multi-faceted impact of globalization on industrial supply chains, the role of multinational corporations, the risks inherent in globalized operations, and strategies to strengthen network robustness.

8.7.1 Globalization and Its Effects on Industrial Supply Chains and Networks

Globalization has fundamentally reshaped industrial supply chains, breaking down traditional barriers and enabling firms to operate on a global scale. Companies now source raw materials, manufacture components, and assemble products across multiple countries, leveraging cost advantages and specialized expertise from different regions (Vargas-Hernández & Vargas-González, 2024). This interconnectedness has led to unprecedented efficiencies, innovation, and access to markets.

One key benefit of globalization is cost optimization. By outsourcing production to countries with lower labor and operational costs, companies can reduce expenses and allocate resources to other value-adding activities. For example, global apparel brands like Nike and H&M have established extensive supply chains that span continents, capitalizing on cost-effective manufacturing in Asia while focusing on branding and innovation in their home markets (DFreight, 2023).

Globalization has also fostered innovation by facilitating knowledge exchange and collaboration across borders. Companies can tap into global talent pools and benefit from technological advancements in various regions. In the automotive industry, collaboration between German engineering firms and Asian electronics manufacturers has driven the development of advanced electric vehicles.

However, globalization has also introduced challenges, such as increased supply chain complexity and dependency on international logistics. Disruptions in one part of the chain can have cascading effects, as seen during the COVID-19 pandemic when factory closures and transportation delays caused widespread shortages (Shih, 2020). While globalization has unlocked significant opportunities, it also necessitates robust strategies to manage its inherent risks.

8.7.2 The Role of Multinational Corporations and Cross-Border Collaborations

Multinational corporations (MNCs) are central to the globalization of industrial chains, acting as key facilitators of cross-border trade, investment, and

Table 8.12 *Pros and cons of globalization in industrial supply chains*

Aspect	Benefits	Challenges
Cost Efficiency	Lower manufacturing costs via outsourcing	Potential exploitation of labor markets
Market Access	Easier expansion into international markets	Compliance with complex foreign regulations
Innovation	Global knowledge-sharing drives innovation	Increased dependence on foreign suppliers
Supply Chain Complexity	Greater efficiency with distributed production	High risk of disruptions (e.g., pandemics)

collaboration. MNCs leverage their global presence to optimize production, access new markets, and drive innovation by coordinating activities across diverse regions (Svystunova et al., 2024). These corporations often serve as hubs within industrial networks, connecting suppliers, manufacturers, and distributors across continents.

One significant advantage of MNCs is their ability to create economies of scale by centralizing high-volume production and distributing goods efficiently. For example, Apple's global supply chain integrates manufacturing in Asia, R&D in the United States, and retail operations worldwide. This interconnected system allows Apple to maintain high-quality standards while benefiting from regional cost advantages.

Cross-border collaborations also play a crucial role in industrial innovation. Strategic partnerships between companies in different countries enable the sharing of resources, expertise, and technology. For instance, the aerospace collaboration between Boeing and Embraer combines American innovation with Brazilian manufacturing capabilities to produce cost-effective and advanced aircraft (Bickers & Alencar, 2018).

Despite their advantages, MNCs and cross-border collaborations face challenges such as cultural differences, regulatory complexities, and political risks. These factors can hinder effective coordination and lead to inefficiencies. Addressing these challenges requires robust governance structures, strong communication channels, and adaptive strategies.

By fostering collaborative networks and leveraging their global reach, MNCs and cross-border partnerships contribute to the resilience and adaptability of industrial chains in an increasingly interconnected world.

Table 8.13 Key multinational corporations and their global supply chains

Corporation	Headquarters	Manufacturing Locations	Key Global Strategy
Apple	USA	China, India, Vietnam	Centralized R&D, decentralized production
Tesla	USA	USA, Germany, China	Localized manufacturing for regional markets
Nike	USA	China, Vietnam, Indonesia	Low-cost manufacturing with strong branding

8.7.3 Risks Posed by Geopolitical Shifts, Trade Wars, and Global Supply Chain Disruptions

Globalization has increased the exposure of industrial chains to external risks, including geopolitical shifts, trade wars, and supply chain disruptions. These risks can significantly impact the stability and efficiency of global operations, posing challenges for businesses reliant on international networks (Rasshyvalov et al., 2024).

Geopolitical shifts, such as changes in government policies or political instability, can disrupt trade flows and industrial operations (GVR, 2024). For instance, Brexit created uncertainty for businesses operating between the UK and the European Union, necessitating adjustments in supply chains to account for new trade regulations. Similarly, escalating tensions between the US and China have led to trade wars, resulting in tariffs, regulatory barriers, and increased costs for companies reliant on goods from these regions.

Supply chain disruptions, as exemplified by the COVID-19 pandemic, highlight the vulnerabilities of globalized networks. Factory shutdowns, transportation delays, and workforce shortages caused severe shortages in critical industries, such as healthcare and technology. The semiconductor shortage, driven by increased demand and supply constraints, further underscores the fragility of industrial chains reliant on specialized components (Kaya, 2024).

These risks emphasize the importance of building resilient and adaptable industrial networks. Companies must assess vulnerabilities within their supply chains and develop strategies to mitigate potential disruptions, ensuring continuity and stability in the face of unforeseen challenges.

8.7.4 Strategies for Mitigating Risks and Enhancing Resilience in Industrial Networks

To address the risks associated with globalization, industrial networks must adopt strategies that enhance resilience and adaptability. These strategies include diversifying supply chains, investing in technology, and fostering strong relationships with partners.

Diversification is a critical approach to mitigating risks. By sourcing from multiple suppliers and regions, companies can reduce dependency on any single entity and ensure continuity in case of disruptions (Wang et al., 2021). For example, automotive manufacturers have diversified their semiconductor suppliers to avoid bottlenecks caused by regional shortages.

Investing in digital technologies such as blockchain, the IoT, and AI can also strengthen supply chain resilience (Kumar et al., 2023). Blockchain provides transparency and traceability, enabling real-time tracking of goods and mitigating risks of counterfeiting or delays. IoT sensors and AI-powered

Source: Author's own illustration.

Figure 8.5 *Risks posed by geopolitical shifts, trade wars, and supply chain disruptions*

analytics allow companies to monitor operations, predict disruptions, and respond proactively.

Building strong relationships with suppliers and partners enhances trust and collaboration, fostering a shared commitment to managing risks (Ankura,

Table 8.14 Strategies for strengthening global supply chains

Strategy	Implementation Method	Benefit
Diversification	Sourcing from multiple suppliers and regions	Reduces reliance on a single country
Technology Adoption	Using AI, blockchain, and the IoT	Improves real-time monitoring and risk mitigation
Stronger Partnerships	Establishing long-term contracts with suppliers	Enhances trust and supply chain stability
Supply Chain Flexibility	Creating adaptable production models	Enables rapid adjustments during disruptions

2024). Companies can establish contingency plans and conduct joint risk assessments to prepare for potential disruptions. For instance, during the COVID-19 pandemic, companies with robust partnerships were better positioned to navigate supply chain challenges.

Finally, fostering a culture of flexibility and innovation is essential. By prioritizing adaptability, companies can quickly pivot in response to changing circumstances, ensuring their industrial networks remain robust in a dynamic global environment.

These strategies underscore the importance of proactive risk management and collaborative efforts in navigating the complexities of globalization. By implementing these measures, industrial networks can capitalize on the opportunities globalization offers while safeguarding against its inherent risks.

8.8 SUSTAINABILITY AND CIRCULAR ECONOMY IN INDUSTRIAL NETWORKS

Sustainability has become a cornerstone of innovation in industrial networks as businesses face increasing pressure to address environmental challenges while maintaining economic competitiveness. The shift toward sustainable practices is driven by regulatory requirements, consumer expectations, and the urgent need to mitigate the environmental impact of industrial activities. Central to this transformation is the adoption of circular economy principles, which emphasize reducing waste, reusing resources, and recycling materials to create closed-loop systems. These principles are further supported by green supply chains that integrate environmentally friendly practices across all stages of production and distribution (ITCC, 2024). Industries worldwide are adopting these approaches, with sectors such as electric vehicles and sustainable agriculture leading the way in implementing innovative, sustainable solutions (Hubbart, 2023). This unit explores the importance of sustainability in industrial chains, the role of circular economy principles, the development of green supply chains, and real-world examples of industries embracing sustainable practices.

8.8.1 The Growing Importance of Sustainability in Industrial Chain Innovation

Sustainability is no longer an optional consideration but a strategic imperative for industrial networks. As global concerns about climate change, resource depletion, and pollution intensify, businesses are under mounting pressure to adopt practices that minimize their environmental footprint while enhancing operational efficiency and competitiveness. This shift reflects a growing recognition that sustainable practices are not only ethically necessary but also economically advantageous.

Industrial chain innovation now prioritizes the integration of sustainable technologies and practices. For instance, advancements in energy-efficient manufacturing processes, renewable energy adoption, and sustainable material sourcing have enabled industries to reduce their carbon emissions significantly. In sectors such as construction, the development of sustainable building materials, such as low-carbon concrete and recycled steel, exemplifies how innovation can align with environmental goals (Allgood, 2025).

Sustainability also drives cost efficiencies by reducing waste and optimizing resource utilization. For example, companies adopting lean manufacturing techniques often find that minimizing waste leads to both environmental and financial benefits (Rotondo & Chow, 2025). Furthermore, sustainable practices can enhance brand reputation, attracting environmentally conscious consumers and investors who prioritize corporate social responsibility (CSR).

Table 8.15 Benefits and challenges of sustainability in industrial networks

Aspect	Benefits	Challenges
Environmental Impact	Reduces carbon footprint	High initial cost of green technologies
Regulatory Compliance	Meets government and industry standards	Constantly evolving policies and requirements
Economic Efficiency	Minimizes waste, reduces energy consumption	Transitioning from traditional supply chains
Consumer Appeal	Increases demand for sustainable products	Requires consumer education and awareness

The transition to sustainability, however, poses challenges, including the upfront costs of adopting green technologies and the need to reconfigure traditional industrial networks. Despite these hurdles, the long-term benefits of sustainability—enhanced resilience, market differentiation, and regulatory compliance—make it a crucial focus for innovation in industrial chains.

8.8.2 Circular Economy Principles: Reducing Waste, Reusing Resources, and Recycling

The circular economy represents a transformative approach to industrial chain innovation, emphasizing the need to shift from a linear "take-make-dispose" model to a regenerative system where resources are continuously reused. Circular economy principles aim to minimize waste, extend product lifecycles, and create value from materials that would otherwise be discarded (Edirisinghe et al., 2024).

Reducing waste is a foundational element of the circular economy. Companies are increasingly designing products with end-of-life considerations, ensuring that materials can be recovered and repurposed. For example, in the electronics industry, manufacturers like Dell and HP have introduced modular designs that make it easier to repair, upgrade, and recycle devices, reducing electronic waste.

Reusing resources involves repurposing materials and components to extend their usefulness. The fashion industry, traditionally known for its high environmental impact, has begun to adopt circular practices by promoting second-hand markets and creating products from recycled textiles. This shift not only reduces waste but also appeals to environmentally conscious consumers.

Recycling is another critical component, enabling materials to re-enter the production cycle rather than ending up in landfills. Advanced recycling technologies, such as chemical recycling for plastics, have significantly improved the quality and range of materials that can be recycled. Industries like automotive manufacturing are leading the way, with companies like BMW and Tesla incorporating recycled materials into their vehicles, reducing reliance on virgin resources.

Circular economy principles not only reduce environmental impact but also create economic opportunities by turning waste into valuable inputs. By adopting these principles, industrial networks can contribute to a more sustainable and resource-efficient future (Torres Curado et al., 2024).

Table 8.16 Examples of circular economy adoption in different industries

Industry	Circular Economy Practice	Impact
Automotive	Battery recycling & remanufacturing	Reduces need for new raw materials
Electronics	Modular device designs for easy repair	Extends product lifespan
Fashion	Use of recycled textiles & second-hand markets	Reduces textile waste
Construction	Recycled steel and low-carbon concrete	Cuts emissions in infrastructure projects

8.8.3 Green Supply Chains and Their Role in Promoting Environmentally Friendly Industrial Practices

Green supply chains integrate sustainability into every stage of the production and distribution process, ensuring that environmental considerations are prioritized alongside traditional business objectives. This approach involves sourcing eco-friendly materials, optimizing energy use, minimizing emissions, and managing waste effectively (Komal & Khandare, 2024).

One example of green supply chain practices is the adoption of renewable energy sources in manufacturing facilities. Companies like IKEA have committed to powering their operations entirely with renewable energy, reducing their carbon footprint and setting an example for the industry. Similarly, logistics firms are transitioning to electric and hybrid delivery vehicles, contributing to cleaner transportation networks.

Sustainable sourcing is another critical aspect of green supply chains. Industries are increasingly adopting practices that prioritize ethical and environmentally responsible suppliers. For instance, the food industry has embraced certifications such as Fair Trade and Rainforest Alliance to ensure sustainable agricultural practices and fair treatment of workers.

Green supply chains also benefit from digital technologies, such as blockchain, which enhances transparency and traceability. By using blockchain, companies can track the origins of raw materials, ensuring they meet sustainability standards and avoiding unethical practices like deforestation or exploitation (Henry et al., 2023).

Implementing green supply chains presents challenges, including higher initial costs and the need for collaboration among diverse stakeholders. However, the long-term benefits—reduced environmental impact, improved efficiency, and enhanced brand reputation—make it a crucial strategy for achieving sustainability in industrial networks.

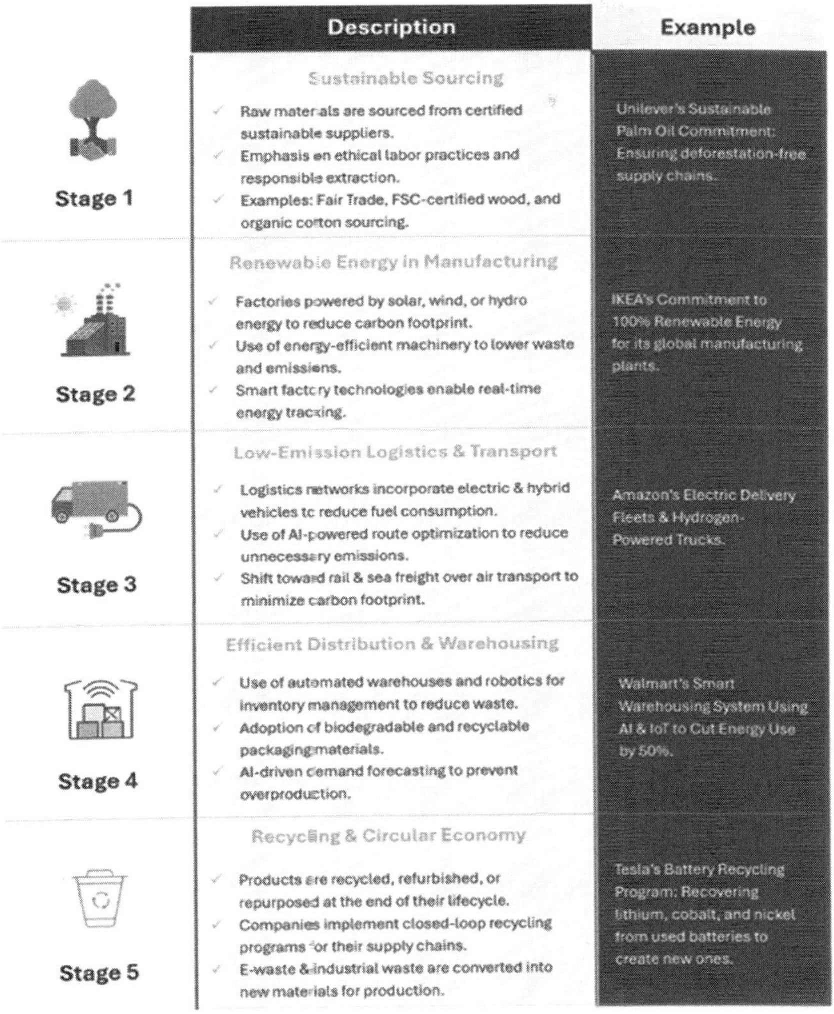

Source: Author's own illustration.

Figure 8.6 *Stages of green supply chains in industrial networks*

Table 8.17 Digital technologies enabling green supply chains

Technology	Application in Green Supply Chains	Example
Blockchain	Enhancing supply chain transparency	Tracking ethical sourcing of raw materials
AI & Big Data	Predicting supply-demand for efficient inventory	Reducing overproduction in fashion
IoT Sensors	Real-time energy and waste tracking	Monitoring emissions in logistics
Automation	Optimizing warehouse operations	Reducing packaging waste

8.8.4 Case Studies on How Industries Are Adopting Sustainable Practices

The adoption of sustainable practices within industrial networks highlights how innovation and strategic rethinking can reduce environmental impacts while enhancing efficiency and productivity. Two prominent examples—the electric vehicle (EV) supply chain and sustainable agriculture—demonstrate how businesses are leveraging advanced technologies, circular economy principles, and resource optimization to promote sustainability.

In the EV sector, companies like Tesla and Rivian exemplify how industrial chains can integrate sustainability at every stage of their operations. Tesla's vertically integrated supply chain is a cornerstone of its sustainability efforts (Oluwafunmilayo & Talabi, 2024). By controlling critical stages of production, Tesla ensures environmentally responsible practices, such as sourcing raw materials for batteries from suppliers adhering to strict environmental and ethical standards. Moreover, Tesla actively recycles components from end-of-life vehicles, recovering valuable materials like lithium, nickel, and cobalt to reduce reliance on virgin resources and minimize waste.

Additionally, Tesla invests heavily in renewable energy to power its operations, including solar farms and energy storage systems. This not only reduces the carbon footprint of its manufacturing processes but also aligns with its mission to accelerate the global transition to renewable energy. The integration of circular economy principles in the EV supply chain—reducing waste, reusing resources, and recycling materials—demonstrates the potential for industrial networks to achieve both environmental and economic benefits.

Rivian, another leader in the EV sector, is similarly committed to sustainability. The company incorporates sustainable design into its vehicles, emphasizing recyclability and reducing the environmental impact of manufacturing (King, 2023). Rivian's partnerships with renewable energy providers and its focus on creating charging infrastructure powered by clean energy further reinforce its commitment to sustainable industrial practices.

In sustainable agriculture, organizations like Driscoll's and Indigo Agriculture are transforming traditional farming practices by adopting innovative, environmentally friendly approaches. Driscoll's, a leader in berry production, utilizes advanced irrigation systems that optimize water usage, significantly reducing waste in water-scarce regions (Babbitt, 2019). The company also employs natural pest control methods, such as introducing beneficial insects, minimizing chemical pesticide use, preserving biodiversity, and reducing soil contamination.

Indigo Agriculture takes sustainability a step further by leveraging digital tools and data-driven insights to optimize crop yields while promoting regenerative farming techniques (Belousova, 2023). These methods, such as cover cropping and reduced tillage, improve soil health, increase carbon sequestration, and reduce greenhouse gas emissions. By combining technology with sustainable practices, Indigo Agriculture addresses critical challenges in global food production while enhancing the long-term viability of agricultural lands.

Key Insights from the Case Studies: Both the EV and sustainable agriculture sectors illustrate that sustainability and innovation are not mutually exclusive but are, in fact, mutually reinforcing. Tesla and Rivian demonstrate how integrating sustainability into product design, resource management, and energy use can enhance brand value, reduce costs, and contribute to global decarbonization efforts. Similarly, Driscoll's and Indigo Agriculture highlight the importance of adopting technologies that optimize resource use while prioritizing environmental health.

Table 8.18 *Key insights from sustainable industrial practices*

Company	Sustainability Initiative	Impact on Industry
Tesla	Battery recycling and renewable-powered manufacturing	Reducing dependency on virgin materials
Rivian	Carbon-neutral vehicle production	Setting sustainability benchmarks
Driscoll's	Advanced water-saving irrigation	Lower water waste in agriculture
Indigo Agriculture	AI-driven regenerative farming	Improving soil health and sustainability

These examples underscore the transformative potential of sustainable practices in industrial networks. By adopting circular economy principles, investing in renewable energy, and leveraging data-driven tools, industries can address environmental challenges while enhancing operational efficiency. The success of these companies sets a benchmark for others, showing that sustainability is not just a moral obligation but also a strategic advantage in the modern industrial landscape.

8.9 FUTURE TRENDS IN INDUSTRIAL NETWORK INNOVATION

The evolution of industrial networks is being propelled by rapid technological advancements, which are reshaping the way organizations operate, collaborate, and innovate. Emerging trends such as autonomous systems, AI, and machine learning are driving unprecedented levels of automation and efficiency in industrial chains. Additionally, breakthroughs in connectivity technologies like 5G and edge computing are enhancing network performance, enabling real-time data processing and decision-making. Predictive analytics and real-time insights are becoming integral to proactive management within industrial networks, helping businesses anticipate challenges and seize opportunities (Sari et al., 2020). Looking ahead, possibilities such as fully automated factories, self-repairing systems, and predictive maintenance promise to revolutionize industrial operations further. This unit explores these transformative trends and their implications for the future of industrial network innovation (Åkerberg et al., 2021).

8.9.1 Emerging Trends: Autonomous Systems, Artificial Intelligence, and Machine Learning in Industrial Chains

Autonomous systems, AI, and machine learning are revolutionizing industrial networks by introducing automation and intelligence at unprecedented scales. Autonomous systems, such as automated guided vehicles (AGVs) and drones, are increasingly being used in logistics and manufacturing to streamline operations, reduce costs, and improve efficiency. For example, warehouses operated by companies like Amazon use fleets of AGVs to transport goods seamlessly, minimizing human intervention and maximizing throughput (Stone, 2025).

AI and machine learning further enhance industrial networks by enabling data-driven decision-making and predictive capabilities. AI algorithms analyze vast amounts of data generated within industrial networks, identifying patterns and trends that humans might overlook. For instance, in supply chain management, AI-powered tools optimize inventory levels, forecast demand, and manage logistics more efficiently. Machine learning models continuously

Source: Author's own illustration.

Figure 8.7 *The evolution of industrial networks through AI and automation*

improve these predictions by learning from historical and real-time data, enabling adaptive and responsive industrial chains (Masulis, 2024).

The integration of autonomous systems and AI is particularly transformative in industries such as automotive manufacturing, where self-driving cars are both a product and a production tool (Sriram, 2025). Autonomous robots collaborate with human workers on assembly lines, performing repetitive or hazardous tasks with precision and consistency. These advancements not only enhance productivity but also reduce workplace risks and operational costs.

Despite their potential, adopting these technologies requires overcoming challenges, such as integrating legacy systems with new automation tools, addressing cybersecurity risks, and ensuring workforce readiness for AI-driven environments. However, the benefits—enhanced efficiency, reduced costs, and greater adaptability—make autonomous systems, AI, and machine learning critical to the future of industrial networks.

8.9.2 The Role of 5G and Edge Computing in Enhancing Network Performance

The advent of 5G technology and edge computing is transforming industrial networks by enabling ultra-fast connectivity, low latency, and real-time data processing. These technologies are particularly impactful in environments where speed and responsiveness are crucial, such as smart factories and automated logistics hubs.

5G technology provides the high-speed, reliable connectivity needed for industrial networks to support advanced applications like IoT devices, autonomous systems, and augmented reality (AR). In manufacturing, 5G enables seamless communication between machines, sensors, and controllers, creating highly synchronized production environments (Shaw, 2024). For example, automotive assembly plants equipped with 5G networks can monitor and adjust processes in real time, ensuring optimal efficiency and reducing downtime.

Edge computing complements 5G by processing data closer to its source rather than relying on centralized data centers. This reduces latency, enhances security, and improves the reliability of industrial networks. For instance, in predictive maintenance, edge computing allows IoT sensors to analyze data on-site, enabling immediate responses to equipment anomalies without delays caused by transmitting data to remote servers (Kurduban, 2023).

The combined power of 5G and edge computing also supports emerging technologies like digital twins, which require real-time data to simulate and optimize industrial processes (Nguyen et al., 2021). Additionally, these technologies enable advanced applications like remote monitoring and AR-assisted maintenance, enhancing operational flexibility and reducing costs.

Table 8.19 *Differences between traditional cloud computing and edge computing in industrial networks*

Feature	Cloud Computing	Edge Computing
Data Processing	Centralized (data centers)	Localized (near source of data)
Latency	Higher due to network delays	Ultra-low latency for real-time actions
Use Cases	Long-term storage, analytics	Predictive maintenance, real-time AI
Example	Google Cloud for Industrial AI	Edge AI in Tesla's self-driving cars

However, implementing 5G and edge computing requires substantial investment in infrastructure and cybersecurity measures to safeguard against potential vulnerabilities. Despite these challenges, the benefits of enhanced connectivity and real-time data processing position these technologies as foundational pillars of future industrial networks.

8.9.3 Predictive Analytics and Real-Time Data for Decision-Making in Industrial Networks

Predictive analytics and real-time data processing are becoming essential tools for decision-making in industrial networks, enabling organizations to anticipate challenges, optimize operations, and improve resilience. Predictive analytics uses advanced algorithms and machine learning to analyze historical and current data, identifying trends and making forecasts that guide strategic and operational decisions.

One of the most significant applications of predictive analytics is in supply chain management. By analyzing demand patterns, inventory levels, and logistics data, predictive models can anticipate potential disruptions, such as delays or shortages, and recommend proactive measures (Puica, 2023). For example, during the COVID-19 pandemic, companies that had implemented predictive analytics were better equipped to navigate supply chain disruptions by adjusting production schedules and sourcing alternative suppliers.

Real-time data further enhances decision-making by providing up-to-the-minute insights into network performance. IoT devices and sensors embedded throughout industrial networks generate continuous streams of data, enabling businesses to monitor equipment, track inventory, and oversee production processes in real time (Lauzier, 2020). This immediacy allows organizations to respond swiftly to emerging issues, such as equipment failures or unexpected shifts in demand.

The integration of predictive analytics with real-time data creates a powerful feedback loop that improves both short-term responsiveness and long-term planning. For instance, manufacturers use predictive maintenance systems to detect early signs of equipment wear and schedule repairs before breakdowns occur, reducing downtime and maintenance costs (IIoT-world, 2024).

To fully harness the potential of predictive analytics and real-time data, organizations must invest in advanced data analytics platforms, robust IT infrastructure, and skilled personnel capable of interpreting complex datasets. By doing so, industrial networks can enhance their agility, efficiency, and resilience in an increasingly dynamic environment.

8.9.4 Future Possibilities for Industrial Chain Innovation: Fully Automated Factories, Self-Repairing Systems, and Predictive Maintenance

The future of industrial network innovation lies in groundbreaking advancements such as fully automated factories, self-repairing systems, and predictive maintenance. These possibilities promise to redefine efficiency, reliability, and productivity in industrial chains.

Fully automated factories, also known as "lights-out manufacturing," operate with minimal human intervention, relying entirely on robotics, AI, and advanced automation systems. These facilities optimize production processes, reduce operational costs, and maintain consistent quality (McGrew, 2021). Companies like FANUC, a leading robotics manufacturer, have already implemented lights-out factories where robots build other robots with little human oversight. As automation technology advances, these factories are expected to

Table 8.20 Key uses of predictive analytics in industrial networks

Use Case	How Predictive Analytics Helps	Example
Supply Chain Management	Forecasting demand & optimizing inventory	Walmart's AI-driven demand prediction
Predictive Maintenance	Preventing machine failures	GE's AI-powered turbine maintenance
Energy Optimization	Adjusting power consumption in factories	Tesla's AI-driven energy grid management
Quality Control	Detecting defects early	Intel's semiconductor AI inspections

Table 8.21 Comparison of fully automated factories vs. self-repairing systems

Feature	Fully Automated Factories	Self-Repairing Systems
Main Objective	Operate with minimal human intervention	Extend equipment lifespan, reduce downtime
Key Technology	AI, robotics, smart logistics	IoT sensors, self-healing materials
Implementation Challenges	High setup costs, cybersecurity risks	Requires AI-driven monitoring and automation
Example	FANUC's "Lights-Out" Factory in Japan	Boeing's self-repairing aircraft materials

become more widespread across industries, particularly in high-volume manufacturing sectors like electronics and automotive.

Self-repairing systems represent another transformative innovation. These systems leverage IoT sensors, AI, and advanced materials to detect and address issues without human intervention (Pit, 2024). For example, machinery equipped with self-repairing capabilities can identify stress fractures, initiate automated repairs using specialized materials, and restore functionality without disrupting production. This reduces downtime and extends the lifespan of equipment, leading to significant cost savings.

Predictive maintenance, powered by AI and the IoT, is already gaining traction and is expected to become a standard practice in industrial networks (Villareal, 2020). By continuously monitoring equipment performance, predictive maintenance systems identify potential failures before they occur, enabling timely interventions. This not only reduces downtime but also lowers maintenance costs and improves overall network efficiency.

While these advancements hold immense promise, their implementation requires overcoming challenges such as high initial costs, workforce adaptation, and cybersecurity concerns. However, the potential benefits—unparalleled efficiency, enhanced reliability, and reduced operational risks—make these innovations key drivers of the future of industrial networks. By embracing these possibilities, organizations can position themselves at the forefront of industrial transformation.

8.10 CONCLUSION

The evolution of industrial networks has been shaped by advancements in technology, globalization, and an increasing emphasis on sustainability. This chapter explored the transformative trends and strategies driving innovation across industrial chains, highlighting the growing importance of collaboration, adaptability, and the integration of advanced technologies such as AI, the IoT, and blockchain. From the adoption of sustainable practices to the emergence of fully automated factories, industrial networks are undergoing profound changes that position them to address future challenges and opportunities.

One of the key takeaways is the pivotal role of technology in reshaping industrial networks. Tools such as predictive analytics, real-time data processing, and edge computing enable organizations to make informed decisions, optimize operations, and enhance resilience. These innovations are complemented by the rise of autonomous systems and machine learning, which have introduced new levels of efficiency and precision in production and logistics. Moreover, technologies like 5G and digital twins have transformed connectivity and process simulation, allowing industrial chains to operate with greater agility and coordination.

Equally significant is the shift toward sustainability and circular economy principles within industrial networks. The integration of environmentally friendly practices, such as reducing waste, reusing resources, and recycling, is not just a regulatory requirement but also a strategic advantage. Industries such as electric vehicles and agriculture demonstrate how businesses can align economic growth with environmental stewardship by leveraging innovation and collaboration.

Collaboration and adaptability emerge as critical themes for the future success of industrial networks. The complexity of globalized supply chains and the rapid pace of technological change necessitate strong partnerships among diverse stakeholders, including businesses, governments, research institutions, and civil society. Open innovation, co-creation, and the development of innovation hubs and clusters underscore the need for shared knowledge and collective problem-solving to drive breakthroughs in industrial processes and products.

Adaptability, in particular, is essential in a world characterized by uncertainty and disruption. Geopolitical shifts, trade wars, and supply chain crises, such as those experienced during the COVID-19 pandemic, highlight the vulnerabilities of globalized industrial networks. Companies must build resilience by diversifying supply chains, leveraging digital tools, and fostering a culture of innovation that embraces change. Flexibility and proactive risk management will enable industrial networks to navigate future uncertainties and seize emerging opportunities.

As industrial chains continue to evolve, new possibilities such as self-repairing systems, predictive maintenance, and fully automated factories will redefine the boundaries of efficiency and innovation. These advancements promise to reduce costs, enhance reliability, and create value in ways previously unimaginable. However, their successful implementation will require organizations to address challenges such as workforce adaptation, cybersecurity, and the ethical implications of automation.

Looking ahead, industrial networks will increasingly serve as dynamic ecosystems that balance technological innovation, economic competitiveness, and sustainability. The ability to integrate cutting-edge technologies, collaborate across boundaries, and adapt to a rapidly changing global landscape will define the leaders of tomorrow's industrial networks. By embracing these principles, organizations can ensure that their industrial chains remain resilient, efficient, and ready to meet the demands of the future.

In conclusion, the future of industrial networks lies in their capacity to innovate, collaborate, and adapt. The challenges are significant, but so are the opportunities. By fostering an environment of shared purpose and continuous improvement, industrial chains can play a vital role in driving sustainable economic growth and addressing the global challenges of the 21st century.

REFERENCES

Abdel-Basset, M., Mohamed, R. & Chang, V., 2024. A Multi-Criteria Decision-Making Framework to Evaluate the Impact of Industry 5.0 Technologies: Case Study, Lessons Learned, Challenges and Future Directions. *Information Systems Frontiers*. https://doi.org/10.1007/s10796-024-10472-3.

Abishek, B. A. et al., 2023. Collaborative Robots and Cyber Security in Industry 5.0. *2023 2nd International Conference on Advancements in Electrical, Electronics, Communication, Computing and Automation (ICAECA)*, Coimbatore, India, pp. 1–6. https://doi.org/10.1109/ICAECA56562.2023.10200319.

Abrahamsen, M. H., Henneberg, S. C. & Naudé, P., 2012. Using Actors' Perceptions of Network Roles and Positions to Understand Network Dynamics. *BI Open*. http://dx.doi.org/10.1016/j.indmarman.2012.01.008.

Acebes, F. et al., 2021. On the Project Risk Baseline: Integrating Aleatory Uncertainty into Project Scheduling. *Computers & Industrial Engineering*, 160, 107537. https://doi.org/10.1016/j.cie.2021.107537.

Adel, A. & HS Alani, N., 2024. Human-Centric Collaboration and Industry 5.0 Framework in Smart Cities and Communities: Fostering Sustainable Development Goals 3, 4, 9, and 11 in Society 5.0. *Smart Cities*, 7(4), 1723–1775. https://doi.org/10.3390/smartcities7040068.

Agampodi, S. et al., 2024. Global Pandemic Preparedness: Learning from the COVID-19 Vaccine Development and Distribution. *Expert Review of Vaccines*, 23(1), 761–772. https://doi.org/10.1080/14760584.2024.2395546.

AI Guardian, 2024. The Pivotal Role of an AI Ethics Committee: Navigating AI Dilemmas. https://www.aiguardianapp.com/ai-ethics-committee.

Ainsley Lawrence, 2024. Leveraging Digital Twins for Predictive Maintenance in Smart Manufacturing. *ISA Interchange*. https://blog.isa.org/leveraging-digital-twins-for-predictive-maintenance-in-smart-manufacturing.

Åkerberg, J. et al., 2021. Future Industrial Networks in Process Automation: Goals, Challenges, and Future Directions. *Applied Sciences*, 11(8), 3345. https://doi.org/10.3390/app11083345.

Akter, R., Rathnayaka, S. & Ahmadi, Z., 2023. The Effect of Leadership and Organisational Culture on Organisational Innovation. *International Journal of Services Technology and Management*, 28, 360–388. https://doi.org/10.1504/IJSTM.2023.135084.

Allgood, K., 2025. Supply Chain and Manufacturing Transformation: Key Takeaways from Davos 2025. *World Economic Forum*. https://www.weforum.org/stories/2025/01/manufacturing-transformation-sustainability-innovation/?

Alqudhaibi, A. et al., 2023. Cybersecurity Threats in Critical Infrastructure for Industry 4.0: A Proactive Approach Based on Attacker Motivations. *Sensors*, 23(9), 4539. https://doi.org/10.3390/s23094539.

Alqudhaibi, A. et al., 2025. Securing Industry 4.0: Assessing Cybersecurity Challenges and Proposing Strategies for Manufacturing Management. *Cyber Security and Applications*, 3. https://doi.org/10.1016/j.csa.2024.100067.

Alzate-Mejía, N., Santos-Boada, G. & de Almeida-Amazonas, J., 2021. Decision-Making under Uncertainty for the Deployment of Future Hyperconnected Networks: A Survey. *Sensors*, 21, 3791. https://doi.org/10.3390/s21113791.

Amos, Z., 2024. *Why Collaboration Is Essential for Cybersecurity Teams*. International Society of Automation (ISA).

Ankura, 2024. 7 Strategies to Overcome Supply Chain Disruptions: Mitigate Risk While Enhancing Resilience and Adaptability. *JDsupra*. https://www.jdsupra.com/legalnews/7-strategies-to-overcome-supply-chain-6337392/?

Anon., 2025. *Norwegian Ecosystem for Secure IT-OT Integration (NESIOT)*. https://www.ntnu.edu/norcics/it-ot-integration-nesiot

Applied CAx, 2023. Case Study: AeroTEC's Digital Transformation Journey. *Applied CAx*. https://www.appliedcax.com/case-study-aerotecs-digital-transformation-journey/?

Arthur, C., 2012. Google to Pay Record $22.5m Fine to FTC over Safari Tracking. *The Guardian*. https://www.theguardian.com/technology/2012/aug/09/google-record-fine-ftc-safari.

Aschenbroich, A. & Dintelman, M., 2023. Success in Joint Ventures. *KPMG*. https://kpmg.com/kpmg-us/content/dam/kpmg/pdf/2023/success-joint-ventures.pdf?.

Augusto, C. & Souza, J., 2015. Transaction Cost Economics and Resource Based View: Complementary Aspects in the Treatment of Governance Structures. *REBRAE*, 8, 173. https://doi.org/10.7213/rebrae.08.002.AO04.

Awati, R. & Cole, A., 2022. North American Electric Reliability Corporation Critical Infrastructure Protection (NERC CIP). *TechTarget*. https://www.techtarget.com/searchsecurity/definition/North-American-Electric-Reliability-Corporation-Critical-Infrastructure-Protection-NERC-CIP.

Babbitt, C., 2019. How Driscoll's, the World's Largest Berry Company, Is Becoming a Leader in Water Conservation. *Environmental Defense Fund*. https://blogs.edf.org/growingreturns/2019/01/23/driscolls-berry-company-water-conservation/.

Badman, A., 2024. Data Protection Strategy: Key Components and Best Practices. *IBM*. https://www.ibm.com/think/insights/data-protection-strategy?

Balbaa, M. & Abdurashidova, M., 2024. The Impact of Artificial Intelligence in Decision Making: A Comprehensive Review. *EPRA International Journal of Economics, Business and Management Studies*, 11, 27–38. https://doi.org/10.36713/epra15747.

Bansal, A., 2024. GDPR vs. HIPAA vs. CCPA vs. PCI: Compliance Differences. *Clouddefense. AI*. https://www.clouddefense.ai/gdpr-vs-hipaa-vs-ccpa-vs-pci/?

Beerman, J., Berent, D., Falter, Z. & Bhunia, S., 2023. A Review of Colonial Pipeline Ransomware Attack. *IEEE/ACM 23rd International Symposium on Cluster, Cloud and Internet Computing Workshops (CCGridW)*, Bangalore, India, pp. 8–15. https://doi.org/10.1109/CCGridW59191.2023.00017.

Belousova, M., 2023. How Data and Technology Bring Value to Sustainable Farming Practices. *Indigo.* https://www.indigoag.com/blog/how-data-and-technology-bring-value-to-sustainable-farming-practices.

Bertello, A., De Bernardi, P. & Ricciardi, F., 2024. Open Innovation: Status Quo and Quo Vadis – An Analysis of a Research Field. *Review of Managerial Science. Review of Managerial Science,* 18, 633–683. https://doi.org/10.1007/s11846-023-00655-8.

Bibi, P., 2024. Establishing Transparency and Accountability in AI: Ethical Standards for Data Governance and Automated Systems. https://doi.org/10.13140/RG.2.2.25599.83366.

Bickers, C. & Alencar, V., 2018. Boeing and Embraer to Establish Strategic Aerospace Partnership to Accelerate Global Aerospace Growth. *Embraer.* https://embraer.com/global/en/news/?slug=1206396-boeing-and-embraer-to-establish-strategic-aerospace-partnership-to-accelerate-global-aerospace-growth.

Bingham, C. B. & McDonald, R. M., 2022. Mastering Innovation's Toughest Trade-Offs. *MIT Sloan Management Review.* https://sloanreview.mit.edu/article/mastering-innovations-toughest-trade-offs/.

Boeckl, K. et al., 2019. Considerations for Managing Internet of Things (IoT) Cybersecurity and Privacy Risks. *NIST (National Institute of Standards and Technology.* https://doi.org/10.6028/NIST.IR.8228.

Boubaker, K. B., 2023. Industry 5.0: where does cybersecurity fit in? *Stormshield.* https://www.stormshield.com/news/industry-5-0-where-does-cybersecurity-fit-in/?

Bouhdada, J. & Ayala, M., 2024. Securing Industrial Control Systems and Safety Instrumented Systems: A Practical Guide for Safeguarding Mission and Safety Critical Systems. *IEEE Books.* https://ieeexplore.ieee.org/servlet/opac?bknumber=10769223.

Briand, L. et al., 2012. Research-Based Innovation: A Tale of Three Projects in Model-Driven Engineering. *Model Driven Engineering Languages and Systems. 15th International Conference, MODELS 2012*, Innsbruck, Austria, September 30–October 5, 2012, Proceedings Berlin, Heidelberg: Springer, pp. 793–809.

Brook, C., 2024. IP Theft: Definition and Examples. *Fortra Digital Guardian.* https://www.digitalguardian.com/blog/ip-theft-definition-and-examples.

Burova, E., Grishunin, S., Suloeva, S. & Stepanchuk, A., 2021. The Cost Management of Innovative Products in an Industrial Enterprise Given the Risks in the Digital Economy. *International Journal of Technology*, 12, 1339. https://doi.org/10.14716/ijtech.v12i7.5333.

Burrus, D., 2024. What Is Industry 4.0? SAP. https://www.sap.com/products/scm/industry-4-0/what-is-industry-4-0.html?

Carayannis, E., Acikdilli, G. & Ziemnowicz, C., 2020. Creative Destruction in International Trade: Insights from the Quadruple and Quintuple Innovation Helix Models. *Journal of the Knowledge Economy*, 1, 1489–1508. https://doi.org/10.1007/s13132-019-00599-z.

Carayannis, E. & Campbell, D., 2012. Triple Helix, Quadruple Helix and Quintuple Helix and How Do Knowledge, Innovation and the Environment Relate To Each Other? *International Journal of Social Ecology and Sustainable Development*, 1, 41–69. https://doi.org/10.4018/jsesd.2010010105.

Carayannis, E. & Campbell, D., 2021. Democracy of Climate and Climate for Democracy: The Evolution of Quadruple and Quintuple Helix Innovation Systems. *Journal of the Knowledge Economy*, 12, 2050–2082. https://doi.org/10.1007/s13132-021-00778-x.

Carayannis, E. & Campbell, D., 2021. Democracy of Climate and Climate for Democracy: The Evolution of Quadruple and Quintuple Helix Innovation Systems. *Journal of the Knowledge Economy*, 12, 2050–2082. https://doi.org/10.1007/s13132-021-00778-x.

Carayannis, E. G. & Campbell, D. F., 2009. Mode 3 and Quadruple Helix: Toward a 21st Century Fractal Innovation Ecosystem. *International Journal of Technology Management*, 46, 201–234.

Carayannis, E. G., Canestrino, R. & Magliocca, P., 2024. From the Dark Side of Industry 4.0 to Society 5.0: Looking "Beyond the Box" to Developing Human-Centric Innovation Ecosystems. *IEEE Transactions on Engineering Management*, 71, 6695–6711. https://doi.org/10.1109/TEM.2023.3239552.

Carayannis, E. G., Dumitrescu, R., Falkowski, T. & Zota, N. -R., 2024. Empowering SMEs "Harnessing the Potential of Gen AI for Resilience and Competitiveness". *IEEE Transactions on Engineering Management*, 71, 14754–14774. https://doi.org/10.1109/TEM.2024.3456820.

Carayannis, E., Kostis, P. & Dinçer, H., 2024. Quality Function Deployment-Oriented Strategic Outlook to Sustainable Energy Policies Based on Quintuple Innovation Helix. *Journal of the Knowledge Economy*, 15, 6761–6779. https://doi.org/10.1007/s13132-023-01394–7.

Carayannis, E., Papamichail, G., Zotas, N. & Askounis, D., 2025. Corporate Foresight: Navigating Uncertainty in a VUCA World. *Journal of the Knowledge Economy*. https://doi.org/10.1007/s13132-024-02587-4.

Carinus, L., Ngongoni, C. N. & Saartjie Grobbelaar, S. S., 2022. Towards a Strategic Decision Support Tool for Innovation Ecosystems Stakeholder Management. *2022 IEEE 28th International Conference on Engineering, Technology and Innovation (ICE/ITMC) & 31st International Association For Management of Technology (IAMOT) Joint Conference*, Nancy, France.

CCCS, 2024. *Security Considerations for Research and Development Organizations* (ITSAP.00.130). Canadian Centre for Cyber Security. https://www.cyber.gc.ca/en/guidance/security-considerations-research-and-development-itsap00130?

Chaube, S. et al., 2024. An Overview of Multi-Criteria Decision Analysis and the Applications of AHP and TOPSIS Methods. *International Journal of Mathematical Engineering and Management Sciences*, 9, 581–615. https://doi.org/10.33889/IJMEMS.2024.9.3.030.

Chen, H., Mehra, A., Tasselli, S. & Borgatti, S. P., 2022. Network Dynamics and Organizations: A Review and Research Agenda. *Journal of Management*, 48(6), 1602–1660. https://doi.org/10.1177/01492063211063218.

Chowdhury, E. et al., 2022. The Contribution of Innovation Hubs Towards Strengthening the Regional Development in Sweden. *International Journal of Innovation and Technology Management*, 20. https://doi.org/10.1142/S0219877023500104.

Ciechan-Kujawa, M., Buszko, M. & Taranowska, K., 2018. Sensitivity Analysis in Business Risk Assessment in Practice of Polish Companies. *Ekonomiczne Problemy Usług*, 133, 39–50. https://doi.org/10.18276/epu.2018.133/2-04.

Constantin, L., 2014. *New Havex Malware Variants Target Industrial Control System and SCADA Users.*

Costa, F. S., 2021. *A Practical Approach to Adopting the IEC 62443 Standards*. s.l.:s.n.

Cristofaro, M., Leoni, L. & Giardino, P. L., 2022. Cognitive Biases' Influence on Employees' Product Creativity and Product Performance: Evidences from Italian Manufacturing Technology Firms. *Journal of Manufacturing Technology Management*, 33, 675–695. https://doi.org/10.1108/JMTM-10-2020-0414.

Curley, M. & Salmelin, B., 2017. *Open Innovation 2.0: The New Mode of Digital Innovation for Prosperity and Sustainability*. Springer Nature.

Dal Molin, P., 2024. Cyberattack on Industrial Systems: A Growing Threat. *Lumiun*. https://www.lumiun.com/blog/en/cyberattack-on-industrial-systems-is-a-growing-threat/.

Daradkeh, M. & Abul-Huda, B., 2017. Incorporating Uncertainty into Decision-Making: An Information Visualisation Approach, 74–87. https://doi.org/10.1007/978-3-319-57487-5_6.

Dawood, M. et al., 2023. Cyberattacks and Security of Cloud Computing: A Complete Guideline. *Symmetry*, 15(11), 1981. https://doi.org/10.3390/sym15111981.

De Bettignies, J.-E., Liu, H. F., Robinson, D. T. & Gainullin, B., 2022. Competition and Innovation in Markets for Technology. *Management Science*, 69(8), 4753–4773. https://doi.org/10.1287/mnsc.2022.4574.

Decybr, 2023. Protecting Intellectual Property: Cybersecurity for Research and Development. https://decybr.com/protecting-intellectual-property-cybersecurity-for-research-and-development/?

Deloite, 2019. Cybersecurity for Smart Factories: Tools for Managing Cyber Threats to Manufacturing. https://www2.deloitte.com/content/dam/Deloitte/us/Documents/energy-resources/cybersecurity-for-smart-factories-mfg.pdf.

Departementene, 2019. Regjeringen.no. https://www.regjeringen.no/contentassets/8ed748d37e504a469874ce936551b4f8/nasjonal-strategi-for-digital-sikkerhetskompetanse.pdf

DeRose, R., 2024. JIT vs Lean Manufacturing: What's the Difference. https://www.l-tron.com/jit-versus-lean-manufacturing-whats-the-difference/? *L-tron*.

Develaki, M., 2024. Uncertainty, Risk, and Decision-Making. *Science & Education*, 1–32. https://doi.org/10.1007/s11191-024-00544-w.

DFreight, 2023. An Insight Into Nike's Supply Chain Strategy. *Digital Freight Forwarder*. https://dfreight.org/blog/an-insight-into-nikes-supply-chain-strategy/?

DigitalDefynd, 2025. 5 Digital Transformation in FMCG Case Studies [2025]. *DigitalDefynd*. https://digitaldefynd.com/IQ/digital-transformation-in-fmcg/?

DoD CIO, n.d. *Chief Information Officer, U.S. Department of Defense*. DoD CIO.

Easterly, J. & Fanning, T., 2023. *The Attack on Colonial Pipeline: What We've Learned & What We've Done Over the Past Two Years*. Cybersecurity & Infrastructure Security Agency "CISA". https://www.cisa.gov/news-events/news/attack-colonial-pipeline-what-weve-learned-what-weve-done-over-past-two-years?

Eberz, S., Lang, S., Breitenmoser, P. & Niebert, K., 2023. Taking the Lead into Sustainability: Decision Makers' Competencies for a Greener Future. *Sustainability*, 15, 4986. https://doi.org/10.3390/su15064986.

EC-Council University, 2024. *Staying Ahead of the Curve: Emerging Cybersecurity Technologies*. EC-Council University.

Edirisinghe, L., de Alwis, A., Wijayasundara, M. & Hemali, N., 2024. Quantifying Circularity Factor of Waste: Assessing the Circular Economy Potential of Industrial Zones. *Cleaner Environmental Systems*, 12. https://doi.org/10.1016/j.cesys.2023.100160.

Emma, L., 2024. Big Data Analytics for Real-Time Insights and Strategic Business Planning.https://www.researchgate.net/publication/386336003_Big_data_analytics_for_real-time_insights_and_strategic_business_planning.

Emtrain, 2024. The Importance of Data Privacy Training for Employees. *Emtrain.* https://emtrain.com/blog/code-of-conduct/data-privacy-training-for-employees/?

EPA, 2024. *Lean Thinking and Methods – JIT/Kanban.* EPA – United States Environmental Protection Agency. https://www.epa.gov/sustainability/lean-thinking-and-methods-jitkanban?

Epicor, 2024. What is Industry 4.0—the Industrial Internet of Things (IIoT)? *Epicor.* https://www.epicor.com/en-us/blog/technology-and-data/what-is-industry-4-0/?

EUR-Lex, n.d. The EU Cybersecurity Act. https://eur-lex.europa.eu/legal-content/EN/TXT/?uri=legissum:4398780

Fadia, A., Nayfeh, M. & Noble, J., 2020. *How Governments Can Combat Intensifying Cybersecurity Risks.* Mckinsey & Company. https://www.mckinsey.com/industries/public-sector/our-insights/follow-the-leaders-how-governments-can-combat-intensifying-cybersecurity-risks.

Ferraioli, J., 2022. *Megatrends: Opportunities on the Front Lines of Cybersecurity.* Morgan Stanley.

Ferreira, J., Coelho, A. & Moutinho, L., 2020. The Influence of Strategic Alliances on Innovation and New Product Development through the Effects of Exploration and Exploitation. *Management Decision.* ahead-of-print. https://doi.org/10.1108/MD-09-2019–1239.

Finegan, N., 2019. How Globalization Impacts Supply Chain Management. *Sflow Space.* https://flow.space/blog/globalization-supply-chain/?

Flores-García, E., Bruch, J., Wiktorsson, M. & Jackson, M., 2019. Decision-making approaches in process innovations: an explorative case study. *Journal of Manufacturing Technology Management.* ahead-of-print. https://doi.org/10.1108/JMTM-03-2019-0087.

Fluchs, S. et al., 2022. Security by Design Integration Mechanisms for Industrial Control Systems. *IECON 2022 – 48th Annual Conference of the IEEE Industrial Electronics Society,* Brussels, Belgium, pp. 1–6. https://doi.org/10.1109/IECON49645.2022.9968406.

Forbes, 2024. Return on Investment of Cybersecurity: Making the Business Case. *Forbes Technology Council.* https://councils.forbes.com/blog/roi-of-cybersecurity.

Fragapane, G. et al., 2022. Increasing Flexibility and Productivity in Industry 4.0 Production Networks with Autonomous Mobile Robots and Smart Intralogistics. *Annals of Operations Research,* 308, 125–143. https://doi.org/10.1007/s10479-020-03526-7.

Gale, T., 2023. *Cybersecurity Risk Assessment Strategies in Industrial Control Systems.* AIChE. https://www.aiche.org/resources/publications/cep/2023/december/cybersecurity-risk-assessment-strategies-industrial-control-systems?

Gausdal, A. H., Svare, H. & Möllering, G., 2016. Why Don't All High-Trust Networks Achieve Strong Network Benefits? A Case-Based Exploration of Cooperation in Norwegian SME Networks. *Journal of Trust Research,* 6(2), 194–212. https://doi.org/10.1080/21515581.2016.1213173.

Giaccone, S. & Magnusson, M., 2021. Unveiling the Role of Risk-Taking in Innovation: Antecedents and Effects. *R&D Management,* 52. https://doi.org/10.1111/radm.12477.

González, C. V., Robina, R. R., Gibaja, R. D.-E. & Sánchez, O. S. M., 2023. The Quintuple Helix Model: Cooperation System for a Sustainable Electric Power

Industry in Mexico. *Frontiers in Sustainable Energy Policy*, 1, 1047675. https://doi.org/10.3389/fsuep.2022.1047675.

Gordon, J., 2024. The Evolving Threat Landscape – From Ransomware to State-Sponsored Espionage. *Industrial Cyber*. https://industrialcyber.co/analysis/the-evolving-threat-landscape-from-ransomware-to-state-sponsored-espionage/?

Gorschek, T., Garre, P., Larsson, S. & Wohlin, C., 2006. A Model for Technology Transfer in Practice. *IEEE Software*, 23(6), 88–95.

Goud, N., 2024. *The Rising Threat of Cloud Ransomware: A Global Concern for Businesses of All Sizes.*

Greenberg, A., 2018. The Untold Story of NotPetya, the Most Devastating Cyberattack in History. *Wired*. https://www.wired.com/story/notpetya-cyberattack-ukraine-russia-code-crashed-the-world/.

Gregersen, E., 2024. Stuxnet. Britannica. https://www.britannica.com/technology/Stuxnet?

Guess, G., 2022. The Rise of IT/OT Convergence in Industry 4.0. *engineering.com*. https://www.engineering.com/the-rise-of-it-ot-convergence-in-industry-4-0/?

GVR, 2024. The Impact of Geopolitical Factors and Trade Risks on Global Supply Chain. *Grand View Research*. https://www.grandviewresearch.com/research-insights/geopolitical-factors-trade-risks-impact-supply-chain.

Hall, A., 2024. *Legal Compliance and Data Protection in Employee Data Privacy*. Aaron Hall Attorney.

Hampl, N., Hoffmann, W. H., Knoll, T. & Reuer, J. J., 2024. Alliance Re-Evaluation in the Context of Outside Partnering Opportunities: Decision Heuristics and the Impact of Environmental Uncertainty. *Journal of Management Studies*. https://doi.org/10.1111/joms.13090.

Han, J. & Kang, R., 2021. Market Uncertainty, Innovation of Firms in Alliance and Alliance Partner Characteristics. *European Journal of Innovation Management*, 24(5), 1883–1905. https://doi.org/10.1108/EJIM-05-2020-0195.

Hatoum, M. B. & Nassereddine, H., 2024. *Determining Decision-Making Factors for Technology Adoption in the Construction Industry*. IntechOpen. https://doi.org/10.5772/intechopen.1004365.

Henry, W., Kathawate, R., Chen, E. & Coulter, J., 2023. Using Blockchain to Drive Supply Chain Transparency. *Deloitte*. https://www2.deloitte.com/us/en/pages/operations/articles/blockchain-supply-chain-innovation.html?

Hubbart, S., 2023. *Going Green with Electric Vehicles*. Neef USA. https://www.neefusa.org/story/sustainability/going-green-electric-vehicles?

Hu, S. et al., 2024. Digital Twins Enabling Intelligent Manufacturing: From Methodology to Application. *Intelligent and Sustainable Manufacturing*, 1, 10007. https://doi.org/10.35534/ism.2024.10007.

Huston, L. & Sakkab, N. Y., 2006. Connect and Develop: Inside Procter & Gamble's New Model for Innovation. *Harvard Business Review*.

Hyland, A., 2024. Fortescue Spies Sifted Through Personal Mail of Ex-Staff, Followed Family Members to Kmart: Court Told. *The Age*. https://www.theage.com.au/business/companies/fortescue-seeks-to-suppress-600-page-document-detailing-spying-on-ex-staff-20240710-p5jsiu.html.

Hyseni, V., 2024. A Comprehensive Guide to Cybersecurity Incident Response Plan. *Pecb*. https://pecb.com/article/a-comprehensive-guide-to-cybersecurity-incident-response-plan.

Ieremchuk, O. & Iaskova, D., 2024. Building a Resilient Data Management Strategy: Key Steps and Best Practices. *Trinetix*. https://www.trinetix.com/insights/building-a-resilient-data-management-strategy-key-steps-and-best-practices?

IIoT-world, 2024. Predictive Maintenance in IIoT: Leveraging Time Series Data for Equipment Longevity. *IIoT-world*. https://www.iiot-world.com/predictive-analytics/predictive-maintenance/predictive-maintenance-iiot-time-series-data/?

Industry Risk, 2019. Risk Assessment Matrix. *Industry Risk*. https://industryrisk.com.au/risk-assessment-matrix/?

Inspira, 2024. *Importance of Security-by-Design for IT and OT Systems in Building a Security Resilient Framework*. s.l.:Inspira Eenterprise. https://inspiraenterprise.com/importance-of-security-by-design-for-it-and-ot-systems-in-building-a-security-resilient-framework/?

ISA, n.d. *ISA/IEC 62443 Series of Standards*. ISA.

ISO Standards, 2022. *ISO/IEC 27001:2022*. https://www.iso.org/standard/27001

ITCC, 2024. *A Circular Economy: Moving from Supply and Value Chains to Networks*. IEEE Technology Climate Center (ITCC). https://itcc.ieee.org/blog/a-circular-economy-moving-from-supply-and-value-chains-to-networks/?

Jalonen, H., 2011. The Uncertainty of Innovation: A Systematic Review of the Literature. *Journal of Management Research*, 4. https://doi.org/10.5296/jmr.v4i1.1039.

Jena, B. K., 2024. SolarWinds Attack and all the Details You Need to Know about it. *Simplilearn*. https://www.simplilearn.com/tutorials/cryptography-tutorial/all-about-solarwinds-attack.

Jwo, J.-S., Lee, C.-H. & Lin, C.-S., 2022. Data Twin-Driven Cyber-Physical Factory for Smart Manufacturing. *Sensors*, 22(8), 2821. https://doi.org/10.3390/s22082821.

Kahneman, D. & & Tversky, A., 1979. Prospect Theory: An Analysis of Decision under Risk. *Econometrica*, 47(2), 263–291. https://doi.org/10.2307/1914185.

Kapletia, D., Felici, M. & Wainwright, N., 2014. An Integrated Framework for Innovation Management in Cyber Security and Privacy. Communications in Computer and Information Science. *Communications in Computer and Information Science*, 470, 135–147. https://doi.org/10.1007/978-3-319-12574-9_12.

Katz, B. & Wagner, J., 2014. *The Rise of Innovation Districts*. Metropolitan Policy Program at Brookings. https://c24215cec6c97b637db6-9c0895f07c3474f6636f95b6bf3db172.ssl.cf1.rackcdn.com/content/metro-innovation-districts/~/media/programs/metro/images/innovation/innovationdistricts1.pdf.

Kaya, A., 2024. How Are Geopolitical Risks Affecting the World Economy? *Economics Observatory*. https://www.economicsobservatory.com/how-are-geopolitical-risks-affecting-the-world-economy?

Khan, M., 2021. *Data Minimization—A Practical Approach*. ISACA. https://www.isaca.org/resources/news-and-trends/industry-news/2021/data-minimization-a-practical-approach?

Kim, C., 2017. Keynote Speaker 1: Cyber-resilient ICS through Diversified Redundancy and Intrusion Detection. *2017 12th International Conference for Internet Technology and Secured Transactions (ICITST)*, Cambridge, pp. 15–15. https://doi.org/10.23919/ICITST.2017.8356331.

King, C., 2023. Rivian Shift Global Energy Attitudes Towards Renewables. *Energy Digital*. https://energydigital.com/articles/rivian-shift-global-energy-attitudes-towards-renewables.

Klen, E., 2009. Co-creation and Co-innovation in a Collaborative Networked Environment. Conference: Leveraging Knowledge for Innovation in Collaborative

Networks, 10th IFIP WG 5.5 Working Conference on Virtual Enterprises, PRO-VE 2009, pp. 33–40. https://doi.org/10.1007/978-3-642-04568-4_4.
Komal, D. & Khandare, D. M., 2024. Green Supply Chain Management: Strategies for Eco-Friendly Business Practices. *Journal of Advanced Zoology*, 45, 215–223. https://doi.org/10.53555/jaz.v45iS4.4187.
Koudriachov, C., Tam, C. & Aparicio, M., 2025. Success with Agile Project Management: Looking back and into the future,. *Journal of Systems and Software*, 226112428. https://doi.org/10.1016/j.jss.2025.112428.
Krykavskyy, Y. & Stasiuk, K., 2022. Digital Transformation in the Automotive Supply Chain: Trends and Cases. *Scientific Journal of Bielsko-Biala School of Finance and Law*. Bielsko-Biała, PL, 26(4), 113–117. https://doi.org/10.19192/wsfip.sj4.2022.17.
Kumar, P., Aziz, S. & Khan, A., 2023. Analyzing The Impact of Digital Technologies on Enhancing Supply Chain Resilience in the Post-Pandemic Era. *Journal of Fundamental and Applied Sciences*, 16, 15–35. https://doi.org/10.4314/jfas.1358.
Kurduban, V., 2023. 5G Edge Computing: How It's Setting the Stage for Industry 4.0. *Digi*. https://www.digi.com/blog/post/5g-edge-computing-for-industry-4-0?
Kushner, D., 2024. The Real Story of Stuxnet. *IEEE Spectrum*. https://spectrum.ieee.org/the-real-story-of-stuxnet.
Kuzmenko, V., 2023. Data Privacy Paradox: Balancing Innovation with Protection in the Age of AI. *Hyperight*. https://hyperight.com/data-privacy-paradox-balancing-innovation-with-protection-in-age-of-ai/.
Kwon, S., Youtie, J., Porter, A. & Newman, N., 2022. How does Regulatory Uncertainty Shape the Innovation Process? Evidence from the Case of Nanomedicine. *The Journal of Technology Transfer*. https://doi.org/10.1007/s10961-022-09980–8.
Laage-Hellman, J., Lind, F. & Perna, A., 2021. The Role of Openness in Collaborative Innovation in Industrial Networks: Historical and Contemporary Cases. *Journal of Business & Industrial Marketing*, 36(13): 116–128.
Lähteenmäki, J. & Töyli, J., 2023. Platform based Innovation Ecosystems: Value Network Configuration Perspective. *Journal of Innovation Management*, 11, 68–97. https://doi.org/10.24840/2183-0606_011.001_0004.
Lauzier, J., 2020. Predictive Analytics in Manufacturing: Use Cases and Benefits. *Machine Metrics*. https://www.machinemetrics.com/blog/predictive-analytics-in-manufacturing?
Lee, J. & Lee, T., 2023. Trustful Competitor & Distrustful Cooperator: Impacts of Assessment Gaps on Trustworthy Coopetition in Policy Network. *Cogent Social Sciences*, 10(1). https://doi.org/10.1080/23311886.2023.2293308.
Lindemulder, G. & Kosinski, M., 2024. *What Is Role-based Access Control (RBAC)?* s.l.:IBM, https://www.ibm.com/think/topics/rbac.
Lipovsky, R., 2017. Seven years after Stuxnet: Industrial Systems Security Once Again in the Spotlight. https://www.welivesecurity.com/2017/06/16/seven-years-stuxnet-industrial-systems-security-spotlight/?
Liu, R., 2013. Cooperation, Competition and Coopetition in Innovation Communities. *Prometheus*, 31(2), 91–105. https://doi.org/10.1080/08109028.2013.818788.
Li, W., Guo, X. & Cao, D., 2021. The Complexity of Technological Innovation Decision-Making in Emerging Industries. Complexity. 2021. 1–14. https://doi.org/10.1155/2021/3611921.
Maayan, G. D., 2024. 10 Risks of IoT Data Management. The Data Administration Newsletter. https://tdan.com/10-risks-of-iot-data-management/32157?
Malik, V., 2024. Secure by Design: Implementing Zero Trust Principles in Cloud-Native Architectures. *Cloud Security Alliance*. https://cloudsecurityalliance.org

/blog/2024/10/03/secure-by-design-implementing-zero-trust-principles-in-cloud-native-architectures?

Maradin, D., Malnar, A. & Kaštelan, A., 2022. Sustainable and Clean Energy: The Case of Tesla Company. *Journal of Economics, Finance and Management Studies*, 5. https://doi.org/10.47191/jefms/v5-i12-https://doi.org/10.

Masulis, R., 2024. Industrial Artificial Intelligence and Machine Learning. *Wesco*, 6. Automation Insights. https://www.wesco.com/us/en/knowledge-hub/articles/industrial-artificial-intelligence-and-machine-learning.html?

Maurer, C. & Valkenburg, R., 2013. Approaches To Networked Innovation. *International Journal of Innovation and Technology Management,* 11. https://doi.org/10.1142/S0219877014400045.

Mbanefo, C. & Grobbelaar, S., 2024. Unveiling the Core Elements of Platform Ecosystem Development: A Systemic Lens for Value Co-Creation in Small and Medium Enterprises and Orchestrators. *Management Review Quarterly*. https://doi.org/10.1007/s11301-024-00416–1.

Mbanyele, W. & Fengrong, W., 2022. Economic Policy Uncertainty and Industry Innovation: Cross Country Evidence. *The Quarterly Review of Economics and Finance*, 84. https://doi.org/10.1016/j.qref.2022.01.012.

McGrew, G., 2021. *Lights-Out Manufacturing*. AMT. https://www.amtonline.org/article/lights-out-manufacturing?

McKinsey & Company, 2022. *What are Industry 4.0, the Fourth Industrial Revolution, and 4IR?* McKinsey & Company. https://www.mckinsey.com/featured-insights/mckinsey-explainers/what-are-industry-4-0-the-fourth-industrial-revolution-and-4ir?

Minaya, P., Avella, L. & Trespalacios, J., 2024. Synthesizing Three Decades of Digital Servitization: A Systematic Literature Review and Conceptual Framework Proposal. *Service Business*, 18, 193–222. https://doi.org/10.1007/s11628-024-00559-x.

Minz, N. et al., 2024. Platform Business Models and Service Innovation: A Comprehensive Review of Digital Ecosystems. In *Book: Innovative Technologies for Increasing Service Productivity* (pp. 27–40). https://doi.org/10.4018/979-8-3693-2019-8.ch002.

Moeti, M., 2024. The Impact of Cybersecurity on Industrial Operations Caused by Digital Transformation from Industry 4.0 to Industry 5.0. https://doi.org/10.5772/intechopen.114961.

Möller, D., 2023. Cybersecurity in Digital Transformation. In: *Guide to Cybersecurity in Digital Transformation. Advances in Information Security* (Vol. 103). Springer. https://doi.org/10.1007/978-3-031-26845-8_1.

Monticone, F. et al., 2024. Harvesting Connections: The Role of Stakeholders' Network Structure, Dynamics and Actors' Influence in Shaping Farmers' Markets. *Agriculture and Human Values*, 41, 1503–1520. https://doi.org/10.1007/s10460-024-10563–6.

Motyka, M., Keefe, T. L., Hardin, K. & Amon, C., 2024. 2025 Renewable Energy Industry Outlook, Renewables Race to Fill Resource Gap as Demand for Clean Energy Is Outpacing Supply. *Deloitte*. https://www2.deloitte.com/us/en/insights/industry/renewable-energy/renewable-energy-industry-outlook.html?

Mourtzis, D., Angelopoulos, K. & Zogopoulos, V., 2019. Mapping Vulnerabilities in the Industrial Internet of Things Landscape. *Procedia CIRP*, 84, 265–270. https://doi.org/10.1016/j.procir.2019.04.201.

MST, 2021. *Cyber Case Study: Hack at Steel Mill Causes Physical Damage*. MST Insurance Solutions.

Nankya, M., Chataut, R. & Akl, R., 2023. Securing Industrial Control Systems: Components, Cyber Threats, and Machine Learning-Driven Defense Strategies. *Sensors*, 23(21), 8840. https://doi.org/10.3390/s23218840.

National Institute of Standards and Technology, 2024. *The NIST Cybersecurity Framework (CSF) 2.0.* https://nvlpubs.nist.gov/nistpubs/CSWP/NIST.CSWP.29.pdf

Ng, A. & Sisco, J., 2024. Justice Department Sues TikTok over Alleged Kids' Privacy Violations. *POLITICO.* https://www.politico.com/news/2024/08/02/doj-sues-tiktok-00172483?

Nguyen, H., Trestian, R., To, D. & Tatipamula, M., 2021. Digital Twin for 5G and Beyond. *IEEE Communications Magazine.* https://doi.org/10.1109/MCOM.001.2000343.

Niculescu, G. & Marcau, F., 2024. Behavioral Factors That Can Significantly Influence the Decision-making Process. https://www.researchgate.net/publication/378373343_behavioral_factors_that_can_significantly_influence_the_decision-making_process.

Nie, C., Zhao, F., Li, C. & Chen, T., 2024. Research on Integration of Innovation Chain, Industrial Chain, Fund Chain, and Talent Chain. *Bulletin of Chinese Academy of Sciences* (Chinese Version), 39(2), Article 5. https://doi.org/10.16418/j.issn.1000-3045.20231008002.

NIST Cybersecurity Framework, n.d. *Cybersecurity Framework.* https://www.nist.gov/cyberframework

NORCICS Underway Assessment Panel, 2025. *Panel's report: NORCICS SFI Norwegian Centre for Cybersecurity in Critical Sectors.* https://www.ntnu.edu/documents/1294734959/0/SFI+NORCICS_mideval.pdf/ee1bf85e-9972-b99d-5a81-90b663b191e6?t=1744619139801

Norges Forskningråd, 2011. *Innovasjon.* https://www.forskningsradet.no/siteassets/publikasjoner/1253970499777.pdf

Norwegian Ministeries, 2019. *National Cyber Security Strategy for Norway.* https://www.regjeringen.no/contentassets/c57a0733652f47688294934ffd93fc53/national-cyber-security-strategy-for-norway.pdf

Norwegian Ministry of Digitalisation and Public Governance, 2024. *Government.no.* https://www.regjeringen.no/contentassets/c499c3b6c93740bd989c43d886f65924/en-gb/pdfs/digitaliseringsstrategi_eng.pdf

Obaid, A. & Al-Husseini, K., 2024. Monte Carlo Simulation for Risk Management in Agile Software Development. *International Journal of Computers and Informatics*, 3, 63–78. https://doi.org/10.59992/IJCI.2024.v3n3p3.

Ohanu, C. P., Rufai, S. A. & Oluchi, U. C., 2024. A Comprehensive Review of Recent Developments in Smart Grid Through Renewable Energy Resources Integration. *Heliyon*, 10(3). https://doi.org/10.1016/j.heliyon.2024.e25705.

Oluwafunmilayo, A. & Talabi, S., 2024. Tesla's Supply Chain Management Model: A Lesson for Smart Manufacturing. *International Journal of Engineering Research & Technology (IJERT)*, 13(05). https://doi.org/10.17577/IJERTV13IS050293.

Parker, S., 2024. The Strategic Value of Treating Cybersecurity as an Investment. *Agileblue.* https://agileblue.com/the-strategic-value-of-treating-cybersecurity-as-an-investment/.

Parthasarathy, S., 2024. Building Trust in Digital Strategy: A Key to Competitive Advantage and Long-Term Success. *CXOToday.* https://cxotoday.com/interviews/building-trust-in-digital-strategy-a-key-to-competitive-advantage-and-long-term-success/.

Patel, M., 2024. The Ethics of AI Addressing Bias, Privacy, and Accountability in Machine Learning. *cloudthat*. https://www.cloudthat.com/resources/blog/the-ethics-of-ai-addressing-bias-privacy-and-accountability-in-machine-learning?

Perry, N., 2024. Toyota's Approach to Lean Procurement and Production. *Procurement Magazine*. https://procurementmag.com/articles/toyotas-approach-to-lean-procurement-and-production.

Piacentini, R. D. & Della Ceca, L. S., 2017. The Use of Environmental Sustainability Criteria in Industrial Processes. *Drying Technology*, 35(1), 1–3. https://doi.org/10.1080/07373937.2016.1243446.

Pit, R., 2024. Self-Healing Machines and Materials are Creating a More Resilient Future. *Copperberg*. https://www.copperberg.com/self-healing-machines-and-materials-are-creating-a-more-resilient-future/?

Pittenger, L. M. et al., 2022. Bounded Rationality: Managerial Decision-Making and Data. *Journal of Computer Information Systems*, 63(4), 890–903. https://doi.org/10.1080/08874417.2022.2111380.

Pliatsios, D., Sarigiannidis, P., Lagkas, T. & Sarigiannidis, A. G., 2020. *A Survey on SCADA Systems: Secure Protocols, Incidents, Threats and Tactics*. IEEE.

Pochmara, J. & Świetlicka, A., 2024. Cybersecurity of Industrial Systems —A 2023 Report. *Electronics*, 13, 1191. https://doi.org/10.3390/electronics13071191.

Produção, G. et al., 2022. Decision Making in the Process of Choosing and Deploying Industry 4.0 Technologies. *Gestão & Produção*, 29. https://doi.org/10.1590/1806-9649-2022v29e163.

Puica, E., 2023. Predictive Analytics Functionalities in Supply Chain Management. *Proceedings of the International Conference on Business Excellence*, 17, 986–996. https://doi.org/10.2478/picbe-2023-0090.

PWC, 2020. Zero Trust Architecture: A Paradigm Shift in Cybersecurity and Privacy. https://www.pwc.ch/en/publications/2020/ch-pwc-zero-trust-architecture-a-paradigm-shift.pdf?

Raimundo, R. J. & Rosário, A. T., 2022. Cybersecurity in the Internet of Things in Industrial Management. *Applied Sciences*, 12(3), 1598. https://doi.org/10.3390/app12031598.

Ramadan, M., 2023. A Decision Support System for Selecting Suitable Management Processes and Tools in the Case of Telework for Software Developers. *Conference: Fintech and Closing the Digital GapAt: The 13th International Conference on ICT in Our Lives*. Conference Reference.

Rambus Press, 2022. What Is OTA in Automotive? Over the Air Updates Explained. *Rambus*. https://www.rambus.com/blogs/ota-updates-explained/.

Rangen, C., 2021. Building An Innovation Cluster. *strategytools*. https://www.strategytools.io/building-an-innovation-cluster/?

Rasshyvalov, D. et al., 2024. Navigating Geopolitical Risks: Implications for Global Supply Chain Management. *Multidisciplinary Reviews*, 7, 2024spe017. https://doi.org/10.31893/multirev.2024spe017.

Raza, Z., 2024. Just-in-Time Manufacturing: Driving Efficiency and Lean Innovation. *Converged by Propel*. https://converged.propelsoftware.com/blogs/just-in-time-manufacturing-driving-efficiency-and-lean-innovation?

Reed, J., Svedberg, P. & Nygren, J., 2025. Enhancing the Innovation Ecosystem: Overcoming Challenges to Introducing Information-Driven Technologies in Health Care. *Journal of Medical Internet Research*, 27, e56836.

Ricadela, A., 2023. 6 Industry 4.0 Challenges and Risks. *Oracle*. https://www.oracle.com/industrial-manufacturing/industry-4-challenges/?

Rijwani, T. et al., 2024. Industry 5 0: A Review of Emerging Trends and Transformative Technologies in the Next Industrial Revolution. *International Journal on Interactive Design and Manufacturing (IJIDeM)*, 19, 667–679. https://doi.org/10.1007/s12008-024-01943-7.

Rosin, F., Forget, P., Lamouri, S. & Pellerin, R., 2022. Enhancing the Decision-Making Process through Industry 4.0 Technologies. *Sustainability*, 14, 461. https://doi.org/10.3390/su14010461.

Rotondo, D. & Chow, P., 2025. Unlocking Green Growth: Sustainability as a Key Driver of Corporate Innovation. *World Economic Forum*. https://www.weforum.org/stories/2025/01/unlocking-sustainability-green-growth-innovative-strategies/?

Safitra, M. F., Lubis, M. & Fakhrurroja, H., 2023. Counterattacking Cyber Threats: A Framework for the Future of Cybersecurity. *Sustainability*, 15(18), 13369. https://doi.org/10.3390/su151813369.

Sánchez-Obando, J., Castillo-Ossa, L., Duque-Méndez, N. & Carrillo Zambrano, E., 2024. Design of a conceptual model of open innovation for the decentralization of the science, technology, and innovation system in Colombia from an organizational ecology perspective. Journal of Innovation and Entrepreneurship volume 13, Article number: 67. https://doi.org/10.1186/s13731-024-00428-x.

Sangkhro, R. & Agrawal, A. K., 2023. Cybersecurity in Industrial Control Systems: A Review of the Current Trends and Challenges. *10th International Conference on Computing for Sustainable Global Development (INDIACom)*, New Delhi, India, *pp. 355–359.*

SANS Cyber Defense, 2023. *What Is Zero Trust Architecture?* SANS. https://www.sans.org/blog/what-is-zero-trust-architecture/?

Sargiotis, D., 2024. Data Security and Privacy: Protecting Sensitive Information. In: *Data Governance*. Springer. https://doi.org/10.1007/978-3-031-67268-2_6.

Sari, A., Lekidis, A. & Butun, I., 2020. Industrial Networks and IIoT: Now and Future Trends. In: *Industrial IoT, Challenges, Design Principles, Applications, and Security* (pp.3–55). https://doi.org/10.1007/978-3-030-42500-5_1.

Sarı, T., 2019. Multi-Criteria Decision Making for Innovation Decisions. In: *A New Perspective in Social Sciences* (pp.158–166). Frontpage Publications. https://www.researchgate.net/publication/362263506_Multi-Criteria_Decision_Making_for_Innovation_Decisions.

Savchuk, V., 2023. Real Options Technique as a Tool of Strategic Risk Management. https://doi.org/10.48550/arXiv.2303.09176.

Schott, S., 2022. TIA Portal for Improved Cyber Security in an Industrial Setting // TIA Portal für mehr Cybersicherheit im industriellen Umfeld. *Siemens*. https://blog.siemens.com/2022/01/tia-portal-for-improved-cyber-security-in-an-industrial-setting-tia-portal-fur-mehr-cybersicherheit-im-industriellen-umfeld/?

Seka, N., 2024. The Network Connection Between Apple and Foxconn. *Medium*. https://medium.com/%40nareshnavinash/the-network-connection-between-apple-and-foxconn-4c2956e5187b.

Sharghivand, N. & Derakhshan, F., 2021. Data Security and Privacy in Industrial IoT. In: H. Karimipour & F. Derakhshan (eds.) *AI-Enabled Threat Detection and Security Analysis for Industrial IoT*. Springer. https://doi.org/10.1007/978-3-030-76613-9_3.

Sharma, D., 2024. Top 10 Data Governance Best Practices for the Manufacturing Industry. *ScikiQ*. https://Top 10 Data Governance Best Practices for the Manufacturing Industry com/blog/top-10-data-governance-best-practices-for-manufacturing-industry/?

Sharma, S., Srivastava, P. & Kumar, A., 2021. Supply Chain Vulnerability Assessment for Manufacturing Industry. *Annals of Operations Research*, 326, 653–683. https://doi.org/10.1007/s10479-021-04155-4.

Shaw, K., 2024. How 5G and Edge Computing Can Help Improve Manufacturing Productivity. *Verizon Business*. https://www.verizon.com/business/resources/articles/s/how-5g-and-edge-computing-can-help-improve-manufacturing-productivity/.

Shih, W., 2020. *Is It Time to Rethink Globalized Supply Chains?* MIT SMR. https://sloanreview.mit.edu/article/is-it-time-to-rethink-globalized-supply-chains/?

Shilenge, M. C. & Telukdarie, A., 2022. Optimization of Operational and Information Technology Integration Towards Industry 4.0. *IEEE 31st International Symposium on Industrial Electronics (ISIE)*, Anchorage, AK, pp. 1076–1081. https://doi.org/10.1109/ISIE51582.2022.9831605.

Siman, E. et al., 2023. Blockchain-Enabled Edge Computing: Bridging the Gap for Secure and Efficient Decentralized Systems. Conference: *National Conference on Nation Building & Development*. https://www.researchgate.net/publication/374003589_blockchain-enabled_edge_computing_bridging_the_gap_for_secure_and_efficient_decentralized_systems.

Smith, D., 2013. Power-by-the-Hour: The Role of Technology in Reshaping Business Strategy at Rolls-Royce. *Technology Analysis and Strategic Management*, 25, 987–1007. https://doi.org/10.1080/09537325.2013.823147.

Sobers, R., 2024. Ransomware Statistics, Data, Trends, and Facts. *Varonis*. https://www.varonis.com/blog/ransomware-statistics.

Sriram, A., 2025. Waabi Ties Up with Volvo to Roll Out Self-driving Trucks. *Reuters*. https://www.reuters.com/business/autos-transportation/waabi-ties-up-with-volvo-roll-out-self-driving-trucks-2025-02-04/?

Stach, J., 2021. Ford and Google Partner to Reinvent the Connected Vehicle Experience. *engineering.com*. https://www.engineering.com/ford-and-google-partner-to-reinvent-the-connected-vehicle-experience/.

Staves, A. et al., 2022. A Cyber Incident Response and Recovery Framework to Support Operators of Industrial Control Systems. *International Journal of Critical Infrastructure Protection*, 37. https://doi.org/10.1016/j.ijcip.2021.100505.

Stone, M., 2025. Amazon's Robots Could Help it Save $10 billion a year by 2030, Morgan Stanley Analysts Say. *Business Insider*. https://www.businessinsider.com/amazon-robots-could-save-10-billion-a-year-2025-2?

Størkersen, et al., 2023. Hvordan styrke SFI-enes bidrag til innovasjon? Råd og anbefalinger. https://ntnuopen.ntnu.no/ntnu-xmlui/bitstream/handle/11250/3126685/SFI_Rapport_B5_30.08.pdf?sequence=1&isAllowed=y

Svystunova, L., Muratova, Y., Fortwengel, J. & Edwards, T., 2024. Multinational Corporations' Interactions with Host Institutions: Taking Stock and Moving Forward. *Management International Review*, 64, 3–33. https://doi.org/10.1007/s11575-023-00525-1.

Szemzo, H., Mosquera, J., Polyák, L. & Hayes, L., 2022. Flexibility and Adaptation: Creating a Strategy for Resilience. *Sustainability*, 14, 2688. https://doi.org/10.3390/su14052688.

Takahashi, S. & Takahashi, V., 2022. Integrated Co-creation Process with Multiple Stakeholders in Innovation Networks. *Innovation & Management Review*, 19(4), 382–399. https://doi.org/10.1108/INMR-10-2020-0142.

Talamo, C., Paganin, G., Atta, N. & Rota, F., 2019. Epistemic Uncertainty, Risk Management and Information: the Role of the Detailed Design. *TECHNE – Journal of Technology for Architecture and Environment*, 18, 164–173. https://doi.org/10.13128/techne-7523.

Tao, F., Qi, Q., Wang, L. & Nee, A., 2019. Digital Twins and Cyber–Physical Systems toward Smart Manufacturing and Industry 4.0: Correlation and Comparison. *Engineering*, 5, 653–661. https://doi.org/10.1016/j.eng.2019.01.014.

TechRepublic Staff, 2020. Facebook Data Privacy Scandal: A Cheat Sheet. *TechRepublic*. https://www.techrepublic.com/article/facebook-data-privacy-scandal-a-cheat-sheet/.

Tertulino, R., Ivaki, N. & Morais, H., 2024. Design a Software Reference Architecture to Enhance Privacy and Security in Electronic Health Records. *IEEE Access*, 12, 112157–112179. https://doi.org/10.1109/ACCESS.2024.3441751.

The Associated Press, 2024. *LinkedIn Hit With 310 Million Euro Fine for Data Privacy Violations From Irish Watchdog*, s.l.: s.n.

The Research Council of Norway, 2021. *The Research Council of Norway*. https://www.forskningsradet.no/siteassets/generelle-krav-og-vilkar-for-foi-prosjekter/generelle-vilkar-01012021-eng-ny.pdf

The Research Council of Norway, 2025. *Centre for Research-based Innovation – SFI V – Phase 2*. https://www.forskningsradet.no/en/call-for-proposals/2025/centre-for-research-based-innovation-sfi-v-phase-2/

Thu, H. D., 2025. AI and Data Privacy: Balancing Innovation with Security. *Smartdev*. https://smartdev.com/ai-and-data-privacy-balancing-innovation-with-security/.

TLI, 2024. Alibaba's Cainiao Logistics Powerhouse Redefining Global Delivery. *Transportation & Logistics International*. https://tlimagazine.com/news/alibabas-cainiao-logistics-powerhouse-redefining-global-delivery/?

Torkington, S., 2024. 5 Cybersecurity Risks Posed by Emerging Technology – and How We Can Defend Against Them. *WEF (World Economic Forum)*. https://www.weforum.org/stories/2024/10/cyber-resilience-emerging-technology-ai-cybersecurity/.

Torres Curado, M., Resende, R. & Rato, V. M., 2024. Circular Economy: Current View From the Construction Industry Based on Published Definitions. *Sustainability: Science, Practice and Policy*, 20(1). https://doi.org/10.1080/15487733.2024.2364954.

Tripathi, D. & Nishad, D., 2019. Digital Twin Technology: Concepts and Applications. *Turkish Journal of Computer and Mathematics Education (TURCOMAT)*, 10, 1660–1665. https://doi.org/10.61841/turcomat.v10i3.14627.

Tronvoll, B., Sklyar, A., Sörhammar, D. & Kowalkowski, C., 2020. Transformational Shifts through Digital Servitization. *Industrial Marketing Management*, 89, 293–305. https://doi.org/10.1016/j.indmarman.2020.02.005.

UNODC, n.d. *International Cooperation on Cybersecurity Matters*.

Uzonwanne, F., 2022. Rational Model of Decision-Making. In: A. Farazmand (ed.) *Global Encyclopedia of Public Administration, Public Policy, and Governance*. Springer. https://doi.org/10.1007/978-3-030-66252-3_2474.

Van Niekerk, M., 2024. From Source to Stomach: How Blockchain Tracks Food Across the Supply Chain and Saves Lives. *World Economic Forum*. https://www.weforum.org/stories/2024/08/blockchain-food-supply-chain/?

Van Rooyen, M. & Van der Lingen, E., 2024. Reducing Uncertainty Associated With Managing Technology Innovation. *Social Sciences & Humanities Open*, 9. https://doi.org/10.1016/j.ssaho.2023.100771.

Vargas-Hernández, J. & Vargas-González, O., 2024. *Global Supply, Production and Value Chains. International Trade, Economic Crisis and the Sustainable*

Development Goals, Emerald Publishing Limited, Leeds (pp. 277–297). https://doi.org/10.1108/978-1-83753-586-620241019.

Varghese, S. A. et al., 2022. Digital Twin-based Intrusion Detection for Industrial Control Systems. arxiv. https://doi.org/10.48550/arXiv.2207.09999.

Varnado, L. & Matthew, R., 2024. *Navigating Cybersecurity and Corporate Espionage Risks to the Oil and Gas Industry.* Reuters.

Vijayan, J., 2017. Ransomware Attack on Merck Caused Widespread Disruption to Operations. *Dark Reading.* https://www.darkreading.com/cyberattacks-data-breaches/ransomware-attack-on-merck-caused-widespread-disruption-to-operations?

Villareal, N., 2020. Self-service Predictive Analytics: An Industrial Fortune Teller. *Processing Magazine.* https://www.processingmagazine.com/maintenance-safety/preventive-predictive-maintenance/article/21144338/self-service-predictive-analytics-an-industrial-fortune-teller?

Wai, E. & Lee, C. K. M., 2023. Seamless Industry 4.0 Integration: A Multilayered Cyber-Security Framework for Resilient SCADA Deployments in CPPS. *Applied Sciences*, 13(21), 12008. https://doi.org/10.3390/app132112008.

Wang, C., Wang, Q., Feng, T. & Zhang, Y., 2021. The Influence of Service Category, Consumers' Narcissism and Processing Mode on Service Customization Consumption. *Asia Pacific Journal of Marketing and Logistics*, 33(7), 1556–1577. https://doi.org/10.1108/APJML-04-2020-0263.

Waqar, M., Khan, A. H., Bhatti, I. & Lucas, M., 2024. Self-Adaptive AI Systems for Autonomous Decision-Making in Dynamic Environments. https://www.researchgate.net/publication/386076276_Self-Adaptive_AI_Systems_for_Autonomous_Decision-Making_in_Dynamic_Environments.

Whitfield, G., 2022. The History of Global Supply Chains. All Things Supply Chain. https://www.allthingssupplychain.com/the-history-of-global-supply-chains/.

Więckowski, J. et al., 2023. Recent Advances in Multi-Criteria Decision Analysis: A Comprehensive Review of Applications and Trends. *International Journal of Knowledge-Based and Intelligent Engineering Systems*, 27(4), 367–393. https://doi.org/10.3233/KES-230487.

Woods, E., 2018. *Secure by Design – Security Design Principles for the Working Architect,* s.l.: s.n.

Wu, J.-Z. &., Lin, K.-S. & Wu, C.-Y., 2015. Integration of Scenario Planning and Decision Tree Analysis for New Product Development: A Case Study of a Smartphone Project in Taiwan. *The International Journal of Industrial Engineering: Theory, Applications and Practice*, 22, 616–627.

Wulf, A. & Butel, L., 2017. Knowledge Sharing and Collaborative Relationships in Business Ecosystems and Networks: A Definition and a Demarcation. *Industrial Management & Data Systems*, 117. https://doi.org/10.1108/IMDS-09-2016-0408.

Xu, X., Lu, Y., Vogel-Heuser, B. & Wang, L., 2021. Industry 4.0 and Industry 5.0—Inception, Conception and Perception. *Journal of Manufacturing Systems,* 61, 530–535.

Zhurer, Y., 2024. Industrial & Corporate Espionage: What Is It? Cases & Best Prevention Practices. *Syteca.* https://www.syteca.com/en/blog/prevent-industrial-espionage.

Zhu, S., Susan, M., Mikhail, M. & Mikhail, M., 2020. Team Decision Making: The Dynamic Effects of Team Decision Style Composition and Performance via Decision Strategy. *Journal of Management*, 47. https://doi.org/10.1177/0149206320916232.

9. Decision-making in industrial innovation under multiple criteria and uncertainty

Elias G. Carayannis and Nikos R. Zotas

9.1 INTRODUCTION: DECISION-MAKING COMPLEXITY IN INDUSTRIAL INNOVATION

Decision-making lies at the heart of industrial innovation, shaping the trajectory of businesses as they navigate the challenges of developing, refining, and deploying new technologies, products, and processes. Every stage of the innovation cycle, from ideation to commercialization, requires strategic choices that determine the success or failure of industrial enterprises. These decisions impact not only the internal operations of a company but also its position in the market, competitive dynamics, and long-term sustainability.

In today's fast-paced industrial landscape, decision-making is more complex than ever due to rapid technological advancements, shifting consumer demands, and evolving regulatory environments. Companies must consider multiple factors simultaneously, balancing cost-efficiency, technical feasibility, market viability, and sustainability (Li et al., 2021). These decision criteria often present conflicting objectives. For instance, while accelerating product development may provide a competitive edge, it may also compromise quality or increase operational risks. Similarly, investing in sustainable innovation can enhance brand reputation and ensure regulatory compliance; yet it may also require significant upfront capital and long-term commitment.

Beyond the inherent complexity of multiple decision criteria, industrial innovation is further complicated by uncertainty. Companies frequently operate in environments where future technological trends, consumer behaviors, and regulatory frameworks are unpredictable. A firm investing in the development of a new material or manufacturing technology, for example, may face uncertainties regarding its scalability, customer adoption, and the potential emergence of superior alternatives. These uncertainties, whether technical, market-related, regulatory, or economic, introduce an element of risk that makes strategic planning and decision-making particularly challenging.

Given the intricate nature of industrial innovation, companies must adopt structured approaches to decision-making to mitigate risks and enhance the likelihood of success. Decision-making frameworks provide a systematic way to evaluate options, prioritize objectives, and assess risks. Among the most widely used frameworks are rational decision-making models, which emphasize logical analysis and data-driven choices, and bounded rationality approaches, which acknowledge human cognitive limitations and the need for practical, satisficing solutions (Flores-García et al., 2019). Additionally, prospect theory and heuristic-based models recognize that decision-makers often rely on experience, intuition, and simplified mental shortcuts when faced with uncertainty.

This chapter explores the complexity of decision-making in industrial innovation, addressing the interplay of multiple decision criteria and the challenges posed by uncertainty. By examining key decision-making frameworks and their practical applications, it aims to provide a structured perspective on how industrial firms can navigate the intricate and often unpredictable innovation landscape.

9.2 THE NATURE OF UNCERTAINTY IN INDUSTRIAL INNOVATION

Industrial innovation is inherently uncertain, requiring businesses to make critical decisions with incomplete information about future technological developments, market conditions, and regulatory landscapes. Unlike routine operational choices, which often rely on historical data and established trends, innovation decisions involve venturing into uncharted territory (Jalonen, 2011). Uncertainty in industrial innovation manifests in multiple forms—technical, market, regulatory, and economic—each of which influences the decision-making process. Additionally, different types of uncertainty, such as aleatory and epistemic, require distinct approaches to risk management and strategic planning.

9.2.1 Forms of Uncertainty in Industrial Innovation

9.2.1.1 Technical uncertainty

Technical uncertainty arises from the unpredictability of whether a new technology, product, or process will function as intended. Companies investing in emerging fields such as artificial intelligence (AI), nanotechnology, or advanced robotics must grapple with unknowns related to feasibility, performance, and scalability (Van Rooyen & Van der Lingen, 2024). For example, in the semiconductor industry, the transition to smaller transistor sizes presents technical challenges related to heat dissipation, quantum effects, and fabrication precision. Similarly, the development of autonomous vehicles involves uncertainties regarding sensor accuracy, machine learning reliability, and real-world adaptability.

Technical uncertainty is particularly high in the early stages of research and development (R&D), where unforeseen technical limitations may arise, requiring continuous experimentation and iteration. Companies mitigate this uncertainty through prototyping, computational simulations, and controlled pilot programs before full-scale deployment.

9.2.1.2 Market uncertainty

Even when a technology is technically feasible, its commercial success depends on market acceptance. Market uncertainty arises when businesses struggle to predict customer preferences, competitive responses, and adoption rates (Han & Kang, 2021).

Consumer behavior is influenced by various factors, including brand perception, economic conditions, and shifts in societal values. For example, while electric vehicles are increasingly popular today, their early adoption was hindered by concerns over battery life, charging infrastructure, and cost. Similarly, augmented reality (AR) and virtual reality (VR) technologies have faced adoption uncertainty due to unclear value propositions for mainstream consumers.

Market uncertainty can also stem from competitive dynamics. An innovative product may quickly become obsolete if a competitor releases a superior alternative. To address this, companies use techniques such as market research, beta testing, and customer co-creation to refine their offerings before large-scale commercialization.

9.2.1.3 Regulatory uncertainty

Regulatory environments play a crucial role in shaping industrial innovation, and uncertainty in policy changes can significantly impact investment decisions. Governments worldwide implement laws and standards to ensure safety, environmental compliance, and fair market practices. However, regulatory frameworks are often subject to shifts, creating uncertainty for companies developing new technologies (Kwon et al., 2022). For example, in the pharmaceutical industry, drug approval processes vary between regions, and changes in clinical trial regulations can affect the time and cost of bringing a new drug to market. Similarly, the renewable energy sector depends on government incentives, subsidies, and carbon taxation policies, which may change with political transitions.

To manage regulatory uncertainty, businesses engage in regulatory foresight, lobbying, and collaboration with policymakers. In highly regulated industries, legal teams and compliance experts play a crucial role in navigating evolving requirements.

9.2.1.4 Economic uncertainty

Economic conditions, including inflation, interest rates, currency fluctuations, and global trade policies, introduce financial uncertainty for industrial innovators. During economic downturns, consumer spending declines, investors become risk-averse, and supply chains face disruptions. Conversely, periods of economic growth may lead to increased demand but also heightened competition and rising operational costs (Mbanyele & Fengrong, 2022).

Industrial firms often make long-term capital investments in R&D, infrastructure, and talent acquisition. Economic uncertainty complicates these decisions, as future returns on investment are difficult to predict. For instance, during the 2008 financial crisis, many technology firms postponed ambitious innovation projects due to funding constraints. More recently, the COVID-19 pandemic disrupted supply chains and altered market demands, forcing industries to reassess their innovation strategies. Mitigating economic uncertainty requires scenario planning, financial risk assessment, and portfolio diversification. Some firms hedge against economic fluctuations by investing in multiple markets or maintaining flexible manufacturing capabilities to adapt to changing demand conditions.

9.2.2 Types of Uncertainty: Aleatory vs. Epistemic

Uncertainty in industrial innovation can be classified into two fundamental types: aleatory uncertainty and epistemic uncertainty.

9.2.2.1 Aleatory uncertainty (randomness and variability)

Aleatory uncertainty arises from inherent randomness or variability in processes. This type of uncertainty is often irreducible, meaning that no amount of additional information can eliminate its unpredictability. Examples include fluctuations in raw material costs, unexpected delays in supply chains, and natural disasters disrupting production. Since aleatory uncertainty cannot be entirely controlled, companies focus on risk mitigation strategies, such as building redundancy into supply chains, maintaining financial reserves, and adopting flexible production systems (Acebes et al., 2021). For example, semiconductor manufacturers often establish multiple fabrication plants in different regions to minimize risks associated with geopolitical instability.

9.2.2.2 Epistemic uncertainty (lack of knowledge and information gaps)

Epistemic uncertainty, on the other hand, stems from incomplete knowledge or information gaps. Unlike aleatory uncertainty, epistemic uncertainty can be reduced through research, experimentation, and data collection. For example, when developing a new drug, pharmaceutical companies initially have limited information on its long-term side effects (Talamo et al., 2019). Through rigorous clinical trials and patient studies, they gradually reduce epistemic uncertainty and gain confidence in the drug's safety and efficacy. Similarly, in aerospace engineering, computational models and wind tunnel testing help reduce uncertainty regarding an aircraft's aerodynamics before full-scale production.

To address epistemic uncertainty, industrial firms invest in big data analytics, AI, and real-time monitoring systems to enhance decision-making. By continuously gathering and analyzing information, companies can make more informed choices and adjust their strategies accordingly.

Uncertainty is an inevitable component of industrial innovation, influencing decisions across technical, market, regulatory, and economic dimensions. Distinguishing between aleatory and epistemic uncertainty allows firms to develop appropriate risk management strategies, leveraging technology and data-driven insights to reduce knowledge gaps. By adopting adaptive decision-making approaches and strategic flexibility, industrial firms can navigate uncertainty more effectively, ensuring long-term innovation success in an ever-changing landscape.

9.3 MULTIPLE DECISION CRITERIA IN INDUSTRIAL INNOVATION

Decision-making in industrial innovation is a multidimensional process that requires companies to evaluate multiple, often conflicting, factors before committing to a course of action Unlike traditional business decisions that may prioritize a single objective, innovation decisions must integrate technical feasibility, financial investment, market demand, and sustainability considerations. Each of these factors plays a crucial role in shaping the long-term success of new technologies and products, making trade-offs inevitable (Sarı, 2019). Prioritizing one criterion often comes at the expense of another, requiring businesses to strike a balance between competing objectives such as time to market, cost efficiency, and product quality. To navigate these complexities, structured decision-making frameworks such as Multi-Criteria Decision Analysis (MCDA) help businesses assess multiple factors simultaneously and optimize strategic choices.

9.3.1 Key Decision Criteria in Industrial Innovation

Industrial innovation is rarely driven by a single factor. Instead, companies must consider multiple dimensions simultaneously to ensure that new products, processes, or technologies align with business objectives and market demands (Produção et al., 2022). Technical performance, cost efficiency, market viability, and sustainability are among the most significant decision criteria that influence the success of innovation efforts.

9.3.1.1 Technical performance

Technical feasibility plays a crucial role in determining whether an innovation can be successfully implemented. A product or process must meet industry standards and demonstrate improvements over existing alternatives to be considered viable. The reliability, efficiency, and scalability of new technologies must be evaluated to ensure long-term functionality and market competitiveness (Hatoum & Nassereddine, 2024).

Advanced manufacturing techniques, for instance, have enabled the development of lighter yet more durable materials for aerospace and automotive applications. In the semiconductor industry, improvements in microchip architecture enhance processing speed and energy efficiency, enabling more powerful and compact electronic devices. However, despite the potential benefits, new technologies often face unforeseen technical challenges that require rigorous testing and refinement before large-scale adoption.

9.3.1.2 Cost considerations

Financial constraints are a major determinant in industrial innovation, as companies must assess whether the potential returns justify the investment required. The cost of research and development, production, and long-term operational expenses must be carefully managed to maintain financial sustainability (Burova et al., 2021). High development costs can be a barrier to innovation, particularly in industries that require significant capital expenditures.

The pharmaceutical industry provides an example of how cost considerations influence innovation decisions. Drug development involves extensive clinical trials and regulatory approvals, leading to high upfront costs and uncertain financial returns. Companies must evaluate whether to pursue high-risk, high-reward projects or invest in incremental improvements with more predictable outcomes. Similarly, electric vehicle manufacturers must weigh the costs of developing advanced battery technologies against consumer willingness to pay for extended range and performance.

9.3.1.3 Market demand and competitive positioning

Market demand plays a vital role in determining the success of an innovation. Even the most technologically advanced product can fail if it does not align with consumer preferences or if existing competitors dominate the market. Companies must conduct thorough market research to understand customer needs, emerging trends, and potential barriers to adoption (De Bettignies et al., 2022).

The renewable energy sector illustrates how market demand influences innovation decisions. Although solar and wind power have gained widespread adoption, their growth has been influenced by government incentives, infrastructure investments, and shifting public attitudes toward sustainability. Similarly, in consumer electronics, manufacturers must anticipate user preferences for battery life, camera quality, and software capabilities to maintain market leadership. Without a clear understanding of demand trends, innovation investments can result in significant financial losses.

9.3.1.4 Sustainability and environmental impact

Sustainability has become an increasingly important criterion in industrial innovation as companies face growing regulatory pressures and consumer expectations for environmentally responsible products. Businesses must assess the environmental impact of their innovations, including energy consumption, material usage, and carbon emissions (Piacentini & Della Ceca, 2017).

The transition to electric vehicles, for example, has been driven not only by advancements in battery technology but also by policies aimed at reducing greenhouse gas emissions. Similarly, industries such as packaging and materials science are investing in biodegradable alternatives to traditional plastics to ensure compliance with stricter environmental regulations. Companies that integrate sustainability into their innovation strategies not only reduce environmental risks but also enhance their reputation and competitiveness in an evolving market.

9.3.2 Trade-Offs in Industrial Innovation

Balancing competing priorities is a fundamental challenge in industrial innovation. Decision-makers frequently encounter situations where optimizing one aspect requires compromising another. Managing these trade-offs effectively is essential for achieving long-term success (Bingham & McDonald, 2022).

One of the most common trade-offs involves speed versus quality. In industries with short product life cycles, such as consumer electronics and software development, rapid innovation is often necessary to maintain a competitive edge. Companies release new models frequently, sometimes prioritizing speed to market over perfecting every detail. However, in sectors such as aerospace and pharmaceuticals, safety and reliability are paramount, requiring extensive testing and validation before a product can be launched. The balance between speed and quality depends on factors such as industry dynamics, regulatory requirements, and competitive pressures.

Cost versus performance is another critical trade-off in industrial innovation. Advanced technology often comes with higher development and production costs, forcing businesses to decide whether premium features justify the additional expenses. Semiconductor manufacturers, for instance, must balance the pursuit of cutting-edge microchip designs with the economic feasibility of mass production. Similarly, automakers must determine whether to invest in high-performance electric vehicle batteries or focus on cost reduction to improve accessibility and market penetration.

Risk versus reward also plays a key role in innovation decisions. Some companies pursue disruptive technologies with high uncertainty but the potential for significant competitive advantage. Others adopt a more conservative approach, focusing on incremental improvements that carry lower risk but may not provide breakthrough advancements. Startups and tech disruptors often embrace high-risk innovations, such as AI and blockchain applications, while established corporations may prioritize steady improvements in existing products to sustain market leadership.

9.3.3 Multi-Criteria Decision Analysis (MCDA) in Industrial Innovation

To navigate the complexity of multiple decision criteria, companies rely on structured decision-making frameworks such as MCDA. These methodologies provide a systematic approach to evaluating trade-offs and optimizing innovation strategies (Chaube et al., 2024).

The Analytic Hierarchy Process (AHP) is one of the most widely used MCDA methods. It allows decision-makers to prioritize different factors by assigning weights to each criterion. This approach ensures that strategic decisions are aligned with business objectives and industry trends. In the automotive industry, for example, AHP is used to assess powertrain options, comparing internal combustion engines, hybrid systems, and fully electric drivetrains based on efficiency, cost, regulatory compliance, and consumer demand.

Another commonly applied MCDA method is Technique for Order of Preference by Similarity to Ideal Solution (TOPSIS), which ranks decision alternatives based on their proximity to an ideal solution. This method is particularly useful in sectors such as manufacturing and energy, where companies must balance cost-effectiveness, sustainability, and performance. Renewable energy firms, for instance, use TOPSIS to select the best investment opportunities by assessing financial returns, environmental impact, and technological feasibility.

9.3.4 Industry Applications of Multi-Criteria Decision Analysis

MCDA is widely applied across industries to enhance decision-making by evaluating multiple factors such as technical feasibility, cost, risk, sustainability, and market potential. By providing a structured approach, MCDA helps businesses optimize resource allocation, minimize uncertainties, and align innovation efforts with strategic objectives.

Across these industries, MCDA plays a crucial role in balancing trade-offs, improving innovation outcomes, and ensuring long-term competitiveness. As markets and technologies evolve, structured decision-making frameworks will remain essential for guiding complex industrial innovations (Więckowski et al., 2023).

Table 9.1 Key applications of MCDA in various industries

Industry	Key Applications	Decision Criteria Considered
Pharmaceutical	Evaluating drug development pipelines, prioritizing treatments, and managing regulatory approvals	Clinical efficacy, regulatory approval likelihood, production scalability, market demand, and financial risks
Automotive	Assessing alternative powertrain technologies (electric, hybrid, hydrogen) and optimizing vehicle design	Fuel efficiency, emissions compliance, production costs, infrastructure readiness, and consumer adoption
Renewable Energy	Selecting between solar, wind, and hydrogen energy projects, optimizing energy storage solutions	Energy output, environmental impact, cost-effectiveness, policy incentives, and grid compatibility
Aerospace & Defense	Guiding investment in aircraft development, space exploration, and military technologies	Technical performance, safety, cost-effectiveness, regulatory compliance, and geopolitical considerations
Manufacturing	Prioritizing Industry 4.0 transformations, including AI-driven automation and smart factories	ROI, integration complexity, labor impact, scalability, and operational efficiency

9.4 DECISION-MAKING FRAMEWORKS FOR INDUSTRIAL INNOVATION

Effective decision-making is fundamental to industrial innovation, as it determines the successful adoption, commercialization, and sustainability of new technologies. Given the complexity and uncertainty inherent in innovation processes, companies rely on structured frameworks to guide strategic and operational decisions. Commonly applied frameworks include the rational decision-making model, bounded rationality, satisficing approaches, and prospect theory, each offering distinct perspectives on decision-making behavior (Abdel-Basset et al., 2024). Additionally, practical tools such as decision trees and scenario planning support organizations in managing uncertainty and evaluating potential outcomes systematically. By exploring these frameworks and tools, industrial firms can enhance their capacity to handle complex innovation challenges, ultimately driving sustainable competitive advantage.

9.4.1 Rational Decision-Making Model

The rational decision-making model represents a structured, analytical approach commonly used in industrial innovation, particularly when clarity, detailed data, and precision are essential. This model involves clearly defining problems, establishing decision criteria, generating alternative solutions, systematically evaluating these alternatives, and choosing the most optimal solution based on evidence and logical reasoning (Uzonwanne, 2022).

In industrial settings, rational decision-making is particularly valuable for well-defined technical challenges, such as selecting appropriate manufacturing equipment or optimizing production processes. Companies in advanced manufacturing, for instance, leverage rational analysis to decide on investments in robotics, additive manufacturing (3D printing), or advanced materials. Detailed evaluations based on quantifiable metrics like cost-benefit analyses, Return on Investment (ROI) calculations, and feasibility studies ensure informed decisions that align with strategic objectives.

However, the rational model assumes decision-makers have access to complete information and sufficient time for analysis—conditions rarely met in fast-paced, dynamic innovation environments. Thus, while the rational model remains essential for structured decision contexts, organizations frequently complement it with approaches better suited to complexity and uncertainty.

9.4.2 Bounded Rationality and "Satisficing"

Recognizing that perfect rationality is often unattainable, the concept of bounded rationality acknowledges human cognitive limitations, incomplete information, and time constraints. Introduced by Herbert Simon, bounded rationality proposes that decision-makers operate within practical limitations and thus cannot consistently achieve optimal solutions. Instead, they aim for "satisficing," or identifying solutions that are satisfactory and sufficiently effective rather than perfectly optimal (Pittenger et al., 2022).

In industrial innovation, bounded rationality often drives pragmatic decisions. Companies frequently rely on heuristic approaches—simplified rules of thumb—to quickly evaluate new technologies or respond to unforeseen market changes. For example, when a company considers adopting a new manufacturing technology like automated guided vehicles (AGVs), rather than exhaustively comparing every possible alternative, managers might settle for solutions that meet key requirements, such as affordability, ease of integration, and immediate availability. This approach enables faster decisions in dynamic environments, allowing organizations to maintain flexibility without getting overwhelmed by excessive analysis.

Industries characterized by rapid technological advancements, such as consumer electronics, often employ satisficing strategies to accelerate product development cycles. Companies quickly iterate prototypes, accepting solutions that adequately meet customer expectations rather than continually seeking perfection. Such an approach balances speed and practicality in highly competitive markets.

9.4.3 Prospect Theory and Decision Heuristics under Uncertainty

Prospect theory, developed by Daniel Kahneman and Amos Tversky, offers insights into how decision-makers respond to uncertainty, particularly in contexts involving risk and potential losses. Unlike rational models, prospect theory suggests that decisions are influenced by how alternatives are presented and perceived rather than purely objective assessments. Individuals tend to be risk-averse when considering potential gains but risk-seeking when attempting to avoid certain losses (Kahneman & Tversky, 1979). Thus, the framing of innovation opportunities—whether presented as potential gains or losses—can significantly influence managerial decision-making.

In industrial innovation, prospect theory explains behaviors such as companies hesitating to abandon failing projects due to "loss aversion." Organizations may continue investing in struggling innovations to avoid acknowledging previous losses, potentially exacerbating financial and operational risks. Conversely, framing an innovation as a pathway to recover from existing competitive disadvantages (loss avoidance) can encourage bolder, riskier investments.

Decision heuristics—mental shortcuts used to simplify complex decisions—further influence how companies handle uncertainty. Common heuristics include the availability heuristic, where decision-makers rely on recent experiences or easily recalled information, and anchoring, in which initial reference points heavily influence subsequent decisions. For instance, a company deciding to invest in blockchain technology may anchor its decision on early success stories, potentially overlooking critical operational complexities and challenges. Understanding these behavioral tendencies enables managers to recognize potential biases and make more balanced innovation decisions.

9.4.4 Decision Trees and Scenario Planning in Innovation Management

Decision trees and scenario planning are practical tools commonly used in industrial innovation to systematically manage complexity, assess uncertainty, and evaluate strategic options. Decision trees provide visual representations of decisions and their potential outcomes, allowing organizations to map alternatives, probabilities, and associated payoffs clearly. In innovation management, companies utilize decision trees to evaluate complex investment decisions, such as whether to expand production capacity, invest in new product lines, or pursue strategic acquisitions. For example, a firm considering smart manufacturing technologies like Internet of Things (IoT)-enabled machinery may use decision trees to compare different implementation scenarios, analyzing cost implications, integration risks, and potential operational benefits under varying market conditions (Wu et al., 2015).

Scenario planning complements decision trees by encouraging organizations to anticipate and prepare for multiple possible futures rather than relying on single-point forecasts. Through scenario planning, companies systematically explore diverse market, technological, regulatory, and competitive developments, creating strategic narratives about plausible future states. This approach is particularly useful in rapidly evolving sectors such as renewable energy, biotechnology, and digital manufacturing. For instance, automotive companies use scenario planning to explore different futures shaped by electric vehicle adoption rates, infrastructure development, regulatory changes, and consumer preferences, allowing them to remain flexible and responsive to emerging trends (Carayannis et al., 2025).

9.4.5 Industry Examples of Decision-Making Frameworks in Innovation

Industries across various sectors leverage decision-making frameworks to address complex innovation challenges and strategic uncertainties. By applying rational decision-making models, bounded rationality principles, prospect theory insights, and scenario planning techniques, companies enhance their strategic decision-making capabilities and improve innovation outcomes.

In the automotive industry, rational decision-making frameworks dominate due to the critical nature of safety, regulatory compliance, and performance standards. Companies evaluating investments in advanced driver-assistance systems (ADAS), autonomous vehicles, or electric mobility perform rigorous technical analyses and detailed cost-benefit evaluations. By systematically assessing reliability, scalability, and market viability, automotive manufacturers such as Tesla, BMW, and Toyota ensure their strategic decisions align with regulatory requirements and consumer safety expectations.

Smart manufacturing sectors, characterized by rapidly evolving technologies like AI, robotics, and Industry 4.0 solutions, often rely on bounded rationality and satisficing approaches. Given high uncertainty, complexity, and time constraints, firms adopt incremental, iterative innovation cycles. Instead of seeking perfect solutions, companies like Siemens and Bosch frequently implement practical, sufficiently effective technologies that deliver immediate productivity gains and flexibility, enabling rapid adaptation in highly dynamic environments.

In the pharmaceutical and biotechnology industries, decision-making is heavily influenced by prospect theory and decision heuristics. Companies face high-risk, high-reward scenarios, where potential losses significantly affect decisions. Firms may continue investments in struggling drug development projects due to loss aversion—reluctance to acknowledge sunk costs and accept perceived failures. Alternatively, framing biotechnology innovations as critical for competitive positioning or avoiding strategic losses motivates bold investments despite uncertainty. Pharmaceutical leaders such as Pfizer, Johnson & Johnson, and Moderna navigate these behavioral dynamics, balancing strategic risk-taking with prudent resource allocation.

The energy sector extensively employs scenario planning due to long investment horizons, regulatory complexity, and market volatility. Energy companies like Shell, BP, and Vestas systematically explore multiple plausible future scenarios, considering technological advancements, regulatory shifts, economic fluctuations, and environmental impacts. Scenario planning enables these companies to proactively adapt strategies for sustainable energy transitions, investment in renewable sources, and resilience against market disruptions.

Table 9.2 summarizes key industry applications of these decision-making frameworks:

Table 9.2 Key applications of decision-making frameworks

Industry	Framework Applied	Innovation Decisions & Applications	Companies & Examples
Automotive	Rational decision-making	Advanced driver-assistance systems (ADAS), autonomous vehicle technologies, electric vehicle investments	Tesla, Toyota, BMW
Smart Manufacturing	Bounded rationality, satisficing	Adoption of robotics, AI-driven process improvements, iterative technology implementations	Siemens, Bosch, General Electric (GE)
Pharmaceutical & Biotechnology	Prospect theory, decision heuristics	Investment in drug research, managing high-risk R&D projects, strategic persistence despite setbacks	Pfizer, Johnson & Johnson, Moderna
Energy Sector	Scenario planning	Renewable energy transitions, infrastructure investments, regulatory and market uncertainty management	Shell, BP, Vestas, Iberdrola
Aerospace & Defense	Rational decision-making, scenario planning	Aircraft development, satellite technology, military systems procurement, strategic foresight in technological innovation	Boeing, Airbus, Lockheed Martin

Across these diverse sectors, structured decision-making frameworks help organizations navigate innovation complexity, manage uncertainty, and align strategic investments with industry dynamics and future opportunities. By integrating analytical rigor with practical heuristics and scenario-based thinking, industries enhance their capacity to innovate sustainably and competitively.

Industrial innovation requires sophisticated decision-making frameworks to navigate complexity, uncertainty, and strategic risks effectively. Rational decision-making models, bounded rationality, satisficing approaches, prospect theory, and heuristic-driven decisions each offer valuable insights and methodologies. Tools like decision trees and scenario planning further enhance organizational capabilities to systematically evaluate innovation options and future scenarios. By combining structured analytical methods with behavioral insights, industrial companies can improve innovation outcomes, strengthen competitive positioning, and successfully manage uncertainty in rapidly evolving business environments.

9.5 RISK MANAGEMENT AND DECISION-MAKING UNDER UNCERTAINTY

Industrial innovation involves navigating complex environments characterized by uncertainty, risk, and rapid change. Decision-makers must balance the potential rewards of innovation against possible risks such as technological failures, market rejection, regulatory hurdles, or economic disruptions. To effectively manage these uncertainties, businesses adopt structured approaches and advanced analytical techniques, including sensitivity analysis, Monte Carlo simulations, and real options analysis. Incorporating risk management into strategic decision-making enables organizations to identify, analyze, and proactively mitigate risks, improving innovation outcomes and enhancing resilience (Develaki, 2024). Practical insights from healthcare, information technology, and renewable energy industries illustrate successful risk management strategies in high-stakes innovation contexts.

9.5.1 The Role of Risk in Industrial Innovation Decisions

Risk significantly influences industrial innovation by shaping strategic choices, investment priorities, and resource allocations. Organizations pursuing innovative technologies face uncertainties related to technical performance, market acceptance, regulatory environments, and broader economic conditions (Giaccone & Magnusson, 2021). These uncertainties introduce substantial risks that, if unmanaged, can lead to financial losses, reputational damage, or missed opportunities.

For example, in the automotive sector, the shift toward autonomous driving technologies introduces considerable risk concerning safety regulations, liability frameworks, and consumer trust. Companies investing in autonomous vehicles must carefully weigh potential legal, technological, and reputational risks against future market opportunities. Similarly, in pharmaceuticals, clinical trials present significant financial and operational risks. Failure to achieve regulatory approval can result in substantial financial losses and strategic setbacks. Effective risk management enables firms to navigate these complexities confidently, ensuring informed, balanced decision-making.

9.5.2 Techniques for Risk Management in Innovation

Organizations use several sophisticated methods to identify, quantify, and mitigate innovation-related risks. Sensitivity analysis, Monte Carlo simulations, and real options analysis are three widely adopted techniques that provide valuable insights into uncertain environments.

9.5.2.1 Sensitivity analysis

Sensitivity analysis systematically evaluates how variations in specific parameters impact overall project outcomes. Decision-makers vary critical inputs—such as demand forecasts, production costs, and regulatory timelines—to identify factors most significantly affecting innovation performance. This helps managers prioritize risks and design targeted mitigation strategies (Ciechan-Kujawa et al., 2018).

For example, in product development, sensitivity analysis can highlight how fluctuations in raw material costs or delays in component availability could impact profitability and market competitiveness. In renewable energy projects, sensitivity analyses are performed on energy price assumptions, government subsidies, or operational efficiency metrics to identify the most influential factors that determine financial viability. By recognizing which variables have the greatest impact, companies focus their strategic planning and risk mitigation resources more effectively.

9.5.2.2 Monte Carlo simulations

Monte Carlo simulations offer a powerful approach to capturing uncertainty by generating thousands of potential scenarios based on probability distributions for critical input variables. These simulations provide a comprehensive picture of potential outcomes, allowing businesses to understand the probability of achieving specific targets or incurring losses (Obaid & Al-Husseini, 2024).

In the pharmaceutical industry, companies routinely apply Monte Carlo simulations during clinical trial planning to model uncertainties such as patient recruitment rates, trial durations, and regulatory approval probabilities. These simulations enable firms to better understand the likelihood of successful drug development and market entry timelines. Similarly, energy companies use Monte Carlo simulations to predict the financial performance of renewable energy projects under varying conditions, including fluctuating electricity prices, changing weather patterns, and shifting regulatory environments. This approach helps companies quantify risks, improve contingency planning, and make informed strategic decisions.

9.5.2.3 Real options analysis

Real options analysis provides an advanced method for valuing managerial flexibility in innovation projects, acknowledging that companies can adapt decisions in response to changing conditions. Unlike traditional methods that rely on fixed forecasts, real options analysis explicitly incorporates the strategic value of delaying, scaling, abandoning, or expanding projects as new information emerges (Savchuk, 2023).

This technique is especially valuable in high-risk, capital-intensive industries. For instance, technology firms often use real options analysis when developing cutting-edge solutions such as AI platforms or blockchain infrastructures. Companies initially invest in pilot programs or proof-of-concept projects, maintaining the option to scale up based on performance indicators and market feedback. Similarly, in infrastructure-intensive sectors like energy or aerospace, real options enable firms to strategically phase investments, adjusting project scope or timing as technological, market, or regulatory conditions evolve, reducing financial exposure and increasing strategic flexibility.

9.5.3 Incorporating Uncertainty into Strategic Decision-Making in Innovation Projects

To effectively manage innovation risks, companies must systematically integrate risk management techniques into their strategic planning processes. Incorporating uncertainty involves continuously assessing potential risks, conducting rigorous scenario analyses, and maintaining flexibility in strategy execution.

Proactive risk management includes establishing dedicated cross-functional teams responsible for ongoing risk monitoring, evaluation, and adaptation. These teams leverage sensitivity analyses, scenario planning, Monte Carlo simulations, and real options analysis to develop strategic foresight, identify emerging threats, and design robust mitigation plans (Daradkeh & Abul-Huda, 2017). For example, automotive manufacturers continuously monitor regulatory trends affecting electric vehicle subsidies, infrastructure developments, and consumer behavior shifts, enabling timely strategic adjustments to maintain competitiveness.

Likewise, technology companies regularly update risk assessments as new market data emerges, adjusting innovation roadmaps and investments accordingly. This dynamic approach ensures continuous preparedness for emerging risks, promoting resilience and adaptability within rapidly changing innovation environments.

9.6 CASE STUDIES OF SUCCESSFUL RISK MANAGEMENT STRATEGIES IN INNOVATION

Successful risk management strategies are critical for navigating uncertainty and achieving innovation objectives across industries. Real-world examples from healthcare, information technology, and renewable energy demonstrate how structured approaches like sensitivity analysis, Monte Carlo simulations, and real options analysis can significantly enhance strategic decision-making and innovation outcomes. These case studies illustrate practical applications of risk management tools, highlighting their effectiveness in addressing high-stakes scenarios, adapting to unforeseen challenges, and ensuring long-term competitive advantage.

1. **Healthcare Industry—Pfizer's COVID-19 Vaccine Development:** Pfizer's rapid COVID-19 vaccine development represents a prime example of effective risk management under intense uncertainty. Facing unprecedented time pressures and regulatory hurdles, Pfizer employed comprehensive sensitivity analysis and Monte Carlo simulations to forecast potential outcomes for clinical trials, manufacturing scale-up, and global distribution logistics. Real options analysis guided decisions to concurrently scale up manufacturing capacity and initiate clinical trials, balancing risks of financial loss against the potential reward of accelerated vaccine deployment. These structured risk management practices enabled Pfizer to successfully deliver a globally impactful innovation under challenging conditions.
2. **Information Technology—Amazon Web Services (AWS):** Amazon's strategic decision to launch AWS involved significant market, technological, and competitive uncertainties. Initially, Amazon adopted a cautious investment strategy, launching pilot projects internally before gradually expanding AWS's external offerings. Real options analysis allowed Amazon to retain strategic flexibility, enabling incremental scaling based on real-time customer feedback and market adoption data. Sensitivity analyses and scenario planning also informed AWS's ongoing investments, considering competitive responses, technological advancements, and market acceptance. Amazon's structured risk management facilitated informed strategic decision-making, transforming AWS into a global leader in cloud computing.
3. **Renewable Energy—Ørsted's Transformation:** Ørsted's transformation from a fossil-fuel energy company to a global renewable energy leader demonstrates successful risk management in strategic innovation. Ørsted leveraged scenario planning, Monte Carlo simulations, and sensitivity

Table 9.3 Overview of risk management strategies across industries

Industry	Company/Case	Innovation Context	Risk Management Techniques Used	Outcomes Achieved
Healthcare	Pfizer—COVID 19 Vaccine Development	Accelerated vaccine development and global deployment amid high uncertainty	Sensitivity analysis, Monte Carlo simulations, real options analysis	Rapid and successful global vaccine rollout, minimized operational risks
Information Technology	Amazon—Amazon Web Services (AWS)	Cloud computing platform launch with market and technological uncertainty	Real options analysis, sensitivity analysis, scenario planning	Strategic scalability, market leadership, reduced financial exposure
Renewable Energy	Ørsted—Renewable Energy Transition	Strategic shift from fossil fuels to offshore wind and renewable energy	Scenario planning, Monte Carlo simulations, sensitivity analysis, real options analysis	Successful transformation into global renewable energy leader, reduced exposure to regulatory and market risks

analysis to evaluate multiple possible futures involving regulatory shifts, technological advancements, and market conditions. Real options analysis guided incremental investments in offshore wind projects, enabling Ørsted to scale capacity and technology selectively based on evolving market conditions and regulatory incentives. These risk management strategies significantly reduced uncertainty and positioned Ørsted as a global renewable energy leader.

Effective risk management is crucial to successful innovation, requiring structured approaches and sophisticated analytical techniques. Sensitivity analysis, Monte Carlo simulations, and real options analysis provide organizations with robust methods for systematically evaluating, quantifying, and mitigating risks. Integrating these tools into strategic decision-making processes enhances organizational resilience, adaptability, and strategic agility, enabling companies across industries to confidently navigate uncertainty. Successful applications in healthcare, information technology, and renewable energy industries illustrate the importance of proactive risk management, positioning businesses for sustainable innovation success amidst dynamic environments.

9.7 BEHAVIORAL FACTORS IN DECISION-MAKING

Decision-making in industrial innovation is not purely a rational process driven by data and logical evaluation. Human psychology, cognitive tendencies, group dynamics, organizational culture, and leadership styles all significantly influence how decisions are made, often introducing biases and inefficiencies. These behavioral factors can either enhance or hinder the innovation process, impacting a company's ability to adapt to market changes, manage risks, and sustain competitive advantages (Niculescu & Marcau, 2024). Understanding and addressing these behavioral influences is critical for organizations to make more informed, balanced, and effective innovation decisions.

This section explores the key human factors that affect decision-making in industrial innovation, including cognitive biases, group decision-making dynamics, and the role of organizational culture and leadership. It also examines real-world case studies that highlight the impact of these factors on industrial innovation success or failure.

9.7.1 Human Factors Influencing Decision-Making in Industrial Innovation

The process of making decisions in industrial innovation is often affected by various human limitations, including cognitive biases and group decision-making challenges. These factors can shape how decision-makers perceive risk, evaluate opportunities, and respond to uncertainty.

9.7.1.1 Cognitive biases in industrial innovation

Cognitive biases are subconscious mental shortcuts that lead individuals to make decisions based on preconceived notions rather than objective analysis. While these biases can sometimes help streamline decision-making, they frequently introduce errors that negatively impact innovation strategies (Cristofaro et al., 2022).

- **Confirmation Bias:** This occurs when decision-makers seek out or favor information that supports their preexisting beliefs while disregarding contradictory evidence. In industrial innovation, confirmation bias can result in overcommitment to failing projects because executives ignore warning signs and resist contrary data. A classic example is Kodak's failure to embrace digital photography, as company leaders remained convinced that film-based photography would continue to dominate despite mounting evidence to the contrary.
- **Availability Heuristic:** Decision-makers tend to overestimate the importance of information that is most easily recalled or recently encountered. This can lead to overreaction to recent industry trends while ignoring longer-term patterns. For example, a company might invest heavily in AI after seeing a competitor succeed with AI-powered applications, without fully evaluating whether AI aligns with its strategic needs.
- **Overconfidence Bias:** Many leaders in industrial innovation overestimate their ability to predict market trends, technological feasibility, or consumer behavior. This overconfidence can lead to excessive risk-taking without adequate contingency planning. The downfall of Blackberry exemplifies this bias, as executives were overly confident that their existing technology and business model would continue to dominate the mobile industry, underestimating the disruptive power of touchscreen smartphones.

To mitigate these biases, companies can implement structured decision-making frameworks, encourage diverse perspectives in strategic discussions, and require evidence-based validation before making major innovation investments.

9.7.1.2 Group decision-making dynamics

While collaboration in decision-making is often beneficial, certain group dynamics can negatively affect innovation strategies by suppressing dissent, reducing accountability, or reinforcing flawed assumptions (Zhu et al., 2020).

- **Groupthink:** When a team prioritizes consensus over critical evaluation, it can lead to poor decision-making. Groupthink discourages dissenting opinions, stifles innovation, and increases the likelihood of strategic blind spots. An example is Boeing's response to safety concerns with the 737 MAX aircraft, where internal teams failed to challenge flawed assumptions, ultimately resulting in disastrous consequences.
- **Social Loafing:** In large innovation teams, some individuals may exert less effort, assuming that others will contribute sufficiently. This diffusion of responsibility can slow down decision-making and dilute accountability. In industrial R&D projects, social loafing may result in delayed timelines or half-hearted experimentation, reducing the effectiveness of innovation initiatives.

Organizations can counteract these issues by fostering an open culture where critical feedback is encouraged, assigning clear roles and accountability within teams, and incorporating structured decision-making methodologies to ensure thorough evaluation of options.

9.7.2 Impact of Organizational Culture and Leadership on Innovation Decisions

An organization's culture and leadership style play a crucial role in shaping how innovation decisions are made. The degree of risk tolerance, flexibility, and openness to new ideas directly impacts a company's ability to innovate effectively (Akter et al., 2023).

- **Risk-Tolerant vs. Risk-Averse Cultures:** Companies that foster a risk-tolerant culture encourage experimentation, view failure as a learning opportunity, and empower employees to pursue novel ideas. On the other hand, risk-averse cultures tend to emphasize stability, avoid uncertainty, and prioritize efficiency over exploration. While risk aversion can protect companies from reckless decisions, it can also stifle innovation by discouraging bold initiatives. Google's 20% time policy, which allows employees to spend a portion of their work time on independent projects, exemplifies how fostering a risk-tolerant culture can lead to groundbreaking innovations such as Gmail and Google Maps.
- **Hierarchical vs. Decentralized Decision-Making:** In hierarchical organizations, decision-making is often slow and bureaucratic, limiting the ability to respond quickly to innovation opportunities. In contrast, decentralized structures empower employees at all levels to make innovation-related decisions, fostering agility and creativity. Tesla's fast-paced

innovation cycle is an example of how decentralized decision-making can accelerate technological advancements and market responsiveness.

- **Leadership Influence:** The behavior and mindset of company leaders significantly impact innovation outcomes. Transformational leaders inspire teams to embrace change, challenge assumptions, and experiment with new ideas. In contrast, authoritarian leadership styles may suppress alternative perspectives, reducing creativity and adaptability. Leaders like Elon Musk and Jeff Bezos have successfully built innovation-driven organizations by setting ambitious goals, promoting experimentation, and fostering cultures that encourage calculated risk-taking.

To cultivate an innovation-friendly culture, companies should reward creativity, encourage cross-functional collaboration, and ensure leadership actively supports new ideas.

9.7.3 Case Examples of Behavioral Factors Influencing Decision Outcomes in Industrial Innovation

Real-world examples illustrate how behavioral factors such as cognitive biases, group decision-making dynamics, and organizational culture influence innovation decisions—sometimes leading to groundbreaking success and, in other cases, to strategic failures. By examining these cases, companies can learn valuable lessons about the importance of addressing biases, fostering a culture of critical thinking, and implementing structured decision-making frameworks. The following case studies highlight both positive and negative impacts of behavioral factors on industrial innovation, demonstrating how businesses can either leverage or mitigate these influences to improve decision outcomes.

1. **Nokia's Downfall—The Cost of Confirmation Bias and Groupthink:** Nokia's leadership was convinced that its existing mobile phone technology and market dominance were unshakable. Confirmation bias led executives to dismiss the competitive threat of smartphones, while groupthink prevented employees from challenging prevailing assumptions. As a result, Nokia failed to adapt to the rise of touchscreen smartphones, losing its competitive edge and eventually being acquired by Microsoft.
2. **SpaceX's Success—Overcoming Overconfidence and Encouraging Risk-Taking:** While ambitious, SpaceX's leadership implemented structured risk-taking strategies that countered overconfidence bias. By embracing failure as a learning mechanism and iteratively refining rocket designs, the company achieved significant breakthroughs in reusable rocket technology. SpaceX's decentralized decision-making structure also

empowered engineers to contribute ideas, fostering a culture of continuous innovation.

3. **Toyota's Lean Innovation Culture—Mitigating Social Loafing and Enhancing Collaboration:** Toyota's success in automotive innovation is rooted in its Toyota Production System (TPS), which emphasizes continuous improvement, employee accountability, and structured problem-solving. By encouraging workers at all levels to identify inefficiencies and propose solutions, Toyota has maintained a culture of innovation while ensuring operational excellence.

Behavioral factors significantly influence decision-making in industrial innovation. Cognitive biases, such as confirmation bias and overconfidence, can distort judgment, while group dynamics, including groupthink and social loafing, can hinder effective collaboration. Organizational culture and leadership further shape how innovation decisions are made, determining whether a company fosters agility, creativity, and risk tolerance.

By actively recognizing and mitigating these behavioral influences, organizations can improve decision-making processes, enhance innovation outcomes, and sustain long-term competitiveness. Case studies from Nokia, SpaceX, and Toyota highlight both the risks and advantages of behavioral dynamics in innovation. Companies that integrate behavioral insights into their strategic

Table 9.4 Overview of case examples of behavioral factors influencing decision outcomes in industrial innovation

Case Study	Key Behavioral Factors	Impact on Innovation Decision
Nokia's Downfall	Confirmation bias, groupthink	Ignored the smartphone revolution, resisted adopting touchscreen technology, and underestimated competitors, leading to market failure
SpaceX's Success	Overcoming overconfidence, embracing risk-taking	Adopted iterative testing, acknowledged failures as learning opportunities, and encouraged bottom-up innovation, leading to breakthrough advancements in reusable rocket technology
Toyota's Lean Innovation Culture	Counteracting social loafing, fostering accountability	Empowered employees to contribute process improvements through its Toyota Production System (TPS), maintaining efficiency and continuous innovation in manufacturing

decision-making will be better equipped to navigate uncertainty and drive technological advancements.

9.8 DECISION-MAKING TOOLS AND TECHNOLOGIES FOR INDUSTRIAL INNOVATION

The digital revolution has fundamentally reshaped how industries approach decision-making, particularly in the context of innovation. As industrial markets grow increasingly complex, organizations must navigate an environment filled with technological advancements, volatile economic conditions, global competition, and evolving regulatory landscapes. Traditional decision-making processes that relied on intuition and historical data are no longer sufficient. Instead, companies are leveraging decision-support systems (DSS), AI, machine learning (ML), big data analytics, and predictive modeling to enhance accuracy, efficiency, and strategic foresight (Rosin et al., 2022).

These advanced tools allow businesses to process massive amounts of data, simulate future scenarios, optimize resource allocation, and make real-time, evidence-based decisions. The ability to integrate technology into decision-making has provided companies with an unparalleled competitive advantage, enabling them to manage uncertainty proactively rather than reactively.

This chapter explores the role of modern decision-making technologies in industrial innovation, examining how businesses utilize digital tools to improve operational efficiency, enhance strategic choices, and optimize innovation processes. Through an in-depth analysis, we highlight the critical applications of AI, big data, predictive modeling, and decision-support systems across industries such as manufacturing, logistics, energy, pharmaceuticals, and automotive.

9.8.1 Decision-Support Systems and Digital Tools

Decision-support systems (DSS) and digital tools have revolutionized the way industrial organizations analyze data, assess risks, and optimize business strategies. These systems provide structured methodologies for processing complex information, automating decision workflows, and integrating real-time analytics into strategic planning (Ramadan, 2023).

In industrial innovation, DSS play a crucial role in enhancing efficiency, reducing uncertainty, and improving long-term decision-making. These systems can be rule-based, data-driven, or AI-powered, offering solutions tailored to specific industry needs. Companies leverage DSS for predictive maintenance, resource allocation, supply chain management, and operational optimization.

Table 9.5 Types of decision-support systems and their applications across industries

Type of Decision-Support System	Description	Industry Applications
Expert Systems	AI-powered platforms that mimic human decision-making using rule-based logic and vast knowledge databases	Troubleshooting industrial processes, financial risk assessment, regulatory compliance in pharmaceuticals
Business Intelligence (BI) Tools	Platforms that analyze business data, track key performance indicators (KPIs), and generate real-time insights	Retail demand forecasting, logistics optimization, energy consumption monitoring
Simulation and Modeling Software	Digital tools that create virtual models of industrial processes to predict outcomes before real-world implementation	Factory layout optimization, vehicle crash testing, supply chain risk assessment
Cloud-Based Decision-Support Platforms	Platforms that provide global accessibility and real-time decision-making capabilities through cloud computing	Distributed team collaboration, remote production monitoring, predictive analytics for industrial trends

These decision-support tools significantly enhance decision accuracy, speed, and strategic flexibility. By integrating DSS into their daily operations, companies can streamline complex decision processes, improve risk assessment capabilities, and optimize innovation strategies.

9.8.2 Role of AI and Machine Learning in Decision-Making under Uncertainty

AI and machine learning (ML) have emerged as game-changers in industrial decision-making, providing companies with the ability to process vast amounts of structured and unstructured data, identify patterns, and generate predictive insights (Balbaa & Abdurashidova, 2024). Unlike traditional decision-making models that depend on fixed rules, AI-driven systems continuously evolve, refining their accuracy as they learn from real-time data and previous experiences.

9.8.2.1 AI-powered decision-making in industrial innovation

Industries face multiple layers of uncertainty—from fluctuating market demand to evolving technological advancements and unforeseen disruptions such as supply chain breakdowns. AI enhances decision-making by identifying correlations between variables, forecasting trends, and making adaptive recommendations based on live data streams.

AI-driven decision-making is transforming industries in the following ways:

1. Predictive Maintenance: Manufacturing and logistics companies use AI-powered sensors and IoT devices to monitor equipment performance. By predicting failures before they occur, organizations reduce downtime, lower maintenance costs, and increase operational reliability.
2. Supply Chain Optimization: AI algorithms analyze supplier performance, delivery schedules, and market fluctuations to adjust procurement strategies dynamically. This ensures faster deliveries, cost reductions, and resilience to disruptions.
3. Automated Quality Control: In sectors such as pharmaceuticals and electronics manufacturing, AI systems inspect production lines in real time, identifying defects at microscopic levels. This significantly reduces waste, enhances product quality, and increases efficiency.
4. Market Intelligence and Strategic Planning: AI tools scan global data sources, identifying emerging trends and competitive threats. This allows executives to anticipate changes, make proactive investments, and pivot strategies in response to shifting industry dynamics.

AI-driven decision-making not only improves efficiency but also eliminates human biases, enhances speed, and provides decision-makers with real-time adaptive intelligence, ensuring companies remain agile in volatile industrial landscapes.

9.8.3 Big Data Analytics and Predictive Modeling for Real-Time Decision-Making

Big data analytics and predictive modeling have revolutionized how businesses forecast trends, assess risks, and optimize operations. These technologies process extensive datasets—often too large and complex for traditional analytics—allowing companies to extract meaningful patterns, generate forecasts, and make informed decisions (Emma, 2024).

9.8.3.1 The power of big data in industrial decision-making

The industrial sector generates enormous amounts of data from IoT-connected devices, production sensors, financial transactions, customer interactions, and regulatory compliance records. Without advanced analytical capabilities, much of this data remains underutilized.

Big data analytics applies machine learning algorithms, statistical models, and AI-driven automation to turn raw information into actionable insights. Predictive modeling, in particular, enables businesses to anticipate disruptions, optimize supply chains, and refine investment strategies. For example, in renewable energy, predictive analytics help optimize wind and solar power generation by forecasting weather conditions, energy demand, and grid stability. In healthcare, pharmaceutical companies use predictive modeling to streamline drug development, optimize clinical trials, and improve patient outcomes.

9.8.3.2 Real-time predictive decision-making

Industries require instant responses to emerging risks and opportunities. Real-time predictive decision-making enables businesses to make adjustments dynamically based on live data inputs. This capability is particularly valuable in:

- Financial markets, where predictive analytics guide investment strategies in response to market fluctuations.
- Retail and logistics, where AI-powered demand forecasting prevents stock shortages and overproduction.
- Disaster response, where AI models predict environmental hazards, optimizing emergency preparedness.

By adopting big data analytics and predictive modeling, businesses enhance their ability to operate with agility, precision, and foresight, ensuring sustainable innovation and long-term growth.

The adoption of AI, machine learning, big data analytics, and decision-support systems has revolutionized industrial decision-making, enabling organizations to make data-driven strategic choices with greater precision and efficiency. These technologies help businesses navigate uncertainty, optimize operations, reduce risks, and drive innovation success.

As industries continue to embrace digital transformation, organizations that leverage these advanced tools will gain a competitive advantage, improve resource allocation, and enhance long-term decision-making strategies. In the future, businesses that integrate AI-driven insights and predictive analytics into their decision-making frameworks will be better equipped to innovate, adapt, and lead in highly competitive industrial markets.

9.9 STRATEGIC DECISION-MAKING IN INNOVATION ECOSYSTEMS

Innovation in modern industries does not take place in isolation; it is embedded within interconnected industrial ecosystems that involve multiple stakeholders, including governments, businesses, academic institutions, and civil society. The complexity of today's innovation landscape requires companies to navigate technological advancements, regulatory frameworks, market fluctuations, and societal demands. Unlike traditional decision-making, which often takes place within the boundaries of a single organization, strategic decision-making in innovation ecosystems is inherently collaborative, requiring engagement between different actors who bring diverse expertise, resources, and perspectives (Carinus et al., 2022).

As industries become increasingly interdependent, companies must adopt systemic approaches to decision-making, integrating external knowledge networks, forming cross-sector partnerships, and engaging in multi-stakeholder governance structures. The Quadruple and Quintuple Helix frameworks provide structured models for understanding how decision-making unfolds in industrial innovation ecosystems. These models emphasize the role of collective intelligence, shared responsibilities, and sustainable development in shaping the future of industrial innovation. Decision-making in this context is no longer about optimizing outcomes for a single firm; it is about co-creating value within a broader network, ensuring that innovation contributes to economic growth, environmental sustainability, and societal well-being.

A successful innovation ecosystem thrives on collaborative decision-making, where actors coordinate their efforts to tackle complex challenges, reduce uncertainty, and accelerate the commercialization of new technologies. Companies that leverage partnerships, alliances, and knowledge-sharing platforms gain a competitive advantage by mitigating risks, improving resource efficiency, and enhancing the scalability of their innovations. By examining how strategic decision-making operates within interconnected ecosystems, we can better understand the mechanisms that drive industrial transformation and long-term competitiveness.

9.9.1 Decision-Making in the Context of Interconnected Industrial Ecosystems

Industrial ecosystems are not static entities but dynamic networks where multiple stakeholders—including businesses, governments, research institutions, and civil society—interact to foster technological advancements, shape policy frameworks, and drive market adoption. The success of industrial innovation is no longer determined solely by the internal capabilities of individual firms; instead, it hinges on the strength of relationships, knowledge-sharing mechanisms, and collaborative decision-making processes within the broader ecosystem.

As industries become more complex and interdependent, traditional decision-making models—which focus on optimizing internal resources and corporate strategies—are proving inadequate. Instead, firms must align their strategic choices with external stakeholders, ensuring that their innovation efforts are not only coordinated and scalable but also responsive to long-term societal needs and environmental imperatives.

To better understand how decision-making unfolds within these interconnected industrial environments, scholars and policymakers have developed structured models that provide a conceptual framework for innovation governance. Two of the most widely recognized models are the Quadruple Helix and the Quintuple Helix (Carayannis & Campbell, 2012). These frameworks go beyond conventional corporate strategies by integrating a multi-stakeholder approach to decision-making, ensuring that industrial transformation aligns with economic, technological, social, and environmental priorities (Carayannis & Campbell, 2021).

9.9.1.1 The Quadruple Helix model: integrating civil society into innovation decision-making

The Quadruple Helix model builds upon the Triple Helix framework, which traditionally emphasized the interactions between universities, industry, and government in driving innovation. While the Triple Helix model was instrumental in shaping knowledge economies and industrial policies, it did not fully account for the role of civil society—a critical player in determining the acceptance, ethical implications, and societal impact of new technologies.

In the Quadruple Helix model, civil society is introduced as the fourth major actor in innovation ecosystems. This inclusion is essential because innovation is not merely a technological and economic process; it is also a social process that affects—and is affected by—public attitudes, cultural norms, and ethical considerations.

The role of civil society in decision-making includes:

- Ensuring Public Acceptance: Many innovations fail not due to technological shortcomings but because they lack societal legitimacy. Public resistance to genetic engineering, AI, or nuclear energy highlights the necessity of engaging citizens early in the decision-making process.

- Enhancing Ethical Governance: Ethical concerns, such as data privacy in AI-driven applications or the social implications of automation, require civil society involvement to ensure that innovation aligns with public values.
- Co-Designing User-Centric Solutions: By integrating citizen feedback into industrial decision-making, companies can develop solutions that are more relevant, inclusive, and accessible.

The Quadruple Helix model, therefore, bridges the gap between industrial priorities and societal expectations, ensuring that technology adoption and policy frameworks are shaped by both economic feasibility and social desirability.

9.9.1.2 The Quintuple Helix model: incorporating environmental sustainability in industrial decision-making

While the Quadruple Helix model introduced civil society as a key player, the Quintuple Helix model takes this a step further by recognizing the natural environment as a crucial dimension in innovation decision-making. This expansion reflects the increasing urgency of climate change, biodiversity loss, and resource depletion, which demand that industries adopt eco-innovation strategies that balance technological and economic growth with environmental sustainability.

In this model, the environment is not merely an external constraint that firms must comply with; rather, it is a foundational component of industrial decision-making that influences:

- Regulatory Pressures: Governments worldwide are implementing stricter environmental regulations (for example, carbon pricing, emissions targets, circular economy mandates), requiring businesses to embed sustainability into their innovation strategies.
- Market Demands for Green Technologies: Consumer preferences are shifting toward sustainable products and services, driving industries to invest in renewable energy, waste reduction, and eco-friendly manufacturing processes.
- Resource Efficiency and Circular Economy: As finite natural resources become scarcer, industries are exploring circular economy models that emphasize reuse, recycling, and responsible production practices.

By integrating environmental sustainability as a central factor in decision-making, the Quintuple Helix model ensures that industrial growth does not come at the cost of ecological degradation. Instead, firms are encouraged to pursue innovation pathways that are resilient, climate-friendly, and aligned with the principles of long-term sustainability.

9.9.1.3 Strategic implications for firms operating in innovation ecosystems

Both the Quadruple Helix and Quintuple Helix models highlight the fact that industrial innovation is no longer just about technological breakthroughs or financial returns. Instead, success depends on a firm's ability to navigate the complexities of multi-stakeholder decision-making, align innovation strategies with societal needs, and ensure environmental responsibility.

Companies that embrace these models are better positioned to co-create solutions that are scalable, resilient, and globally relevant. Some of the key strategic takeaways for firms operating within innovation ecosystems include:

- Expanding Decision-Making Beyond Corporate Boundaries: Organizations must engage with external partners, including research institutions, policymakers, and advocacy groups, to create an inclusive innovation ecosystem that benefits multiple stakeholders.
- Embedding Sustainability as a Core Business Strategy: Industrial leaders must recognize that sustainability is no longer a corporate social responsibility (CSR) initiative but a fundamental aspect of long-term competitiveness.
- Leveraging Public–Private Collaboration for Innovation Acceleration: Firms should participate in government-led R&D programs, cross-industry alliances, and university research partnerships to access funding, knowledge, and market opportunities that drive technological progress.
- Developing Ethical and Responsible Innovation Frameworks: Integrating ethical impact assessments, consumer engagement mechanisms, and transparent governance structures ensures that industrial innovation remains accountable and socially beneficial.

As industrial ecosystems become increasingly interconnected, decision-making within innovation networks must move beyond traditional corporate silos and embrace collaborative, multidimensional approaches. The Quadruple Helix model provides a framework for aligning innovation with societal expectations, ensuring that industrial advancements are not only economically viable but also socially responsible. Meanwhile, the Quintuple Helix model extends this vision by incorporating environmental sustainability as a guiding principle in strategic decision-making.

For firms operating in these complex ecosystems, the ability to integrate external knowledge, leverage cross-sector collaboration, and align innovation with global priorities is critical to long-term success. Companies that adopt ecosystem-based decision-making will not only enhance their competitiveness and resilience but also contribute to a more inclusive, sustainable, and future-ready industrial landscape.

9.9.2 Collaborative Decision-Making among Government, Industry, Academia, and Civil Society

The interconnected nature of industrial innovation requires decision-makers to engage in collaborative governance, ensuring that strategic choices reflect the interests and expertise of multiple stakeholders. Unlike traditional corporate decision-making, which is often hierarchical and profit-driven, collaborative decision-making involves consensus-building, shared risk-taking, and knowledge co-creation.

Government institutions play a critical role in setting policy frameworks, funding R&D initiatives, and establishing regulatory conditions that shape the innovation landscape. Public agencies provide grants, tax incentives, and procurement programs that incentivize businesses to invest in cutting-edge technologies while ensuring compliance with safety, ethical, and environmental standards.

Industry players contribute market-driven insights, capital investments, and commercialization expertise, ensuring that research-based innovations transition from laboratory settings to real-world applications. In many cases, private sector collaboration with academia leads to the development of new intellectual property, spin-off companies, and technology transfer initiatives that accelerate industrial transformation.

Academia serves as a knowledge hub, generating new ideas, training highly skilled professionals, and conducting fundamental research that lays the groundwork for technological breakthroughs. Through public–private research partnerships, startup incubators, and industry-sponsored projects, universities play a crucial role in shaping the next generation of industrial innovations.

Civil society influences decision-making by advocating for ethical considerations, consumer protection, and social accountability. Public engagement is particularly important in industries such as healthcare, AI, and biotechnology, where societal concerns about data privacy, safety, and accessibility can determine the success or failure of new innovations. Companies that actively engage with civil society organizations, consumer groups, and advocacy networks can build trust, enhance transparency, and improve public perception of their innovations.

By fostering collaborative decision-making, innovation ecosystems ensure that technological advancements are not only economically competitive but also socially responsible and environmentally sustainable.

9.9.3 The Role of Partnerships, Alliances, and Networks in Shared Decision-Making under Uncertainty

The interconnected nature of industrial innovation requires decision-makers to engage in collaborative governance, ensuring that strategic choices reflect the interests, expertise, and priorities of multiple stakeholders. Unlike traditional corporate decision-making, which is often hierarchical, profit-driven, and confined within individual firms, collaborative decision-making operates across multiple sectors, facilitating consensus-building, shared risk-taking, and knowledge co-creation (Hampl et al., 2024).

Industrial ecosystems function as multi-actor environments where government agencies, industry leaders, research institutions, and civil society organizations collectively influence the direction, funding, and implementation of new technologies. Given the high level of uncertainty, long investment cycles, and global interconnectedness of modern industries, no single entity can drive innovation in isolation. Collaboration is essential to address regulatory challenges, ensure responsible innovation, and create scalable, sustainable, and inclusive technological solutions.

By integrating diverse perspectives into the decision-making process, industrial ecosystems can accelerate the development and adoption of breakthrough technologies, reduce systemic risks, and align innovation with social, economic, and environmental goals. Each stakeholder plays a distinct yet complementary role, contributing specialized knowledge, financial resources, regulatory oversight, and public engagement mechanisms that ensure that innovation is not only economically competitive but also socially responsible and environmentally sustainable.

9.9.3.1 The strategic value of partnerships and alliances in innovation ecosystems

Strategic partnerships and alliances are essential for organizations that operate in industries with long development cycles, high capital requirements, and complex regulatory constraints. These collaborations allow companies to share investment burdens, reduce development costs, and leverage each other's strengths. Partnerships also enhance firms' ability to navigate uncertainty by providing access to new knowledge, technologies, and market insights that might otherwise be unavailable (Ferreira et al., 2020).

A notable case in the pharmaceutical industry is the development of new drugs, which is an expensive and time-consuming process that requires extensive research, clinical trials, and regulatory approvals. To manage the uncertainties associated with drug discovery, large pharmaceutical companies often establish alliances with biotech startups, universities, and government agencies. These partnerships provide smaller firms with financial support and regulatory expertise, while larger companies gain access to cutting-edge research that can lead to the next breakthrough treatment.

Likewise, in the automotive sector, the push for electric vehicles and autonomous driving technologies has led to unprecedented levels of collaboration between traditional car manufacturers, software developers, and semiconductor companies. Given the high costs and technological uncertainties involved, forming strategic alliances allows companies to jointly invest in battery innovation, AI-powered navigation systems, and smart mobility infrastructure, ensuring that no single entity bears the full burden of risk.

Beyond corporate partnerships, public–private partnerships play a crucial role in fostering industrial innovation, particularly in sectors such as clean energy, infrastructure development, and digital transformation. Governments often co-fund R&D projects, create regulatory sandboxes, and provide incentives to encourage industry players to invest in high-risk, high-reward innovations. By collaborating with public institutions, companies gain regulatory clarity, secure financial backing, and align their innovations with national or global priorities.

9.9.3.2 The power of innovation networks in decision-making under uncertainty

While partnerships and alliances provide structured collaboration between a few key players, innovation networks enable broader knowledge exchange across entire industries and regions. These networks consist of research consortia, startup incubators, technology clusters, and industry associations that facilitate shared learning, joint problem-solving, and collective decision-making (Alzate-Mejía et al., 2021).

A well-known illustration of this concept is Silicon Valley, where continuous collaboration between tech giants, venture capitalists, academic institutions, and early-stage startups has created an environment that fosters knowledge transfer and rapid experimentation. The ability to access diverse expertise and funding sources helps firms navigate the inherent risks of high-tech innovation while maintaining a competitive edge in the global market.

In Europe, industrial clusters such as Germany's automotive sector, the Nordic clean energy ecosystem, and the UK's AI and fintech hubs demonstrate how geographic proximity and shared industry goals enhance collective decision-making. By participating in regional innovation networks, companies can collaborate on pre-competitive research, align regulatory strategies, and share insights on emerging industry trends, ultimately reducing uncertainty and increasing the likelihood of success.

Moreover, digital transformation has enabled the emergence of virtual innovation networks, where companies, researchers, and policymakers collaborate globally through online platforms, data-sharing agreements, and open innovation initiatives. These digital networks break down traditional barriers to collaboration, allowing firms to access global expertise and make informed decisions despite geographical and market uncertainties.

9.9.3.3 Overcoming challenges in shared decision-making

Despite the many advantages of partnerships, alliances, and networks, collaborative decision-making is not without its challenges. Some of the most common obstacles include intellectual property (IP) disputes, misaligned objectives, governance complexities, and competitive tensions between partners. Organizations must establish clear legal agreements, transparent communication protocols, and structured decision-making processes to ensure that collaborations remain productive and mutually beneficial (Reed et al., 2025).

For instance, technology consortia often establish shared IP frameworks, where all contributing partners receive fair access to new discoveries while ensuring that proprietary knowledge remains protected. Similarly, multinational companies involved in cross-border collaborations must navigate different legal and regulatory environments, requiring careful negotiation and compliance management to avoid conflicts.

Additionally, successful partnerships require long-term trust-building and cultural alignment. Firms that engage in alliances must be willing to embrace open communication, align incentives, and foster a spirit of co-creation rather than competition. This is particularly important in industries where collaboration spans multiple sectors, such as the intersection of AI, healthcare, and cybersecurity, where different players must balance technological advancements with ethical considerations and public trust.

9.10 FUTURE TRENDS AND EVOLVING APPROACHES TO DECISION-MAKING IN INDUSTRIAL INNOVATION

The landscape of industrial innovation is evolving at an unprecedented pace, driven by technological advancements, market volatility, sustainability imperatives, and geopolitical shifts. Traditional decision-making approaches, which relied heavily on linear processes, long-term strategic planning, and historical data analysis, are becoming less effective in the face of rapid change and uncertainty. Instead, companies are shifting toward adaptive, data-driven, and autonomous decision-making models that enhance their agility, flexibility, and responsiveness (Rijwani et al., 2024).

With the transition toward Industry 5.0, businesses are embracing new approaches that integrate human intelligence, AI-driven analytics, and sustainability principles into decision-making processes. This shift reflects a growing recognition that economic success, technological innovation, and environmental responsibility must be harmonized to ensure long-term competitiveness and resilience. Moreover, as industries become more interconnected, the ability to navigate uncertainty, leverage predictive insights, and optimize real-time decision-making will become a defining characteristic of successful industrial leaders.

This chapter explores the future trends shaping decision-making in industrial innovation, focusing on adaptive and flexible decision-making approaches, the rise of sustainability as a core strategic driver, the transition toward Industry 5.0, and the growing influence of AI-driven and autonomous decision-making systems.

9.10.1 The Shift toward Adaptive, Agile, and Flexible Decision-Making

The complexity of modern industrial ecosystems requires businesses to abandon rigid, one-size-fits-all decision-making models and embrace adaptive, agile, and flexible strategies. Traditional decision-making frameworks were often structured around fixed long-term plans, predefined market assumptions, and extensive feasibility studies, which, while effective in stable environments, struggle to accommodate rapid technological shifts, fluctuating market dynamics, and unexpected disruptions (Koudriachov et al., 2025).

Adaptive decision-making is a dynamic, real-time approach that enables organizations to adjust strategies, optimize processes, and pivot based on evolving conditions. Unlike traditional methods that rely on static decision trees, adaptive decision-making incorporates continuous learning, real-time data analysis, and iterative testing to ensure that organizations remain competitive in uncertain and volatile markets.

Industries such as renewable energy, biotechnology, and advanced manufacturing have already begun implementing scenario-based decision models that account for multiple possible futures. These models allow firms to assess various market conditions, regulatory environments, and technological advancements, enabling them to make smarter, risk-mitigated choices that enhance long-term sustainability and profitability.

In addition to adaptability, agility and flexibility are becoming core tenets of industrial decision-making. Companies must empower decentralized teams, leverage real-time insights, and build modular innovation strategies that allow them to scale operations up or down based on demand, technological breakthroughs, and supply chain constraints. The ability to rapidly test, iterate, and refine business models will define the success of next-generation industrial enterprises.

9.10.2 Sustainability as a Core Decision-Making Driver

The global climate crisis, growing environmental concerns, and stricter regulatory frameworks have made sustainability an integral part of industrial innovation and decision-making. In the past, sustainability was often treated as a secondary consideration, but today, it has become a primary strategic driver, shaping investment priorities, product development processes, and corporate governance models (Eberz et al., 2023).

Industries are being forced to reevaluate their supply chains, energy consumption, and waste management strategies, as both government regulations and consumer expectations demand higher levels of transparency and accountability. Regulatory bodies across the world are implementing carbon pricing, emissions caps, circular economy mandates, and eco-friendly production incentives, all of which require organizations to integrate sustainability criteria into their decision-making frameworks.

Sustainability is also reshaping investment and financial decision-making, as stakeholders place greater emphasis on Environmental, Social, and Governance (ESG) metrics. Institutional investors, banks, and venture capital firms are prioritizing businesses that demonstrate strong commitments to sustainability, ethical production, and social responsibility. Companies that fail to align with green policies and low-carbon strategies risk losing access to capital, facing regulatory penalties, and suffering reputational damage in increasingly eco-conscious markets.

The shift toward sustainability-driven decision-making is particularly evident in industries such as automotive, construction, consumer electronics, and chemicals, where businesses are exploring alternative materials, renewable energy sources, and resource-efficient production methods. Firms are developing carbon-neutral manufacturing processes, sustainable packaging solutions, and circular economy business models that emphasize waste reduction, recyclability, and long-term resource conservation.

As industries continue to embed sustainability into their strategic frameworks, decision-making processes will become increasingly focused on balancing profitability with environmental impact, aligning business objectives with climate policies, and integrating renewable energy solutions into industrial operations.

9.10.3 Industry 5.0 and the Future of Industrial Innovation

The transition from Industry 4.0 to Industry 5.0 marks a significant evolution in industrial decision-making and technological innovation. While Industry 4.0 was centered around automation, data analytics, and cyber-physical systems, Industry 5.0 reintroduces the human element into industrial ecosystems, focusing on human-AI collaboration, personalization, resilience, and sustainability (Carayannis et al., 2024).

One of the defining features of Industry 5.0 is its emphasis on human-centric decision-making, where advanced AI and automation technologies do not replace human intelligence but rather complement it. Unlike earlier industrial revolutions that prioritized efficiency, cost reduction, and full-scale automation, Industry 5.0 integrates human creativity, ethical considerations, and adaptive intelligence into decision-making processes. This shift is particularly important in industries such as healthcare, advanced manufacturing, and robotics, where complex, nuanced decisions require a combination of data-driven insights and human expertise.

Another fundamental aspect of Industry 5.0 is the focus on personalization and customer-driven innovation. Companies are increasingly using real-time consumer insights, behavioral analytics, and AI-powered recommendation engines to design customized products and services that cater to individual preferences. Decision-making is no longer solely top-down and production-driven but rather demand-driven, responsive, and iterative.

Industry 5.0 also brings a renewed emphasis on supply chain resilience and risk management. In recent years, global supply chains have experienced disruptions due to trade conflicts, pandemics, and resource shortages, highlighting the need for more flexible, localized, and digitally optimized supply chain models. Businesses are leveraging predictive analytics, blockchain technology, and AI-driven logistics optimization to anticipate supply chain risks, enhance operational agility, and ensure continuity in production and distribution.

9.10.4 AI-Driven and Autonomous Decision-Making Systems

AI, ML, and big data analytics are revolutionizing industrial decision-making, enabling organizations to make faster, more accurate, and data-driven choices. The increasing complexity of industrial environments, coupled with the explosion of real-time data streams, has made AI-driven decision models indispensable in optimizing production processes, market strategies, and operational efficiency (Waqar et al., 2024).

Predictive analytics allows businesses to analyze vast datasets, detect patterns, and forecast market trends with unprecedented precision. Companies can now anticipate consumer behavior shifts, supply chain vulnerabilities, and regulatory developments, enabling them to proactively adjust strategies and mitigate potential risks. AI-powered decision models are also being used to automate repetitive tasks, optimize resource allocation, and enhance business intelligence, reducing human error and improving overall efficiency.

In industrial settings, autonomous decision-making systems are becoming increasingly prevalent, particularly in smart factories, digital logistics networks, and AI-driven supply chains. These systems leverage self-learning algorithms, robotic process automation, and real-time sensor data to adjust workflows, detect inefficiencies, and optimize production without human intervention.

However, as AI-driven decision-making becomes more prevalent, industries must address ethical concerns, data privacy regulations, and the need for human oversight. While AI models can process information and execute decisions at unprecedented speed and scale, they still require ethical governance frameworks, accountability measures, and bias mitigation strategies to ensure responsible implementation.

9.11 CONCLUSION

Industrial innovation is undergoing a profound transformation, shaped by technological advancements, sustainability imperatives, and evolving decision-making methodologies. The increasing complexity of global markets, rapid technological disruptions, and shifting regulatory frameworks demand that businesses move beyond traditional decision-making models and embrace adaptive, data-driven, and collaborative approaches.

One of the fundamental themes explored in this chapter is the growing need for agility, flexibility, and responsiveness in industrial decision-making. In an era characterized by volatility, uncertainty, complexity, and ambiguity (VUCA), companies can no longer rely on rigid, long-term strategic plans. Instead, they must adopt adaptive decision-making frameworks, which allow them to analyze real-time data, experiment with different strategies, and pivot when necessary. This approach ensures that businesses remain competitive even in highly dynamic and unpredictable environments.

A critical component of modern decision-making is the integration of sustainability as a core strategic driver. The rise of environmental concerns, regulatory pressures, and consumer demand for responsible business practices has forced industries to rethink how they innovate, manufacture, and distribute products and services. Companies that embed sustainability into their decision-making processes—whether through carbon-neutral strategies, circular economy models, or ESG-driven investment decisions—will be better positioned to achieve long-term resilience and regulatory compliance.

Another emerging trend shaping the future of industrial decision-making is the shift from Industry 4.0 to Industry 5.0. While Industry 4.0 emphasized automation, digitalization, and AI-driven manufacturing, Industry 5.0 reintroduces human intelligence, ethical considerations, and sustainable innovation into the equation. Decision-making in Industry 5.0 will focus on balancing automation with human expertise, integrating AI as a decision-support tool, and prioritizing ethical and socially responsible innovation strategies.

The increasing role of AI-driven decision-making and autonomous systems has also been explored in this chapter. With the rise of big data, machine learning, and real-time predictive analytics, businesses now have access to unprecedented levels of information to enhance decision-making accuracy. AI-powered models can detect market trends, predict operational inefficiencies, and optimize supply chains, enabling businesses to make faster, more precise, and data-driven decisions. However, the widespread adoption of AI and automation also raises ethical concerns, regulatory challenges, and the need for human oversight, emphasizing the importance of responsible AI governance frameworks in industrial settings.

Another key aspect discussed is the importance of collaboration and interconnected innovation ecosystems in navigating complexity and uncertainty. No single organization can innovate in isolation—industries must engage in cross-sector partnerships, strategic alliances, and public–private collaborations to share knowledge, mitigate risks, and accelerate technological advancements. The Quadruple and Quintuple Helix models illustrate how governments, businesses, academia, civil society, and the natural environment must work together to shape industrial decision-making in a way that is sustainable, inclusive, and future-oriented.

As industries continue to evolve, decision-makers must cultivate a mindset of continuous learning, strategic adaptability, and foresight-driven innovation. Companies that embrace emerging decision-making approaches, integrate sustainability as a core value, and leverage AI-driven insights will be better positioned to lead in the next era of industrial transformation. By navigating complexity with strategic agility and cross-sector collaboration, businesses can drive technological progress while ensuring economic, social, and environmental sustainability.

In conclusion, industrial innovation in the modern era requires a shift in mindset, tools, and strategic approaches. Decision-makers must move beyond static, one-dimensional strategies and adopt a multi-faceted, forward-thinking approach that integrates technological intelligence, sustainability imperatives, and collaborative governance. By doing so, industries can successfully navigate complexity, seize emerging opportunities, and drive meaningful innovation in an ever-evolving global landscape.

REFERENCES

Abdel-Basset, M., Mohamed, R., & Chang, V. (2024). A multi-criteria decision-making framework to evaluate the impact of Industry 5.0 technologies: Case study, lessons learned, challenges and future directions. *Information Systems Frontiers*. https://doi.org/10.1007/s10796-024-10472-3.

Acebes, F., Poza, D., González-Varona, J., Pajares, J., & Paredes, A. (2021). On the project risk baseline: Integrating aleatory uncertainty into project scheduling.

Computers & Industrial Engineering, 160, 107537. https://doi.org/10.1016/j.cie.2021.107537.

Akter, R., Rathnayaka, S., & Ahmadi, Z. (2023). The effect of leadership and organisational culture on organisational innovation. *International Journal of Services Technology and Management,* 28, 360–388. https://doi.org/10.1504/IJSTM.2023.135084.

Alzate-Mejía, N., Santos-Boada, G., & de Almeida-Amazonas, J. (2021). Decision-making under uncertainty for the deployment of future hyperconnected networks: A survey. *Sensors,* 21, 3791. https://doi.org/10.3390/s21113791.

Balbaa, M., & Abdurashidova, M. (2024). The impact of artificial intelligence in decision making: A comprehensive review. *EPRA International Journal of Economics, Business and Management Studies,* 11, 27–38. https://doi.org/10.36713/epra15747.

Bingham, C., & McDonald, R. (2022). Mastering innovation's toughest trade-offs. *MIT Sloan Management Review.* https://sloanreview.mit.edu/article/mastering-innovations-toughest-trade-offs/.

Burova, E., Grishunin, S., Suloeva, S., & Stepanchuk, A. (2021). The cost management of innovative products in an industrial enterprise given the risks in the digital economy. *International Journal of Technology,* 12, 1339. https://doi.org/10.14716/ijtech.v12i7.5333.

Carayannis, E., & Campbell, D. (2012). Triple helix, quadruple helix and quintuple helix and how do knowledge, innovation and the environment relate to each other? *International Journal of Social Ecology and Sustainable Development,* 1, 41–69. https://doi.org/10.4018/jsesd.2010010105.

Carayannis, E., & Campbell, D. (2021). Democracy of climate and climate for democracy: The evolution of quadruple and quintuple helix innovation systems. *Journal of the Knowledge Economy,* 12, 2050–2082. https://doi.org/10.1007/s13132-021-00778-x.

Carayannis, E., Canestrino, R., & Magliocca, P. (2024). From the dark side of Industry 4.0 to Society 5.0: Looking "beyond the box" to developing human-centric innovation ecosystems. *IEEE Transactions on Engineering Management,* 71, 6695–6711. https://doi.org/10.1109/TEM.2023.3239552.

Carayannis, E., Papamichail, G., Zotas, N., & Askounis, D. (2025). Corporate foresight: Navigating uncertainty in a VUCA world. *Journal of the Knowledge Economy.* https://doi.org/10.1007/s13132-024-02587-4.

Carinus, L., Ngongoni, C., & Saartjie Grobbelaar, S. (2022). Towards a strategic decision support tool for innovation ecosystems stakeholder management. *2022 IEEE 28th International Conference on Engineering, Technology and Innovation (ICE/ITMC) & 31st International Association For Management of Technology (IAMOT) Joint Conference*, Nancy, France.

Chaube, S., Kumar, A., Singh, M., Kotecha, K., & Kumar, A. (2024). An overview of multi-criteria decision analysis and the applications of AHP and TOPSIS methods. *International Journal of Mathematical Engineering and Management Sciences,* 9, 581–615. https://doi.org/10.33889/IJMEMS.2024.9.3.030.

Ciechan-Kujawa, M., Buszko, M., & Taranowska, K. (2018). Sensitivity analysis in business risk assessment in practice of Polish companies. *Ekonomiczne Problemy Usług,* 133, 39–50. https://doi.org/10.18276/epu.2018.133/2-04.

Cristofaro, M., Leoni, L., & Giardino, P. (2022). Cognitive biases' influence on employees' product creativity and product performance: Evidences from

Italian manufacturing technology firms. *Journal of Manufacturing Technology Management*, 33, 675–695. https://doi.org/10.1108/JMTM-10-2020-0414.
Daradkeh, M., & Abul-Huda, B. (2017). *Incorporating uncertainty into decision-making: An information visualisation approach*, pp. 74–87. https://doi.org/10.1007/978-3-319-57487-5_6.
De Bettignies, J.-E., Liu, H., Robinson, D., & Gainullin, B. (2022). Competition and innovation in markets for technology. *Management Science,* 69(8), 4753–4773. https://doi.org/10.1287/mnsc.2022.4574.
Develaki, M. (2024). Uncertainty, risk, and decision-making. *Science & Education,* 1–32. https://doi.org/10.1007/s11191-024-00544-w.
Eberz, S., Lang, S., Breitenmoser, P., & Niebert, K. (2023). Taking the lead into sustainability: Decision makers' competencies for a greener future. *Sustainability,* 15, 4986. https://doi.org/10.3390/su15064986.
Emma, L. (2024). Big data analytics for real-time insights and strategic business planning. https://www.researchgate.net/publication/386336003_Big_data_analytics_for_real-time_insights_and_strategic_business_planning.
Ferreira, J., Coelho, A., & Moutinho, L. (2020). The influence of strategic alliances on innovation and new product development through the effects of exploration and exploitation. *Management Decision. ahead-of-print.* https://doi.org/10.1108/MD-09-2019-1239.
Flores-García, E., Bruch, J., Wiktorsson, M., & Jackson, M. (2019). Decision-making approaches in process innovations: An explorative case study. *Journal of Manufacturing Technology Management. ahead-of-print.* https://doi.org/10.1108/JMTM-03-2019-0087.
Giaccone, S., & Magnusson, M. (2021). Unveiling the role of risk-taking in innovation: Antecedents and effects. *R&D Management*, 52. https://doi.org/10.1111/radm.12477.
Hampl, N., Hoffmann, W., Knoll, T., & Reuer, J. (2024). Alliance re-evaluation in the context of outside partnering opportunities: Decision heuristics and the impact of environmental uncertainty. *Journal of Management Studies.* https://doi.org/10.1111/joms.13090.
Han, J., & Kang, R. (2021). Market uncertainty, innovation of firms in alliance and alliance partner characteristics. *European Journal of Innovation Management*, 24(5), 1883–1905. https://doi.org/10.1108/EJIM-05-2020-0195.
Hatoum, M., & Nassereddine, H. (2024). Determining decision-making factors for technology adoption in the construction industry. *IntechOpen.* https://doi.org/10.5772/intechopen.1004365.
Jalonen, H. (2011). The uncertainty of innovation: A systematic review of the literature. *Journal of Management Research,* 4. https://doi.org/10.5296/jmr.v4i1.1039.
Kahneman, D., & Tversky, A. (1979). Prospect theory: An analysis of decision under risk. *Econometrica,* 47(2), 263–291. https://doi.org/10.2307/1914185.
Koudriachov, C., Tam, C., & Aparicio, M. (2025). Success with agile project management: Looking back and into the future. *Journal of Systems and Software,* 226. https://doi.org/10.1016/j.jss.2025.112428.
Kwon, S., Youtie, J., Porter, A., & Newman, N. (2022). How does regulatory uncertainty shape the innovation process? Evidence from the case of nanomedicine. *The Journal of Technology Transfer.* https://doi.org/10.1007/s10961-022-09980-8.
Li, W., Guo, X., & Cao, D. (2021). The complexity of technological innovation decision-making in emerging industries. *Complexity,* 2021, 1–14. https://doi.org/10.1155/2021/3611921.

Mbanyele, W., & Fengrong, W. (2022). Economic policy uncertainty and industry innovation: Cross country evidence. *The Quarterly Review of Economics and Finance,* 84. https://doi.org/10.1016/j.qref.2022.01.012.

Niculescu, G., & Marcau, F. (2024). Behavioral factors that can significantly influence the decision-making process. https://www.researchgate.net/publication/378373343_behavioral_factors_that_can_significantly_influence_the_decision-making_process.

Obaid, A., & Al-Husseini, K. (2024). Monte Carlo simulation for risk management in agile software development. *International Journal of Computers and Informatics,* 3, 63–78. https://doi.org/10.59992/IJCI.2024.v3n3p3.

Piacentini, R. D., & Della Ceca, L. S. (2017). The use of environmental sustainability criteria in industrial processes. *Drying Technology*, 35(1), 1–3. https://doi.org/10.1080/07373937.2016.1243446.

Pittenger, L., Glassman, A., Mumbower, S., Merritt, D., & Bollenback, D. (2022). Bounded rationality: Managerial decision-making and data. *Journal of Computer Information Systems*, 63(4), 890–903. https://doi.org/10.1080/08874417.2022.2111380.

Produção, G., Silva, J., Silva, F., Silva, D., Rocha, L., & Ritter, Á. (2022). Decision making in the process of choosing and deploying industry 4.0 technologies. *Gestão & Produção*, 29. https://doi.org/10.1590/1806-9649-2022v29e163.

Ramadan, M. (2023). A decision support system for selecting suitable management processes and tools in the case of telework for software developers. *Conference: Fintech and Closing the Digital GapAt: The 13th International Conference on ICT in Our Lives.* Conference Reference.

Reed, J., Svedberg, P., & Nygren, J. (2025). Enhancing the innovation ecosystem: Overcoming challenges to introducing information-driven technologies in health care. *J Med Internet Res,* 27, e56836.

Rijwani, T., Kumari, S., Srinivas, R., Abhishek, K., Iyer, G., Vara, H., . . . Gupta, M. (2024). Industry 5.0: a review of emerging trends and transformative technologies in the next industrial revolution. *International Journal on Interactive Design and Manufacturing (IJIDeM)*, 19, 667–679. https://doi.org/10.1007/s12008-024-01943-7.

Rosin, F., Forget, P., Lamouri, S., & Pellerin, R. (2022). Enhancing the decision-making process through Industry 4.0 technologies. *Sustainability,* 14, 461. https://doi.org/10.3390/su14010461.

Sarı, T. (2019). Multi-criteria decision making for innovation decisions. In *A new perspective in social sciences* (pp. 158–166). Frontpage Publications. https://www.researchgate.net/publication/362263506_Multi-Criteria_Decision_Making_for_Innovation_Decisions.

Savchuk, V. (2023). Real options technique as a tool of strategic risk management. https://doi.org/10.48550/arXiv.2303.09176.

Talamo, C., Paganin, G., Atta, N., & Rota, F. (2019). Epistemic uncertainty, risk management and information: The role of the detailed design. *TECHNE – Journal of Technology for Architecture and Environment*, 18, 164–173. https://doi.org/10.13128/techne-7523.

Uzonwanne, F. (2022). Rational model of decision-making. In A. Farazmand (Ed.), *Global encyclopedia of public administration, public policy, and governance.* Springer. https://doi.org/10.1007/978-3-030-66252-3_2474.

Van Rooyen, M., & Van der Lingen, E. (2024). Reducing uncertainty associated with managing technology innovation. *Social Sciences & Humanities Open*, 9. https://doi.org/10.1016/j.ssaho.2023.100771.

Waqar, M., Khan, A., Bhatti, I., & Lucas, M. (2024). Self-adaptive AI systems for autonomous decision-making in dynamic environments. https://www.researchgate.net/publication/386076276_Self-Adaptive_AI_Systems_for_Autonomous_Decision-Making_in_Dynamic_Environments.

Więckowski, J., Sałabun, W., Kizielewicz, B., Bączkiewicz, A., Shekhovtsov, A., Paradowski, B., & Wątróbski, J. (2023). Recent advances in multi-criteria decision analysis: A comprehensive review of applications and trends. *International Journal of Knowledge-Based and Intelligent Engineering Systems*, 27(4), 367–393. https://doi.org/10.3233/KES-230487.

Wu, J.-Z., Lin, K.-S., & Wu, C.-Y. (2015). Integration of scenario planning and decision tree analysis for new product development: A case study of a smartphone project in Taiwan. *The International Journal of Industrial Engineering: Theory, Applications and Practice*, 22, 616–627.

Zhu, S., Susan, M., Mikhail, M., & Mikhail, M. (2020). Team decision making: The dynamic effects of team decision style composition and performance via decision strategy. *Journal of Management,* 47, Article 014920632091623. https://doi.org/10.1177/0149206320916232.

PART III

Future-oriented strategies and transformations

10. Disruption, foresight, and I2E: Strategic navigation through complexity and change

Elias G. Carayannis and Nikos R. Zotas

10.1 INTRODUCTION

The 21st century has emerged as an era of intensified turbulence, complexity, and accelerating change across industrial systems, value chains, and governance landscapes. In this volatile environment, the capacity to innovate is no longer defined solely by the ability to create novel technologies or streamline production. Instead, it is increasingly shaped by an organization's or system's ability to anticipate disruption, adapt strategically, and realign innovation processes in real time. This chapter explores three deeply interlinked concepts that are essential to navigating the present and future of industrial transformation: disruption, strategic foresight, and the Innovation–Intelligence–Execution (I2E) framework.

While previous chapters have highlighted the technological and systemic dimensions of industrial innovation—such as Industry 4.0, Industry 5.0, Society 5.0, and the Quintuple Innovation Helix—this chapter shifts focus to the dynamic navigation mechanisms that underpin innovation resilience. In particular, it responds to a growing imperative for industries and institutions to move beyond reactive responses to change and toward proactive, anticipatory governance built on strategic foresight.

Disruption, once regarded as episodic or exogenous, has become a structural feature of the industrial innovation landscape. From the diffusion of artificial intelligence and generative technologies to geopolitical decoupling and planetary-scale environmental crises, shocks are no longer isolated but interconnected. They reverberate across sectors, geographies, and institutional domains, challenging traditional innovation models and decision-making architectures.

Against this backdrop, strategic foresight has emerged not as a peripheral planning tool but as a critical form of innovation intelligence—a mode of seeing, sensing, and preparing for multiple, plausible futures. Strategic foresight equips institutions with the capacity to detect weak signals, scan emerging trends, and construct scenario-based pathways that inform agile and robust decision-making.

To convert insight into action, however, foresight must be embedded into the core architecture of innovation systems. This is where the I2E framework becomes vital. It positions foresight (Intelligence) as an integral input into innovation design (Innovation) and execution strategies (Execution), creating a dynamic loop that is both forward-looking and grounded in action. The I2E approach offers a structured yet flexible model for navigating high-uncertainty environments—particularly those characterized by rapid technological convergence, shifting societal values, and asymmetric shocks.

This chapter will unfold in four parts. First, it dissects the anatomy of disruption, categorizing its forms and illustrating its impact across industrial ecosystems. Second, it explores the operationalization of strategic foresight, highlighting its role in transforming prediction into preparedness. Third, it introduces the I2E framework as a methodological bridge between insight generation and innovation implementation. Finally, it proposes a model of systemic futures thinking as a foundation for next-generation innovation governance—one that builds institutional resilience, distributes intelligence, and aligns industrial innovation with long-term public value creation.

By the end of the chapter, the reader will have a comprehensive understanding of how disruption can be recontextualized as a trigger for transformative innovation, how foresight can serve as a navigational compass, and how I2E can convert uncertainty into strategic advantage. The ideas presented here also serve as a conceptual bridge to the final chapter, where the discussion will turn to the deeper techno-societal paradigms and sustainability imperatives shaping the long-term trajectory of industrial innovation in a post-digital, post-linear world.

10.2 UNDERSTANDING DISRUPTION IN THE INNOVATION LANDSCAPE

In contemporary industrial dynamics, disruption has transcended its earlier meaning as a localized or sectoral phenomenon. It now occupies a central position in how innovation processes are conceptualized, mobilized, and governed. This section offers a comprehensive analytical account of disruption: its evolving character, typological classification, emblematic cases, and structural consequences for value chains and industrial sectors (Kivimaa et al., 2021). By doing so, it provides the groundwork for understanding why foresight and strategic intelligence are becoming core capabilities in navigating complexity and innovation governance.

10.2.1 The Nature of Disruption

Disruption, in the context of industrial innovation, is not merely a disturbance or deviation from the norm—it represents a profound transformation of systems, paradigms, and expectations. Unlike incremental change, which enhances or optimizes existing processes, disruption often breaks with the logic of the status quo, forcing actors to adapt, abandon, or reimagine their approaches to value creation, governance, and societal impact (Godart & Pistilli, 2024). In the 21st-century innovation landscape, disruption has emerged not only as a defining feature but as a catalytic force shaping the trajectory of industries, institutions, and entire economies.

At its core, disruption entails a reconfiguration of relationships—between technologies and users, producers and markets, norms and practices. It is the process by which entrenched models become obsolete, either through the introduction of radically new alternatives or through the erosion of the contextual conditions that once sustained them (Lyytinen & Rose, 2003). Disruption can be externally imposed or internally generated, sudden or gradual, visible or latent. What distinguishes it from other forms of change is the depth and scope of its impact: disruption does not merely alter variables within a system—it alters the system's structure, assumptions, and future potential.

In recent decades, the term "disruption" has often been used colloquially to describe anything new, unexpected, or technologically advanced. However, in a scholarly and policy-oriented context, a more precise conceptualization is necessary. Disruption, as a transformative force, must be understood through a set of defining characteristics that differentiate it from incremental change, adaptation, or cyclical shifts.

First, disruption is inherently non-linear. While incremental change tends to follow predictable trajectories, often grounded in past performance or controlled experimentation, disruption unfolds through feedback loops, tipping points, and emergent behaviors. Small triggers may generate disproportionate consequences, especially when they interact with complex systems that are tightly coupled or under strain. This non-linear quality makes disruption difficult to anticipate through traditional forecasting tools, necessitating more advanced foresight and systems thinking methodologies.

Second, disruption is often convergent in nature. It rarely emerges from a single domain or technological breakthrough; rather, it is the product of interrelated shifts across multiple fronts—technological, societal, geopolitical, ecological. For example, the disruption of traditional retail was not only the result of e-commerce platforms but also of mobile payment systems, logistics automation, changing consumer expectations, and the social normalization of digital transactions. Convergence amplifies the force of disruption, making it more difficult for incumbents to respond within their established strategic or operational frameworks.

Third, disruption is frequently asymmetric in its effects. It does not impact all actors equally, nor does it unfold in a uniform or democratic fashion. Some industries, regions, or social groups may benefit from disruptive change—gaining access to new markets, capabilities, or efficiencies—while others experience displacement, marginalization, or obsolescence. The asymmetric nature of disruption poses challenges for policy design, particularly in ensuring inclusive transitions and avoiding systemic inequities.

Fourth, disruption often challenges institutional and regulatory frameworks, which are typically designed for stability, predictability, and incremental adjustment. Disruptive innovations such as synthetic biology, decentralized finance, or autonomous mobility strain existing legal categories, governance mechanisms, and public values. They force regulators and policymakers to rethink core principles—such as liability, consent, or risk assessment—in light of novel configurations of power, responsibility, and uncertainty.

To understand how disruption differs from incremental change, it is helpful to place both within a broader theory of innovation trajectories. Incremental change involves improvements within an existing paradigm: faster processors, more efficient engines, better supply chain software. These changes enhance performance without fundamentally altering the architecture of the system or the logic of its value proposition. They are often driven by continuous research and development (R&D), optimization strategies, or user feedback loops. Incremental innovation is essential for competitiveness, but it operates within bounded horizons.

Disruption, by contrast, involves a paradigmatic shift. It redefines not only what is possible but what is desirable, viable, or legitimate. Disruption alters the dominant design of a product or service, the institutional context in which it is embedded, and the social meanings attached to it. In many cases, it also changes the identities and roles of the actors involved. For example, the rise of platform-based models in transport, hospitality, or media has turned consumers into producers, centralized control into decentralized coordination, and regulatory norms into evolving negotiation arenas.

Another key difference lies in the temporal dynamics of change. Incremental change tends to be continuous and cumulative, often following the innovation diffusion curve and aligning with investment cycles, policy reviews, or market feedback. Disruption, on the other hand, is often punctuated—it may appear suddenly after a long gestation period or emerge rapidly in response to external shocks. The COVID-19 pandemic, for example, served as a catalyst for digital disruption that had been developing for years, accelerating trends such as remote work, online education, and telehealth from marginal to mainstream in a matter of months.

This punctuated character of disruption aligns with theories of punctuated equilibrium and technological discontinuities, which argue that periods of stability are interrupted by episodes of radical change that reset the evolutionary trajectory of systems. In such moments, traditional success factors—such as market share, brand loyalty, or operational efficiency—offer limited protection. Instead, resilience, agility, and anticipatory capacity become critical.

Disruption also reconfigures power relations within innovation systems. It often empowers new entrants—startups, civic innovators, or non-traditional actors—who are unencumbered by legacy infrastructures or organizational inertia. At the same time, it can destabilize incumbents, whose scale and path dependency make adaptation costly or slow. This power shift is not only economic but also epistemic: disruption challenges the dominant narratives about what constitutes progress, expertise, or legitimacy in innovation.

From a governance perspective, disruption demands institutional reflexivity—the capacity of systems to reflect on their own assumptions, adapt their norms, and reorient their strategies in light of emergent realities. This includes not only the adaptation of specific rules or programs but the transformation of the underlying logic by which innovation is governed. In this sense, disruption functions as both a stress test and an opportunity: it reveals institutional weaknesses but also opens space for experimentation, reform, and learning.

Finally, disruption must be understood as both threat and opportunity. While it often entails economic loss, social upheaval, or regulatory uncertainty, it also catalyzes innovation, democratizes access, and enables the articulation of alternative futures. The net impact of disruption depends on the capacity of actors and institutions to absorb shocks, learn from them, and reconfigure themselves in more resilient, inclusive, and sustainable directions.

In conclusion, disruption is not an anomaly to be managed at the margins of innovation policy. It is a central dynamic of the 21st-century industrial landscape—an expression of the underlying volatility, complexity, and acceleration that characterize our era. Differentiating disruption from incremental change is essential for designing governance frameworks, innovation strategies, and institutional capacities that are capable of not only surviving but thriving amid transformative change. As the next sections will show, doing so requires a deep integration of strategic foresight, systemic intelligence, and adaptive execution into the architecture of innovation systems.

10.2.2 Types of Disruption

Disruption in the industrial innovation landscape is not a monolithic phenomenon. It materializes through multiple vectors, each interacting with others to reshape systems, displace incumbents, and generate new possibilities and risks. Among the most analytically distinct yet interrelated forms are technological disruption, societal disruption, and geopolitical disruption (Millar et al., 2017). These types do not exist in isolation but often co-evolve, producing complex transformation dynamics that industrial actors and policymakers must learn to navigate holistically.

10.2.2.1 Technological disruption

Technological disruption is perhaps the most visible and studied form, driven by the introduction and diffusion of innovations that transform production processes, business models, and user experiences (Rohn, 2025). It is rooted in breakthroughs that go beyond incremental improvement to alter the foundational capabilities of an industrial system.

Historically, major waves of technological disruption have reshaped economic and social orders—from the steam engine to electricity, and from the internal combustion engine to digital computing. In the 21st century, a new generation of general-purpose technologies (GPTs) is once again redefining industrial boundaries. Among these, artificial intelligence (AI) and quantum computing stand out as particularly transformative.

AI, particularly in its contemporary machine learning and generative forms, is disrupting sectors as diverse as manufacturing, healthcare, law, education, logistics, and creative industries. It automates cognitive labor, enhances decision-making through predictive analytics, and enables real-time responsiveness in complex systems. Beyond efficiency, AI changes how knowledge is produced, how authority is distributed, and how trust is negotiated—raising not only economic but also epistemological and ethical questions.

Quantum computing, though still emerging, represents a radical leap in processing power and problem-solving capacity. Its potential to break current encryption standards, simulate molecular structures with precision, or optimize logistics at unprecedented scale poses significant implications for national security, pharmaceutical development, and financial modeling. When realized, quantum technologies will not merely enhance existing capabilities—they will necessitate a comprehensive redesign of software, hardware, and organizational practices across multiple sectors.

Technological disruption also includes platformization, blockchain decentralization, 3D printing, bioengineering, and other domain-specific transformations. What unites them is their capacity to displace existing technological regimes, reorganize production logics, and redefine competitive advantage. Importantly, these disruptions do not unfold in a vacuum; their trajectories are shaped by regulation, public acceptance, business model innovation, and geopolitical rivalry.

The challenge for institutions is not only to adopt new technologies but to manage their convergence, anticipate their spillover effects, and address the societal implications they generate. This requires an innovation governance approach that is simultaneously agile, inclusive, and anticipatory.

10.2.2.2 Societal disruption

While often less immediately visible than technological upheaval, societal disruption exerts profound influence on the evolution of industrial systems. It arises from shifts in social norms, collective behaviors, demographic trends, and cultural expectations. These changes can alter the direction and legitimacy of innovation, reshape labor markets, and challenge institutional arrangements (Schrijvers et al., 2021).

A key driver of societal disruption is the generational shift in values and worldviews. Younger generations—often more digitally native, climate-conscious, and socially engaged—are reshaping labor expectations, consumer behavior, and political participation. They demand not only convenience or performance but also ethical alignment, transparency, and inclusivity from the organizations they work for and buy from. This alters the competitive landscape, forcing firms to engage with issues such as sustainability, equity, and digital rights not merely as compliance obligations but as strategic imperatives.

Digital activism is another powerful vector of societal disruption. Enabled by social media and mobile connectivity, citizens now mobilize around causes with unprecedented speed and scale, influencing corporate behavior, regulatory agendas, and innovation priorities. Movements around data privacy, algorithmic fairness, platform accountability, and labor rights in the gig economy exemplify how societal actors can exert pressure on technology developers and industrial platforms. Digital activism destabilizes traditional hierarchies of expertise and authority, democratizing innovation while also introducing new forms of conflict and contestation.

Demographic transitions, including aging populations in developed economies and youth bulges in others, also contribute to disruption. These shifts affect labor force dynamics, social protection systems, healthcare innovation, and education delivery. The rise of hybrid work models, lifelong learning platforms, and health-tech solutions is a response not only to technological opportunity but to demographic necessity.

In addition, crises such as pandemics or climate-related disasters act as societal accelerants. They often expose underlying inequalities, institutional weaknesses, and value misalignments, prompting rapid shifts in public expectations and behaviors. For example, the COVID-19 pandemic accelerated the normalization of remote work, telehealth, and virtual education—technologies that had existed for years but lacked widespread social uptake. It also sparked debates about public goods, trust in science, and the balance between individual rights and collective responsibilities.

Societal disruption compels innovation systems to become more responsive, participatory, and ethically attuned. It pushes institutions beyond performance metrics and market share, toward legitimacy, accountability, and cultural resonance. This kind of disruption cannot be addressed through technological fixes alone; it requires institutional innovation, values-sensitive design, and a reimagining of the relationship between innovation and society.

10.2.2.3 Geopolitical disruption

Geopolitical disruption refers to the transformation of the international system in ways that affect the governance, distribution, and development of innovation. It reflects changes in the global order—shifts in power, contestation over resources, and realignment of alliances—that create uncertainty for firms, regulators, and innovation ecosystems (Pham & Hsu, 2025).

One of the most visible forms of geopolitical disruption in recent years has been strategic decoupling. This process, exemplified by the technological rivalry between the United States and China, has led to the fragmentation of global supply chains, the weaponization of technological standards, and the politicization of data and digital infrastructure. Export controls, investment restrictions, and trade barriers are not simply economic tools—they are mechanisms of strategic control in the race for technological supremacy.

The consequences of such decoupling are far-reaching. Firms are compelled to reevaluate their R&D partnerships, manufacturing locations, and intellectual property strategies. Governments are investing in technological sovereignty, attempting to build domestic capabilities in critical areas such as semiconductors, AI, biotech, and quantum computing. This shift disrupts the global innovation system, which had long relied on open collaboration, cross-border flows, and globalized value chains.

Digital sovereignty is another dimension of geopolitical disruption. As states seek to assert control over data governance, cloud infrastructure, and algorithmic accountability, divergent regulatory models are emerging. The European Union's General Data Protection Regulation (GDPR), China's Cybersecurity Law, and the United States' sectoral approaches reflect distinct philosophies about privacy, control, and platform responsibility. For multinational firms and innovators, navigating this regulatory patchwork introduces complexity, compliance costs, and strategic uncertainty.

Geopolitical instability also affects innovation financing and infrastructure. Conflicts, sanctions, and currency volatility disrupt investment flows and create barriers to international collaboration. Moreover, geopolitical shifts influence public perceptions, shaping the narratives and trust levels surrounding technologies, especially those perceived as foreign or strategically sensitive.

Climate geopolitics is an emerging vector of disruption. As countries compete and cooperate over clean energy technologies, carbon markets, and adaptation strategies, new patterns of industrial competition and alignment are emerging. Innovation in renewable energy, climate modeling, or circular economy practices is increasingly shaped not only by technological feasibility but by geopolitical interest and access to critical minerals and supply chains.

In sum, geopolitical disruption introduces a new layer of complexity into innovation governance. It blurs the boundaries between economic policy, security strategy, and technological development (Shreya, 2025). It forces institutions to think not only in terms of market competition but also in terms of sovereignty, resilience, and systemic interdependence.

10.2.3 Case Illustrations

To grasp the multifaceted and interlocking nature of disruption in industrial innovation systems, it is instructive to examine empirical cases that capture its real-world dynamics. Disruption does not manifest solely in abstract trends or theoretical models—it materializes in specific events, technologies, and geopolitical confrontations that reconfigure institutional behaviors, market structures, and governance paradigms. This section explores three emblematic cases: the proliferation of generative AI and its impact on knowledge work; the COVID-19 pandemic as a systemic shock that restructured global supply chains; and the strategic decoupling between the United States and China as a geopolitical disruption with deep technological implications. Each case illustrates a unique constellation of forces, actors, and consequences, while reinforcing the systemic interconnectedness of technological, societal, and geopolitical disruption.

10.2.3.1 Case 1: generative AI and the automation of white-collar work

The rapid emergence and adoption of generative AI systems—particularly large language models (LLMs) such as OpenAI's GPT, Google's Gemini, or Anthropic's Claude—marks a fundamental disruption in the landscape of knowledge-intensive work. Traditionally, automation was associated with blue-collar labor and routine physical tasks. However, generative AI extends automation into domains once thought to be the exclusive preserve of human cognitive abilities: language comprehension, creative generation, decision-making, and adaptive problem-solving (Kinder et al., 2024).

The implications of this disruption are profound. Generative AI tools are capable of drafting legal documents, producing software code, generating marketing content, and even designing technical schematics. This challenges the traditional boundaries between human expertise and machine capacity. It reconfigures labor markets by reshaping job roles, upskilling requirements, and productivity expectations across professions such as law, journalism, education, customer service, and software development.

From an innovation governance perspective, the generative AI disruption raises a number of critical issues. First, it accelerates the need for regulatory foresight and anticipatory governance. Concerns over intellectual property, misinformation, bias, accountability, and the erosion of professional standards demand new institutional responses. Questions arise over who bears responsibility for AI-generated content, how transparency and traceability can be maintained in algorithmic decision-making, and how equitable access to these technologies can be ensured.

Second, generative AI highlights the growing significance of infrastructure politics. The capabilities of these systems are dependent on massive datasets, advanced computing infrastructure (including GPUs and data centers), and access to proprietary algorithmic models. This creates new asymmetries of power between Big Tech firms and smaller market players, as well as between countries with AI infrastructure and those without. The concentration of model development and deployment in a handful of corporations raises issues of democratic oversight, economic concentration, and technological dependency.

Third, the rise of generative AI has profound implications for human capital development. It challenges education systems to rethink curriculum design, skill development, and the role of human creativity and critical thinking. As AI becomes a co-pilot in many white-collar professions, the future of work is not simply about displacement, but about redefinition—how humans collaborate with intelligent systems, how cognitive labor is valued, and how productivity is measured.

In short, generative AI exemplifies a disruption that is simultaneously technological, societal, and ethical. It transforms not only what machines can do, but what humans are expected to do—and how institutions must evolve to govern the interplay between the two.

10.2.3.2 Case 2: pandemic-induced supply chain restructuring

The COVID-19 pandemic, which unfolded globally between 2020 and 2022, represents one of the most consequential systemic disruptions in recent history. While initially perceived as a public health emergency, its ripple effects rapidly extended into virtually every aspect of the global economy. Among its most lasting impacts was the disruption of global supply chains—a development that exposed structural vulnerabilities and catalyzed new forms of industrial organization and innovation governance (Niu et al., 2023).

The pandemic interrupted production flows, transportation systems, and labor availability across continents. Critical shortages in medical supplies, semiconductors, consumer electronics, and agricultural products revealed the fragility of globalized, just-in-time supply chain models. What had once been celebrated as efficient and optimized systems suddenly appeared brittle and over-extended.

In response, both public and private actors began to reconfigure supply chains based on the principles of resilience, redundancy, and regionalization. Firms started to diversify suppliers, invest in nearshoring strategies, and adopt digital tools for real-time monitoring and forecasting. Governments launched initiatives to re-domesticate the production of critical goods, from vaccines to microchips, in the name of national security and public health preparedness.

From an innovation policy perspective, the pandemic marked a shift from efficiency-oriented industrial strategy to resilience-oriented governance. National and regional strategies began to prioritize strategic autonomy in key sectors, incentivizing domestic innovation capabilities and rethinking global dependency structures. Innovation funding mechanisms were redirected toward supply chain intelligence, smart logistics, automation technologies, and critical material substitution.

Furthermore, the pandemic accelerated the digitalization of industrial operations, including the adoption of digital twins, predictive analytics, blockchain-based traceability, and AI-enabled logistics management. These innovations were not simply technological responses—they were strategic enablers of a new paradigm that balances global integration with local adaptability.

Finally, the pandemic also triggered a broader societal conversation about risk, equity, and public value in innovation. Vaccine development and distribution highlighted both the power of rapid R&D collaboration and the disparities in access. The crisis prompted reflection on the governance of innovation ecosystems—who benefits, who is included in the innovation process, and how trust in institutions is maintained during emergencies (Onea, 2022).

In sum, the pandemic did not merely interrupt existing systems—it compelled a rethinking of the very foundations of industrial production and innovation governance. Its legacy is not only a restructured supply chain but a transformed logic of innovation under uncertainty.

10.2.3.3 Case 3: US–China tech decoupling and strategic autonomy

The strategic rivalry between the United States and China, particularly in the realm of high technology, exemplifies geopolitical disruption with direct consequences for industrial innovation. What began as a trade conflict has evolved into a broader process of technological decoupling, wherein the world's two largest economies pursue divergent paths in semiconductors, telecommunications, artificial intelligence, and quantum technologies (Bateman, 2022).

This decoupling is driven by concerns over national security, data sovereignty, and economic competitiveness. The United States has implemented export controls on advanced semiconductor manufacturing equipment, restricted investment flows into Chinese tech firms, and sought to curb China's access to critical R&D partnerships. In parallel, China has doubled down on its ambition for technological self-reliance, launching major policy programs such as "Made in China 2025," the "Dual Circulation" strategy, and the development of domestic chipmaking and AI capacity (Vyas, 2025).

The implications of this decoupling are far-reaching. First, it introduces fragmentation into the global innovation system, which for decades has been characterized by open collaboration, cross-border knowledge flows, and integrated supply chains. Companies operating in both markets are now forced to adopt dual-track strategies, localize technology stacks, and hedge against political risk in their innovation portfolios.

Second, it drives national investments in strategic technologies, leading to a surge in public R&D funding, industrial policy instruments, and techno-nationalist rhetoric. Innovation becomes a field of geopolitical contestation rather than neutral problem-solving, with implications for global governance, standard-setting, and ethical norms.

Third, the decoupling process challenges the governance of global technology platforms. Issues such as internet fragmentation, data localization, cross-border AI regulation, and intellectual property disputes take on new salience. Innovation is no longer governed solely by market logic or multilateral norms—it is increasingly shaped by national interests and strategic calculus.

This case illustrates how geopolitics can become a primary driver of innovation disruption—not merely as a background variable but as a direct and intentional force. It compels governments, firms, and researchers to navigate a landscape where innovation strategy, national policy, and global stability are tightly intertwined.

These three cases—generative AI, pandemic-induced supply chain restructuring, and US–China technological decoupling—demonstrate how disruption operates through distinct but overlapping channels. Each case reflects a different type of disruption—technological, societal, geopolitical—but all reveal the need for integrated innovation governance that is adaptive, anticipatory, and resilient. They underscore the urgency of embedding strategic foresight and systemic intelligence into the heart of industrial innovation policy.

10.2.4 Impacts on Value Chains and Sectors

Disruption—whether technological, societal, or geopolitical—has profound implications for how value is produced, distributed, and governed within and across industries. The traditional architecture of global production and innovation systems, built on assumptions of stability, predictability, and efficiency, is increasingly challenged by emergent volatility and transformation. As a result, value chains are undergoing deep reconfiguration. This shift is not merely a logistical adjustment—it reflects a broader reorientation in industrial priorities, governance mechanisms, and strategic imperatives.

Table 10.1 Contemporary disruptions and their implications for innovation governance

Case	Type of Disruption	Main Impacts	Innovation Governance Implications
Generative AI and White-Collar Automation	Technological	Automation of knowledge work (e.g., legal, design, coding) Redefinition of professional roles and cognitive labor Concentration of AI infrastructure and power	Need for anticipatory regulation (ethics, IP, accountability) Demand for new skills and education strategies Governance of AI infrastructure and transparency
Pandemic-Induced Supply Chain Restructuring	Societal/Systemic	Disruption of global logistics and production Shift from efficiency to resilience and redundancy Accelerated digital transformation of industry	Reorientation of industrial strategy toward resilience Adoption of digital tools in operations and forecasting Greater state involvement in innovation and production
US–China Tech Decoupling	Geopolitical	Fragmentation of global technology systems Dual-track development strategies by firms Race for technological sovereignty and IP control	Rise of techno-nationalism and industrial policy Strategic investment in critical and frontier technologies Politicization of innovation standards and data governance

10.2.4.1 Reconfiguration of production and logistics

Over the past three decades, the globalization of production was underpinned by the pursuit of cost optimization and scale. Firms disaggregated their operations across borders, relying on complex just-in-time (JIT) logistics systems and lean inventory models (Bednarski et al., 2023). This model, while efficient under conditions of stability, proved fragile when confronted with systemic shocks such as the COVID-19 pandemic, climate-related events, or geopolitical tensions.

In the current landscape of disruption, firms and governments are rethinking this model. One of the most visible changes is the shift from efficiency-driven to resilience-oriented supply chain design. Companies are now prioritizing redundancy, transparency, and flexibility. Multi-sourcing strategies are replacing single-supplier dependencies, buffer stocks are being reintroduced where necessary, and digital tools—such as predictive analytics and blockchain-based traceability—are increasingly deployed to enhance visibility and responsiveness across the supply network.

Manufacturing is similarly evolving. Advanced manufacturing technologies such as additive manufacturing (3D printing), industrial robotics, and AI-driven process optimization are enabling decentralized and modular production models. These allow firms to produce closer to the point of consumption, reduce transportation dependencies, and customize outputs for local market conditions. The factory of the future is not only smart but distributed, resilient, and capable of adapting in real time to shifting demands or constraints.

Moreover, logistics infrastructure is being recalibrated to accommodate these shifts. Ports, warehouses, and freight corridors are being digitized, integrated with sensor networks, and reimagined as nodes in intelligent, self-optimizing systems. The rise of "logistics-as-a-service," drone-based delivery, and autonomous freight solutions signals a departure from static models of distribution toward dynamic, data-rich, and anticipatory systems.

These transformations do not occur uniformly across sectors. Industries with high dependence on physical inputs and long global supply chains—such as automotive, aerospace, and electronics—are especially affected. Conversely, sectors more digitally mediated—such as media, software, and financial services—experience different forms of reconfiguration, focused more on platform governance, cybersecurity, and algorithmic accountability.

Ultimately, the reconfiguration of production and logistics is both a response to disruption and a driver of further change, as new capabilities, interdependencies, and vulnerabilities emerge.

10.2.4.2 New vulnerabilities and resilience strategies

The experience of cascading disruptions has foregrounded the concept of resilience in industrial discourse. Resilience, however, is not simply about withstanding shocks—it is about learning from them, adapting institutional and operational logics, and recovering with greater robustness and agility (Habibi et al., 2025).

New vulnerabilities are emerging in multiple dimensions. Cybersecurity has become a critical concern, particularly as production systems become digitized and connected through the Internet of Things (IoT) and industrial control systems. The risk of cyber-physical attacks on smart factories or supply chain infrastructure has elevated resilience to a matter of national security.

Climate-related risks are also reshaping production logic. Extreme weather events disrupt transportation, damage infrastructure, and affect the availability of raw materials. In response, firms are incorporating climate resilience metrics into site selection, logistics planning, and supplier management. Sustainability is no longer a reputational concern—it is increasingly integrated into operational continuity and compliance strategies.

The vulnerability of global logistics to geopolitical events—such as sanctions, embargoes, or territorial disputes—has added a further layer of complexity. Industries dependent on rare earth minerals, semiconductors, or other strategically sensitive components face heightened exposure to diplomatic instability. This has prompted investments in critical material substitution, recycling technologies, and stockpiling strategies.

In response to these vulnerabilities, a range of resilience strategies is being deployed. Some are technological—such as the deployment of AI-based risk-monitoring tools, digital twins for scenario planning, or blockchain for enhanced transparency. Others are institutional—such as reshoring policies, strategic public–private partnerships, and the creation of industry-level resilience frameworks.

Firms are also adopting organizational strategies, including the diversification of supplier bases, the geographic dispersion of production sites, and the institutionalization of crisis response teams. Resilience is no longer seen as a cost burden but as a strategic asset—a source of competitive differentiation and long-term sustainability.

Notably, resilience strategies are most effective when proactive rather than reactive. Institutions that integrate foresight, contingency planning, and systems thinking into their innovation governance structures are better positioned to anticipate, absorb, and adapt to disruption.

10.2.4.3 Rise of local and regional industrial strategies

Another major impact of disruption has been the reassertion of local and regional industrial strategies, challenging the orthodoxy of global integration as the default mode of industrial organization. This resurgence is not driven by protectionism alone, but by a complex mix of political, environmental, social, and technological factors (Bailey et al., 2023).

From a political standpoint, the experience of over-dependence on foreign suppliers for critical goods—whether vaccines, semiconductors, or energy components—has led many governments to pursue strategic autonomy. Policy instruments such as reshoring incentives, regional innovation clusters, and mission-oriented procurement are increasingly deployed to rebuild domestic production capacities and reduce strategic vulnerabilities.

Environmental concerns further reinforce this trend. The localization of production reduces transport-related emissions and facilitates the implementation of circular economy models, where materials are reused, recycled, or remanufactured within regional ecosystems. Sustainable industrial policy increasingly involves regional planning, lifecycle analysis, and place-based innovation strategies.

Social factors are also at play. Localized production supports employment, community engagement, and democratic accountability. It aligns with broader movements toward "slow" and ethical production, as consumers become more attuned to the origins, methods, and impacts of what they buy.

Technologically, the viability of local industrial strategies has been boosted by the proliferation of flexible, scalable, and digitalized production technologies. Modular factories, cloud-based design systems, and AI-assisted customization allow firms to operate efficiently at smaller scales and closer to markets.

As a result, industrial policy is shifting from a one-size-fits-all approach to one that emphasizes regional differentiation and specialization. Smart specialization strategies in the European Union, state-level industrial plans in the United States, and the development of city-based innovation districts reflect this territorial turn in innovation governance.

The implication is not the end of globalization, but a rebalancing. Global supply chains are being supplemented by regional value webs, combining global scale with local resilience. Innovation systems must now be designed to navigate this hybrid geography—leveraging global flows while anchoring capabilities in local institutions, infrastructures, and ecosystems.

The impacts of disruption on value chains and sectors are neither uniform nor temporary—they represent a long-term transformation of industrial systems and governance paradigms. The reconfiguration of production and logistics, the emergence of new vulnerabilities, and the rise of regional strategies are reshaping how and where value is created. They challenge the foundations of the global innovation architecture and compel a rethinking of industrial policy, corporate strategy, and institutional design.

10.3 STRATEGIC FORESIGHT AS INNOVATION INTELLIGENCE

The previous subsection explored the multifaceted disruptions reshaping industrial ecosystems and the systemic reconfigurations of value chains in response to technological, societal, and geopolitical volatility. These dynamics underscore the inadequacy of conventional planning tools and reactive governance models in navigating 21st-century challenges. Innovation systems today require more than adaptability—they demand anticipation. This is where strategic foresight becomes essential, not as a speculative exercise but as a structured and actionable form of innovation intelligence.

Strategic foresight equips institutions with the methodologies, mindsets, and mechanisms necessary to interpret weak signals, explore plausible futures, and convert long-term insights into present-day strategy. It shifts the focus from short-term optimization to long-term preparedness, aligning innovation processes with emerging needs, systemic transformations, and societal values (Linares & De la Vega, 2024).

10.3.1 Key Tools of Strategic Foresight

Strategic foresight is not defined by a single method or discipline but by a meta-competency: the ability to imagine, assess, and act upon multiple possible futures in order to make better decisions in the present. Its strength lies in its methodological pluralism and systemic scope (Carayannis et al., 2025). Foresight combines qualitative and quantitative approaches, engages diverse stakeholders, and operates across temporal horizons. In this section, we examine three foundational tools of strategic foresight: horizon scanning and emerging issue identification, trend mapping and weak signal analysis, and scenario planning and backcasting. Each plays a vital role in helping innovation actors make sense of uncertainty and complexity.

10.3.1.1 Horizon scanning and emerging issue identification

Horizon scanning is the entry point of most foresight processes. It involves the systematic exploration of the external environment to detect early signs of potentially important developments. Unlike conventional environmental scanning, which focuses on known variables and established trends, horizon scanning seeks to capture the uncertain, the weak, and the emergent—elements that may not yet be visible in mainstream data but could signal deeper transformations underway (Bengston et al., 2024).

The practice of horizon scanning typically uses frameworks such as Political, Economic, Social, Technological, Legal, Environmental (PESTLE) or Social, Technological, Economic, Environmental, Political (STEEP) to ensure a comprehensive view across sectors and domains. It draws on a wide range of sources—academic research, patents, media analysis, startup ecosystems, regulatory proposals, citizen discourse, and expert consultations. Increasingly, horizon scanning is augmented by AI and natural language processing tools that analyze large datasets, detect semantic shifts, and map novelty patterns in real time.

Emerging issues identified through scanning may at first appear marginal or speculative. However, when tracked systematically and contextualized within broader systems, they can reveal discontinuities, blind spots, and leverage points for innovation. For example, early signals of digital biosecurity, emotional AI, or decentralized governance models may point to future areas of disruption or opportunity.

The value of horizon scanning lies not only in what it detects but in how it challenges assumptions, surfaces hidden drivers, and opens up strategic conversations. It sensitizes organizations to what lies beyond their immediate strategic vision and prepares them to engage with a wider range of plausible futures.

10.3.1.2 Trend mapping and analysis of weak signals

While horizon scanning identifies potential novelties, trend mapping organizes this information into patterns of change. Trends are continuous developments with observable trajectories, which may span technological, demographic, economic, or socio-cultural domains (Zhao et al., 2024). Foresight practitioners often categorize trends by their level of maturity (emerging, accelerating, plateauing), scope (local, regional, global), and impact (low, moderate, transformative).

Trend mapping serves two functions. First, it helps contextualize emerging signals within broader narratives. Second, it enables strategic alignment—ensuring that innovation efforts are not only novel but resonant with deeper societal, technological, or ecological shifts. Trend analysis is particularly powerful when integrated with systems thinking: trends are not static trajectories but dynamic elements embedded in complex systems of interaction, feedback, and mutual influence.

A complementary tool in this process is the identification and interpretation of weak signals—subtle indicators of change that may lack scale or visibility but contain significant strategic insight. Weak signals are often precursors to future trends or disruptions. They challenge conventional wisdom, reveal nascent shifts in values or behaviors, and highlight emerging stakeholder expectations.

For example, growing online communities discussing neurodivergent design, early prototypes of climate-adaptive architecture, or localized experiments in post-capitalist economies may each represent weak signals of broader cultural or systemic evolution. Recognizing and nurturing these signals enables organizations to pre-position themselves before such shifts become mainstream or unavoidable.

Foresight processes that integrate both trend mapping and weak signal analysis build a more nuanced and layered understanding of change. They allow actors to track the present, anticipate the near future, and identify inflection points for intervention or transformation.

10.3.1.3 Scenario planning and backcasting

Scenario planning is one of the most recognized tools in strategic foresight. It involves constructing multiple, plausible narratives of the future—not to predict what will happen, but to explore what could happen under different assumptions, drivers, and uncertainties. Scenarios are designed to stretch thinking, test strategy robustness, and facilitate decision-making under conditions where extrapolation is unreliable (Cordova-Pozo & Rouwette, 2023).

A robust scenario process typically begins with the identification of key drivers and uncertainties. These are then combined into scenario axes (for example, centralized vs. decentralized governance; high vs. low ecological crisis) to generate a set of differentiated futures. Each scenario is elaborated into a narrative that includes political, economic, technological, social, and environmental dimensions.

Scenarios are not forecasts—they are exploratory constructs used to illuminate blind spots, challenge strategic assumptions, and prepare institutions for a range of future contexts. For example, scenarios on the future of industrial automation might consider futures where global labor markets fragment, where AI becomes tightly regulated, or where ecological collapse redirects investment away from digital solutions.

Backcasting complements scenario planning by working in reverse: instead of starting with present trends, it begins with a desired future state (for example, carbon-neutral manufacturing by 2040) and then maps the necessary steps to achieve it. Backcasting is particularly useful for normative or mission-oriented innovation, where the goal is not to adapt to the future but to create it. It helps align innovation portfolios with long-term societal goals and ensures coherence between short-term actions and long-term outcomes (Kim & Srivastava, 2024).

When used together, scenario planning and backcasting provide both exploratory and normative lenses. Scenarios expand the field of possibilities; backcasting focuses on pathways and feasibility. This dual perspective strengthens the strategic capacity of innovation systems by integrating imagination with implementation.

The tools of strategic foresight—horizon scanning, trend and signal analysis, scenario development, and backcasting—form the methodological backbone of future-oriented innovation intelligence. They offer structured ways to engage with complexity, uncertainty, and long-term transformation. However, tools alone are not sufficient. The following part will examine how these methods support a shift from prediction to preparedness and enable the evolution of anticipatory governance frameworks in both public and private institutions.

Table 10.2 Comparative matrix of foresight instruments for innovation planning

Foresight Tool	Purpose	Key Features	Strategic Application
Horizon Scanning	Detect early signs of change across domains	Identifies emerging issues and discontinuities; uses frameworks like PESTLE/STEEP; incorporates diverse data sources	Sensing emerging risks and opportunities; challenging assumptions; guiding early innovation agenda-setting
Trend Mapping	Understand patterns of change over time	Classifies trends by maturity, scale, and impact; links developments across sectors; informs systemic perspectives	Strategic alignment with evolving societal and technological conditions; prioritizing innovation focus areas
Weak Signal Analysis	Capture subtle, early indicators of future disruptions or transformations	Often qualitative and low visibility; highlights marginal, novel, or unexpected dynamics	Revealing blind spots; inspiring experimentation and early-stage R&D; informing scenario development
Scenario Planning	Explore multiple plausible futures	Constructs narratives around key uncertainties and drivers; combines systemic and contextual factors	Testing strategy robustness; fostering institutional reflexivity; preparing for discontinuity and volatility
Backcasting	Design pathways from preferred futures to present-day action	Starts from a desired end-state and works backward; supports mission-driven innovation	Roadmapping long-term transitions; aligning policy and innovation with sustainability and equity goals

10.3.2 From Prediction to Preparedness

As innovation ecosystems confront increasing complexity, ambiguity, and disruption, there is a growing recognition that traditional planning paradigms—rooted in prediction, linear extrapolation, and control—are insufficient for guiding long-term strategy. Strategic foresight offers an alternative. It does not seek to predict the future as a fixed endpoint, but to prepare for multiple futures by embracing uncertainty as a strategic resource (Carvalho & Woeffray, 2023). This part explores the conceptual and practical shift from prediction to preparedness, and how this transition is operationalized through the principles of anticipatory governance.

The conventional logic of prediction assumes that the future is knowable, quantifiable, and—given sufficient data—forecastable. This logic underpins many dominant tools of strategic management: trend extrapolation, forecasting models, risk matrices, and time series analysis. While these methods are useful in stable environments or for short-term tactical decision-making, they are deeply limited in contexts marked by deep uncertainty, long-term societal transformation, or the convergence of multiple disruptive forces.

In contrast, preparedness starts from the premise that the future is fundamentally indeterminate. It treats uncertainty not as a deficit to be eliminated, but as a condition to be engaged creatively. Preparedness does not discard evidence or analysis, but it situates them within broader narratives of possibility, reflexivity, and adaptation. The goal is not to narrow the future to a single optimal path, but to widen the horizon of options and to build the institutional and cognitive capacity to act across scenarios.

10.3.2.1 The shift from forecasting to foresight-driven resilience

The distinction between forecasting and foresight is often misunderstood. Forecasting is typically focused on probability: projecting what is likely to happen based on historical trends and known variables. Foresight, by contrast, is focused on plausibility and preparedness. It asks what could happen, how we might respond, and what capabilities we need to build today to thrive under different conditions (Carayannis et al., 2025).

This shift has major implications for innovation strategy. Under a forecasting paradigm, innovation investment may follow expected market trajectories—focusing on scaling existing technologies, optimizing efficiency, or maintaining competitive parity. Under a foresight paradigm, innovation is oriented toward transformation, system-shaping, and strategic resilience. It supports moonshot projects, anticipatory research, and cross-sectoral experimentation that may not have short-term commercial viability but are vital for long-term societal preparedness.

For example, consider the domain of climate-related innovation. Forecasting models may suggest incremental adaptation measures based on expected warming trends. Foresight, on the other hand, would explore high-uncertainty climate tipping points, socio-political upheaval, and ecological collapse scenarios—prompting more radical innovation in regenerative design, carbon-negative technologies, or adaptive urbanism.

Preparedness also encourages portfolio thinking. Instead of investing in a few high-probability bets, organizations diversify across multiple plausible pathways. This logic aligns closely with the I2E framework introduced in the following section: intelligence informs innovation, which feeds into adaptive execution under uncertainty. The foresight-preparedness paradigm underpins this iterative, feedback-rich approach.

10.3.2.2 Anticipatory governance as a systemic capability

At the heart of preparedness is the concept of anticipatory governance. Introduced in the early 2000s in the context of emerging technologies, anticipatory governance refers to the capacity of institutions to systematically explore, assess, and shape future developments before they fully materialize. It bridges foresight with decision-making and connects long-term visioning with near-term implementation.

Anticipatory governance is distinct from reactive or crisis-driven governance. It requires embedding futures thinking into policy design, institutional procedures, regulatory frameworks, and public discourse. Rather than waiting for evidence of disruption, anticipatory systems actively monitor early signals, develop adaptive plans, and mobilize cross-sectoral coordination in advance.

There are several key components to anticipatory governance:

1. Futures Integration: This involves embedding foresight outputs—such as scenarios, trend analyses, and backcasting roadmaps—into strategic planning, budgeting, and policy evaluation processes. For example, urban planning departments might use climate adaptation scenarios to inform zoning codes, infrastructure investment, or emergency response systems.
2. Institutional Reflexivity: Anticipatory governance depends on an organization's capacity to question its own assumptions, revise its models, and accept that plans must evolve. This is not always easy. Institutions often face cognitive inertia, risk aversion, or bureaucratic constraints. Reflexivity requires leadership commitment and a culture that supports experimentation, learning, and iteration.
3. Stakeholder Engagement and Co-creation: Anticipation must be inclusive. Engaging multiple perspectives—scientific, indigenous, civil society, business, youth—enhances both the robustness and the legitimacy of future-oriented planning. Participatory foresight, deliberative scenario development, and citizen assemblies are increasingly used to democratize anticipation and align innovation with public values.
4. Adaptive Regulation and Policy Experimentation: Governing futures involves flexibility. Anticipatory systems often employ "regulatory sandboxes," foresight-informed impact assessments, or dynamic licensing schemes to accommodate emerging technologies without stifling innovation. This approach shifts regulation from a gatekeeping role to an enabling

function—guiding innovation toward ethical and socially beneficial trajectories.

5. Monitoring, Evaluation, and Feedback Loops: Finally, anticipatory governance relies on ongoing evaluation. Futures literacy and preparedness are not one-off achievements but dynamic capacities that must be cultivated over time. Institutions must invest in monitoring systems that track how scenarios evolve, how policies perform under uncertainty, and how foresight inputs are used in practice.

These components enable institutions to move beyond prediction as a narrow technical function and toward anticipation as a governance paradigm. They help shift the focus from risk avoidance to opportunity cultivation, from control to stewardship, and from linearity to complexity-embracing systems logic.

10.3.2.3 The role of resilience in innovation governance

Preparedness is deeply linked to the concept of resilience. In foresight-informed innovation systems, resilience is not simply the capacity to withstand shocks but the ability to absorb disturbance, reorganize, and learn. This perspective draws from ecological, organizational, and complexity theories that view resilience as a dynamic, adaptive quality rather than a fixed state (Zumbrunn, 2023).

Foresight enhances resilience by providing organizations with early warning systems, optionality, and strategic depth. Rather than committing to a single future, institutions build the capacity to pivot, recombine resources, and navigate uncertainty without paralysis or collapse. Resilience becomes a design principle for innovation portfolios, institutional structures, and policy regimes.

In this context, innovation governance shifts from optimizing for known goals to preparing for contingent futures. It integrates foresight into technology assessment, scenario stress testing into program evaluation, and anticipatory ethics into R&D governance. This new governance model is not without tensions—it must balance stability with flexibility, expert insight with stakeholder deliberation, and long-term vision with short-term accountability.

Nevertheless, the reward is significant: systems that are not only better prepared for disruption, but better positioned to shape the future in desirable, just, and sustainable ways.

Strategic foresight enables the evolution from prediction to preparedness—not merely by offering new tools, but by reframing how innovation systems think, act, and govern under uncertainty. Through the logic of anticipatory governance, institutions can convert foresight into adaptive strategy, enabling innovation to become more resilient, inclusive, and future-aligned.

10.3.3 Building Organizational Foresight Capabilities

As strategic foresight becomes central to navigating complexity and enabling preparedness, the question arises: how can organizations—not only governments, but also firms, research institutions, and civil society actors—develop the internal capabilities to use foresight effectively and sustainably? While foresight methods such as scenario planning or horizon scanning can be applied through one-off initiatives or external consultants, true resilience and anticipatory capacity depend on the institutionalization of foresight practices within organizations. Foresight must evolve from a tool to a capability, from an episodic exercise to a structural and cultural feature of innovation governance.

This subsection explores the practical challenges and strategic pathways for embedding foresight in organizations. It focuses on three key dimensions: the integration of foresight into institutional architectures and processes; the development of skills, mindsets, and cultures that support futures thinking; and the design of mechanisms to evaluate foresight maturity and effectiveness over time.

10.3.3.1 Embedding foresight in institutions

The integration of foresight into organizational structures requires more than the creation of future scenarios or periodic trend reports. It involves a reconfiguration of decision-making logics and planning systems so that long-term, systemic, and reflexive thinking becomes embedded in how strategies are formulated, investments allocated, and policies designed (De Smedt & Van den Broeck, 2024).

In public institutions, foresight integration often takes place through the establishment of dedicated foresight units, strategic foresight teams within policy departments, or inter-ministerial futures committees. These bodies act as hubs of intelligence, responsible for translating external scanning into actionable insights, designing participatory foresight processes, and advising leadership on long-term implications of current decisions. For example, Finland's parliament has institutionalized foresight through its Committee for the Future, while the European Commission integrates foresight into each stage of its policy cycle.

In the private sector, organizational foresight is increasingly located within strategy, R&D, innovation, or corporate development departments. Some firms—particularly in the energy, aerospace, finance, and technology sectors—have established internal foresight labs, trend observatories, or scenario teams tasked with exploring futures aligned to strategic priorities. These units often operate at the interface between long-term visioning and immediate business development, connecting abstract foresight with concrete product planning, risk management, and market entry strategies.

Crucially, embedding foresight requires building organizational interfaces. Foresight insights must reach across silos and be translated into the language of decision-makers. This means integrating foresight outputs into budgeting processes, board-level deliberations, Key Performance Indicators (KPI) development, and innovation portfolio assessments. Tools such as future impact statements, strategic alignment dashboards, and scenario stress tests help institutionalize this integration.

Foresight is most effective when it is linked to the core purposes and missions of an organization. Rather than functioning as a separate intelligence function, it becomes a way of aligning long-term goals, strategic resilience, and value creation. In mission-oriented innovation, for example, foresight helps define the nature of the mission, assess alternative pathways, and evaluate unintended consequences. In regulatory bodies, it supports adaptive rule-making that evolves alongside technological change.

10.3.3.2 Skills and cultural prerequisites for futures thinking

Building foresight capability also entails investment in human capital—specifically, in the development of skills, cognitive capacities, and cultural norms that support futures literacy and systemic thinking. Organizations cannot rely solely on external foresight consultants; they must cultivate internal champions, transversal foresight literacy, and a shared understanding of how to engage with the future constructively.

The key competencies required for organizational foresight include:

- **Futures literacy**: The ability to recognize that the future is not predetermined and to work with alternative futures constructively.
- **Systems thinking**: The capacity to identify feedback loops, interdependencies, and emergent behaviors within complex systems.
- **Sensemaking**: The ability to interpret weak signals, make sense of ambiguous data, and identify patterns in uncertainty.
- **Strategic imagination**: The creative capability to envision novel possibilities, challenge dominant paradigms, and articulate alternative trajectories.
- **Reflexive judgment**: The ability to critically assess one's own assumptions, values, and institutional biases when thinking about the future.

Beyond individual skills, fostering a culture of foresight is essential. This involves shifting organizational mindsets from control to exploration, from linear planning to iterative learning, and from short-termism to long-term stewardship. Leadership plays a critical role in modeling this shift—by legitimizing uncertainty, rewarding long-term thinking, and opening space for speculative dialogue.

Cultural change can be supported through deliberate practices. Regular futures workshops, cross-departmental scenario co-creation, storytelling exercises, and speculative prototyping help normalize futures thinking. Celebrating experiments—even those that "fail"—signals that innovation is exploratory by nature. Organizations that treat uncertainty as an opportunity rather than a threat are better positioned to navigate volatile environments.

Importantly, organizational foresight must be inclusive and participatory. Futures are not the domain of elite experts alone; they belong to all stakeholders who are affected by the consequences of today's decisions. Inclusive foresight helps surface marginalized perspectives, broaden the range of considered outcomes, and foster collective ownership over strategic direction. Participatory foresight methods—such as futures games, citizen panels, or stakeholder mapping—enrich the process and deepen impact.

10.3.3.3 Measuring foresight maturity and effectiveness

To sustain and evolve foresight capabilities, organizations must also be able to measure and evaluate their foresight maturity. This involves assessing not only whether foresight activities are taking place, but whether they are embedded, impactful, and adaptive. Foresight maturity models, similar to those used in digital transformation or innovation management, can guide this evaluation (Fasoli & Poli, 2024).

Foresight maturity can be assessed along several dimensions:

- **Institutionalization**: To what extent is foresight integrated into planning, budgeting, and governance structures?
- **Methodological diversity**: Does the organization employ a range of foresight tools appropriate to its context and strategic needs?
- **Capacity development**: Are foresight skills and literacies cultivated across departments and roles?
- **Decision impact**: Are foresight outputs used to inform key decisions, shape investment, or anticipate emerging challenges?
- **Learning and adaptation**: Is foresight activity evaluated, updated, and iterated in response to feedback and changing conditions?

Evaluation methods may include surveys, maturity self-assessments, case studies, internal audits, or external reviews. Some organizations use foresight audits to trace how scenarios or horizon scans have influenced policy outcomes or project trajectories. Others use impact indicators to assess whether foresight contributes to resilience, agility, and innovation alignment.

Crucially, measuring foresight is not about proving predictive accuracy. Rather, it is about assessing the quality of preparedness, the depth of engagement, and the robustness of strategic thinking. It is about whether the organization has the capacity to sense, interpret, and act on signals of change—and to do so in ways that are inclusive, ethical, and future-oriented.

Foresight capability is not a fixed asset but a dynamic institutional function—one that must be cultivated, integrated, and evaluated over time. By embedding foresight into structures, developing futures-oriented skills and culture, and systematically measuring impact, organizations can become more adaptive, resilient, and strategically aligned with long-term transformations.

In the following section, we transition from the tools and organizational integration of foresight to the I2E framework—which connects foresight (intelligence) with innovation development and strategic execution. It offers a systemic model for navigating disruption and building innovation ecosystems capable of sensing, shaping, and stewarding complex futures.

10.4 THE I2E FRAMEWORK: FROM INSIGHT TO EXECUTION

The previous section established the centrality of strategic foresight as a form of innovation intelligence—an essential capability for navigating complexity, anticipating disruption, and embedding preparedness into the design of policies, technologies, and institutional strategies. Yet foresight, while critical, is not sufficient on its own. Anticipating change must be coupled with the capacity to innovate in response to emergent futures and to translate ideas into scalable actions. This requires a more integrated and systemic model for innovation governance—one that connects forward-looking intelligence with experimental creativity and with real-world execution. The I2E framework—Intelligence, Innovation, and Execution—offers such a model.

This section develops the I2E framework in depth. It introduces its conceptual architecture, defining each of its three components and explaining how they interact in a continuous cycle of adaptive innovation. It explores how I2E can be operationalized in diverse contexts, from policymaking and R&D to innovation ecosystems aligned with societal goals such as sustainability, digital rights, and resilience. Finally, it examines how the framework supports the management of innovation portfolios under uncertainty—balancing exploration and exploitation, radical and incremental innovation, and risk and opportunity.

10.4.1 Conceptualizing I2E

In increasingly volatile and interdependent innovation environments, linear models of technology development and policy planning are no longer adequate. Traditional approaches that treat foresight, ideation, and implementation as separate phases struggle to respond to dynamic change, emergent challenges, and complex stakeholder landscapes. The I2E framework responds to this limitation by offering a dynamic, non-linear model that integrates three mutually reinforcing capacities: Intelligence, Innovation, and Execution. Together, these constitute a circular and iterative system for transformative innovation governance.

10.4.1.1 Intelligence: foresight as strategic input

The first component of the I2E framework, Intelligence, refers to the systemic foresight capabilities discussed in the previous chapter. Intelligence involves scanning the horizon, analyzing weak signals, constructing scenarios, mapping system dynamics, and interpreting long-term trends. It is not confined to data analytics or predictive modeling—it includes interpretive, imaginative, and participatory dimensions.

Strategic intelligence allows organizations to move from reactive problem-solving to anticipatory positioning. It helps redefine the problem space, identify emergent opportunities, and clarify the values and risks embedded in different innovation paths. Importantly, intelligence is not neutral or technical—it is shaped by worldview, institutional perspective, and cultural narrative. For this reason, inclusive and reflexive foresight processes are critical to ensure that intelligence reflects a plurality of futures and not just dominant imaginaries.

Within the I2E model, intelligence is not a preliminary input that disappears once innovation begins. It is a continuous function that informs each phase of the innovation cycle—guiding ideation, contextualizing experiments, and shaping execution strategies. Intelligence also evolves over time: feedback from innovation and implementation updates the foresight landscape, enabling dynamic learning and adjustment.

10.4.1.2 Innovation: ideation, design, and experimentation

The second component, Innovation, represents the creative, generative core of the framework. It encompasses ideation, design thinking, prototyping, and experimental action. Innovation, in the I2E context, is not limited to technological breakthroughs or commercial product development. It includes organizational, institutional, social, and policy innovation—new ways of solving problems, organizing relationships, and delivering value.

Crucially, innovation is framed not as an isolated act of invention but as a systemic process. Ideas emerge within contexts shaped by foresight, informed by stakeholder needs, and enabled by experimentation platforms such as living labs, sandboxes, or co-design processes. Rather than focusing on novelty alone, innovation in the I2E framework emphasizes relevance, adaptability, and transformative potential.

This approach to innovation requires a shift from the pursuit of efficiency or short-term return to a logic of exploration and learning. It values partial solutions, iterative development, and failure as a source of insight. Innovation becomes a means of engaging with uncertainty, testing hypotheses, and building capabilities for change.

Foresight enhances innovation by redefining the parameters of what is possible and desirable. It pushes innovation beyond path dependency, encouraging the reimagination of systems. For instance, rather than optimizing the current food system, intelligence-informed innovation might explore regenerative agriculture, decentralized food networks, or synthetic biology under alternative climate or demographic futures.

10.4.1.3 Execution: implementation, scaling, and institutionalization

The third component of the I2E model is Execution. This refers to the implementation, diffusion, and institutional embedding of innovations in real-world settings. Execution is often the most under-theorized and under-supported phase of innovation—but without it, foresight and ideation remain abstract.

Execution includes activities such as pilot testing, scaling up, regulatory integration, public procurement, and stakeholder mobilization. It involves overcoming technical, financial, political, and cultural barriers to make innovations operational. Execution also requires governance mechanisms, including accountability structures, feedback loops, and performance monitoring, to ensure that innovation aligns with strategic goals and social values.

In the I2E framework, execution is not the endpoint of a process—it is part of an ongoing cycle. Implementation generates new intelligence about what works, what fails, and what adapts in complex environments. These insights feed back into foresight and innovation, creating a system of reflexive governance.

Execution also includes institutionalization—the embedding of successful innovations into policies, standards, routines, and social norms. This step is critical for long-term impact. Without institutional support, even the most promising innovations risk stagnation or reversal. Embedding requires alignment with legal frameworks, fiscal mechanisms, cultural narratives, and stakeholder interests.

Strategic execution requires more than management capacity; it requires adaptive leadership, multi-sectoral coordination, and mission coherence. In mission-driven innovation—such as climate neutrality, digital equity, or pandemic resilience—execution is a political and social process as much as a technical one. It involves coalition building, legitimacy negotiation, and value reconciliation.

10.4.1.4 The systemic nature of I2E

What distinguishes the I2E model from traditional innovation frameworks is its non-linear, iterative, and systemic character. Intelligence does not simply feed into innovation, and innovation does not automatically lead to execution. Instead, each component interacts continuously with the others:

- Intelligence shapes innovation by defining future-oriented challenges and identifying systemic opportunities.
- Innovation informs intelligence by generating real-world insights, revealing blind spots, and testing assumptions.
- Execution tests both intelligence and innovation under real constraints, generating feedback that reshapes strategy and foresight.

This dynamic loop enables continuous learning, adaptation, and resilience. It aligns with complexity science and systems thinking approaches, which emphasize the need for feedback-rich, decentralized, and flexible governance structures in high-uncertainty environments.

Moreover, the I2E model emphasizes purpose-driven innovation. Intelligence is not just about risk avoidance but about value generation; innovation is not just about novelty but about relevance; and execution is not just about rollout but about transformative embedding. This purpose orientation allows the I2E model to align with public missions, societal goals, and ethical imperatives.

The I2E framework offers a robust conceptual foundation for future-oriented innovation governance. By integrating foresight (intelligence), experimentation (innovation), and implementation (execution) into a continuous, adaptive cycle, it enables institutions to navigate complexity with strategic clarity and operational agility.

How this framework can be operationalized will be explored next—across different institutional settings, from government ministries and corporate innovation units to R&D labs and multi-stakeholder consortia—and how it aligns with broader societal goals such as the Sustainable Development Goals, environmental transitions, and digital governance.

10.4.2 Operationalizing I2E

Having established the conceptual architecture of the I2E framework—linking Intelligence (foresight), Innovation (experimentation), and Execution (scaling and institutionalization)—the challenge turns to implementation. How can this framework be embedded in practice, particularly within the structures of public policymaking, R&D, and real-world innovation ecosystems? Operationalizing

I2E requires deliberate interventions in governance design, institutional processes, and strategic alignment mechanisms.

This part explores how I2E can be translated into actionable systems across multiple contexts. First, it examines how I2E logic can be embedded in public policy cycles, R&D agendas, and innovation laboratories. Second, it considers how this framework supports the alignment of innovation governance with broad societal goals such as the Sustainable Development Goals (SDGs), green transitions, and ethical digitalization. Operationalizing I2E is not simply a managerial task—it is a transformation of how innovation systems understand and govern change.

10.4.2.1 Embedding I2E in policymaking, R&D cycles, and innovation labs

The most immediate arena for I2E operationalization is the domain of public policy. In recent years, governments and intergovernmental institutions have recognized the need to move beyond reactive regulation and toward anticipatory, mission-oriented innovation systems. The I2E framework offers a model for integrating long-term strategic intelligence with short-cycle policy and program execution.

In policymaking, this means embedding foresight practices (intelligence) not only in agenda-setting but throughout the policy cycle—from ex-ante impact assessment to mid-course evaluation and adaptive revision. This can take the form of institutional foresight units, national scenario exercises, or participatory visioning platforms. For example, the European Commission's foresight framework feeds directly into its strategic planning and Horizon Europe R&D funding priorities, ensuring that policy choices are responsive to long-term transformations.

Once foresight has shaped the direction of travel, policymakers must support experimentation and innovation. Here, the I2E framework calls for the institutionalization of experimentation spaces within policy systems: "regulatory sandboxes" for new technologies, "policy labs" for social innovation, or "challenge platforms" for mission-driven R&D. These spaces allow governments to test solutions in real-world conditions, iterate based on feedback, and assess broader systemic implications before full-scale deployment.

Execution, the third leg of the framework, takes place through strategic program implementation, procurement systems, public–private partnerships, and institutional reform. Execution is not an end-point but a phase of learning, enabling policy feedback loops, investment adaptation, and policy integration across sectors. Critically, public-sector execution must also involve capacity building—ensuring that agencies have the leadership, infrastructure, and skills to deliver on foresight-informed innovation agendas.

In R&D contexts, operationalizing I2E involves a deliberate shift from purely curiosity- or market-driven research to strategic and mission-aligned research ecosystems. Intelligence functions in this context include foresight-based priority setting, technology roadmapping, and socio-technical impact assessment. Research funding agencies, such as the UKRI in the UK or BMBF in Germany, are increasingly integrating foresight exercises into calls for proposals and program evaluations.

Innovation occurs in R&D through not only technological experimentation but also through methodological pluralism, interdisciplinary co-creation, and open science approaches. Execution, in this domain, is supported through translational research centers, startup accelerators, industrial testbeds, and innovation diffusion networks. The result is a continuous cycle of knowledge generation, validation, and application informed by foresight and societal demand.

Innovation laboratories—whether hosted by universities, corporations, or public agencies—provide fertile ground for I2E operationalization. These labs serve as microcosms of the framework: they combine horizon scanning and problem sensing, iterative design and rapid prototyping, and real-world experimentation and scaling. The best examples incorporate stakeholder foresight exercises, living lab methods, and adaptive business models to align experimentation with strategic relevance and practical uptake.

What distinguishes I2E-aligned labs from conventional incubators or think tanks is their systemic orientation and policy connectivity. They do not merely aim to produce innovative outputs, but to test governance models, embed ethics, and contribute to institutional learning. Operationalizing I2E in such settings requires leadership that embraces uncertainty, facilitates cross-sectoral collaboration, and prioritizes transformative over incremental outcomes.

10.4.2.2 Strategic alignment with the SDGs, green innovation, and digital ethics

Beyond institutional embedding, the operationalization of I2E must be aligned with the broader transformational challenges facing society. These include climate change, biodiversity loss, social inequality, digital disruption, and democratic decline. Strategic alignment with these macro-objectives ensures that innovation governance is not only technically effective but socially legitimate and future-proof (Hariyani et al., 2025).

The Sustainable Development Goals (SDGs), adopted by the United Nations in 2015, offer a globally recognized reference point for aligning foresight, innovation, and execution with long-term societal well-being. Operationalizing I2E in this context involves several strategies:

1. **Foresight-informed SDG mapping:** Linking emerging trends and disruptions to SDG targets, identifying where future risks may undermine progress or where new opportunities may accelerate achievement.
2. **Mission-oriented innovation for SDGs:** Framing R&D programs, innovation investments, and policy missions around cross-cutting SDG challenges—such as clean energy, circular economy, or inclusive education.
3. **Execution through cross-sectoral coalitions:** Scaling innovation through partnerships among governments, civil society, industry, and academia, mobilizing diverse resources and perspectives for SDG implementation.

Similarly, green innovation is a domain where I2E alignment is both urgent and complex. Achieving climate neutrality, decarbonization, and ecological restoration requires not only new technologies but new economic models, infrastructures, and behaviors. Foresight in this context anticipates climate risks, resource constraints, and ecological tipping points. Innovation explores alternatives to current extractive practices—such as renewable energy systems, regenerative agriculture, or biomaterials. Execution demands changes in investment norms, industrial policy, infrastructure planning, and lifestyle incentives.

The European Green Deal, for instance, operationalizes I2E by combining long-term strategic objectives (climate neutrality by 2050) with policy foresight (climate scenarios and transition pathways), innovation funding (for example, Horizon Europe's Green Missions), and regulatory execution (carbon pricing, green taxonomy, circularity standards). This integration exemplifies the I2E logic at scale.

Digital transformation presents another field for operationalizing I2E, particularly regarding ethical governance. Foresight here identifies emerging challenges related to AI bias, data colonialism, algorithmic transparency, and digital labor displacement. Innovation includes privacy-preserving technologies, platform cooperatives, and public-interest algorithms. Execution requires digital rights frameworks, anticipatory regulation, ethical tech procurement, and public engagement in technology assessment.

Operationalizing I2E in this context ensures that digital innovation is aligned not only with economic efficiency but with democratic values, equity, and inclusion. It reinforces the idea that ethical innovation is not a constraint but a condition for legitimacy and adoption in the digital age.

10.4.2.2.1 Barriers and enablers

While the potential of I2E is substantial, operationalization faces real barriers. These include institutional inertia, siloed governance structures, short-term political pressures, and a lack of futures literacy. Many organizations lack the cross-cutting coordination mechanisms or data-sharing platforms needed to align intelligence, innovation, and execution across departments and sectors.

Enablers of operationalization include leadership commitment, inter-ministerial task forces, dedicated foresight capacity, policy labs, flexible funding mechanisms, and inclusive governance processes. Learning from global exemplars and tailoring the I2E framework to local institutional contexts can accelerate adoption and scale.

Importantly, operationalization is not a one-time event but an ongoing practice. It evolves as foresight deepens, innovation ecosystems mature, and governance capacity grows.

Operationalizing the I2E framework bridges the gap between conceptual ambition and institutional practice. By embedding intelligence, enabling innovation, and supporting strategic execution, I2E transforms how governments, firms, and innovation ecosystems respond to disruption and advance long-term missions. When aligned with societal goals such as the SDGs, climate resilience, and digital justice, the I2E model becomes not only a governance tool—but a framework for transformative impact.

10.4.3 Managing Innovation Portfolios

The I2E framework—integrating Intelligence, Innovation, and Execution—offers a structured model for aligning foresight, experimentation, and implementation. Yet its value is most fully realized when applied not only to discrete projects but to the strategic management of innovation portfolios. As innovation ecosystems become more complex and exposed to multiple, overlapping disruptions, single-solution thinking gives way to portfolio-based governance: a systemic approach that balances exploration and exploitation, short-term feasibility with long-term transformation, and risk mitigation with opportunity cultivation.

This part explores how organizations—whether public agencies, research institutions, corporations, or transnational alliances—can use the I2E model to design, manage, and evaluate innovation portfolios under conditions of uncertainty and volatility. It focuses on three interrelated priorities: balancing radical and incremental innovation; navigating uncertainty through flexible investment and feedback loops; and embracing portfolio diversification as a resilience and impact strategy.

10.4.3.1 Balancing radical and incremental innovation

Innovation portfolios are often skewed toward either incremental improvements—which optimize existing systems—or radical innovations—which seek to reconfigure them. Both types are essential, but they carry different timelines, levels of risk, and degrees of organizational disruption. Managing an effective portfolio requires deliberately balancing the two, ensuring that core operations remain competitive while future capabilities are actively cultivated (Lennon, 2022).

Incremental innovation focuses on efficiency, performance enhancement, or customer experience optimization. It is typically low-risk, with clear market pathways and measurable short-term gains. However, it often reinforces existing paradigms and may fail to prepare organizations for systemic change or existential disruption.

Radical innovation, on the other hand, explores unproven technologies, governance models, or socio-technical systems. It challenges assumptions, opens new markets, and may generate breakthrough value. However, it is uncertain, resource-intensive, and politically sensitive—often lacking immediate profitability or institutional support.

The I2E framework supports this balancing act by grounding innovation choices in strategic foresight. Intelligence (I) clarifies which domains are most exposed to disruption or transformation, helping organizations decide where radical innovation is necessary. At the same time, it identifies areas where existing systems remain resilient and where incremental innovation may suffice.

For example, in the energy sector, foresight might suggest that solar and wind technologies are entering maturity and suited for incremental innovation (for example, efficiency improvements, storage integration). Meanwhile, emergent areas like hydrogen, bioenergy with carbon capture, or fusion may require radical R&D investment and long-term experimentation.

Managing both tracks within a single portfolio avoids over-reliance on either optimization or speculation. It reflects the principle of strategic ambidexterity: the ability to exploit existing assets while exploring new frontiers.

10.4.3.2 Navigating uncertainty with flexible investment and feedback loops

Uncertainty is not a static variable but a dynamic condition. Innovations evolve under shifting policy regimes, market signals, technological trajectories, and societal norms. Portfolio governance, therefore, must be designed to adapt to change—not by rigid planning, but by creating real-time feedback mechanisms, decision flexibility, and learning capacity (Stanton & Roelich, 2021).

The I2E framework enables this through continuous iteration. Intelligence (foresight) is not a one-time input at the start of innovation cycles; it is updated through monitoring, sense-making, and stakeholder engagement. This adaptive intelligence feeds back into innovation design and informs execution strategies.

In portfolio terms, this allows for dynamic rebalancing. Projects can be accelerated, paused, redesigned, or exited based on updated assumptions or external changes. For instance, a foresight-informed dashboard might track scenario alignment, technology readiness, stakeholder sentiment, or policy signals, triggering real-time adjustments.

This approach parallels real options thinking in finance—treating each project not as a binary success/failure bet, but as a contingent option that may be scaled, pivoted, or deferred. Innovation funding models are evolving accordingly. Some agencies are adopting stage-gated funding or adaptive grant mechanisms, linking resource allocation to ongoing alignment with strategic foresight or emerging risk.

Execution (E), in this system, becomes an experiment in governance itself: flexible procurement, agile policy design, and learning-oriented implementation. Feedback loops may include data analytics, user testing, citizen feedback, participatory evaluation, or third-party audits. The goal is not perfection at launch, but adaptive scaling based on iterative intelligence.

The COVID-19 pandemic illustrated this logic vividly. Innovation portfolios in health, digital services, and education were rapidly restructured as new intelligence emerged—from vaccine efficacy and digital divide data to remote work dynamics and economic resilience patterns. Agile portfolio governance allowed institutions to reallocate resources, scale promising models, and abandon obsolete interventions.

10.4.3.3 Portfolio diversification as risk mitigation and strategic positioning

Diversification has long been a tenet of financial risk management, but in innovation governance, it takes on deeper strategic and systemic dimensions. Innovation portfolios must be diverse not only in project type, but across technologies, actors, time horizons, disciplines, and geographies (Oladimeji & Udosen, 2019). This ensures robustness against shocks, fosters inclusive participation, and enables richer cross-pollination of ideas.

Under the I2E framework, portfolio diversification is informed by foresight (intelligence), co-created through design (innovation), and coordinated through adaptive mechanisms (execution). A well-diversified portfolio might include:

- **Technological diversity:** Investing in a range of competing or complementary technologies to avoid lock-in and hedge against technical failure.
- **Actor diversity:** Engaging large firms, startups, academia, civil society, and public agencies to ensure plural knowledge and value creation.
- **Temporal diversity:** Mixing near-term wins with long-term transformation pathways, balancing immediate impact with systemic change.

- **Risk diversity:** Accepting a mix of low-risk, incremental projects and high-risk, radical ventures based on systemic need and foresight scenarios.
- **Geographical diversity:** Supporting local, regional, and international initiatives to build resilience across ecosystems and avoid over-concentration.

Diversity is not only a safeguard—it is a generator of resilience and innovation capacity. Diverse portfolios are more likely to adapt to unknown future conditions, discover novel combinations, and support equitable distribution of benefits.

For example, the Mission Innovation global platform—a coalition of countries investing in clean energy R&D—illustrates a diversified portfolio approach. Its structure includes various technologies (storage, hydrogen, smart grids), delivery mechanisms (national labs, international collaboration), and governance models (public–private partnerships, philanthropic alliances). The result is not only risk mitigation but a collective strategy for planetary resilience.

Importantly, diversification must be balanced with coherence. Portfolios should not be random assortments of projects, but organized around strategic missions, policy goals, or foresight-informed scenarios. Scenario stress-testing can help assess whether the portfolio as a whole is robust under alternative futures. Mapping interdependencies among projects can reveal synergies or gaps.

Portfolio-level coordination mechanisms—such as innovation councils, cross-sectoral steering groups, or digital portfolio dashboards—support coherence, transparency, and strategic alignment.

Managing innovation portfolios through the lens of the I2E framework enables organizations to balance creativity with coherence, ambition with accountability, and uncertainty with learning. By integrating foresight intelligence, fostering diverse innovation pathways, and embedding execution within flexible, feedback-rich governance systems, I2E transforms portfolio management into a strategic function of anticipatory governance.

This approach equips institutions to not only survive disruption, but to proactively shape desirable futures—through portfolios that are not only innovative, but mission-aligned, socially responsive, and systemically resilient.

10.5 SYSTEMIC FUTURES THINKING FOR INNOVATION GOVERNANCE

The preceding section introduced the I2E framework as a systemic model for linking foresight (intelligence), innovation (ideation and experimentation), and execution (implementation and scaling). Through this lens, innovation governance becomes an iterative, reflexive process that enables institutions to engage proactively with complexity, ambiguity, and long-term transformation. However, to ensure that I2E is not only applied within isolated programs or policy instruments but becomes embedded across entire innovation systems, a broader conceptual and institutional paradigm shift is required. This is the role of systemic futures thinking—a perspective that views the governance of innovation as an adaptive, distributed, and ethically grounded process aimed at collective resilience and long-term societal flourishing. This section develops the principles and implications of systemic futures thinking for innovation governance.

10.5.1 Toward Adaptive Innovation Governance

The governance of innovation has traditionally been conceptualized in technocratic and instrumental terms—focused on optimizing investment, enhancing competitiveness, or scaling technological breakthroughs. Yet in the face of structural disruptions such as climate change, geopolitical instability, AI-driven labor transformation, and demographic shifts, these models are no longer sufficient. Governing innovation today requires not only foresight but adaptability, resilience, and reflexivity—qualities that enable systems to anticipate change, learn from feedback, and evolve continuously in response to uncertainty (Janssen & van der Voort, 2016).

10.5.1.1 Defining resilience, adaptability, and reflexivity

Resilience in innovation governance refers to the capacity of systems—whether institutional, organizational, or socio-technical—to absorb shocks, maintain core functions, and reorganize in response to disruptions. It goes beyond robustness (the ability to resist change) and includes transformative resilience—the ability to emerge from crises in new configurations that are better aligned with evolving environmental and societal conditions (Vella & Pai, 2019).

In practical terms, resilience in innovation systems includes redundancy in capabilities, diversification of stakeholders and funding streams, cross-sectoral collaboration, and preparedness for low-probability/high-impact events. A resilient system does not collapse under stress; it adapts, reorients, and often innovates in response to disturbance.

Adaptability, closely related to resilience, involves the ability of institutions to modify strategies, structures, and processes in light of emerging evidence or shifting conditions. Adaptive innovation governance is responsive to feedback and open to experimental approaches. It is not static or rule-bound but operates on principles of contingency, learning, and iteration.

For instance, regulatory agencies that adopt sandbox models for emerging technologies (for example, fintech or AI applications) are practicing adaptive governance. Rather than applying rigid frameworks, they enable real-world experimentation under monitored conditions, adjusting rules as technologies and societal expectations evolve.

Reflexivity adds a further dimension. It refers to the ability of innovation systems to examine their own assumptions, values, and power dynamics. Reflexive governance includes self-evaluation, inclusive deliberation, and the willingness to question established paradigms. It recognizes that decisions about innovation are never purely technical—they are embedded in social values, institutional legacies, and political economies.

Reflexivity becomes especially important when dealing with contested or value-laden innovations: gene editing, surveillance technologies, or geoengineering, for instance. In such cases, foresight must be coupled with ethical inquiry and participatory processes that surface multiple perspectives.

Together, resilience, adaptability, and reflexivity form the backbone of systemic futures thinking in governance. They shift the focus from managing isolated innovations to stewarding complex systems through long-term transformation.

10.5.1.2 Roles of public policy, academia, and civil society

Operationalizing adaptive governance requires distributed responsibility and collaboration across sectors. Each actor—public policymakers, researchers, civil society organizations—plays a distinct but interdependent role in enabling foresight-informed, futures-ready governance.

Public policy has the mandate and resources to shape the broader enabling environment for innovation. Governments are uniquely positioned to set long-term missions, design adaptive regulations, allocate funding, and support intersectoral coordination. When infused with foresight, public policy becomes a platform for anticipatory capacity-building and systemic alignment.

However, traditional policymaking is often constrained by electoral cycles, bureaucratic inertia, or siloed structures. Adaptive innovation governance requires reforming policy institutions to embrace transversal coordination, scenario-based planning, real-time evaluation, and participatory engagement. The establishment of national foresight offices, cross-ministerial strategy units, or open policy labs exemplifies this transition.

Academia contributes through research, critical inquiry, and the cultivation of futures literacies. Universities are both sites of knowledge production and incubators of long-term thinking. They host foresight centers, engage in interdisciplinary experimentation, and provide the evidence base for responsible innovation governance.

Beyond technical expertise, academia plays a key role in fostering reflexivity and ethical awareness. Social scientists, philosophers of technology, and science and technology studies (STS) scholars contribute perspectives that challenge instrumental views of innovation and bring attention to inclusion, power, and justice. Futures thinking is increasingly embedded in curricula, doctoral programs, and transdisciplinary research agendas.

Civil society, often overlooked in traditional innovation governance, is central to adaptive futures. NGOs, community-based organizations, indigenous groups, and digital activists offer grounded knowledge, alternative imaginaries, and public accountability. They surface the social and environmental consequences of innovation, articulate marginalized perspectives, and co-create solutions in real-world contexts.

Civil society actors also foster distributed foresight. Through participatory scenarios, deliberative foresight processes, and citizen assemblies, they democratize the production of futures knowledge. This enriches the legitimacy and relevance of innovation agendas and helps align them with lived realities and social priorities.

The effectiveness of adaptive governance depends not on one actor alone but on their interactions. Public–academic–civic partnerships, foresight-informed missions, and shared governance platforms enable collective sense-making and co-creation. Adaptive innovation governance is therefore not a matter of top-down reform or bottom-up activism alone—it is a systemic coordination challenge, requiring alignment across levels, sectors, and temporalities.

Toward adaptive innovation governance means reimagining how institutions engage with uncertainty, complexity, and transformation. Resilience, adaptability, and reflexivity are not ancillary traits but core capacities for systems that seek to govern innovation in ways that are robust, inclusive, and futures-conscious.

Public institutions, universities, and civil society each contribute critical capabilities—from agenda-setting and evidence generation to ethical scrutiny and participatory foresight. Together, they form the foundation for a distributed, dynamic governance model—one capable of navigating multiple futures while remaining anchored in public value and democratic legitimacy.

10.5.2 Design Principles for Futures-Ready Institutions

In the face of accelerating disruption, uncertainty, and interdependence, institutions must evolve beyond traditional bureaucratic and linear models of governance. While adaptive capacity (as outlined in Section 10.5.1) refers to the behavioral traits of resilient systems—such as flexibility, responsiveness, and reflexivity—these traits must be underpinned by deliberate design principles that structure how institutions are built, how decisions are made, and how knowledge flows. Futures-ready institutions are not reactive organizations; they are proactively constructed systems that embed anticipatory governance in their architecture, culture, and operational logic.

This section explores the core design principles that enable futures literacy and systemic foresight within institutional environments. These principles include distributed intelligence, modularity, feedback loops, futures literacy, and experimental governance. Taken together, they offer a blueprint for creating institutions that can not only withstand turbulence but also shape pathways to inclusive, ethical, and sustainable futures.

10.5.2.1 Distributed intelligence

In traditional hierarchical institutions, strategic insight is often concentrated at the top, and information flows are linear and restricted. This model assumes that senior leadership, central planning units, or specialized analysts possess the authority and knowledge to define future pathways. However, in an era characterized by fast-moving change, non-linear disruption, and distributed expertise, such models become brittle.

Futures-ready institutions are built on the principle of distributed intelligence—the idea that knowledge, insight, and anticipation must be cultivated at multiple levels and across functional boundaries. Strategic foresight is not the sole responsibility of planning departments or think tanks; it must be embedded in project teams, operational units, stakeholder networks, and even frontline service delivery systems.

This requires establishing infrastructure for collective sense-making: internal foresight training, cross-functional futures teams, digital platforms for trend and signal sharing, and open foresight dialogues that span departments and stakeholder groups. These systems ensure that intelligence is co-produced, context-sensitive, and continuously updated as local and global conditions evolve.

Moreover, distributed intelligence supports organizational agility. When insight is localized and diversified, institutions can detect early signals more quickly, experiment with adaptive responses at smaller scales, and escalate successful innovations to broader implementation.

Examples of this principle in action include foresight communities of practice in national ministries, regional scenario networks among municipalities, or corporate strategy units that engage with customers, suppliers, and employees to scan for emerging dynamics.

10.5.2.2 Modularity and structural flexibility

Futures-ready institutions are structurally designed to absorb shocks without collapsing and to reconfigure themselves in response to emerging needs. This is achieved through modularity—a design principle that organizes organizations into semi-autonomous but interoperable units capable of independent function and coordinated integration.

Modular systems contrast with rigid hierarchies or tightly coupled bureaucracies that are vulnerable to cascading failure. In modular designs, a disruption in one domain (for example, climate finance) does not paralyze the entire institution but can be isolated, diagnosed, and addressed locally while the larger system continues to function.

In innovation governance, modularity enables experimentation at the edge of organizations without jeopardizing core operations. For example, a government innovation lab or civic tech unit can pilot new policy tools, regulatory models, or participatory methods, while the broader institution observes, learns, and integrates successful approaches into the mainstream.

Structural flexibility also supports inter-organizational collaboration. Modular institutions can more easily plug into broader networks, engage in multi-stakeholder coalitions, and align with mission-oriented governance platforms. This is essential for tackling complex challenges such as climate adaptation, digital equity, or health system transformation, which require joint action across sectors and scales.

10.5.2.3 Feedback loops and learning systems

One of the most critical design features of futures-ready institutions is the presence of embedded feedback loops. These loops allow organizations to monitor the effects of their decisions, compare outcomes with expectations, and adjust course in real time. Feedback is not only about performance measurement—it is about strategic learning.

Effective feedback systems integrate both quantitative and qualitative data: indicators, KPIs, system dynamics modeling, as well as narrative accounts, stakeholder perceptions, and contextual interpretation. The key is to ensure that feedback is multi-directional, timely, and actionable.

In foresight-informed governance, feedback loops connect the three I2E dimensions. Intelligence (foresight) shapes innovation strategy; execution generates real-world results; and these results are fed back into the intelligence system, updating assumptions, refining scenarios, and triggering new cycles of learning.

To institutionalize feedback, organizations can deploy foresight observatories, innovation dashboards, after-action reviews, and participatory evaluation processes. These mechanisms must be accompanied by a culture that values adaptation over perfection, encourages safe-to-fail experimentation, and treats error as a resource for improvement rather than a trigger for punishment.

10.5.2.4 Futures literacy as a core competency

Beyond structure and process, futures-ready institutions depend on people—on their capacities to think long-term, imagine alternative pathways, and engage with uncertainty productively. Futures literacy, as defined by UNESCO, is "the skill that allows people to better understand the role of the future in what they see and do." It is a cognitive and cultural competency that must be cultivated throughout institutions, not only among specialists.

Futures literacy enables individuals and teams to move beyond deterministic or extrapolative thinking. It allows them to engage in imaginative exploration, critical reflection, and normative visioning. A futures-literate workforce is capable of questioning assumptions, recognizing signals of change, co-creating scenarios, and aligning daily decisions with long-term trajectories.

Institutionalizing futures literacy involves:

- Training and education programs in futures thinking and systems foresight.
- Inclusion of foresight skills in job descriptions, promotion criteria, and performance reviews.
- Leadership development focused on anticipatory capacity, ethical reasoning, and vision-building.
- Integration of futures exercises—such as scenario planning, backcasting, or speculative prototyping—into routine strategy and planning cycles.

By investing in futures literacy, organizations build the internal capacity to engage with complexity not as a threat, but as a field of possibility. This supports both innovation and institutional resilience.

10.5.2.5 Experimental governance and institutional evolution

Finally, futures-ready institutions embrace experimental governance—a mode of operation in which policies, programs, and innovations are treated as hypotheses to be tested, rather than fixed blueprints to be implemented uncritically (Salerno et al., 2021). Experimental governance values iteration, co-creation, and adaptive refinement.

Examples include:

- Policy sandboxes, where regulations are relaxed in controlled environments to test emerging technologies.
- Living labs, where citizens, researchers, and government co-design and test urban innovations in real time.
- Digital twins, where policy interventions are modeled in virtual environments before real-world application.

- Rapid prototyping and agile development within public sector digital teams.

Experimental governance reduces the cost of failure, increases stakeholder engagement, and accelerates learning cycles. It transforms governance from a compliance exercise into a learning system, where evidence-based adaptation replaces rigid implementation.

Critically, experimentation must be conducted ethically. Futures-ready institutions ensure that pilots respect human rights, safeguard vulnerable populations, and include mechanisms for informed consent, impact assessment, and inclusive evaluation.

Designing futures-ready institutions involves more than reorganizing structures—it requires cultivating distributed intelligence, embedding feedback systems, enabling modular resilience, and investing in people's capacity to think anticipatorily. By embracing these principles—distributed intelligence, modularity, feedback loops, futures literacy, and experimental governance—institutions can evolve from reactive bureaucracies into proactive, learning organizations capable of governing transformation with responsibility and foresight.

10.5.3 Linking to the Quintuple Helix and Society 5.0

As innovation systems evolve to address increasingly complex global challenges—climate breakdown, digital disruption, inequality, and democratic decline—governance models must also evolve. Strategic foresight, as we have seen, enables institutions to anticipate, adapt, and act more systemically (Yazıcı, 2023). Yet the full potential of foresight is realized only when it is embedded within broader, collaborative innovation ecosystems that align technology, knowledge, society, and nature toward shared futures.

Two conceptual frameworks offer powerful blueprints for such systemic integration: the Quintuple Innovation Helix and the Japanese policy vision of Society 5.0. Each reflects a vision of innovation not as a siloed technical process, but as a multidimensional, ethically grounded, and ecologically aware endeavor, where foresight becomes a core enabler of co-creation and long-term governance.

This part explores how systemic futures thinking and the I2E framework connect with these models. It examines the roles of the five helices—academia, industry, government, civil society, and the environment—as foresight actors and considers how Society 5.0 reorients digital transformation toward human-centric, inclusive goals. In both cases, foresight is not an auxiliary activity but a shared governance capacity that binds actors across systems and timescales.

10.5.3.1 Foresight as the integrative logic of the Quintuple Helix

The Quintuple Helix Innovation Model builds on earlier models of university–industry–government collaboration (Triple Helix) and their evolution into Quadruple Helix (adding civil society/media) and finally the Quintuple Helix (adding the environment as a co-equal sphere). This framework reflects the understanding that sustainable, inclusive, and anticipatory innovation requires the alignment of five knowledge domains, each with distinct insights, priorities, and functions:

1. **Academia (Education System):** Generates knowledge, cultivates foresight literacy, and develops critical thinking.
2. **Industry (Economic System):** Translates foresight into product development, technological pathways, and business models.
3. **Government (Political System):** Provides regulatory frameworks, public investment, and long-term societal missions.
4. **Civil Society (Media and Culture):** Channels public values, ethical norms, and societal discourse into the innovation agenda.
5. **Natural Environment (Ecological System):** Represents the planetary boundaries, resource constraints, and ecological imperatives that shape viable futures.

Strategic foresight plays a cross-cutting role across all five helices. It enables:

- **Academia** to go beyond research forecasting, embedding anticipatory governance in science policy, and fostering transdisciplinary scenario work.
- **Industry** to engage in market foresight, sustainability transitions, and long-range technology planning aligned with emerging regulations and social expectations.
- **Government** to develop vision-led, mission-oriented innovation strategies, aligning public funding with transformative futures.
- **Civil society** to articulate alternative narratives, mobilize underrepresented voices, and challenge dominant paradigms through participatory foresight.
- **The environment**, though not a direct actor, is to be represented through ecological forecasting, planetary boundaries assessments, and Earth system modeling that guide foresight framing.

In this way, the Quintuple Helix becomes not only a model of institutional interaction, but also a platform for shared anticipation, co-creation, and governance of long-term transitions.

10.5.3.2 Society 5.0: from technology-driven to human-centric futures

Where the Quintuple Helix emphasizes multi-actor governance, the concept of Society 5.0 provides a normative vision of the kind of future society innovation should serve. Developed by Japan's Cabinet Office and Keidanren (Japan Business Federation), Society 5.0 envisions a transformation beyond the information age (Society 4.0) into a super-smart, inclusive, and human-centered society, enabled by AI, IoT, big data, robotics, and biotechnology.

Society 5.0 is not a forecast, but a strategic orientation: a deliberate steering of technological innovation toward social problem-solving and quality-of-life enhancement, rather than pure economic gain or techno-solutionism. It calls for integrating cyber and physical systems in ways that respect human dignity, support well-being, and address inequalities (Carayannis & Morawska-Jancelewicz, 2022).

Foresight is essential in this vision for several reasons:

1. **Framing future challenges and societal needs:** Foresight helps prioritize issues such as aging populations, smart mobility, food security, and disaster resilience, ensuring that innovation targets real and emerging needs.
2. **Shaping responsible technology pathways:** It allows for anticipatory assessment of risks, ethical dilemmas, and unintended consequences—guiding governance toward responsible AI, privacy protection, and human–machine cooperation.
3. **Democratizing futures:** Society 5.0 requires broad societal consensus and engagement. Foresight facilitates this by involving citizens in scenario development, participatory technology assessment, and vision co-design.
4. **Evaluating trade-offs and systemic impact:** Foresight methods help assess interdependencies across sectors, model socio-technical transitions, and ensure that interventions reinforce—not undermine—resilience, equity, and sustainability.

The Society 5.0 paradigm also implicitly reflects a Sixth Helix Logic—where technology itself acts as an enabling infrastructure across the other helices. Yet without foresight, technology becomes autonomous, potentially exacerbating existing inequalities, biases, or vulnerabilities. Foresight ensures that Society 5.0 is not merely technologically advanced, but socially intelligent and ethically governed.

The linkage between the I2E framework and Society 5.0 is clear: intelligence (foresight) defines direction and boundaries; innovation builds the solutions; and execution scales them in alignment with societal values. Society 5.0 thus becomes an operational vision for what I2E, supported by the Quintuple Helix, can achieve.

10.5.3.3 Ethical, ecological, and inclusive futures

Foresight embedded within these frameworks also brings forward the ethical, ecological, and inclusive dimensions of innovation governance—dimensions too often sidelined in techno-economic planning.

- **Ethically**, foresight supports anticipatory reflection: it asks not only what we can do, but what we should do, and who benefits or bears risks. Ethical foresight considers justice, agency, intergenerational equity, and pluralism.
- **Ecologically**, foresight situates innovation within Earth system boundaries. It integrates resilience thinking, degrowth scenarios, biodiversity futures, and regenerative economy pathways. Nature is no longer treated as an externality, but as a co-designer and constraint.
- **Inclusively**, foresight democratizes vision-making. It engages the "long tail" of society—youth, Indigenous peoples, minorities, workers, marginalized communities—whose futures are often decided by others. Inclusive foresight values multiple ways of knowing and fosters legitimacy in decision-making.

By institutionalizing foresight within the governance logics of the Quintuple Helix and Society 5.0, systems can move from fragmented, technocratic planning to coordinated, values-driven transformation. These models provide structure; foresight provides the capability to navigate, align, and evolve.

Linking foresight with the Quintuple Helix and Society 5.0 provides a comprehensive vision for how innovation governance can become collaborative, ethical, and future-oriented. Foresight is not simply a forecasting tool—it is an institutional logic, a cross-sectoral capability, and a democratic process for collectively navigating the future.

10.6 CONCLUSION

The 21st century has exposed the inadequacy of conventional models of innovation governance. Linear planning, technocratic control, and reactive policymaking no longer suffice in a world shaped by intersecting disruptions—from climate collapse and digital transformation to geopolitical realignment and societal fragmentation. This book has argued that innovation, if it is to serve public value and planetary sustainability, must be reimagined as a futures-oriented, reflexive, and systemic enterprise.

At the heart of this reimagination lies the nexus of disruption and foresight. Disruption, as we have seen, is not simply a force to be managed—it is a structural condition of the modern era. It manifests through exponential technologies, shifting demographics, ecological thresholds, and new cultural imaginaries. Its impacts extend far beyond individual firms or technologies; disruption reconfigures entire value chains, policy landscapes, and societal expectations.

In this context, foresight emerges not as a luxury or a speculative tool, but as a governance necessity. Strategic foresight enables institutions to anticipate multiple futures, build resilience against uncertainty, and align innovation trajectories with long-term goals. It reframes innovation governance from a pursuit of efficiency and optimization to a process of preparedness, purpose, and adaptability.

This new governance paradigm is articulated through the I2E framework—Intelligence, Innovation, and Execution. I2E offers a dynamic, non-linear model that links foresight-driven intelligence with ideation, experimentation, and real-world scaling. It supports the construction of strategically aligned innovation portfolios, the embedding of institutional learning and reflexivity, and the fostering of collaborative ecosystems grounded in societal missions.

Across the chapters, we have seen how the I2E logic can be applied in public policy, R&D, innovation labs, and transdisciplinary consortia. We have examined how it enables portfolio diversification, anticipatory regulation, and stakeholder co-creation. And we have connected it with broader paradigms such as the Quintuple Helix and Society 5.0, which recognize that innovation must be inclusive, ethical, and ecologically bounded.

The implications are clear: innovation in the 21st century is no longer a matter of creating the "next big thing." It is a matter of navigating deep uncertainty while holding onto shared futures—futures that are socially just, environmentally regenerative, technologically empowering, and culturally meaningful.

As we now turn to the final chapter of this book, the path forward becomes even more ambitious. We must consider how ethics, sustainability, and techno-societal transformation are not only outcomes of innovation but foundations of future-ready innovation systems.

The final chapter introduces and explores the emerging paradigm of Industry 6.0 and Society 6.0—a vision in which AI, climate intelligence, decentralized governance, and inclusive digital infrastructures converge to reconfigure how we produce, live, and govern. In this vision, innovation is not only smarter, but wiser: rooted in foresight, guided by shared values, and capable of regenerating both the economy and the biosphere.

The journey ahead invites us to ask not only what futures are possible, but what futures are worth building—and how we govern innovation to make those futures real.

REFERENCES

Bailey, D., Pitelis, C. N. & Tomlinson, P. R., 2023. Place-based industrial and regional strategy – levelling the playing field. *Regional Studies*, 57(6), 977–983. https://doi.org/10.1080/00343404.2023.2163260.

Bateman, J., 2022. *U.S.-China technological "decoupling": A strategy and policy framework*. Carnegie Endowment for International Peace. https://carnegieendowment.org/research/2022/04/us-china-technological-decoupling-a-strategy-and-policy-framework?lang=en.

Bednarski, L., Roscoe, S., Blome, C. & & Schleper, M. C., 2023. Geopolitical disruptions in global supply chains: a state-of-the-art literature review. *Production Planning & Control*, 36(4), 536–562. https://doi.org/10.1080/09537287.2023.2286283.

Bengston, D., Mauno, T. & Hujala, T., 2024. Horizon scanning: A process for identifying emerging signals of change shaping the future of natural resources management. *Society & Natural Resources*, 37(7), 1108–1115. https://doi.org/10.1080/08941920.2024.2335392.

Carayannis, E. G. & Morawska-Jancelewicz, J., 2022. The futures of Europe: Society 5.0 and industry 5.0 as driving forces of future universities. *Journal of the Knowledge Economy, Springer; Portland International Center for Management of Engineering and Technology (PICMET)*, 13(4), 3445–3471.

Carayannis, E. G. et al., 2025. Enhancing SME resilience through artificial intelligence and strategic foresight: A framework for sustainable competitiveness. *Technology in Society*, 81. https://doi.org/10.1016/j.techsoc.2025.102835.

Carvalho, P. & Woeffray, O., 2023. The future isn't what it used to be: Here's how strategic foresight can help. *World Economic Forum*. https://www.weforum.org/stories/2023/02/strategic-intelligence-why-foresight-key-future-readiness/.

Cordova-Pozo, K. & Rouwette, E. A., 2023. Types of scenario planning and their effectiveness: A review of reviews. *Futures*, 149. https://doi.org/10.1016/j.futures.2023.103153.

De Smedt, P. & Van den Broeck, F., 2024. *Embedding strategic foresight with a multi-level perspective*. UNU Institute on Comparative Regional Integration Studies. https://cris.unu.edu/embedding-strategic-foresight-multi-level-perspective.

Fasoli, G. & Poli, R., 2024. *Chapter 22: Measuring foresight's maturity: Future orienteering evaluation model*. Elgar Online, Collection: Sociology, Social Policy and Education. https://doi.org/10.4337/9781035301607.00029.

Godart, F. & Pistilli, L., 2024. The multifaceted concept of disruption: A typology. *Journal of Business Research*, 170. https://doi.org/10.1016/j.jbusres.2023.114311.

Habibi, F., Chakrabortty, R. K., Abbasi, A. & Ho, W., 2025. Investigating disruption propagation and resilience of supply chain networks: interplay of tiers and connections. *International Journal of Production Research*, 1–23. https://doi.org/10.1080/00207543.2025.2470348.

Hariyani, D., Hariyani, P. & Mishra, S., 2025. Digital technologies for the sustainable development goals. *Green Technologies and Sustainability*, 3(3). https://doi.org/10.1016/j.grets.2025.100202.

Janssen, M. & van der Voort, H., 2016. Adaptive governance: Towards a stable, accountable and responsive government. *Government Information Quarterly: An International Journal of Information Technology Management, Policies, and Practices*, 33(1), 1–5. https://doi.org/10.1016/j.giq.2016.02.003.

Kim, F. D. & Srivastava, R., 2024. Backcasting from the future: Strategies for accelerating and de-risking discontinuous innovations. *Berkeley-Haass Premier Management Journal*. https://cmr.berkeley.edu/2024/03/backcasting-from-the-future-strategies-for-accelerating-and-de-risking-discontinuous-innovations/.

Kinder, M., Briggs, X. d. S., Muro, M. & Liu, S., 2024. Generative AI, the American worker, and the future of work. *Brookings*. https://www.brookings.edu/articles/generative-ai-the-american-worker-and-the-future-of-work/.

Kivimaa, P., Laakso, S., Lonkila, A. & Kaljonen, M., 2021. Moving beyond disruptive innovation: A review of disruption in sustainability transitions. *Environmental Innovation and Societal Transitions*, 38. https://doi.org/10.1016/j.eist.2020.12.001.

Lennon, N. J., 2022. Balancing incremental and radical innovation through performance measurement and incentivization. *The Journal of High Technology Management Research*, 33(2. https://doi.org/10.1016/j.hitech.2022.100439.

Linares, C. & De la Vega, I., 2024. The impact of strategic foresight on innovation: A systematic literature review. *IEEE Engineering Management Review*, 1–26. https://doi.org/10.1109/EMR.2024.3454630.

Lyytinen, K. & Rose, G., 2003. The disruptive nature of information technology innovations: The case of internet computing in systems development organizations. *MIS Quarterly*, 27, 557–595. https://doi.org/10.2307/30036549.

Millar, C., Lockett, M. & Ladd, T., 2017. Disruption: Technology, innovation and society. *Technological Forecasting and Social Change*, 129. https://doi.org/10.1016/j.techfore.2017.10.020.

Niu, Y. et al., 2023. Global supply chain restructuring during the COVID-19 pandemic. *SSRN Electronic Journal*. https://doi.org/10.2139/ssrn.4564927.

Oladimeji, M. S. & Udosen, I., 2019. The effect of diversification strategy on organizational performance. *Journal of Competitiveness*, 11(4), 120–131. https://doi.org/10.7441/joc.2019.04.08.

Onea, I., 2022. Exploring the COVID-19 pandemic impact on innovation and entrepreneurship – Review and evidence from Global Innovation Index. *Proceedings of the International Conference on Business Excellence*, 16, 527–544. https://doi.org/10.2478/picbe-2022-0051.

Pham, L. & Hsu, K.-C., 2025. Metals of the future in a world in crisis: Geopolitical disruptions and the cleantech metal industry. *Energy Economics*, 141. https://doi.org/10.1016/j.eneco.2024.108004.

Rohn, S., 2025. The impact of disruptive technology: Historical & modern examples. *whatfix*. https://whatfix.com/blog/disruptive-technology/.

Salerno, J. et al., 2021. Adaptation and evolution of institutions and governance in community-based conservation. *Conservation Science and Practice*, 3. https://doi.org/10.1111/csp2.355.

Schrijvers, E., Prins, C. & Passchier, R., 2021. Societal disruption. In: *Preparing for digital disruption: Research for policy*. Springer. https://doi.org/10.1007/978-3-030-77838-5_2.

Shreya, S., 2025. Geopolitical tensions and global supply chain disruptions. https://www.researchgate.net/publication/391566088_Geopolitical_Tensions_and_Global_Supply_Chain_Disruptions.

Stanton, M. C. B. & Roelich, K., 2021. Decision making under deep uncertainties: A review of the applicability of methods in practice. *Technological Forecasting and Social Change*, 171. https://doi.org/10.1016/j.techfore.2021.120939.

Vella, S.-L. & Pai, N., 2019. A theoretical review of psychological resilience: Defining resilience and resilience research over the decades. *Archives of Medicine and Health Sciences*, 7, 233. https://doi.org/10.4103/amhs.amhs_119_19.

Vyas, A., 2025. *US-China economic standoff in 2025: Decoupling, disruption, and global macroeconomic spillovers*. https://ssrn.com/abstract=5221379 or http://dx.doi.org/10.2139/ssrn.5221379.

Yazıcı, A., 2023. The Quintuple Helix, Industrial 5.0, and society 5.0. In: B. Akkaya, S. A. Apostu, E. Hysa & M. Parait (eds.) *Digitalization, sustainable development, and industry 5.0* (pp. 317–336). Emerald Publishing Limited, Leeds, pp. 317–336. https://doi.org/10.1108/978-1-83753-190-520231016.

Zhao, D., Tang, Z. & He, D., 2024. A systematic literature review of weak signal identification and evolution for corporate foresight. *Kybernetes*, 53(10), 3160–3188. https://doi.org/10.1108/K-03-2023-0343.

Zumbrunn, L., 2023. Resilience through foresight: Implications for the public sector. *Swiss Yearbook of Administrative Sciences*, 14, 45–57. https://doi.org/10.5334/ssas.183.

11. Technological futures in the age of Industry 6.0 and Society 6.0

Elias G. Carayannis and Nikos R. Zotas

11.1 INTRODUCTION

The accelerating interplay between technology, society, and planetary systems has pushed innovation governance into uncharted territory. No longer confined to optimizing production systems or enhancing competitiveness, innovation today must grapple with existential dilemmas—climate breakdown, democratic erosion, systemic inequality, and the unintended consequences of emergent technologies. As we look toward the horizon, it becomes increasingly clear that the prevailing paradigms of innovation—rooted in linearity, short-termism, and technological determinism—are no longer adequate. A fundamental shift is underway, one that calls for a new synthesis between technological potential, ethical reasoning, and anticipatory governance.

This final chapter explores the contours of that shift. Building upon the previous chapters' articulation of strategic foresight, the I2E framework, and institutional readiness, we now turn to the governance of emerging technologies within the broader transitions toward Industry 6.0 and Society 6.0. These emerging paradigms represent more than just the next phase of industrial or digital transformation. They signal a reorientation of innovation toward human-centric, ecologically attuned, and ethically informed systems—where value is measured not merely by efficiency or profit, but by resilience, well-being, inclusivity, and long-term societal flourishing.

At the heart of this transformation lies a paradox. On one hand, technologies such as artificial intelligence, quantum computing, synthetic biology, and autonomous systems offer unprecedented capabilities to solve complex global problems. On the other, they introduce profound governance challenges—opacity, bias, power asymmetries, systemic risk, and the erosion of public trust. Navigating this paradox demands more than technocratic regulation; it calls for a foresight-driven, pluralistic approach to governing technology itself as a systemic actor.

In what follows, we chart this terrain in five stages. First, we revisit the trajectory from Industry 5.0 to Industry 6.0, highlighting how innovation is increasingly expected to integrate social, ecological, and democratic values. Second, we examine the governance dilemmas posed by emerging technologies (EmTech), and the institutional tools needed to guide their development responsibly. Third, we explore how strategic foresight and ethical innovation frameworks can be embedded into policymaking, research and development (R&D), and public discourse. Fourth, we delve into the practical dimensions of Society 6.0—a future-oriented vision where technology is mobilized to empower individuals and communities. Fifth, we confront the darker trajectories of techno-authoritarianism and surveillance capitalism, and consider the safeguards needed to uphold democratic, rights-based governance in digital societies.

Finally, we introduce the Sextuple Innovation Helix—a conceptual extension of the Quintuple Helix model that places technology as a sixth, cross-cutting helix—not as a passive enabler, but as an autonomous force shaping innovation ecosystems. While not a central theme, this framework serves as a forward-looking analytical tool for navigating the increasing entanglement of technology, society, and governance in the decades to come.

As the Draghi Report rightly emphasizes, the future of European—and global—competitiveness depends not only on financial investment and industrial autonomy, but on the capacity to govern disruption with foresight, legitimacy, and collective purpose. The innovation systems of tomorrow must be structurally equipped to harness technological progress without compromising democratic values, planetary boundaries, or human dignity.

This chapter invites the reader to confront the fundamental question of the 21st century: Can we govern technological innovation not only effectively, but wisely?

11.2 NAVIGATING THE TRANSITION: FROM INDUSTRY 5.0 TO INDUSTRY 6.0

The evolution of industrial paradigms has historically mirrored shifts in technological capabilities, economic logics, and societal values. From the mechanization of Industry 1.0 to the digitalization of Industry 4.0, each stage has not only redefined how value is created but also reshaped the institutional architectures and governance mechanisms through which societies organize production, labor, and knowledge. In recent years, Industry 5.0 has emerged as a response to the limitations of its predecessor—Industry 4.0—by emphasizing human-centricity, sustainability, and resilience. Yet, even as these ideals gain traction, a deeper transformation is underway. The contours of Industry 6.0 are beginning to take shape: a paradigm where human-AI symbiosis, decentralized innovation ecosystems, and regenerative technological infrastructures become central to how we conceive and govern innovation.

This section explores the emergent transition from Industry 5.0 to Industry 6.0. It assesses the current paradigm's conceptual contributions and limitations, outlines the critical features of the next phase of industrial transformation, and situates this evolution within the broader techno-social visions of Society 6.0. Importantly, it considers how the governance challenges of this transition require a rethinking of institutional foresight, participatory policy frameworks, and innovation metrics beyond economic efficiency. Drawing on insights from EU strategic policy documents, this section also connects the transition to ongoing debates about technological sovereignty, inclusive growth, and sustainable digitalization.

11.2.1 Industry 5.0: Contributions and Constraints

Industry 5.0 was introduced as a corrective to the hyper-automation and efficiency-centric mindset of Industry 4.0. While the fourth industrial revolution prioritized digital integration, real-time data, and cyber-physical systems, it often overlooked social equity, ethical design, and ecological limits. In contrast, Industry 5.0 places the human being at the center of production systems. It advocates for the integration of collaborative robotics, explainable artificial intelligence (AI), sustainable manufacturing, and inclusive work environments (Adel, 2022).

The European Commission, through its "Industry 5.0" communication, emphasized the need for a transition to innovation that respects planetary boundaries and democratic values. It identified three core pillars:

- Human-centricity: technologies should enhance human agency rather than replace it.
- Sustainability: innovation must support ecological regeneration, not just decarbonization.
- Resilience: production systems must be adaptive, distributed, and shock-resistant.

Despite these forward-looking aspirations, Industry 5.0 has faced limitations:

- Its implementation remains patchy, with many firms and sectors still entrenched in Industry 4.0 logics.
- Human-centricity often translates into vague corporate responsibility statements, not structural shifts in power or design.

- The environmental dimension is underdeveloped, with greenwashing still prevalent and few incentives for deep ecological innovation.
- The role of governance is under-theorized, leaving policymakers without robust frameworks for anticipating technological disruptions or ensuring inclusive participation.

Moreover, the diffusion of Industry 5.0 practices remains uneven across regions, sectors, and organizational scales. Large firms in advanced economies may experiment with collaborative robotics and sustainable AI practices, while Small and Medium Enterprises (SMEs) in less connected or resource-constrained contexts may struggle to access the same capacities. As a result, Industry 5.0 risks reinforcing existing inequalities within and between nations if not accompanied by targeted capacity-building, education, and funding mechanisms. The lack of systemic alignment across policy domains—industrial policy, education, labor, environmental regulation—further complicates implementation. In this light, Industry 5.0 must be viewed not as a destination but as a stepping-stone toward a more transformative and integrated industrial vision (Oyekunle et al., 2024).

11.2.2 Toward Industry 6.0: A Paradigm of Techno-Social Synthesis

Industry 6.0 represents a deeper, more transformative rethinking of the industrial paradigm. It recognizes that innovation is no longer confined to factories or digital platforms but is distributed across societies, embedded in ecosystems, and increasingly entangled with existential planetary risks. Unlike Industry 5.0, which retrofits human-centric and ecological goals onto existing systems, Industry 6.0 begins with these imperatives as foundational design principles (Duggal et al., 2021).

Key features of Industry 6.0 include:

- Human–AI Symbiosis: Moving beyond automation, this entails collaborative intelligence, where AI systems are designed to augment human reasoning, empathy, and decision-making. AI is seen not as a substitute for labor, but as a cognitive partner in creativity, problem-solving, and public service delivery. For instance, in healthcare, human-AI collaboration might involve diagnostic support tools that combine medical knowledge with individual patient histories to recommend personalized treatments. In education, intelligent tutoring systems could work alongside teachers to create adaptive learning pathways.
- Regenerative Innovation: Innovation ecosystems under Industry 6.0 are designed to be not only sustainable but restorative. Technologies aim to regenerate natural systems (for example, carbon capture biotechnologies,

ocean clean-up robotics) and social systems (for example, community-centered platform cooperatives). This paradigm is not limited to minimizing harm but is proactively oriented toward creating positive, circular, and resilient outcomes. Regenerative design thus informs everything from urban planning to agriculture and materials science.

- Decentralized Infrastructures: Distributed ledgers, federated learning systems, and edge computing redefine how innovation is governed and scaled. These systems reduce dependence on centralized platforms, enabling more equitable control over data, algorithms, and value flows. Such infrastructures allow localized decision-making, privacy-preserving collaboration, and greater resilience against systemic shocks. They also democratize innovation by opening access to communities and regions historically excluded from centralized industrial systems.
- Value beyond Growth: Metrics of innovation expand to include well-being, ecological impact, community empowerment, and cultural diversity. Gross Domestic Product (GDP) and productivity are complemented by indicators of digital dignity, environmental resilience, and participatory governance. Emerging frameworks such as the Wellbeing Economy Alliance, the Genuine Progress Indicator, and EU social cohesion indices reflect this shift in valuation logic.
- Techno-democratic Governance: Innovation is not governed solely by markets or technocrats but co-shaped through pluralistic foresight, digital deliberation, and public technology assessment. This model views citizens as co-creators of innovation futures, and governance as an open, contested, and iterative process rather than a top-down mechanism.

This transition aligns with broader global debates about the future of capitalism, democracy, and sustainability. It resonates with frameworks such as the UN Sustainable Development Goals (SDGs), Doughnut Economics, and Degrowth, which challenge the primacy of extractive models of value creation. Industry 6.0 provides a unifying platform for advancing these alternatives within an integrated industrial and technological transformation strategy (Carayannis et al., 2024).

11.2.3 Aligning with Society 6.0: Technology for Human and Planetary Flourishing

While Industry 6.0 focuses on the transformation of production systems, Society 6.0 envisions a parallel transformation of social systems. Originating from Japan's national visioning efforts, Society 5.0 proposed the integration of cyber and physical systems to create a super-smart society (Zizek et al., 2021).

Society 6.0 takes this further by embedding values of equity, inclusion, ethics, and ecological responsibility at the core of socio-technical design.

Society 6.0 emphasizes:

- Participatory AI: Technologies that are designed with, not just for, communities. Publics are involved in the design, evaluation, and regulation of systems that impact their lives. Participatory AI includes civic engagement platforms, public consultations on algorithmic fairness, and citizen oversight of AI systems in public administration.
- Digital Commons and Cooperative Platforms: Moving beyond surveillance capitalism to data stewardship, collective ownership, and algorithmic transparency. Examples include open-source AI repositories, municipal digital infrastructures, and cooperative data trusts.
- Well-being Economies: Social policy, public services, and innovation systems converge to enhance quality of life, mental health, and social cohesion. Universal basic services, mental health tech, and inclusive digital education are central pillars.
- Pluralistic Techno-Cultures: Recognizing the cultural specificity of technology adoption, Society 6.0 values diversity in design norms, usage patterns, and ethical standards. This supports technology that is adaptable, respectful of cultural differences, and open to co-design by diverse user communities.

The vision of Society 6.0 is not utopian. It acknowledges the risks of authoritarian techno-politics, AI bias, and techno-solutionism. However, it insists that a different trajectory is possible—one where digital infrastructures enhance democratic life, rather than erode it.

11.2.4 The Draghi Report and the European Strategic Context

In this evolving landscape, the European Union has begun to articulate a vision for competitiveness that aligns with Industry 6.0 principles. The 2024 Draghi Report, commissioned by the European Commission, outlines a new model of EU competitiveness centered on strategic autonomy, inclusive prosperity, and innovation sovereignty (Steinberg & Bergmann, 2024). It calls for a rebalancing of the EU innovation model: from one focused on market efficiency and competition to one grounded in resilience, inclusion, and shared strategic direction. This aligns with the thrust of Industry 6.0 and Society 6.0, suggesting that the institutional conditions for such a transition are beginning to materialize.

11.2.5 Rethinking Governance for Systemic Transformation

The transition to Industry 6.0 cannot be achieved through technology alone. It requires a reconfiguration of governance architectures: how we set innovation agendas, how we regulate complex systems, and how we empower diverse actors to shape the future.

This includes:

- Developing foresight capabilities across public, private, and civil sectors.
- Institutionalizing participatory innovation processes and inclusive design.
- Reforming metrics and incentives to reward long-term, systemic innovation.
- Building new alliances between cities, regions, research institutions, and grassroots networks to co-create transformative solutions.

Critically, it requires rethinking the social contract of innovation. Who decides what problems matter? Who benefits from technological change? Who bears the risk? These questions must be answered not by elites or engineers alone but through deliberative, transparent, and pluralistic processes.

The shift from Industry 5.0 to Industry 6.0 is not a linear upgrade but a paradigmatic reorientation. It challenges the core assumptions of the industrial age—about growth, progress, and control—and replaces them with a more fluid, relational, and anticipatory vision. Industry 6.0, when aligned with Society 6.0, offers a compelling direction for navigating the uncertainty of the coming decades: one that centers human dignity, ecological integrity, and democratic agency in the heart of technological futures.

In the next section, we turn to the governance of emerging technologies themselves—exploring the conditions under which AI, quantum systems, and biotechnologies can serve the public good, and how foresight-driven institutions can ensure that innovation remains accountable, inclusive, and wise.

11.3 EMERGING TECHNOLOGIES AND THE GOVERNANCE CHALLENGE

The accelerating convergence of emerging technologies (EmTech) is reshaping not only markets and industries but also the foundational norms of society. AI, quantum computing, synthetic biology, nanotechnology, and autonomous systems are not merely tools—they are generative infrastructures with the capacity to redefine human agency, institutional legitimacy, and planetary boundaries. Their impact is diffuse, systemic, and often opaque, making them difficult to regulate through traditional mechanisms (Tang & Cao, 2022). As EmTech becomes increasingly central to both economic competitiveness and societal transformation, the governance challenge becomes existential: How do we ensure that emerging technologies serve the public good, rather than undermine democratic values or ecological sustainability?

This section explores the governance dilemmas posed by EmTech, the institutional adaptations required to navigate their complexity, and the principles that should guide anticipatory governance in the era of Industry 6.0 and Society 6.0. It outlines three main dimensions: (1) the intrinsic properties of EmTech that complicate their governability, (2) the emerging institutional innovations for anticipatory regulation, and (3) the design of governance systems that are reflexive, inclusive, and future-oriented. Furthermore, this discussion will expand on the role of supranational organizations, the private sector, and civic movements in shaping governance trajectories.

11.3.1 The Nature of EmTech: Complexity, Opacity, and Irreversibility

Emerging technologies differ from previous waves of innovation in several critical ways. First, they are dual-use and often converge across disciplinary boundaries, generating cascading effects that are hard to anticipate. AI and synthetic biology, for example, can be applied in medicine, agriculture, defense, and surveillance—creating ethical and regulatory ambiguities. Second, EmTech often operate as black-box systems, particularly in machine learning and neural networks, which resist traditional models of transparency and accountability (Le Blanc et al., 2024). Third, their development and deployment frequently exhibit irreversible path dependencies, where early design decisions lock societies into futures that are difficult to reverse or contest.

This complexity renders EmTech partially "ungovernable" by existing legal, ethical, and institutional frameworks. Traditional regulation, which relies on post hoc assessment and risk minimization, is ill-suited for technologies that evolve faster than legislative cycles and outpace public comprehension. The governance of EmTech, therefore, must embrace a new epistemology—one that recognizes uncertainty, emergence, and contested values as fundamental to the innovation process.

Moreover, the geopolitical dimensions of EmTech amplify the governance challenge. The global race for AI supremacy, quantum advantage, and bioengineering capabilities is unfolding in a context of strategic decoupling and techno-nationalism. Governments face pressure to accelerate domestic innovation while balancing the risks of ethical breaches, regulatory arbitrage, and loss of public trust. This creates a tension between technological sovereignty and transnational coordination, making collective action more urgent yet harder to achieve. The increasing weaponization of technology and its role in digital authoritarianism further underscores the fragility of global norms and the need for ethical consensus

Technologies such as generative AI and CRISPR-based gene editing systems highlight how breakthroughs can outpace institutional capacity. The speed at which ChatGPT-like systems entered consumer and enterprise use has raised concerns about misinformation, deepfakes, and labor displacement, while the broad potential of gene editing creates ethical dilemmas around eugenics, biodiversity, and biosecurity. In both domains, the stakes are not only technical but existential—touching on human dignity, autonomy, and ecological balance.

11.3.2 Institutional Innovations in Technology Governance

Addressing the governance deficit in EmTech requires more than reactive regulation; it demands institutional innovation. Around the world, new models are emerging to bridge the gap between technological dynamism and democratic legitimacy (Bokhari & Seunghwan, 2024).

One promising approach is the development of anticipatory governance mechanisms. These include regulatory sandboxes, foresight observatories, ethics-by-design protocols, and algorithmic auditing bodies. Such tools allow for controlled experimentation, participatory scenario-building, and value-sensitive design in real-time. For instance, the UK's Centre for Data Ethics and Innovation and the Netherlands' Rathenau Institute provide platforms for deliberating the societal impacts of AI, while the European Commission's Horizon Scanning and Futures Lab supports policy co-creation based on plausible futures (Rathenau Instituut, 2019).

Another innovation is the rise of digital constitutions—normative frameworks that encode rights, responsibilities, and procedural safeguards into the design of digital systems. These include AI principles articulated by the OECD, UNESCO, and the European Union, which emphasize fairness, explainability, robustness, and human oversight. While largely non-binding, these principles are increasingly being embedded in procurement criteria, funding conditions, and certification schemes. Their diffusion into sectoral standards and corporate governance guidelines is shaping a de facto architecture of tech governance.

Furthermore, some jurisdictions are exploring technocratic-democratic hybrids—institutional designs that combine expert review with public deliberation. Citizens' assemblies on digital ethics, participatory regulatory impact assessments, and community data stewardship models illustrate how governance can become more reflexive and responsive. These models are not merely symbolic; they reconfigure the locus of authority and accountability in technological systems. The inclusion of civic voices in national AI strategies, such as Canada's Algorithmic Impact Assessment tool, represents a shift toward shared stewardship of innovation futures.

At the operational level, organizations are adopting governance-by-design strategies. This includes embedding ethical reflection into R&D workflows, establishing internal ethics boards, and adopting impact assessment tools that go beyond compliance. The Responsible Research and Innovation (RRI) framework in Europe is a notable example, emphasizing anticipation, inclusion, reflexivity, and responsiveness as pillars of governance. The integration of governance into design processes—also known as "ethical prototyping"—is becoming increasingly central in sectors such as autonomous mobility and digital health.

Despite these advances, institutional innovations face challenges of scale, legitimacy, and coordination. Many remain fragmented, underfunded, or marginalized within powerful innovation ecosystems. To become effective, they must be integrated into a broader governance architecture that aligns incentives, builds capacity, and ensures accountability across sectors and borders. This includes the formation of transnational bodies with enforcement mandates and the mobilization of public investments in governance infrastructure, such as open-access regulatory sandboxes and foresight accelerators.

11.3.3 Principles for Foresight-Driven EmTech Governance

To navigate the complexity of EmTech responsibly, governance frameworks must adopt a foresight-driven logic—one that is proactive, pluralistic, and adaptive (OECD, 2025). This involves three interrelated principles:

1. Anticipation over Reaction: Instead of waiting for harms to materialize, governance should cultivate anticipatory capacities that allow stakeholders to explore plausible futures, identify early signals, and act preemptively. This includes institutionalizing horizon scanning, stress-testing policies against different scenarios, and creating adaptive regulatory pathways. Anticipatory governance acknowledges that not all risks can be eliminated but seeks to build resilience and optionality. The goal is not perfect prediction but flexible preparedness.
2. Inclusion over Elitism: EmTech governance must move beyond expert-driven, technocratic models toward more inclusive deliberation. This requires engaging diverse publics—especially marginalized communities—in shaping innovation trajectories. Participatory foresight, deliberative polling, and citizen juries can democratize knowledge and legitimize decision-making. Inclusion also extends to epistemic diversity, recognizing indigenous knowledge, feminist theory, and postcolonial critiques as vital to ethical technology design. A truly inclusive governance model must ensure representation across gender, geography, and generations.

3. Reflexivity over Closure: Governance must remain open to critique, learning, and revision. This entails embedding feedback loops, monitoring systems, and evaluative metrics into innovation ecosystems. It also requires a cultural shift in institutions—from defending decisions to iterative learning and ethical humility. Reflexive governance acknowledges the provisional nature of knowledge and the co-evolution of values and technologies. The creation of institutional memory and foresight repositories can enhance reflexive capacity over time.

These principles align with the broader aims of Industry 6.0 and Society 6.0. They call for a systemic rethinking of how power, knowledge, and responsibility are distributed in the innovation process. They also imply a move from "governing technology" to "governing with technology"—where digital tools themselves become enablers of transparent, inclusive, and adaptive governance.

The governance of emerging technologies stands at a crossroads. The stakes are high: the futures we build will be shaped not only by what technologies we invent but by how we choose to govern them. EmTech governance, therefore, is not just a technical challenge; it is a normative, political, and epistemological project. It demands institutional imagination, democratic renewal, and a commitment to foresight as a public good.

As we transition to Industry 6.0 and Society 6.0, governance must evolve from a peripheral concern to a core pillar of innovation ecosystems. Only then can we ensure that emerging technologies are not only powerful but also legitimate, inclusive, and aligned with the collective futures we aspire to create.

11.4 INSTITUTIONAL FORESIGHT AND ETHICAL GOVERNANCE OF EMTECH

In an era defined by accelerating technological change, increasing systemic risk, and deep societal polarization, the governance of emerging technologies demands more than retrospective regulatory tools or fragmented ethical declarations. What is required is an anticipatory, integrated, and institutionalized framework for managing technological futures—one rooted in strategic foresight and ethical governance. This section explores how foresight can be repositioned not merely as a policy support tool, but as a public good essential for democratic governance and societal resilience in the age of AI, synthetic biology, and other disruptive innovations.

The goal is not just to forecast or mitigate risks, but to create institutional environments where technologies evolve in concert with societal values, planetary boundaries, and long-term human flourishing. The discussion unfolds in four key parts: a reaffirmation of foresight as an indispensable public capability, an examination of novel governance tools including ethical sandboxes and digital constitutions, a mapping of policy bottlenecks at national and European levels, and a proposal to operationalize the Intelligence–Innovation–Execution (I2E) framework for embedding ethics and foresight in innovation ecosystems. This analysis expands on emerging academic frameworks, policy experiments, and institutional best practices across multiple geographies.

11.4.1 Foresight as a Public Good in the Governance of EmTech

Foresight, historically associated with scenario planning and strategic intelligence, is increasingly recognized as a governance capability in its own right. In the context of EmTech, foresight is not a luxury—it is a necessity. Technologies like AI and quantum computing advance so rapidly and pervasively that traditional policy cycles are often outdated before they are implemented. Foresight enables policymakers, institutions, and societies to anticipate emergent properties, test policy assumptions, and explore futures that diverge from dominant trajectories (Sjöblom, 2024).

Unlike forecasting, which aims to predict outcomes based on current trends, foresight is about building preparedness, flexibility, and collective imagination. It encourages a long-term view anchored in normative deliberation and systemic interconnectivity. Foresight helps identify not just probable and plausible futures, but preferred futures—and the pathways to get there. It also acknowledges complexity and ambiguity as central features of socio-technical systems, positioning uncertainty as a governance opportunity rather than a liability.

As a public good, foresight should be institutionalized across multiple layers of governance. At the national level, foresight councils can support anticipatory policymaking in sectors such as health, defense, environment, and education. For instance, South Korea has integrated foresight into its Presidential Commission on the Fourth Industrial Revolution, using scenario exercises to guide economic and innovation policy. In Finland, the Committee for the Future works alongside parliament to engage with long-term strategic issues beyond electoral cycles.

At the municipal and regional level, foresight labs can engage citizens in envisioning locally relevant futures, especially in the context of smart cities and regional innovation hubs. The city of Barcelona has integrated futures thinking into its urban planning processes, using participatory foresight to co-design digital infrastructures that align with citizen values. In the Global South, initiatives such as Africa Foresight Lab help local communities imagine alternative development paths that do not replicate extractive colonial models.

Internationally, networks such as those supported by the OECD, UNDP, and EU Joint Research Centre can facilitate the exchange of anticipatory methodologies and shared policy experimentation. These international foresight ecosystems help harmonize technological norms, bridge regulatory gaps, and promote epistemic pluralism in global innovation governance.

The societal value of foresight also lies in its potential to democratize the future. When embedded in participatory platforms, foresight can amplify marginalized voices, surface ethical dilemmas early, and challenge dominant narratives of technological progress. It becomes a site of contestation and co-creation, rather than elite technocratic planning. For instance, anticipatory citizen assemblies on AI regulation can complement expert panels and legislative reviews, creating a fuller picture of ethical stakes and societal preferences. Indigenous futurism, feminist foresight, and postcolonial imaginaries also offer important correctives to techno-solutionist visions often driven by Silicon Valley or defense-driven paradigms.

11.4.2 Tools and Models for Ethical Governance of EmTech

The application of foresight in EmTech governance must be supported by adaptive, experimental, and inclusive tools. These tools not only manage uncertainty but help shape technology development trajectories through iterative feedback, public engagement, and ethical anchoring.

Ethical sandboxes, for example, are controlled, real-world test environments where emerging technologies can be trialed under close supervision. Unlike traditional regulatory sandboxes that focus on legal compliance, ethical sandboxes foreground societal values, stakeholder participation, and real-time governance adjustments. They are particularly suited to high-risk, high-uncertainty technologies like facial recognition, predictive policing, or genome editing. In the UK, the Financial Conduct Authority has used sandbox models to explore fintech governance, while Estonia and Singapore have tested their applicability to AI-enabled services in e-government platforms. The presence of independent oversight boards and cross-disciplinary advisory panels is central to ensuring that ethical sandboxes do not devolve into deregulatory loopholes.

Anticipatory regulation offers another promising model. It emphasizes proactive, flexible, and participatory rule-making in fast-moving technological domains. This governance style seeks to close the gap between innovation cycles and regulatory responses by enabling co-design of rules, modular compliance pathways, and dynamic updating mechanisms. The Danish Board of Technology has developed anticipatory regulation workshops that bring together innovators, ethicists, and civil servants to simulate and assess the downstream impacts of new technologies.

Digital constitutions represent yet another governance innovation. These are evolving sets of principles, rights, and institutional arrangements that aim to embed democratic values in digital systems. They function as meta-frameworks guiding technical and organizational behavior. The EU's Declaration on Digital Rights and Principles (2022), UNESCO's Recommendation on the Ethics of AI, and the German Bundestag's municipal algorithmic impact charters illustrate this emerging constitutional moment. These charters can be codified into procurement contracts, built into funding criteria for startups, and audited as part of impact assessments. They also provide legitimacy to civil society actors pressing for more radical reform in algorithmic design.

As digital systems become infrastructure-like in their pervasiveness, digital constitutions offer a unique opportunity to renegotiate the terms of social contracts in the digital age. Their transformative potential lies in their ability to translate abstract principles into actionable governance norms that shape both public and private sector practices.

11.4.3 Mapping Institutional Gaps and Bottlenecks in Policy Frameworks

Despite growing awareness, major gaps remain in institutional capacities for governing EmTech. These gaps span both vertical dimensions—across governance levels—and horizontal dimensions—across sectors and domains. They manifest as regulatory lag, enforcement fragmentation, capability deficits, and accountability voids.

At the national level, many ministries lack foresight capacity or dedicated EmTech governance units. Public sector R&D often operates without comprehensive ethical review mechanisms beyond data privacy. Coordination across innovation, digital, justice, and environment departments remains weak. In the US, the federal government's fragmented approach to AI governance illustrates how decentralized structures can impede timely and coordinated responses to emergent risks.

At the EU level, initiatives such as the AI Act, while ambitious, rely heavily on national implementation and lack enforcement clarity. Moreover, foresight remains underutilized in legislative planning, and fragmentation persists between directorates-general such as DG CONNECT, DG RTD, and DG GROW. Even within Horizon Europe, programmatic fragmentation hinders the integration of ethics and foresight across funding calls.

Cross-cutting bottlenecks exacerbate these challenges. There are limited financial resources for ethics and foresight initiatives, weak integration of civil society and SMEs in governance dialogues, and a lack of metrics and key performance indicators for assessing ethical or anticipatory innovation. Moreover, a culture of reactive compliance dominates many sectors, where governance is viewed as a constraint rather than an enabler. This mindset impedes the development of learning systems, where institutions adapt based on real-time feedback and horizon scanning.

To address these gaps, institutional reengineering is essential. Governments should establish inter-ministerial foresight task forces, earmark budgets for ethics capacity-building, mandate public deliberation processes in high-impact domains, and create shared data spaces for algorithmic transparency and auditability. These reforms would signal a shift toward a proactive, inclusive, and futures-oriented governance culture. Lessons can also be drawn from international best practices such as South Africa's ethical AI observatory or Canada's Open Government Partnership initiatives, which link governance to citizen engagement and transparency by design.

11.4.4 Embedding the I2E Framework in Institutional Governance

The I2E framework, introduced in earlier chapters, offers a strategic architecture for embedding foresight and ethics into institutional governance. It integrates strategic foresight, creative experimentation, and scalable action, aligning institutional functions across different time horizons.

Within the I2E framework, the Intelligence phase calls for the creation of foresight cells within agencies, partnerships with futures institutes, and the development of early-warning systems. The Innovation phase involves designing sandbox protocols, investing in experimental funds, and promoting cross-sectoral co-creation. Finally, the Execution phase focuses on defining governance standards, deploying adaptive Key Performance Indicators (KPIs), and mainstreaming continuous learning cycles. The strength of I2E lies in its ability to foster coherence across often siloed decision-making bodies and to enable distributed accountability in innovation governance.

I2E supports portfolio-based governance, wherein institutions manage multiple innovation trajectories with varied risk, return, and time profiles. Ethical and anticipatory criteria are embedded into portfolio selection, funding, and evaluation processes. This mitigates both ethical and reputational risk while enhancing institutional agility. The I2E model aligns with broader European strategic goals, as articulated in the Draghi Report, which advocates for mission-oriented, inclusive, and strategically autonomous innovation frameworks. By embedding foresight and ethics into the DNA of governance, I2E enables a transformation of innovation systems into platforms for systemic societal change.

Furthermore, the I2E approach facilitates alignment with the United Nations SDGs, offering a practical blueprint for integrating global priorities such as climate resilience, equity, and digital inclusion into local governance structures. The dynamic between long-term intelligence, short-term innovation sprints, and sustained execution loops provides a living infrastructure for ethical governance in volatile environments.

Institutional foresight and ethical governance are no longer optional; they are critical competencies for navigating the turbulent and uncertain futures shaped by emerging technologies. As we move deeper into the age of Industry 6.0 and Society 6.0, governance must itself be reimagined as an adaptive, participatory, and anticipatory system.

This transformation demands not just new tools and frameworks, but fundamentally new institutional cultures—ones that embrace learning, humility, inclusion, and long-term thinking. Foresight must become a structural capability embedded in public institutions, private firms, and civic organizations alike. Only then can we ensure that the trajectory of technological change remains accountable to the collective values.

11.5 HUMAN-CENTRIC TRANSFORMATION: SOCIETY 6.0 IN PRACTICE

As technological advancement deepens its reach across all domains of human life, the imperative for a more human-centric innovation paradigm has become undeniable. Society 6.0 is an emerging framework that aims to move beyond the industrial, digital, and knowledge-based economies by integrating human well-being, inclusivity, and sustainability into the heart of technological development. Unlike its predecessors, Society 6.0 is not just about leveraging technology for efficiency or productivity. Instead, it envisions a socio-technical future where technology is aligned with social values, equitable access, ecological sustainability, and individual dignity.

This section translates the aspirational ethos of Society 6.0 into concrete governance and innovation practices. It outlines key intervention areas, showcases illustrative cases of human-centric innovation, and critically examines the emerging metrics for assessing transformative impact. Rather than focusing solely on growth or competitiveness, this chapter explores how indicators like agency, digital equity, ecological balance, and collaborative governance can define success in future societies.

11.5.1 Translating Society 6.0 Principles into Actionable Domains

11.5.1.1 Human–AI collaboration

A central tenet of Society 6.0 is the redesign of the relationship between humans and AI. Instead of substituting human labor, AI must be designed to augment human skills and enhance decision-making while safeguarding accountability and transparency. In the workplace, collaborative AI systems are enabling more nuanced decision support, pattern recognition, and productivity enhancements that preserve human judgment (Kolbjørnsrud, 2023). In education, personalized AI tutors assist teachers by adapting learning modules to the individual pace of students while respecting pedagogical goals.

In governance, predictive analytics and AI-enhanced decision tools can streamline policy development, optimize public services, and identify societal trends. However, these must be deployed within normative frameworks that prioritize democratic accountability, prevent bias, and ensure algorithmic transparency. Only through deliberate design and participatory oversight can AI become a constructive partner in institutional transformation.

11.5.1.2 Digital dignity and inclusive design

Digital dignity, another cornerstone of Society 6.0, refers to the affirmation of individual rights, autonomy, and equity in the digital realm. To achieve this, technological systems must be inclusive by design. Universal design standards should be enforced to ensure accessibility for people with disabilities, the elderly, and other marginalized groups. Platforms must be available in multiple languages, sensitive to cultural diversity, and developed in ways that avoid algorithmic discrimination.

Ensuring digital dignity also entails rethinking consent and data ownership. Ethical data governance policies should be embedded into technology development, offering individuals greater control over their digital identities. Participatory mechanisms such as data trusts and community data governance models are being piloted as ways to give citizens a say in how their data is used and to prevent exploitative data extraction.

11.5.1.3 Decentralized and open infrastructures

Society 6.0 also calls for a reimagination of the technological stack. Rather than centralizing power in platform monopolies, innovation ecosystems should promote decentralized, interoperable, and open digital infrastructures. These infrastructures form the civic backbone of Society 6.0—facilitating equitable access, participatory governance, and community-based innovation.

Open-source software, federated cloud systems, distributed ledgers, and privacy-enhancing technologies are crucial enablers of this vision. They allow for shared ownership and collective innovation without sacrificing sovereignty or resilience. For example, privacy-preserving technologies like zero-knowledge proofs and differential privacy offer alternatives to mass surveillance models, ensuring data utility while protecting individual rights.

Public procurement and standardization bodies also play a decisive role. Governments and international organizations can set the tone by embedding ethical and inclusive criteria in procurement policies and supporting open standards. This reorients market incentives toward innovation practices that reflect the values of Society 6.0.

11.5.2 Case Examples of Human-Centric Innovation

Across the globe, various initiatives are already embodying the values of Society 6.0 in concrete practices. In the Nordic region, countries like Finland and Denmark have pioneered citizen-centered AI models within their digital governance strategies. These models prioritize data minimization, algorithmic transparency, and co-creation with civil society. For instance, Helsinki's AI register allows citizens to view how municipal algorithms operate, what data they use, and how decisions are made—establishing a new standard for algorithmic accountability in the public sector.

Similarly, the Aarhus Model in Denmark integrates environmental foresight and public participation into digital urban planning. This model creates citizen councils that inform smart infrastructure design based on collective priorities like green mobility, data privacy, and intergenerational equity. Such participatory mechanisms reduce governance asymmetries and anchor innovation in local knowledge systems.

Participatory urban technology labs are another fertile ground for human-centric innovation. These labs, often located in mid-sized cities or underserved communities, enable citizens to co-design technologies tailored to local needs. In cities like Amsterdam, Medellín, and Taipei, urban tech labs blend foresight exercises, low-tech experimentation, and cross-sector collaboration. Their projects range from cooperative sensor networks to community-managed mobility platforms and sustainable energy systems. These labs represent both testbeds and catalysts for systemic innovation grounded in local contexts. They promote agile governance and empower grassroots actors to influence technological agendas.

In the field of biotechnology, open-source platforms such as OpenWetWare and DIYBio democratize access to scientific knowledge and experimental tools. Rather than concentrating bioengineering capabilities in proprietary silos, these platforms foster grassroots innovation, ethical experimentation, and global collaboration. They illustrate how biotechnology—often regarded as the domain of elite labs—can be reimagined as a civic science, aligned with public interest and planetary boundaries.

The creation of community-based biohacker spaces in cities like San Francisco, Berlin, and Nairobi has opened new opportunities for inclusive science. These spaces experiment with low-cost lab equipment, cooperative safety norms, and citizen-led scientific agendas. Importantly, they also challenge the cultural assumptions embedded in mainstream bioethics, offering alternative epistemologies and risk perceptions.

Each of these cases reveals a broader principle: that technological development need not be top-down, market-driven, or extractive. It can be participatory, transparent, and inclusive. These models also challenge dominant narratives around innovation, suggesting that societal transformation does not require constant disruption or exponential growth, but rather careful, iterative alignment between social values, technical affordances, and institutional structures. When rooted in dignity, plurality, and equity, technology becomes not only a means of empowerment but also a mirror of democratic maturity.

11.5.3 Evaluating the Metrics of Transformation

One of the defining challenges in advancing Society 6.0 is the development of meaningful metrics that reflect the depth of transformation beyond traditional economic indicators. Historically, innovation has been assessed through indicators such as Gross Domestic Product (GDP), R&D intensity, patent applications, and technology adoption rates. While these metrics offer valuable insight into economic performance and technological progress, they are insufficient in capturing the multidimensional outcomes Society 6.0 seeks—outcomes rooted in well-being, equity, sustainability, and democratic participation (Ruggeri et al., 2020).

New measurement frameworks are required to monitor and guide the transition toward more inclusive, resilient, and ethical innovation systems. These must reflect a broader understanding of societal progress—one that recognizes the importance of social cohesion, environmental stewardship, psychological well-being, and individual agency. In doing so, these frameworks shift the focus from outputs and efficiency to outcomes and values.

11.5.3.1 From growth metrics to well-being indicators

Organizations such as the OECD and UNDP have pioneered composite indexes that offer alternatives to GDP. The OECD Better Life Index includes metrics such as life satisfaction, income distribution, housing quality, and civic engagement. The Human Development Index (HDI), while still anchored in economic indicators, incorporates education and health as foundational elements of development.

In the spirit of Society 6.0, we must go further. Subjective well-being—how people feel about their lives—must be coupled with objective conditions such as access to clean air, safety, and inclusive infrastructure. Countries such as New Zealand have taken the lead in implementing well-being budgets that prioritize public spending based on social impact rather than economic return. These pioneering efforts reveal a growing global consensus that well-being must be at the core of public policy and technological deployment.

11.5.3.2 Agency and participation metrics

Another crucial aspect of transformative evaluation lies in measuring the degree of agency and participatory inclusion individuals experience in innovation ecosystems. Traditional systems often marginalize citizens from key decision-making processes, particularly in the domains of technological design and data governance. Society 6.0 requires participatory technology assessments, deliberative democracy methods, and bottom-up innovation models that empower users.

Metrics of agency might include the percentage of citizens actively participating in technology policy consultations, the presence of community-led innovation platforms, or the degree to which marginalized voices are included in algorithmic governance. Digital participation indexes, civic tech engagement rates, and qualitative measures of perceived influence can help operationalize these dimensions.

Moreover, agency must be disaggregated across different demographic dimensions—gender, age, socio-economic status, and geographic location. Equity-sensitive metrics ensure that digital empowerment is not just a generalized claim but a reality for all segments of society. Monitoring frameworks must include feedback mechanisms to assess whether new technologies genuinely expand the freedom, autonomy, and voice of those who engage with them.

11.5.3.3 Ecological and systemic impact metrics

Equally vital are ecological indicators that evaluate the planetary consequences of innovation. While green innovation is often lauded, the actual sustainability of new technologies varies widely. Metrics such as carbon footprint, energy consumption, lifecycle emissions, and resource circularity must become standard elements in assessing digital infrastructure and product development.

Beyond environmental performance, systemic impact analysis evaluates how innovations affect societal resilience and institutional adaptability. These include indicators related to social trust, regulatory responsiveness, and intergenerational equity. For instance, technologies that promote knowledge sharing across generations, or that enhance community cohesion, contribute positively to systemic resilience even if their immediate economic value is unclear.

Tools like material flow analysis, socio-ecological resilience modeling, and sustainability maturity assessments can be embedded into public procurement evaluations and funding eligibility criteria. By integrating these tools, innovation policy shifts from a reactive to a regenerative mode—anticipating long-term consequences and shaping development in alignment with planetary boundaries.

11.5.3.4 Inclusivity and intersectionality in metrics

Inclusivity is not a singular measure but a multidimensional attribute. It spans accessibility, representation, affordability, usability, and meaningful participation. Evaluating inclusivity requires disaggregated data and nuanced analysis. For instance, internet access may be widespread, but if indigenous languages are not supported, or if AI systems perpetuate biases, digital inclusion remains incomplete.

Intersectional indicators evaluate how innovations serve or exclude at the intersection of identities—how race, gender, class, and disability combine to shape access and impact. Governments, research agencies, and industry must collect and publish intersectional data and integrate equity audits into project evaluations. Moreover, evaluation should incorporate qualitative methodologies—interviews, ethnographies, narrative impact assessments—that capture lived experiences beyond numbers.

11.5.3.5 Participatory evaluation and dynamic feedback

Metrics in Society 6.0 must be co-created with stakeholders. Participatory evaluation processes, including citizen juries, collaborative foresight workshops, and community scorecards, enhance legitimacy and contextual relevance. Technology users, particularly from marginalized communities, must have a say in how innovation is evaluated and governed.

Feedback loops ensure that evaluation is not static but evolves over time. Innovation indicators should be continuously reviewed in light of changing values, technologies, and societal needs. Digital observatories, open dashboards, and peer-learning networks enable real-time monitoring and adaptive governance.

Finally, governance bodies such as national statistical offices, ethics councils, and innovation agencies must coordinate to harmonize frameworks and reduce indicator fatigue. A shared ethical compass, embedded in measurement systems, ensures coherence and fosters global alignment toward the goals of Society 6.0.

In sum, evaluating transformation in the context of Society 6.0 requires a shift from measuring what is produced to understanding for whom and to what end. Only by embedding values into our measurement systems can we guide innovation toward futures that are not only smarter—but also fairer, greener, and more human.

11.6 FUTURE RISKS AND THE GUARDRAILS OF TECHNO-DEMOCRACY

As societies enter the complex terrain of Society 6.0 and increasingly rely on intelligent systems for decision-making and governance, the risks of misalignment between technological capabilities and democratic values become ever more pressing. The promise of a more human-centric, inclusive, and sustainable future cannot be realized unless we also confront the dark undercurrents that emerge from unregulated or misused technologies. This section identifies the key dystopian trajectories that threaten democratic life and outlines actionable safeguards that can serve as institutional and ethical guardrails in a techno-saturated age.

11.6.1 Dystopian Trajectories in the Digital Age

The specter of techno-authoritarianism looms large in the age of AI. While surveillance has long been a feature of state power, emerging technologies have radically altered its scale, precision, and intrusiveness. In authoritarian regimes, AI-powered facial recognition systems, biometric tracking, and predictive analytics are deployed not just for public security, but for the strategic suppression of dissent and the fine-tuned manipulation of behavior. These systems draw on vast data repositories compiled through mobile apps, internet usage, facial cameras in public spaces, and even voice recognition technologies embedded in everyday devices (Hamstra, 2024).

The social credit system in China offers one of the most prominent illustrations. By aggregating data from financial records, online activity, social connections, and even shopping habits, the state can assign behavioral scores to individuals and organizations. These scores determine access to jobs, education, travel, and public services. Such systems embed behavioral nudges into the structure of daily life—ostensibly to promote order and trust—but in practice, they concentrate power and suppress plurality. The danger lies in the quiet normalization of digitally enabled authoritarianism, where rights are algorithmically allocated and dissent becomes a technical anomaly to be corrected.

In more subtle forms, techno-authoritarianism is also emerging in democratic contexts under the guise of national security or pandemic response. Surveillance laws passed under emergency conditions have tended to persist long after the crises that prompted them. AI-driven tools for contact tracing, crowd control, and behavioral forecasting—while useful in public health—are often redeployed with minimal transparency and oversight. Without a strong democratic culture and independent institutions, these capabilities risk becoming embedded instruments of asymmetrical control. The challenge is thus not only about technical safeguards but about institutional ethics and public vigilance.

A key concern is the opacity of these systems. When surveillance is powered by AI and Big Data, its logic becomes inscrutable to the average citizen. Who collects the data? Who decides which behaviors are problematic? What recourse does a wrongly flagged individual have? The answer to these questions is often unclear. Worse, appeals to national security or algorithmic neutrality tend to shield these technologies from democratic scrutiny. In such environments, the very idea of citizenship risks being recast in computational terms: to be a citizen is to be scorable, traceable, and classifiable.

Technological determinism further compounds the issue. When societies assume that more data and smarter algorithms necessarily lead to better outcomes, they sideline normative questions about purpose, fairness, and proportionality. The allure of real-time governance—of dashboards that promise to "see everything"—can seduce policymakers into valuing surveillance over deliberation, efficiency over empathy. Yet democracy thrives not on control, but on trust, dissent, and negotiated values.

The counter to techno-authoritarianism must be grounded in both law and culture. Legally, states must enshrine prohibitions against mass surveillance and ensure meaningful oversight of security apparatuses. Culturally, citizens must be empowered to question the legitimacy of technological interventions, not merely their effectiveness. Civil society, investigative journalism, and academic critique are indispensable in surfacing the silent harms of ubiquitous surveillance. Democracy cannot survive as a black box. The light of scrutiny, contestation, and shared values must remain at its core.

While emerging technologies offer immense potential for positive transformation, they are equally capable of entrenching power asymmetries, curbing freedoms, and destabilizing democratic norms.

Techno-authoritarianism refers to the increasing deployment of surveillance technologies by authoritarian states to monitor, control, and suppress populations. Facial recognition, biometric databases, predictive policing, and social credit systems have created unprecedented levels of state insight into individual behavior. These tools, when coupled with AI and real-time data analytics, allow for granular control over civil liberties and the narrowing of dissent.

Surveillance capitalism, on the other hand, is the logic that drives commercial platforms to extract, analyze, and monetize user data at scale. Dominant digital platforms operate as de facto monopolies, creating vast data asymmetries while manipulating behavior through algorithmic curation and nudge-based personalization. These practices undermine user autonomy, distort public discourse, and erode trust in democratic institutions.

Algorithmic discrimination and systemic bias also threaten to institutionalize inequalities. AI systems trained on biased data or designed without contextual awareness can amplify existing prejudices. Automated decision-making in areas like credit scoring, hiring, policing, and welfare allocation can entrench systemic injustices, particularly affecting marginalized communities (Youvan, 2024). Without rigorous oversight, algorithmic systems risk becoming opaque instruments of inequality.

11.6.1.1 Surveillance capitalism and platform power

Surveillance capitalism has emerged as one of the most dominant—and insidious—economic logics of the digital age. Coined by Shoshana Zuboff, the term refers to a new form of market behavior in which private companies collect and commodify personal data in order to predict, influence, and ultimately control user behavior. Unlike traditional capitalist enterprises that rely on offering goods and services in exchange for money, surveillance capitalism monetizes human experience itself, transforming every digital action into a data point to be harvested and analyzed.

At the heart of this system are the vast platform conglomerates—often referred to as "Big Tech"—which function simultaneously as communication infrastructures, commercial marketplaces, social networks, and content distributors. These companies extract user data at scale, not just through overt channels like search queries or location services, but through ambient mechanisms embedded in apps, devices, and browser metadata. The result is an ever-expanding behavioral surplus—a reservoir of intimate information about thoughts, desires, emotions, and routines (Lyon, 2023).

This surplus is fed into machine learning systems that create detailed psychographic profiles. Algorithms then optimize content, ads, and experiences to nudge users toward behaviors that align with commercial goals—clicks, purchases, time spent on platforms. Over time, these nudges evolve into a form of behavioral modification. Users are not only being observed; they are being shaped.

The consequences of this transformation are profound. First, surveillance capitalism erodes privacy not through abrupt breaches, but through the normalization of extraction. The default condition of digital life becomes one of constant observation, where every scroll, tap, and pause becomes legible to unseen systems. While users may grant consent through terms of service, this consent is rarely informed, and often coerced by the necessity of participation in digital society.

Second, this model reconfigures the architecture of public discourse. Social media platforms, in particular, are designed to prioritize engagement over truth, outrage over nuance, and virality over deliberation. The algorithmic curation of content fragments the public sphere, creating echo chambers and feedback loops that polarize opinion and amplify extremism. What was once envisioned as a democratizing technology has, in many cases, become a vector for disinformation and manipulation.

Third, surveillance capitalism introduces new forms of power asymmetry. Companies that control data flows gain outsized influence over economies, elections, and even cultural norms. Their algorithms remain proprietary and opaque, shielded by trade secrets and weak regulatory oversight. This concentration of informational power undermines democratic accountability and diminishes individual agency.

Crucially, this dynamic is not restricted to advertising. Predictive analytics are increasingly deployed in hiring, insurance pricing, credit scoring, and public services—areas with significant consequences for life chances. When decisions are made on the basis of probabilistic models trained on historical data, existing inequalities are often reproduced and deepened. Discrimination becomes automated, normalized, and difficult to contest.

Resistance to surveillance capitalism is growing, but the response remains fragmented. Some countries have introduced data protection frameworks, such as the EU General Data Protection Regulation (GDPR), which enshrines principles like data minimization, purpose limitation, and the right to be forgotten. Yet enforcement remains inconsistent, and the underlying business models of surveillance capitalism largely persist.

More radical proposals have emerged, including data dividends, public ownership of data, and platform cooperatives. These ideas seek to reimagine data as a collective resource rather than a private commodity. They challenge the notion that convenience and innovation must come at the cost of autonomy and dignity.

Ultimately, confronting surveillance capitalism requires more than regulatory tweaks. It demands a fundamental reconsideration of the values that underlie the digital economy. Do we want technologies that serve human flourishing, or markets that exploit human behavior for profit? Can innovation be decoupled from extraction? These questions go to the heart of the Society 6.0 project. Without answering them, the promise of a more inclusive and democratic technological future will remain elusive.

Surveillance capitalism illustrates that the erosion of democratic life in the digital age does not require jackboots or overt censorship. It can unfold through targeted ads, algorithmic timelines, and predictive analytics that quietly shift our behavior without our awareness. It is governance without consent—rule through data, administered by platforms, and shielded from public scrutiny. To reclaim agency, society must insist on transparency, accountability, and most importantly, alternative models that place people—not predictions—at the center of technological design.

11.6.1.2 Algorithmic discrimination and systemic bias

Beyond overt control and economic exploitation, a subtler yet equally insidious threat emerges in the form of algorithmic discrimination. As AI systems are deployed to manage everything from recruitment and credit scoring to predictive policing and social welfare distribution, the potential for replicating—and even amplifying—existing social biases becomes both widespread and difficult to detect. This is not merely a technical failure; it reflects deeper systemic and epistemic injustices encoded into digital systems (Chen, 2023).

At the core of this issue is the data on which these algorithms are trained. Machine learning systems are not autonomous entities; they learn from patterns in historical data. If that data reflects discrimination—against women in hiring, minorities in criminal sentencing, or lower-income individuals in credit scoring—the algorithm will mirror and institutionalize those patterns. In this way, bias becomes automated, scaled, and obscured by a veil of objectivity. Algorithms often appear neutral, but their outputs are only as just as the data and assumptions they are built upon.

Consider the widely cited example of COMPAS, a criminal risk assessment tool used in the United States. Investigations revealed that it disproportionately labeled Black defendants as high-risk compared to white defendants, even when actual recidivism rates did not support those predictions. In another case, an AI system designed to screen job applicants learned to downgrade resumes that included terms associated with women's colleges or organizations. These incidents are not anomalies; they are symptomatic of a larger problem in how digital systems are designed, deployed, and evaluated.

Algorithmic discrimination is not confined to any single domain. In healthcare, predictive systems have been shown to underestimate the medical needs of Black patients. In education, proctoring software using facial recognition may fail to recognize darker skin tones. In finance, algorithmic credit assessments have penalized individuals from historically marginalized communities. What connects these diverse examples is a lack of scrutiny, a deficit of transparency, and a failure to anticipate social impact.

Moreover, these biases are often compounded by feedback loops. When flawed algorithms are used to make decisions, they generate new data that reflects those flawed outcomes. This data is then fed back into the system, reinforcing the original bias. The result is a self-perpetuating cycle of inequality, difficult to detect and even harder to break.

The opacity of algorithmic systems further complicates the issue. Proprietary models, protected by intellectual property laws, often prevent external audits or public scrutiny. Even when explanations are offered, they are frequently couched in technical jargon inaccessible to laypersons or decision-makers. The problem is not just algorithmic bias, but the epistemic exclusion it enables—denying individuals and communities the right to understand or contest how decisions are made about them.

Tackling algorithmic discrimination demands a multi-layered response. Technically, it requires the development of fairness-aware algorithms, robust testing for disparate impact, and the inclusion of diverse datasets during training. Institutionally, it necessitates independent oversight bodies with the authority to audit, investigate, and sanction. Legally, it involves the extension of anti-discrimination protections to automated decision-making systems.

There is also a need for participatory design processes that include stakeholders from affected communities. These groups bring vital contextual knowledge that can surface risks and harms invisible to developers. Civic engagement, public consultations, and co-creation models offer a pathway toward more democratic technology design.

Ethical frameworks must go beyond abstract principles to address power asymmetries. Who defines fairness? Who decides what constitutes acceptable error? These are not merely engineering problems; they are political and moral questions. Answering them requires the involvement of ethicists, sociologists, legal scholars, and community representatives—not just data scientists.

Ultimately, algorithmic discrimination exposes the limits of a purely technical approach to innovation. The pursuit of efficiency and scalability must not come at the expense of justice, equity, and human dignity. As AI systems become more deeply embedded in the infrastructure of daily life, the demand for fairness cannot remain an afterthought. It must be designed into the very architecture of our digital future (Ferrara, 2024).

In the context of Society 6.0, addressing systemic bias is central to creating a truly inclusive and human-centric technological paradigm. It is not enough to innovate; we must interrogate. We must build systems that not only function but also reflect our highest democratic values. And we must ensure that the march of progress does not trample on the rights of the very people it is meant to serve.

11.6.2 Institutional Safeguards and Ethical Infrastructures

In the face of accelerating technological change and its associated risks, the architecture of techno-democracy must rest on a robust scaffolding of institutional safeguards and ethical infrastructures. These safeguards are not merely reactive tools for harm mitigation—they are foundational elements for ensuring that innovation aligns with democratic principles, social justice, and human well-being (Bauer, 2022).

One of the foundational imperatives is algorithmic transparency. As machine learning and AI systems become deeply embedded in societal decision-making—from judicial processes and loan approvals to medical diagnostics and automated hiring—the need for such systems to be explainable, auditable, and understandable by both experts and the public becomes non-negotiable. Transparency must not be limited to the disclosure of source code or model weights; it must entail mechanisms that allow meaningful interrogation and challenge by affected individuals and oversight bodies. Audit trails, interpretability tools, and public registers of high-risk systems form essential parts of this transparency infrastructure.

Yet, transparency alone is insufficient. A second, equally critical layer is algorithmic accountability. This requires clearly delineated frameworks of liability and responsibility in cases of technological harm or systemic discrimination. As AI systems often involve complex chains of actors—designers, deployers, platform operators, and regulators—accountability can become diffused, undermining justice and redress. Thus, accountability mechanisms must include preemptive impact assessments, redress pathways for citizens, obligations for explainability, and dynamic regulatory sandboxes that allow real-time governance innovation.

Institutional ethical infrastructures extend beyond legal compliance. They include deliberative mechanisms that embed ethical reasoning at each stage of technology development and deployment. These infrastructures may take the form of ethics boards within tech companies, foresight units within government ministries, citizen juries, or cross-sector innovation forums. Their aim is not only to evaluate risk but to co-define desirable futures (Mennella et al., 2024). Ethics must be proactive, not reactive—an anticipatory tool for steering innovation toward the public interest.

The rise of digital rights frameworks marks another significant evolution. In addition to classical rights like privacy and freedom of expression, digital societies must codify new entitlements such as the right to algorithmic explanation, the right to non-biometric surveillance, and the right to refuse automation in critical services. These rights form the bedrock of a digital constitutionalism that prioritizes human dignity in the design and governance of technology.

Innovative governance models such as data trusts and digital commons are emerging as promising instruments for reclaiming collective agency. Data trusts allow communities to manage their data through fiduciary governance, ensuring that data is used in line with community interests. Digital commons propose governance regimes that treat data and digital infrastructure as shared resources rather than private commodities. These models represent a radical shift—from data extraction to data stewardship, from platform capitalism to techno-democracy.

Foresight-based governance bodies institutionalize anticipatory thinking into the regulatory ecosystem. Comprised of diverse stakeholders—scientists, ethicists, citizens, and public officials—these bodies conduct horizon scanning, scenario planning, and impact mapping. Their mandate is to identify not just what is technologically possible, but what is socially desirable and ethically permissible. Embedding such bodies within national parliaments, regulatory agencies, and city governments would significantly enhance anticipatory capacity.

Digital education and civic capacity-building are equally foundational. Ethical infrastructures must be supported by a digitally literate citizenry. This entails integrating curricula on algorithmic reasoning, data ethics, and civic tech into schools, universities, and vocational training. Public awareness campaigns, participatory tech labs, and digital rights advocacy also play key roles. A democracy cannot govern what it does not understand—and so digital pedagogy becomes a cornerstone of sustainable techno-governance.

Finally, public institutions must undergo structural transformation. Bureaucracies must be equipped with technical literacy, agile decision-making structures, and participatory frameworks. Regulatory bodies should adopt a values-by-design approach, integrating ethical considerations into the lifecycle of technology. Cross-ministerial coordination, agile funding streams, and public-private foresight partnerships must become standard practice.

In the era of Society 6.0, institutional safeguards and ethical infrastructures are not luxuries. They are the bedrock upon which inclusive, sustainable, and democratic innovation must be built. Without them, the risks of techno-authoritarianism, surveillance capitalism, and systemic discrimination will not be outliers—they will become structural features of the digital world. Building resilient, rights-based governance models is not just a technical challenge—it is a moral and civic imperative for our time.

11.6.3 Aligning with the European Governance Landscape

Building on the principles discussed in the previous sections—particularly the emphasis on institutional safeguards, digital rights, and ethical foresight—this section turns to the European Union's emerging model of techno-governance. The EU offers a tangible, evolving case of how democratic societies can operationalize the vision of Society 6.0, embedding rights, fairness, and human-centricity into the regulatory fabric of the digital economy. It represents an institutional framework where the ideals of techno-democracy are actively translated into legal and ethical infrastructure.

The General Data Protection Regulation (GDPR), enacted in 2018, established the global benchmark for data protection, affirming the right to privacy, consent, and algorithmic transparency. It laid the groundwork for a more citizen-centered digital ecosystem where data flows are governed not only by commercial imperatives but also by fundamental rights. The GDPR's principles—data minimization, purpose limitation, explicit consent, and the right to be forgotten—reflect a normative vision where individual autonomy and data dignity are foundational.

Building upon this precedent, the EU's Artificial Intelligence Act seeks to construct a horizontal regulatory architecture for AI systems. Classifying applications based on risk—unacceptable, high, limited, and minimal—it mandates specific requirements for high-risk systems, including human oversight, documentation, transparency, and robust data governance. This approach does not attempt to halt innovation but rather to direct it toward ethically acceptable and socially beneficial applications.

Complementary instruments such as the Digital Services Act (DSA) and Digital Markets Act (DMA) address the increasingly structural role of digital platforms. The DSA introduces obligations for platform accountability in content moderation and algorithmic operations, while the DMA seeks to curb anti-competitive behaviors among dominant market actors. These regulatory tools recognize platforms as de facto public infrastructures, demanding governance that serves democratic accountability rather than unchecked corporate power.

To further integrate responsibility into digital transformation, the AI Liability Directive complements the AI Act by establishing mechanisms for redress and civil liability in cases where algorithmic harm occurs. This ensures that legal accountability accompanies technical deployment, closing gaps in justice that often emerge in high-tech contexts.

What makes the EU model particularly relevant to the Society 6.0 agenda is its use of anticipatory and participatory governance. The development of these frameworks has been informed by public consultations, multi-stakeholder foresight exercises, and scenario-based risk evaluations. These processes demonstrate how institutions can actively embed futures thinking into policy, thus linking foresight with implementation—an echo of the I2E model that prioritizes Insight, Innovation, and Execution.

Nevertheless, the EU's approach is not without challenges. Enforcement remains uneven across member states, and institutional capacity often lags behind technological change. The rise of AI, synthetic biology, and quantum computing demands governance models that are not only robust but also agile and adaptive. In response, the EU is investing in regulatory experimentation—through AI sandboxes, ethics observatories, and cross-border data governance initiatives like Gaia-X and European Data Spaces.

Ultimately, the European governance landscape illustrates how the ideals of techno-democracy—previously conceptual—can find institutional expression. It provides a working blueprint for embedding ethical foresight into the core of governance, resisting both surveillance authoritarianism and libertarian deregulation. This is not a finished model, but a living prototype—an evolving demonstration that innovation and ethics, democracy and technology, need not be adversaries but allies in shaping the future.

As the global community grapples with the risks and opportunities of Society 6.0, the European example offers critical lessons. It reveals that rights-based governance, anticipatory regulation, and civic participation are not constraints but enablers of meaningful innovation. In aligning institutional foresight with democratic integrity, the EU showcases how to construct the guardrails necessary for a humane, inclusive, and sustainable digital future.

11.7 CONCLUSION

As we reach the conclusion of this exploration, one insight becomes undeniable: governance in the age of exponential change is no longer a matter of managing linear pipelines of innovation. The complexity, interdependence, and velocity of technological evolution have transformed governance into a systemic endeavor—one that must operate with foresight, be grounded in ethical reasoning, and be inclusive of diverse voices and values. The future will not reward control; it will reward adaptability, wisdom, and collaboration.

Throughout this chapter, we have framed Industry 6.0 and Society 6.0 not as deterministic endpoints or techno-utopian destinations, but as orienting visions—conceptual lighthouses that guide our innovation ecosystems toward deeper goals: human well-being, planetary stewardship, democratic integrity, and shared prosperity. These visions illuminate alternative paths beyond extractive growth logics, inviting us to reimagine productivity, intelligence, and value itself.

We have also introduced the Sextuple Innovation Helix not as a static model, but as a dynamic framework for navigating this complexity. By acknowledging technology as an autonomous actor—capable of shaping norms, amplifying inequalities, and redefining the social contract—we sharpen our tools for innovation governance. We make visible what was previously hidden: that every line of code, every platform protocol, every algorithmic rule carries embedded assumptions about what kind of society we wish to live in.

But no framework, no matter how expansive, can predict or manage the future alone. The real engine of transformation is institutional imagination and societal resolve. It is the continuous effort to ask difficult questions, design inclusive processes, and build infrastructures that can adapt, reflect, and repair. Whether through anticipatory regulation, ethical foresight, or participatory experimentation, the governance of tomorrow must remain anchored in the public interest, not market inertia or technological determinism.

In closing, let us remember that the future is not built by technology alone. It is co-authored—patiently and imperfectly—by institutions that choose learning over inertia, by societies that demand accountability and justice, and by values that place human and planetary flourishing above short-term gains. Our task is not only to innovate, but to govern innovation wisely—with humility, with hope, and with the courage to imagine better worlds.

REFERENCES

Adel, A., 2022. Future of industry 5.0 in society: human-centric solutions, challenges and prospective research areas. *Journal of Cloud Computing, 11*(40). https://doi.org/10.1186/s13677-022-00314-5.

Bauer, J. M., 2022. Toward new guardrails for the information society. *Telecommunications Policy, 46*(5).

Bokhari, S. & Seunghwan, M., 2024. How do institutional and technological innovations influence smart city governance? Focused on stakeholder satisfaction and crime rate. *Sustainability, 16*, 4246. https://doi.org/10.3390/su16104246.

Carayannis, E. G., Posselt, T. & Freissler, S., 2024. Toward Industry 6.0 and Society 6.0: The quintuple innovation helix with embedded AI modalities as enabler of public interest technologies strategic technology management and road-mapping. *IEEE Transactions on Engineering Management*, 1–13. https://doi.org/10.1109/TEM.2024.3406427.

Chen, Z., 2023. Ethics and discrimination in artificial intelligence-enabled recruitment practices. *Humanities and Social Sciences Communications, 10*(567). https://doi.org/10.1057/s41599-023-02079-x.

Duggal, A., et al., 2021. A sequential roadmap to Industry 6.0: Exploring future manufacturing trends. *IET Communications, 16*. https://doi.org/10.1049/cmu2.12284.

Ferrara, E., 2024. Fairness and bias in artificial intelligence: A brief survey of sources, impacts, and mitigation strategies. *Science, 6*(1), 3. https://doi.org/10.3390/sci6010003.

Hamstra, J., 2024. The *end of an anti-utopian era: How digital technology is leading to dystopia*. ALiGN: Alternative Global Network Media Lab. https://carleton.ca/align/2024/the-end-of-an-anti-utopian-era-how-digital-technology-is-leading-to-dystopia/.

Jiao, H., et al., 2025. The relationship between digital technologies and innovation: A review, critique, and research agenda. *Journal of Innovation & Knowledge, 10*(1). https://doi.org/10.1016/j.jik.2024.100638.

Kolbjørnsrud, V., 2023. Designing the intelligent organization: Six principles for human–AI collaboration. *California Management Review*. https://doi.org/10.1177/00081256231211020.

Le Blanc, P., et al., 2024. How emerging technologies shape the future of work. *European Journal of Work and Organizational Psychology, 33*(2), 115–119. https://doi.org/10.1080/1359432X.2024.2324937.

Lyon, D., 2023. Surveillance and the power of platforms. *Cambridge Journal of Regions, Economy and Society, 16*(2), 361–365. https://doi.org/10.1093/cjres/rsad006.

Mennella, C., Maniscalco, U., De Pietro, G. & Esposito, M., 2024. Ethical and regulatory challenges of AI technologies in healthcare: A narrative review. *Heliyon*. https://doi.org/10.1016/j.heliyon.2024.e26297.

OECD, 2025. *Building anticipatory capacity with strategic foresight in government: Lessons from Lithuania, Italy, and Malta*. OECD Publishing. https://doi.org/10.1787/d7eb0bb6-en.

Oyekunle, D., et al., 2024. Industry 5.0: A paradigm shift towards sustainability, adaptability and human-centeredness. Conference: Proceedings of the 12th IPMA

Research Conference "Project Management in the Age of Artificial Intelligence, University of Maryland, College Park, MD. https://doi.org/10.56889/mxee1654.

Rathenau Instituut, 2019. *This is how we put AI into practice based on European values.* Rathenau Instituut. https://www.rathenau.nl/en/digitalisering/how-we-put-ai-practice-based-european-values.

Ruggeri, K., et al., 2020. Well-being is more than happiness and life satisfaction: A multidimensional analysis of 21 countries. *Health Qual Life Outcomes*, *18*, 192. https://doi.org/10.1186/s12955-020-01423-y.

Sjöblom, J., 2024. *Strategic foresight for innovation: International insights to address Sweden's future challenges.* Vinnova – Sweden's Innovation Agency.

Steinberg, F. & Bergmann, M., 2024. *The Draghi report: A strategy to reform the European economic model.* Center for Strategic and International Studies. https://www.csis.org/analysis/draghi-report-strategy-reform-european-economic-model.

Tang, L. & Cao, C., 2022. Prospects and challenges: Introduction to the special issue on "Global governance of emerging technologies." *Global Policy and Governance*, *2*, 261–265. https://doi.org/10.1007/s43508-022-00050-1.

Youvan, D., 2024. Expanding Human Thought Through Artificial Intelligence: A New Frontier in Cognitive Augmentation. https://www.researchgate.net/publication/384399213_Expanding_Human_Thought_Through_Artificial_Intelligence_A_New_Frontier_in_Cognitive_Augmentation.

Conclusion: Toward a new horizon—rethinking innovation for the future

Elias G. Carayannis and Nikos R. Zotas

Industrial innovation in the 21st century is not a discrete event, a singular invention, or a technology awaiting diffusion. It is a vast, evolving field of forces—technical, economic, cultural, ecological—interacting in increasingly complex and uncertain ways. As this book has illustrated across its chapters, the pathways of innovation today are less about linear development than about emergent ecosystems, co-created value, and adaptive transformation. As we stand at the threshold of a new era—one shaped as much by disruption and systemic risk as by opportunity—it becomes clear that innovation is not only what we make of the world, but also how we understand, steward, and ethically navigate its consequences.

The historical trajectory that we have traced throughout this volume reveals a profound transition. Innovation has moved from being seen as the sole province of engineering and industrial science to becoming a domain that intersects with nearly every dimension of life and governance. The early phases of industrial innovation, centered around products, processes, and research and development (R&D) outputs, have given way to broader, more integrated frameworks. Industry 4.0 marked a fundamental reconfiguration of industrial production and logistics, with smart factories, connected systems, data-driven decisions, and algorithmic optimization becoming central to competitiveness. Yet as advanced as these technologies are, they introduce new vulnerabilities, new dependencies, and a need for a more human-centered understanding.

That realization gave rise to Industry 5.0—a response not against technology, but against the tendency to devalue the human in the pursuit of efficiency. Rather than automation for its own sake, Industry 5.0 embraces co-creation between people and machines, the reintroduction of human judgment, and a renewed focus on social well-being and environmental resilience. This shift also converges with the vision of Society 5.0, a future-oriented framework that places technology in the service of solving societal challenges—an inclusive, data-rich society where innovation enhances the quality of life and equity for all.

Alongside these conceptual shifts, the architecture of innovation itself has undergone a parallel transformation. In place of top-down, centralized systems of knowledge and capital, we now observe the rise of innovation ecosystems—adaptive, networked constellations of actors including firms, governments, universities, NGOs, citizens, and increasingly, machines. These ecosystems are not designed like machines; they are grown, shaped by feedback loops, cultural context, and institutional norms. Innovation, under this lens, is not merely about outputs; it is about relationships, co-evolution, and the capacity to respond creatively to uncertainty.

This recognition has been deeply informed by the frameworks discussed in this book, particularly the Quintuple Innovation Helix, which expanded innovation governance beyond the traditional triad of university, industry, and government to include civil society and the natural environment. This expansion was not cosmetic—it reflects the urgent truth that sustainable innovation must account for ecological boundaries and the values of citizens. Innovation that depletes resources or erodes trust cannot be considered progress. Instead, we must embrace the view that innovation is ecological, systemic, and ethical in its orientation.

Moreover, the complex nature of innovation today demands new tools of anticipation and reflection. In an age characterized by discontinuity—be it technological, geopolitical, or environmental—foresight becomes not a luxury, but a necessity. Strategic foresight, as explored in the chapters on preparedness and scenario planning, enables institutions to engage not just with what is probable, but with what is possible and desirable. It shifts the mindset from prediction to preparation, from control to adaptability. By cultivating a longer-term, systems-aware perspective, foresight allows innovation actors to make choices that are not only smart in the short term but wise over time.

This emphasis on insight was further developed through the I2E Framework—Insight to Execution—which proposed a more integrated model for managing innovation across its lifecycle. Insight without execution is impotent; execution without insight is reckless. The dynamic interplay between these two capacities, moderated by organizational learning, culture, and institutional design, is at the heart of modern innovation management. The organizations and ecosystems that thrive will be those that can continuously translate insight into action, while maintaining the humility to adjust and reframe as conditions evolve.

Yet if insight and execution are critical, so too is measurement. Throughout history, we have measured innovation through what is easiest to count: patents, R&D spending, publication metrics. These are useful proxies, but they reveal little about the deeper qualities of innovation—collaboration, inclusivity, social impact, ecological sustainability. This book has made the case for new measurement paradigms, including the M4 Framework, which emphasizes multidimensional, data-rich, and context-sensitive approaches. By measuring what matters, we can better align innovation with societal goals and foster accountability in systems that often move faster than their ethical oversight.

Across all these themes, one unifying insight emerges: innovation is no longer merely about doing more, faster. It is about doing differently, with purpose. The future will not be defined by how quickly we innovate, but by how wisely. We must move beyond speed and disruption as end goals, and toward reflection, responsibility, and regeneration as guiding values. This calls for a deeper shift—from innovation as instrumentality to innovation as stewardship.

The futures of industrial innovation will likely be shaped by several converging forces. The hyper-convergence of technologies such as AI, quantum computing, synthetic biology, and immersive realities will create new possibilities but also new dilemmas. As innovation reaches deeper into biology, cognition, and ecosystems, the line between technical feasibility and ethical permissibility will grow increasingly blurred. In parallel, climate instability, resource scarcity, and global inequality will intensify the call for innovation to serve broader societal missions—missions rooted in justice, resilience, and planetary health.

In response, governance models will need to be reimagined. Governments must become more agile, participatory, and anticipatory. Firms must transcend narrow definitions of competitive advantage and embrace stakeholder value, circular design, and ethical leadership. Universities must evolve into boundary-spanning institutions that foster not just knowledge creation, but the cultivation of innovation literacy and public engagement. Civil society, too, must take an active role—not only advocating for equity and transparency but co-shaping the direction of innovation through participatory foresight, citizen science, and democratic experimentation.

This is the great challenge and opportunity of the coming decades: to transform our innovation systems from extractive to generative, from closed to open, from mechanistic to ecological. It will require courage—to question inherited assumptions; creativity—to design for futures not yet visible; and commitment—to pursue innovation not for its own sake, but for the flourishing of human and planetary life.

The final message of this book is not that we have all the answers, but that we now possess better questions—and better tools to explore them. Industrial innovation in the 21st century will not be governed by templates or blueprints, but by frameworks that are adaptive, inclusive, and reflexive. The terrain is complex, the stakes are high, but the potential—if navigated wisely—is profound.

In the end, innovation is not a destination. It is a journey of becoming. A process of imagining what could be, testing what is possible, and choosing, with intention and integrity, what should be. As we close this volume, let us remember that the future is not something we enter—it is something we co-create. Let us then innovate, not only with speed and scale, but with foresight, responsibility, and care.

Index